DESIGN
and
TECHNOLOGY

Colin Caborn

Deputy Head, Icknield High School, Luton

Ian Mould

Head of Design Services, British School Technology,
Bedfordshire

and John Cave

Head of Technology Education Centre, Middlesex University

Nelson

Thomas Nelson and Sons Ltd
Nelson House   Mayfield Road
Walton-on-Thames   Surrey
KT12 5PL   UK

First published by Thomas Nelson and Sons Ltd 1989

I(T)P ® Thomas Nelson is an International
        Thomson Publishing Company
I(T)P ® is used under licence

ISBN 0-17-448277-9
NPN 9 8 7 6 5 4 3

Printed in China

The authors and publishers wish to thank the following for permission to use
questions from their GCSE papers:
Northern Examining Association (Associated Lancashire Schools Examining Board;
Joint Matriculation Board; Northern Regional Examinations Board; North West
Regional Examinations Board; Yorkshire and Humberside Regional Examinations
Board); London and East Anglian Group; Midland Examining Group; Welsh Joint
Education Committee; Southern Examining Group.

Grateful acknowledgements are made to the following firms:
EMA Ltd, Philip Harris Ltd, Boxford Ltd, Formech Ltd, Smiths Patent Ltd.

Acknowledgements are due to the following for permission to use photographs
and illustrations:

Marion Boyars Publishers Ltd (p. 176) W. Canning Group (p. 340) Bruce Coleman Limited
(cover, space shuttle) Duckworth & Co Ltd (p. 152) Image Bank (cover, computer
backdrop) NFI Group (p. 55) The Photo Source/J Calder/TPS (p. 43, centre left) Tony
Saunders (pp. 27, 28, 29, 30, 31, 34, 36, 37 (top right, centre right, bottom left, right and
centre), 39, 40, 41, 42, 45, 46, 49, 51, 52, 53, 54, 55, 56, 88, 89, 90, 91, 100, 101, 102, 103,
104, 105, 134, 152, 153, 156, 263, 270 (left), 271, 280, 340, 341) Science Photo
Library/George Haling (p. 37); Zefa/J. Fitzchf Agenda Infrared Systems (p. 58); (cover,
computer graphics) Wood Visual Communications (p. 251) John Walmsley (pp. 359, 365,
374, 375) Ford Motor Company (p. 270 right); Topham (p. 163 top left)

Every effort has been made to trace the holders of copyright material. If any have been
inadvertently overlooked, the publishers will be pleased to make the necessary
arrangements at the first opportunity.

Preface

Few textbooks have enjoyed the sustained popularity of the first edition of *Integrated Craft and Design*. In many respects it was a book ahead of its time, and even in its original form remains one of the most comprehensive resources for designing and making in secondary school — and beyond.

The need for a revised edition stems from the many changes that have taken place during the last 10 years, e.g. the rise of technology, the concept of expressing ideas through models and, more recently, the emergence of a National Curriculum.

This new edition, *Design and Technology*, recognises all the merits of the original text. It contains **all** the original material, but in an enlarged and thoroughly updated form. In addition, the book has been significantly expanded to reflect key subject developments. The section on graphics has been extended in **colour** to look at a range of presentation techniques, and a major section on product modelling has been added. Product modelling in the context of schoolwork is one of the most significant recent developments. It involves a fundamental shift of emphasis from 'one-off' designing and making to the design of products capable, in principle, of mass production. It brings the methods of industrial (and engineering) designers firmly into the curriculum.

Major new sections on technology have also been added, and these reflect the new demands of GCSE courses. The selected topics are intended to underpin the activity of designing, and cross-references are therefore made to other sections. Design and technology specialists are pioneering approaches that seek to integrate technology into design at all levels, and the revised edition recognises and encourages this development. Membrane-panel switch technology, for example, is examined in the graphics, modelling and technology sections: it is possible to model highly realistic **working** membrane panels, giving pupils and students enormous opportunities for producing working products that reflect state-of-the-art commercial trends.

Wherever possible, reference is made to new manufacturing concepts, e.g. surface mounting in electronics. Many specialists, in industry as well as in schools, agree that surface mounting of conventional components offers many advantages over conventional PCB construction for prototyping. For most learners it is conceptually far easier and it is, of course, relevant to advanced industrial practices.

All of the examination questions are now up-to-date and most have been taken from GCSE 'Design and Realisation' and 'Design and Technology' exam papers. It should be possible for pupils to rely almost exclusively on *Design and Technology* in answering the questions. The book should also function as a comprehensive guide to and resource for designing.

A number of people have been most helpful in the preparation of this revised edition, and I should like to give special thanks to the following: Richard Tufnell and Peter Shipley, Bill Nicholl, Tim Ford, John Farmer, Peter Stensell, Michael Drugan, Roman Piotrowsky, Joe Firelli, Ted Ditchburn and Philip Drayton.

John Cave, 1989

Contents

1   What is design and technology?   1
2   Communicating through graphics   4
3   Communicating through models   37
4   A vocabulary for design   59
5   Design method   72
6   Design method in action   83
7   Technology for design: Electronics   106
8   Technology for design: Mechanisms and control   134
9   Technology for design: Structures   157
10 Technology for design: Energy   170
11 Introduction to tools, processes and materials   181
12 Classification of common hand tools. Part 1 — marking-out,
    measuring and testing tools   185
13 Classification of common hand tools. Part 2 — holding tools   192
14 Classification of common hand tools. Part 3 — driving tools   197
15 Classification of common hand tools. Part 4 — cutting tools   203
16 Ways of working materials. Part 1A — wasting-hand
    processes   224
17 Ways of working materials. Part 1B — wasting-machine
    processes   240
18 Ways of working materials. Part 2 — deformation   254
19 Ways of working materials. Part 3 — moulding and casting   272
20 Ways of working materials. Part 4 — fabrication   282
21 Materials for design and technology: Wood   309
22 Materials for design and technology: Metal   328
23 Materials for design and technology: Plastics   342
24 GCSE Examination questions   354
    Addresses   404
    Index   405

What is design and technology?

The term 'design and technology' is used to describe a wide range of activities. The specialists involved in the different areas of design and technology, such as graphic design, product design and engineering design, each have their own ideas about what it means. There are therefore many answers to the question, 'What is design and technology?', and it is very easy to become confused.

Design and technology as a problem-solving activity

All the activities grouped under the title of design and technology do, however, share a number of common features: identifying a problem, thinking about it and realising the solution. Improving an electronic circuit, designing a piece of furniture and creating a new range of clothing all have problem solving in common.

The purpose of design and technology

We must be able to think about what we are trying to achieve in solving problems, so that we can learn to judge both our own and other people's solutions in a reasoned way.

Since there would be no point in changing something if it made it function or look worse, it is obvious that the purpose of design and technology is to make things work (and look) better. For example, if a car that was produced was safer, stronger, cheaper, lighter, faster and more economical than existing models, we would all agree that it was a better car. In practice, we would find that many of the design requirements in this example conflicted with one another, and choices would have to be made between them. For example, speed might conflict with economy, and cheapness and lightness with strength and safety. Design and technology, therefore, usually involves compromises. The requirements have to be put in order of importance before producing a solution that fulfils as many of them as possible.

In some cases, after following a design process we may come up with a result very different from our preconceived idea of what the solution should be. This shows that it is important when designing to explore all possible solutions, and not to settle for the first idea that comes to mind. On other occasions, after thoroughly investigating the problem we may find that the best solution is similar to existing ones. A design does not have to be entirely different to be good.

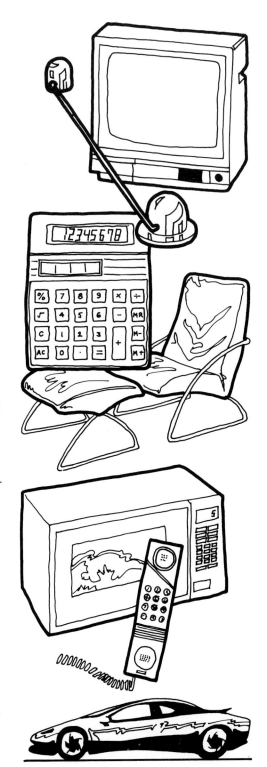

Changes in design and progress in technology

Many of the things we use today have evolved from products first produced a long time ago, and developments have often been slow because of the strong influence of existing designs and because people are sometimes reluctant to accept major steps forward. The motor car is a very good example of how a design has evolved over many years. Changes from year to year have usually been small, but the difference between current models and the carriage-like originals is now very marked.

The rate of change is controlled by two basic factors: first, the development of technology which presents new opportunities for design; and, secondly, changes in the needs of people who will buy the product and thus create a demand for change. Examples of changes in the motor car resulting from new technology include the use of pneumatic tyres (an early change) and the use of electronics — even computers — for engine control (a recent change).

Changes resulting from public demand include the recent switch to smaller and more economical cars because of high fuel costs and increased attention to safety and pollution control because of government action in many countries.

At certain times, cars judged too revolutionary have not been successful even though they were excellent vehicles. This was simply because the public was not ready to accept them.

The effect of design and technology on our lives

In deciding how to use the resources available to us, the designer must sometimes make decisions which could change all our lives. For example, we must choose between the conservation of open spaces and the need for more homes, factories and roads. Design and technology has the power to make or destroy our future, because the results of a mistake when tackling projects of this size could be catastrophic. The chances of a mistake increase when the project gets too big for any one person to oversee and when designers are working at the limits of their knowledge and experience.

For example, a decision was taken in the 1950s to re-house thousands of people in high-rise blocks of flats in order to save land, which could then be used to provide more open spaces, or to prevent towns getting ever larger. This has proved to be a disastrous mistake in many places. Not only were the buildings more difficult and more expensive to build than expected, but they often failed to provide the good low-cost housing which was needed and were unpopular with those forced to live in them. The living conditions they created have been blamed for a large increase in social problems such as vandalism, violence, loneliness, stress and mental illness. Now, many people are no longer prepared to live in them. Also, running repairs to high-rise buildings have proved to be very expensive. As a result, it has at last been admitted that the policy was wrong, and in some cases buildings only a few years old are being demolished to make way for new types of housing.

Understanding design and technology

It is generally agreed that the best way to avoid such mistakes in the future is to encourage more public involvement in decisions which affect everyone's lives, e.g. in architecture, planning and industrial design, so that everyone who is affected can have a say in deciding and influencing what should be done. This will only be possible when the public understand enough about design and technology, and are well-enough informed about important matters, to be able to discuss sensibly and constructively what should be done.

Our understanding of design and our experience of designing will help us to do this. In the same way it will prove valuable in helping us to make decisions about choosing things. Deciding what type of chair to buy, for example, can involve the same careful and objective study of the functional and aesthetic aspects of chair design as is involved in designing one to fit the same situation. Design training is therefore a valuable introduction to making decisions and solving problems in a wide range of situations in later life.

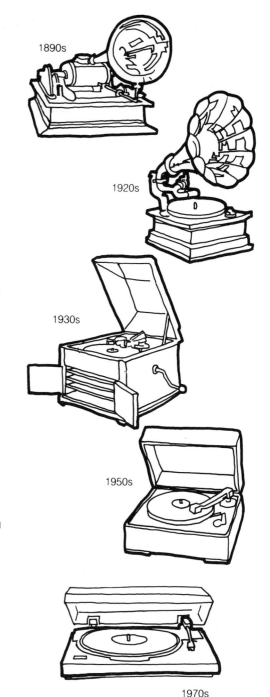

1890s

1920s

1930s

1950s

Evaluating design

Since the success of a design is measured by how well the final solution fulfills the need which the designer set out to meet, and since we are surrounded by examples of professional designers' solutions to what they, or the manufacturers who employ them, saw as the needs of the public, we can learn more about design and develop our own sense of good design by looking carefully and critically at everyday objects such as buildings, cars, bicycles, furniture and electrical equipment. We can make this activity even more valuable by keeping a scrapbook of our own notes, sketches and cuttings from magazines and catalogues to illustrate what we consider to be good designs or parts of designs, and by writing down what we consider to be the good and bad points of a design, together with the reasons for our decisions.

It is also helpful to study the development of things to see how they have improved (or deteriorated). For example, all the products shown on this page are able to reproduce music, but each has advantages over the product it replaced. You might like to write down what you think these advantages are and compare your list with other people's.

1970s

Communicating ideas

1980s

It is wrong to think that we can study or practise design in isolation, because before we can begin to design we must learn how to communicate our ideas clearly and fluently; before we can see a design project through to a successful conclusion we must have a good working knowledge of the materials available to make our solution, together with the tools and processes used to shape, join and finish them; and before we can use our knowledge of design usefully and responsibly, for the benefit of everyone, we must have a sound general knowledge of the needs of our society and of the role of the designer in it.

2 Communicating through graphics

PART 1: Freehand sketching

If we are to design well, we must have efficient ways of recording our ideas and communicating them to other people. Freehand sketching is the quickest way of doing this. However, sketching must not be mistaken for a rough type of drawing, but should be presented carefully.

If you follow a few simple rules, learning to sketch can be quite easy:

1 Decide which of the numerous techniques you wish to use. (If in doubt read through the following pages before going any further.)
2 Choose a suitable pencil (HB) and make sure it has a **sharp** conical point.
3 Hold the pencil correctly as shown in the diagram. This position will enable faint lines to be drawn in any direction.
4 **Crating.** Always start by making a faint framework or box into which details can be drawn simply. Never try to make a finished-looking drawing straight away.
5 **Lining in.** Once you are satisfied that your faint sketch is correct, increase the pressure on the pencil to produce bold outlines and medium detail lines. As some degree of confidence is required when lining in, it is an advantage to be able to move your papers around to the most suitable position for each line to be drawn.
6 **Curves.** Use the wrist as a compass point around which you can pivot your hand.

Sketch in a tidy manner and try to keep the proportions (the relationship of one measurement to another) as accurate as possible.

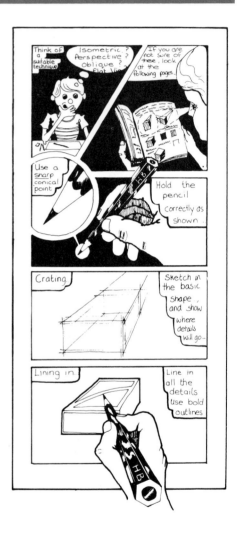

Ways of sketching

In the following sketches we have shown a cube drawn in five different ways. Each projection or method of drawing gives a different view of the cube, and each has advantages and disadvantages over the others. Therefore, you must become familiar with when and how to use each method, so that when sketching you can choose the best one for each purpose. This is in order to show on paper exactly what you want to put over.

One- and two-point perspective offer a good way to start drawing three-dimensional objects, either completely freehand or using ruler and pencil. Simple flat views can be drawn easily provided that you remember to keep the different views lined up with each other as shown.

Formal drawing using instruments will be introduced later.

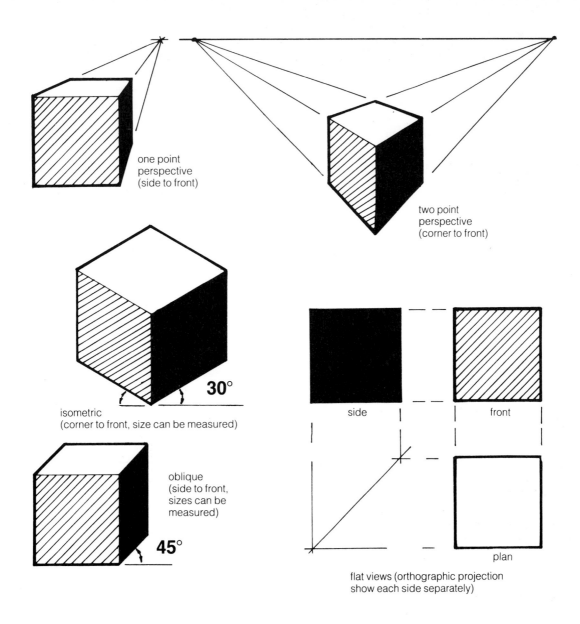

one point perspective (side to front)

two point perspective (corner to front)

30°

isometric (corner to front, size can be measured)

oblique (side to front, sizes can be measured)

45°

side

front

plan

flat views (orthographic projection show each side separately)

Perspective drawing

This allows us to draw shapes quickly and easily in a way which closely resembles their actual appearance. We can, therefore, use it to see what our finished design would look like.

When we look at objects drawn in perspective we see that:

(a) Parallel lines appear to converge (get closer together) as they recede (go away) from us.
(b) Equal lengths at different distances from us no longer look equal, but appear to get smaller as they recede.
(c) Objects of similar size appear to get smaller in size as they recede from us.

Perspective makes objects look solid and gives a sense of depth to the picture.

ONE-POINT PERSPECTIVE

To draw a simple box-shape in one point:

(a) Draw a flat view of one side of the object in faint construction lines. This will be the true shape of the side and can be drawn to scale if required.

(b) Draw the horizon line which represents your eye level as you look at the object. This can be above the flat view if you want to see the top, below it if you want to see the bottom, and through the flat view if you want to make the drawing look as though you are level with it.

(c) Mark the vanishing point somewhere along the horizon line. Its position will determine which side of the completed shape will be seen.

(d) Draw faint lines from each corner of the flat view to the vanishing point.

(e) Complete the shape by drawing the back of the shape, noting that the lines from the flat view towards the vanishing point will be shorter than their true length. You will have to judge the correct lengths for yourself. In this example the back lines are parallel to the front shape.

This example shows how we can alter our view point by raising or lowering the eye level, and vary the amount of each side seen by changing the position of the vanishing point along the eye level. Notice how some views have only two sides showing.

Once you can draw these shapes, practise drawing other three-dimensional geometric forms until you feel confident, and then use them to construct recognisable objects.

(a)

(b)

(c) VP

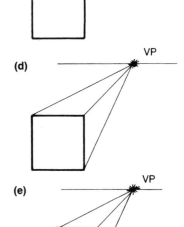

(d) VP

(e) VP

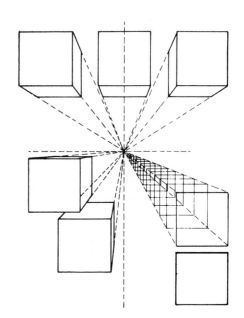

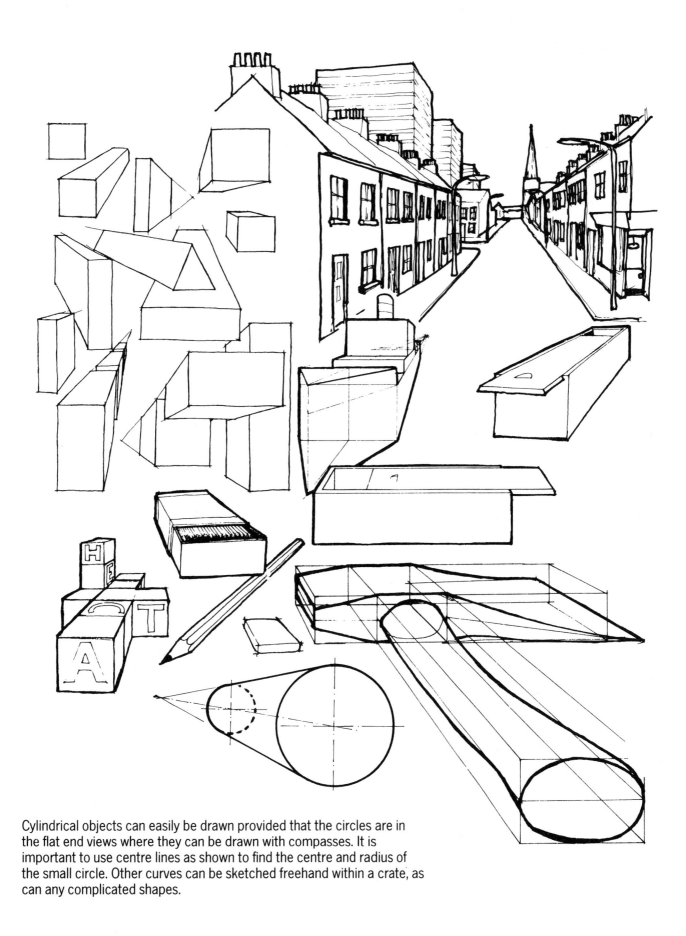

Cylindrical objects can easily be drawn provided that the circles are in the flat end views where they can be drawn with compasses. It is important to use centre lines as shown to find the centre and radius of the small circle. Other curves can be sketched freehand within a crate, as can any complicated shapes.

TWO-POINT PERSPECTIVE

In order to draw a realistic view of an object when all its sides are receding from the spectator, two vanishing points are needed.

The vertical edge nearest to the spectator is the only dimension which can be drawn to scale. All other lines are reduced in length as they recede.

As in one-point perspective, we can draw different views of an object by altering our eye level and view point.

(a)

(b)

(c)

(d)

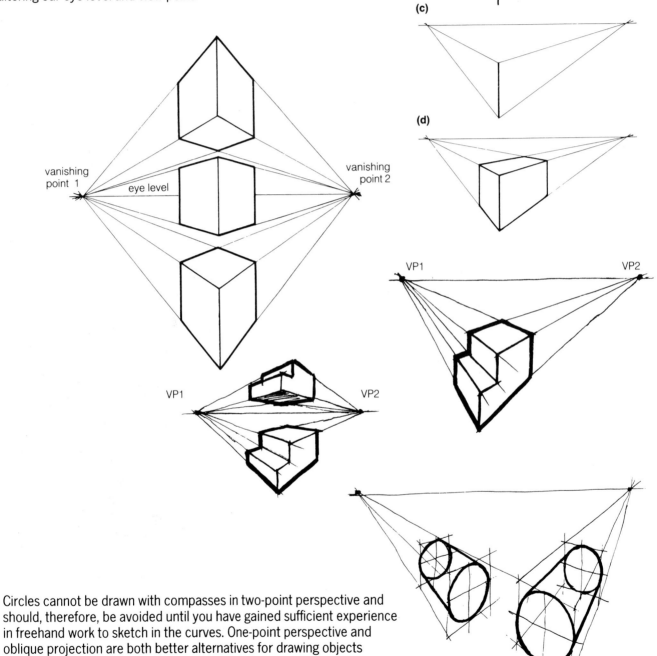

vanishing point 1   eye level   vanishing point 2

VP1   VP2

VP1   VP2

Circles cannot be drawn with compasses in two-point perspective and should, therefore, be avoided until you have gained sufficient experience in freehand work to sketch in the curves. One-point perspective and oblique projection are both better alternatives for drawing objects including curves, at this stage.

If, however, you have to draw curved shapes in two-point, you should use the crating technique used here to sketch cylinders.

Oblique views

These are similar to one-point perspective views in that the true shape of one side is drawn first (see diagram (a)).However, the oblique lines in the drawing (those which are angled between horizontal and vertical) do not recede as they do in perspective drawing. Instead, they are drawn parallel to each other at an angle of 45° (see diagram (b)). This angle will produce a well-shaped realistic drawing. To give the impression of foreshortening, the 45° lines are drawn at half their true length (see diagram (c)). Unless you do this your drawing will look too long from front to back. The shape is then completed.

The main **advantage** of oblique over one-point perspective is that lines can be measured accurately on the front shape and along the 45° lines. The main **disadvantage** is that it does not look quite as realistic as perspective because the lines at the back of the drawing remain the same size as those at the front, when they should be smaller.

Oblique projection, like one-point perspective, is very good for drawing curves as the drawing can usually be arranged so that the curves can be drawn on the flat front face with a compass. Curves on the sloping sides (right) have to be drawn freehand as in isometric and two-point perspective. All the other curves in this section can be drawn with compasses.

CRATING

Oblique and one-point perspective views become a little more difficult to draw when there is no true shape at the front to work from. However, this can be overcome by using the crating technique already introduced (see the example on the right).

Complex detailing is possible when using oblique drawing (see right). In this, oblique is easier than one-point perspective, which would involve reducing the size of the detailing as it receded towards the vanishing point.

(a)

(b)

(c)

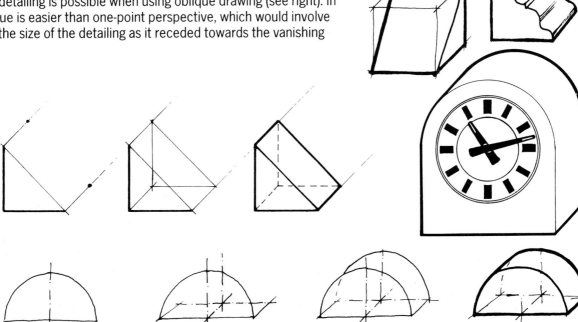

Isometric projection

This allows us to draw views with one corner of an object at the front, as in two-point perspective.

All vertical lines remain vertical while all horizontal lines are angled at 30° to the horizontal (see diagram (a)).

Although none of the sides in an isometric view appear as true shapes, all the sides are measured out to their actual sizes (see diagram (b)). The shape is then completed using more 30° lines (see diagram (c)). One disadvantage of isometric projection is that these lines at the top of the drawing often look as though they are too long because they are drawn full size.

More complicated shapes can easily be drawn using crating, but curves can prove difficult to draw as they usually have to be drawn freehand within a crate.

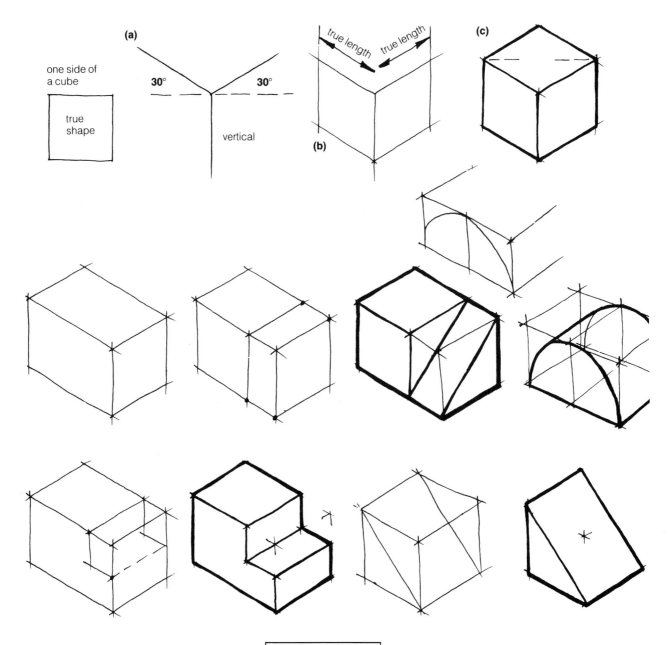

Flat views (orthographic projection)

1 Flat work involving an element of design (e.g. designing the pattern for a tiled table top) can easily be communicated on paper as it only has two dimensions, length and width (see diagram (a)). However, any shape which is to be developed in three dimensions is more difficult to visualise.

2 When we wish to show length, width **and** thickness we have to resort to drawing a second view in order to avoid changing from a flat to a pictorial drawing (see diagram (b)).

3 As the form of the object becomes more complicated, we have to add more views to show all parts of it (see diagram (c)). However, the number of views can often be reduced by using dotted lines to show hidden details (see diagram (d)), and three views — front, plan (top) and one side — are usually sufficient.

We must be careful to keep these views in their correct position in relation to each other, and to project lines across and down from one to the other so that we can see how they fit together to give a complete picture of the design.

Flat views are a simple way of showing an object accurately with all the sides drawn to their correct size. You can add dimensions and notes to give all the information needed to make the object. Therefore, flat views are especially useful for drawing the final solution (see diagram (e)).

As it is often difficult to visualise the appearance of the proposed solution from flat views alone, they are often accompanied by a pictorial view and/or a model (see diagram (f)).

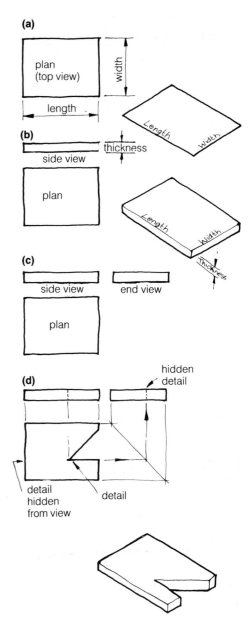

(a) plan (top view), width, length

(b) side view, thickness, plan, Length, Width, Thickness

(c) side view, end view, plan

(d) hidden detail, detail hidden from view, detail

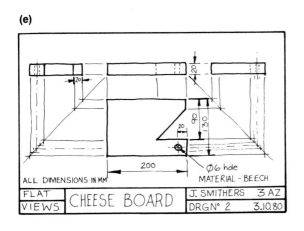

(e)
ALL DIMENSIONS IN MM.
200
Ø6 hole
MATERIAL - BEECH.
FLAT VIEWS · CHEESE BOARD · J. SMITHERS 3 AZ · DRG.N° 2 · 3.10.80

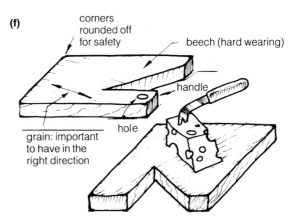

(f)
corners rounded off for safety
beech (hard wearing)
handle
hole
grain: important to have in the right direction

While freehand sketching provides us with a very good way to record and communicate our ideas quickly during the early stages of the design process, it is not always sufficient on its own. There are times during an investigation when more accurate drawing may be needed to work out sizes and to prove whether ideas will work, and the final solution must always be presented sufficiently accurately for it to be made.

In order to produce such accurate drawings quickly we must use the specialist instruments developed for the purpose.

The equipment

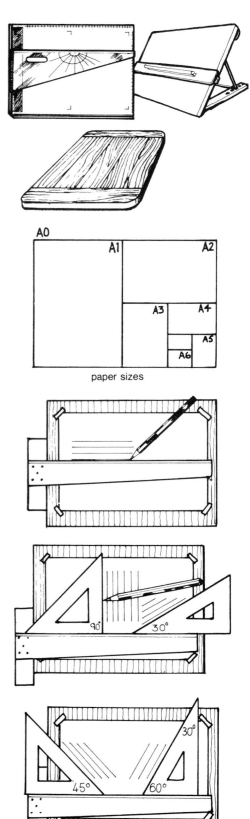

AO

paper sizes

DRAWING BOARDS   vary in size according to the largest size of paper they can be used with, e.g. A1, A2, A3, A4 as shown on the right.

Traditional wooden boards are specially constructed so that they remain flat and have a straight edge at each end. Newer developments in board design include the fitting of a parallel motion mechanism which keeps the tee-square attached to the board and parallel to the top of the board, and portable plastic boards which are light, simple to use and have many of the instruments normally used with a board built in.

TEE-SQUARES   are used to draw horizontal lines. To work accurately the blade and butt must join rigidly at 90° and the drawing edge of the blade must be absolutely straight. Care must be taken not to weaken the joint or chip the edge by misuse.

Before we start drawing we use the tee-square to line the paper up on the drawing board. This ensures that the horizontal edges of the paper are parallel to the tee-square blade and that all subsequent lines drawn on the paper are parallel with its top edge. When using a separate tee-square it is essential that the butt is pressed firmly against the **left-hand edge** of the drawing board during use.

SET SQUARES   are used on the blade of the tee-square to produce vertical lines at right angles to the tee-square and for drawing lines at common angles to the tee-square. There are two types of set square, one with angles of 30°, 60° and 90°, and the other with 45°, 45° and 90° angles. The first is particularly used for isometric drawing and the second for oblique drawing.

THE PROTRACTOR   can be used to construct any angle to the horizontal or vertical, but it is easier to use set squares to construct common angles and any combination of these.

PENCILS are probably the most important items of equipment you will use. If inaccurate drawings are to be avoided it is essential that the correct pencil is chosen for each job and that the correct **sharp point** is maintained throughout its use:

(a) **Conical points** should be used on HB and H pencils for sketching and lettering.

(b) **Chisel points** should be used on harder pencils. These are first sharpened with a knife and then finished on fine emery cloth. These pencils are used for all line work and are essential if a good standard of draughtsmanship is to be maintained.

COMPASSES are of many types, but all must be used with sharp leads sharpened to match the pencils used for straight lines.

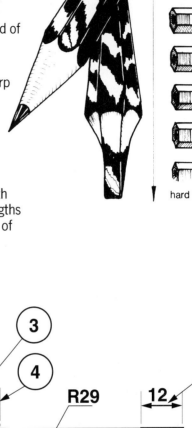

Types of line

Types of line are standardised by British Standard BS 308 along with most of the rules governing engineering drawing. Correct line strengths are a very important part of the language of drawing and each type of line has its own exact meaning. Study the example below carefully, practise using correct line strengths and remember them.

1 Projection lines.
2 Hatching/section lines.
3 Cutting planes.
4 Centre lines.
5 Dimension lines.
6 Hidden detail lines.
7 Outlines.
8 Lettering (see p. 16).

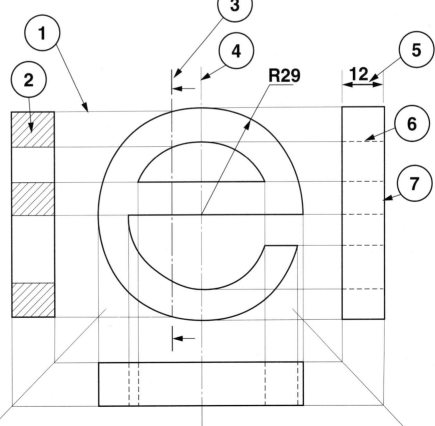

Ways of drawing

When drawing with instruments we use the same five ways of drawing (or projections) already introduced in the section on freehand sketching. You can, therefore, practise drawing with instruments simply by working through the examples given in the previous section and then finding everyday items to measure and draw. It is also valuable to go back to simple design projects for which you prepared only freehand sketches, and draw accurate flat views and pictorial presentation drawings.

It is not possible to provide a complete course in formal drawing here and so we have tried, first, to introduce as many useful drawing techniques as possible in just enough detail for you to start using them. Secondly, we have given fuller details of those not so easily found in readily available technical drawing books.

ORTHOGRAPHIC PROJECTION

Drawings which will be used in the workshop must contain all the information needed to make the design. The simplest way to convey this amount of detail is by using flat views or, to give them their correct name, **orthographic projection.**

There are two types of orthographic projection:

(a) First-angle projection (English).
(b) Third-angle projection (American).

It is important that you understand the basic differences between the two systems, which are described below.

FIRST-ANGLE PROJECTION

Imagine that the letter 'F' is suspended in a box and that we are drawing on the box sides. The final views shown in A4 are constructed by looking at the letter in the directions shown by the arrows in diagram A1, and projecting the images **through** the object onto the inside of the box (diagram A2). This is then opened out (diagram A3).

The important points to note are:
 (i) Start with view F, the front elevation.
 (ii) The view from E, the end elevation, will be drawn to the right of the front elevation.
(iii) When looking down from P, the plan will appear below the front elevation.

Summary
Project **through** the object away from the viewing position.

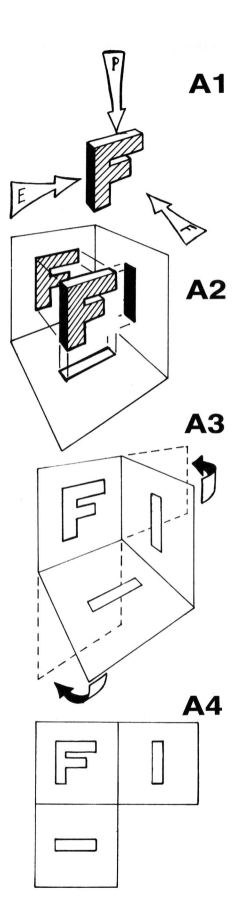

A1

A2

A3

A4

THIRD-ANGLE PROJECTION

In third-angle we construct the final views shown in diagram B4 by looking at the letter from exactly the same angles as before (diagram B1). However, this time the images are projected **back** towards the onlooker through the box onto the outside of it (diagram B2). The box is then opened out (diagram B3). The important points to note are:

 (i) Start with F, the front elevation.
 (ii) The view from E, the end elevation, will be drawn to the left of the front elevation.
(iii) When looking down from P, the plan will appear above the front elevation.

Summary
Project **back** to the viewing position.

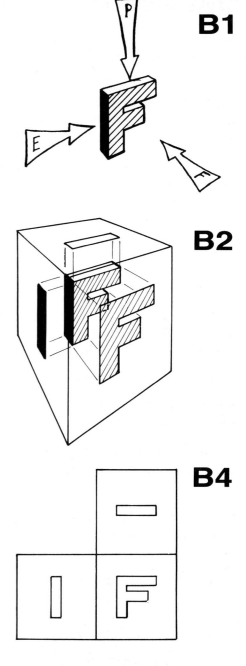

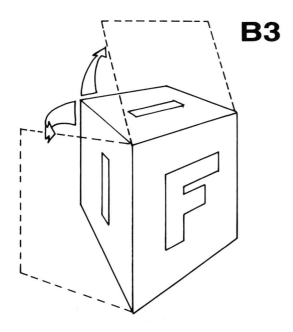

DRAWING TO SCALE

This allows us to see views of an object in true proportion. Drawings need not be full size, but can be enlarged or reduced provided that the scale is printed on the drawing. Full size is shown as 1:1; half size as 1:2; twice full size as 2:1; etc. However, any dimensions on the drawing are always printed **full size**, giving the actual sizes to which the object will be made.

PRESENTATION OF FORMAL DRAWINGS

Follow these steps carefully when presenting formal drawings. Although we have shown an orthographic drawing, these rules apply to all drawings.

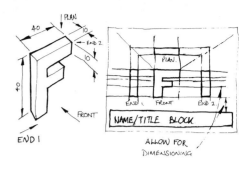

1 Work out the overall sizes and the best way to space the views in rough first. If orthographic projection is being used, as in the example shown, decide now how many elevations will be needed. Also decide if sections or hidden detail are needed to ensure that mistakes are not made on the final drawing. Allow room for dimensioning and other necessary information such as a name/title block, scale and projection used (see right).

2 Using very faint pencil lines (3H or harder) draw in the position of each part (**crating**). Check this arrangement as faintly drawn lines can easily be corrected at this stage. If correct, proceed to **project** further details from one view to another. (Use 45° lines or compasses to project through 90° from plan to end views.) When drawing symmetrical shapes or shapes involving curves, it is often best to start by drawing centre lines to work from. It is essential that you build up your drawing by projecting lines from one view to another and do not construct each view separately. Projection is much more accurate and ensures that each view lines up correctly with the others. Every time you measure there is the chance of making a mistake.

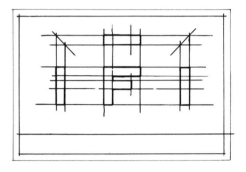

3 Begin to fill in detail with a sharp medium line only when you are certain that everything is correct. Once lined in, lines cannot be changed neatly.

4 Draw around each view with a sharp bold outline.

5 Add limit and dimension lines.

6 Complete name/title block and any additional information (see right).

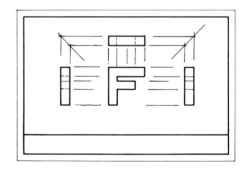

LAYOUT

If visual information is to be communicated efficiently it must be presented neatly and in an organised way. The careful use of projection lines will ensure correct spacing of the various drawing elements involved. However, when written information has also to be included, such as name, date, title, scale, materials, etc., a system of name/title blocks is usually adopted. There are many ways in which these blocks of information can be arranged but in each case the emphasis must be on clarity.

LETTERING

The success of a name/title block will depend almost entirely on the standard of lettering used. For this reason it is important that a simple straightforward letter type is used. Decorative lettering should be avoided. Use guide lines when printing.

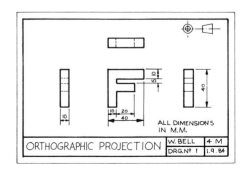

ABCDEFGHIJKLMNOPQRSTUVWXYZ

HIDDEN DETAIL

You may have noticed that very little of the detail on the 'F' block shown on the previous page has been included on the end elevations or plans. This is because these details are hidden when looking from the chosen view points. Hidden detail lines enable us to show this hidden information and may reduce the number of elevations needed.

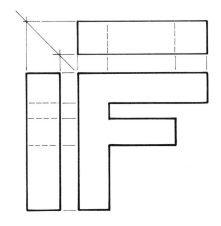

DIMENSIONING

Usually the main purpose of an orthographic projection is to give information as to the size and proportions of an object. Therefore, measurements must be given to indicate the size of the individual parts, and overall length, width and height. As the drawing may be required for continuous reference in the workshops, it is important that dimensions can be easily and quickly read.

Study the following rules carefully when dimensioning drawings:

1 You must be able to read all lettering and dimensions from the bottom or right-hand side of the sheet, so that you do not have to rotate the paper.

2 To avoid confusion, space the dimensions well away from the drawing.

3 All letters and figures should be clear and of the same height (use guide lines which sit above, not on, the dimension lines).

4 Use neat, bold but sharp arrow heads.

5 Leave 1 mm space between the part being dimensioned and the limit lines.

6 Try not to show the same dimension more than once. For further details consult BS 308. It is not necessary to show dimensions which can be easily worked out by adding or subtracting others.

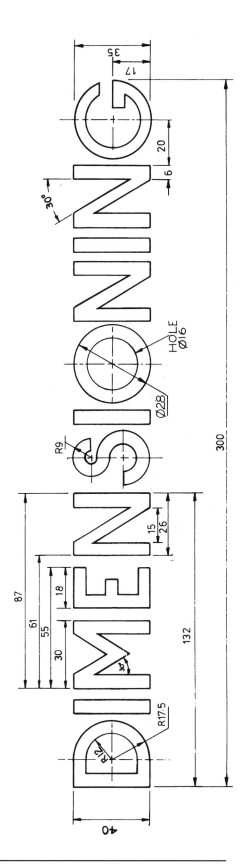

SECTIONAL VIEWS

1 Sometimes additional views and even hidden detail cannot give sufficient information to clearly illustrate the construction of an object. Sectioning provides us with a very good method of seeing inside an object.

2 **Cutting planes**. A cutting plane on one of the elevations or the plan of an orthographic projection indicates where the object is to be sectioned. The arrows attached to the cutting plane indicate the direction from which the section will be viewed.

The position of the sectional elevation on the paper is worked out in the same way as for any of the other elevations shown previously. Surfaces which have been cut through are carefully cross-hatched to make the section show up more clearly.

These examples show sections in different directions through the block (right) in both orthographic and isometric projections.

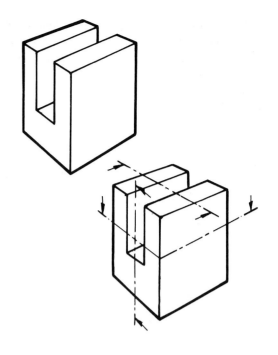

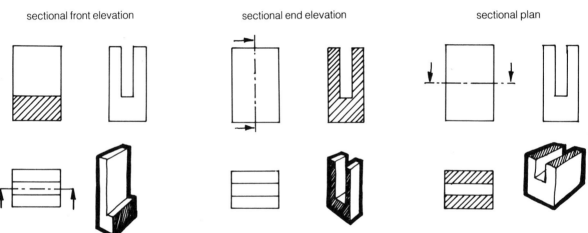

sectional front elevation   sectional end elevation   sectional plan

3 This example shows how a cutting plane is marked on an isometric drawing and how a section can be used to reveal important information which cannot be seen on the normal isometric view.

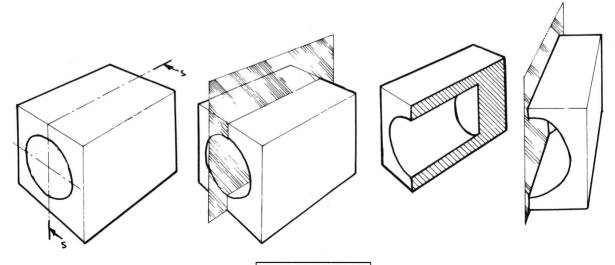

The drawing below illustrates how inadequate a pictorial view alone is compared to an orthographic projection including hidden detail, and the use of orthographic and/or isometric sectional elevations.

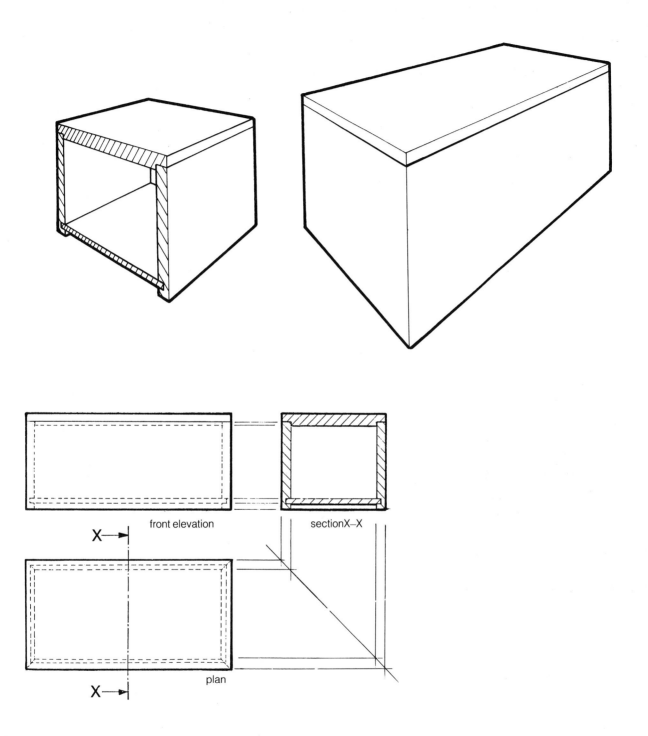

front elevation

sectionX–X

X→

X→

plan

Note: Only the view indicated by the cutting plane X–X appears as a sectional view. The other views must be drawn as complete views unless further cutting planes are added.

WAYS OF DRAWING — A SUMMARY

The exploded view (top) shows a simple toy garage made from several wooden blocks. Compare the different techniques used on this page to show the garage and choose the one most suited to the drawing you want to do.

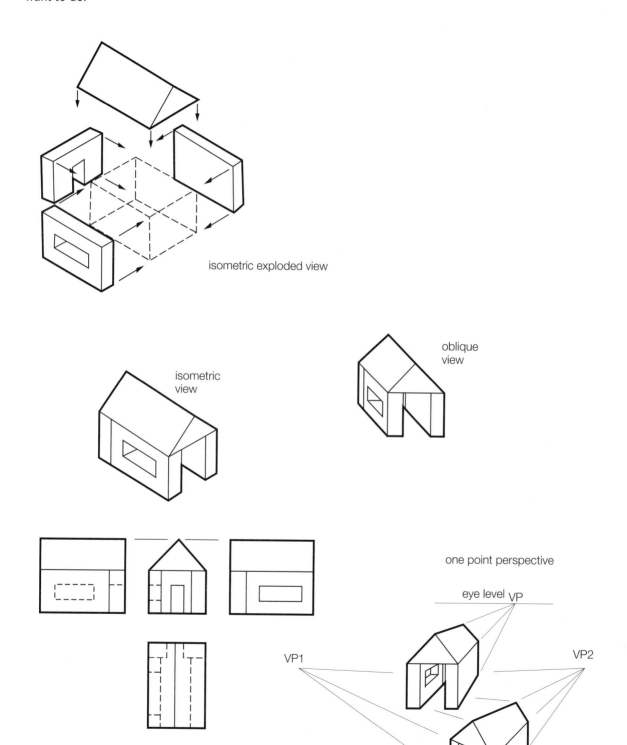

isometric exploded view

isometric view

oblique view

orthographic projection

one point perspective

eye level VP

VP1

VP2

two point perspective

Shading

Simple flat views given in orthographic projection are sufficient to explain the basic proportions of each side of an artefact. Pictorial views are used to give an overall picture of an object. However, as these views are still merely two-dimensional line drawings of three-dimensional objects, they often lack the appearance of being solid. Hence the need for a method of successfully representing an object. There are many ways of achieving this aim using a wide variety of media.

SIMPLE COLOURING AND SHADING

We see objects around us because they reflect light. Therefore, the position of the object and our viewing position in relation to the source of light are primary factors regarding the view we see. A rectangular form, for example, will reflect varying amounts of light from each of its sides as each side is at right angles to the others.

To make possible a simple demonstration of shading, the position of light in each example has been assumed. Shadows that would usually be cast from an object have been left out.

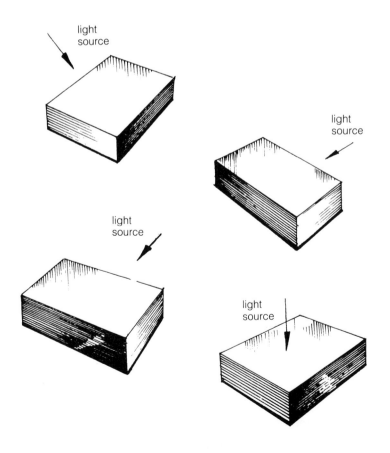

PENCIL AND PENCIL CRAYONS

These can be used to create some very 'professional' results. However, these results can only be achieved by extremely careful use of the media.

Hold the pencil about half-way down its length and at the same time lower the pencil so that the side of the conical point, and not the point itself, comes into contact with the paper. Begin shading/colouring by moving the pencil from one side to the other, merely allowing the weight of the pencil to provide the light pressure needed to build up a faint layer of colour. Repeat this process as many times as is required to sufficiently cover the area being shaded.

In this way it is possible to build up a very flat layer of colour.

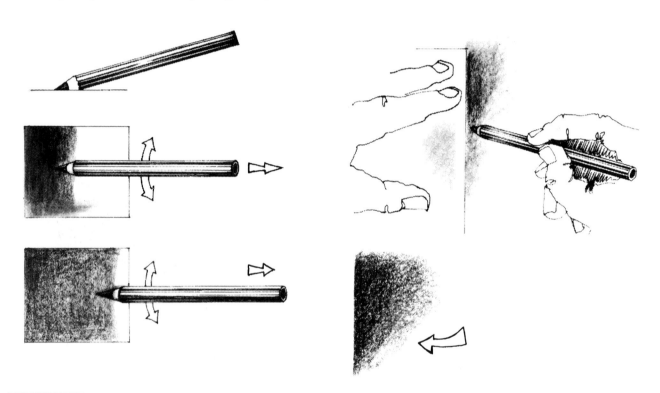

MASKING

It takes quite a lot of skill to colour up to a line, and so the use of a sheet of paper may prove beneficial in giving a good crisp edge.

Using scraps of paper in this way (they must have good straight edges) is a simple method of keeping the background to a drawing clean.

However, if the background has also become shaded and hence the edges of the drawing will appear woolly, this masking technique can be used to correct the situation. Put a piece of paper over your drawing but line one straight edge of the paper up to the edge of the drawing and proceed to erase any unwanted pencil marks. Repeat this process on all edges to give a good clean finish to the drawing. (Of course this technique is more difficult if curves are involved.)

Before you begin to render objects make sure you can control the media first. Practise creating the flat areas of tone described above. Make each one slightly lighter or darker than the next. Now try shading from the faintest tone you can possibly make to the darkest, which should be almost black.

THE CUBE

Follow the instructions below very carefully:

1 Apply a very faint tone over all three surfaces as practised above.
2 Ignoring face A, apply a second tonal layer over faces B and C. Already the cube will have a more solid appearance.
3 Now complete the process by adding a third layer to face C, which should then appear to be in shadow.

For a more three-dimensional effect, graduate the density of tone (using the practice exercise above) so that it looks similar to diagram 4.

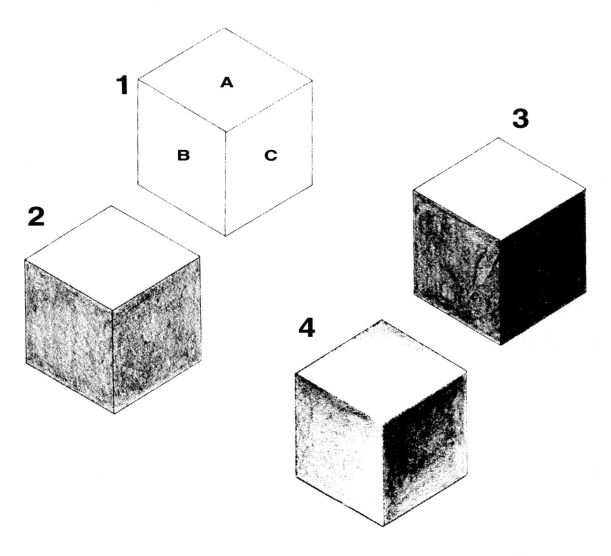

THE CYLINDER

1 Apply a faint layer of tone covering the whole of the drawing.
2 Ignoring the uppermost surface, graduate the tone on the rounded surface so that a light-to-dark effect is gained as illustrated.

Water based paints/ink

Many people are frightened off the idea of using paints because of one or two early disastrous attempts. Indeed, there are more problems involved with paints but the effects of these can be reduced considerably if tackled in an organised way.

There are many types of paint available which are suitable for graphic work, but here are the main ones which you are likely to use.

WATER COLOURS

These can be bought in small tubes as a paste or as a small tablet. (Students and Artists Quality should be used if possible.) A very small amount of pigment is needed to produce a good colour wash. (A large amount of water is used to dilute the pigment into a colour tint.)

This colour wash is applied to faint drawings in the same way as the faint layers of pencil were applied when rendering the cubes. However, each colour wash must be allowed to dry in between coats which have to be added quickly. Thick cartridge, water colour paper or card should be used as a base.

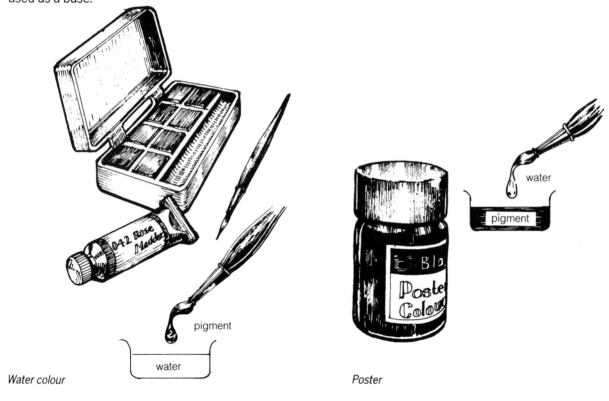

Water colour

Poster

POSTER COLOUR

There are many types and qualities. Unlike water colours, poster colours have to be mixed with a small amount of water. The water merely allows a thick coat of pigment to be applied smoothly over the paper. A good paint, applied correctly, will leave a flat, even colour which does not allow the white of the paper to show through.

Although only one coat should be necessary, poster colour has the disadvantage of having to be mixed to the right colour for each detail on the drawing. A greater degree of accuracy has to be shown and it can very easily look messy if mistakes are made.

DESIGNER'S GOUACHE

This is used in the same way as poster colour, but it can give a very professional finish. It does not make the base paper wrinkle as quickly as the other paints.

INK

Some inks can be used in the same way as water colour, but they do not usually give such a good finish. If waterproof inks are used, be very careful as brush strokes tend to show up. To avoid this work quickly.

Of course ink does not have to be used to form layers of colour as with paints, therefore line techniques can be used.

Nowadays the best way to achieve good line drawings is with the use of one of many makes of **technical pen**. These can be bought with nib widths ranging from less than 0.1 mm to over 2 mm. (They usually go up in 0.05 mm stages.) However, these are very expensive.

Drawing pens with the traditional type of nib are also very useful but are also expensive and difficult to use when doing technical work. They are good for sketching.

Many manufacturers are now producing a wide range of felt-tipped, fibre-tipped and ballpoint pens, some of which are quite suitable for fine drawing work and are relatively inexpensive.

Line rendering can be done with pencils, coloured pencils and pens, but avoid using medium and thick felt- and fibre-tips. Line drawing provides us with a simple method of rendering which can, if handled properly, produce very good results. However, success does rely on accurate spacing of lines. Study the illustrations carefully. Graduation of tone can be gained by fading out lines.

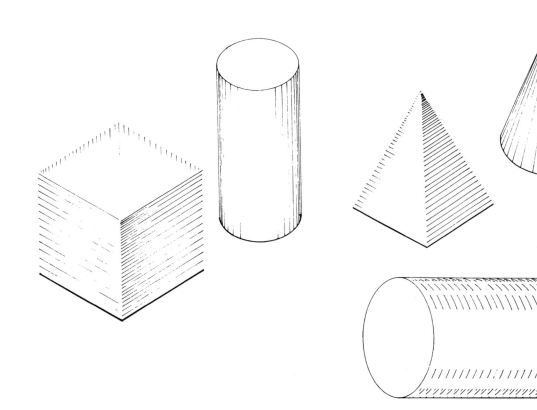

LETTERING

When drawing orthographic projections and other technical work, hand lettering or letters drawn in with the aid of letter guides are quite efficient methods of communicating information.

However, if a lot of time has been spent rendering a final presentation drawing of a design, good tidy lettering will be required to complement the work. Illustrated below are the main alternatives:

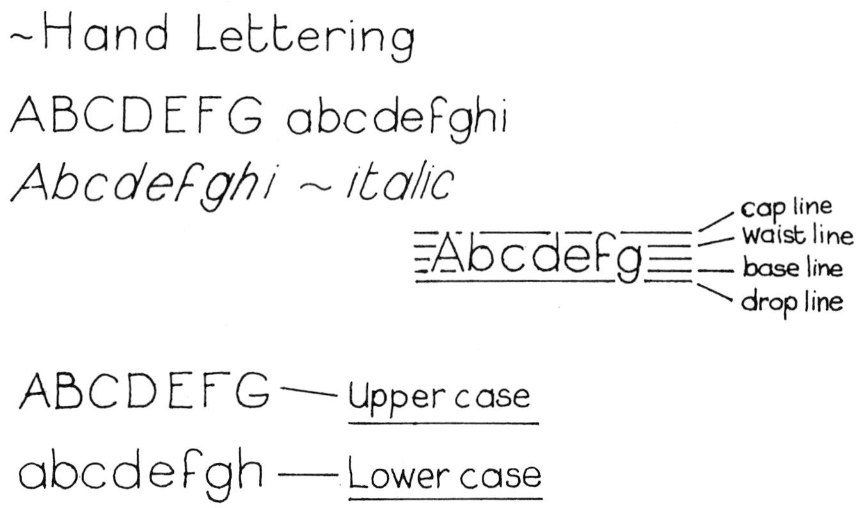

~Hand Lettering

ABCDEFG abcdefghi

Abcdefghi ~ italic

Abcdefg — cap line
— waist line
— base line
— drop line

ABCDEFG — Upper case

abcdefgh — Lower case

transfer letters :

sans serif

Extra Bold **Bold** Medium

Light OUTLINE *Italic* EXTENDED

Serif

Extra Bold **Bold** Medium

OUTLINE *Italic*

DECORATIVE

Old English ★ **Bottleneck**

Palace Script *Flash*

Fancy **DAVIDA**

In recent years the use of colour markers has transformed the way designers can communicate and represent ideas on paper. Just a few simple techniques are needed to begin producing realistic images.

The materials

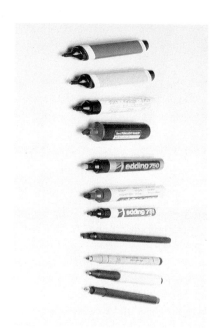

Markers are available in a bewildering variety of shapes, sizes and colours. The main differences are in the type and width of the nib and in the type of ink used. Markers contain either solvent-based inks (permanent) or water-based inks, and are capable of producing line widths between 1 mm and 25 mm.

To begin with, a fine black marker and several markers that give a medium broad line are all that are required. To complete the suggested exercise below, you will also need a soft white pencil and some bleed-proof paper. This limits the penetration and spread of ink and makes it easier to blend larger areas of colour.

As a first exercise, you might like to reproduce the outline of the hairdryer and follow the steps in rendering it. Alternatively, take another object, and apply the same procedure step-by-step.

Rendering a product

Step 1: Draw an outline of the product using a fine black pen. Start to fill in with colour around the outline, but do not go right to the edge: any small gaps can be filled in later.
Step 2: To fill in the red area without leaving streaks, a 'wet edge' has to be maintained. This means working the pen quickly backwards and forwards, keeping it just in contact with the previous stroke while it is still wet. This will require some practice on scrap paper.

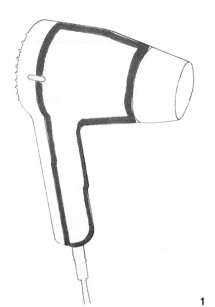

1

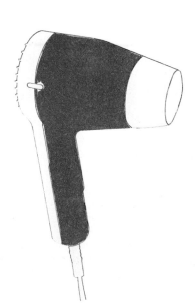

2

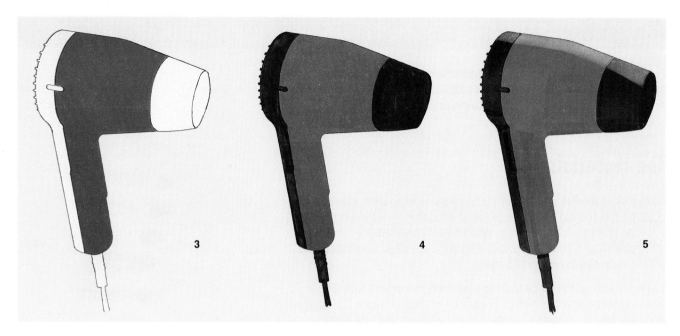

Step 3: The outline edge of the red area can now be filled in with a matching coloured pencil to sharpen up the outline.

Step 4: Fill in the black areas using the above techniques.

Step 5: The photograph shows most of the light falling on top of the hairdryer. This can be represented by colouring with a soft white pencil, taking care to blend the pencil strokes and make the whitening uniform.

Step 6: Using the white pencil slightly more heavily, the other highlights can be picked out. If these appear as straight lines, use a ruler on the drawing to guide the pencil.

Step 7: Finally, additional highlights are added together with small details such as the screw at the front.

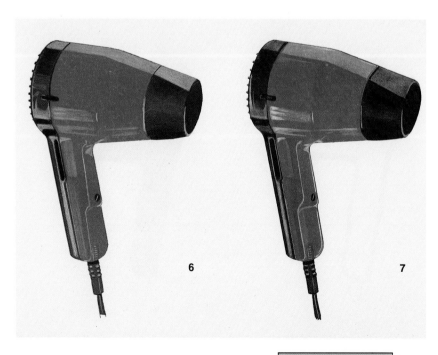

Marker streaking

Streaks are easily produced by a marker when a coloured area is blocked in. This is sometimes undesirable (e.g. the hairdryer), but is often used to good effect to give additional visual interest to rendered surfaces.

Experimentation with the rendering of a small alarm product illustrates the use of streaking. Notice also how darkening and some highlighting (with white pencil) at the edges produce the illusion of roundness. The sharpness of outline of the three images was obtained by cutting them from the original paper and re-mounting them.

Confidence in the use of markers grows if you practise getting particular effects and compare the results. This exercise in marker rendering of a cube pays attention to reflectivity on the surface, shadowing within the hole and appropriate treatment of the edges.

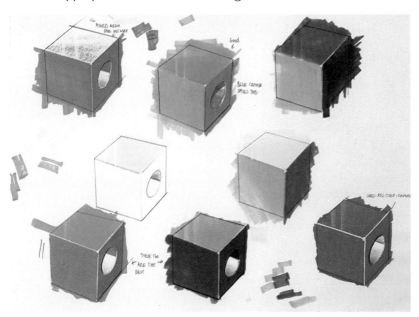

This example of an alarm product shows how a combination of simple techniques can add up to a very professional representation. The basic images have been cut out and re-mounted for sharpness of outline. Highlighting has been done with a soft white pencil and, in one or two places, typists' correction fluid, giving small intense points of white.

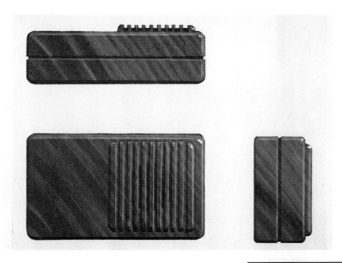

Airbrushing

Airbrushing has a long history and is widely used for creating images on paper — many of which have photographic realism. An airbrush creates a fine aerosol mist of ink that can be controlled to produce a narrow or diffuse spray.

Professional airbrushes can be expensive and difficult to maintain but a new system of airbrushing involves the use of ordinary markers. A small attachment having an air supply and trigger valve is clipped to the marker and directs a jet of air over the nib. This draws out ink and results in a fine spray. The source of air can be a propellant can or a garden sprayer unit if a normal compressor is unavailable.

The simple secret of much successful airbrushing lies in masking. Special low-tack masking films can be cut to the shape of an outline and laid over the paper surface to guarantee a sharp edge after airbrushing.

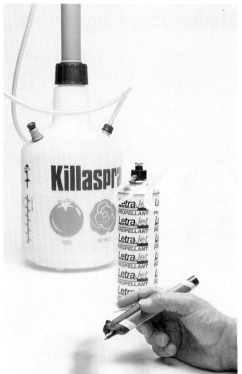

The geometrical shapes illustrated were initially defined by spraying through an accurately cut mask. Assuming that light is falling from the top left-hand corner, the objects are given depth by selective darkening of the surfaces. Careful use of the airbrush makes it possible to obtain almost imperceptible gradations of shade.

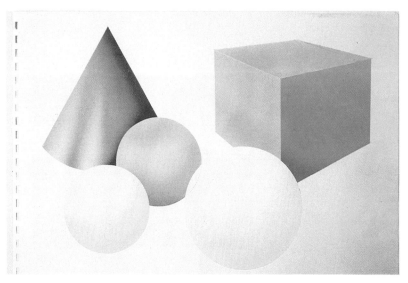

As computers become more powerful, graphic designers are becoming ever more interested in their potential for creating and adapting images. Advanced computers and software are capable of very high resolution (fine detail), and have an almost miraculous facility for adaptation and modification of an idea.

In design and technology, you will probably have access to computers and software packages capable of relatively low resolution work. These can be used very creatively indeed.

The following examples of work were produced using the AMX-SuperArt package. This is an easy to use icon/mouse system. Instructions are given via the mouse to select on-screen menu items and to 'draw' the image.

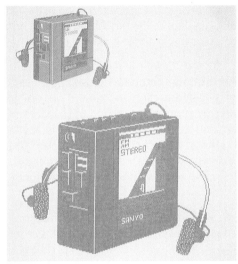

The hard copy was obtained from an ink-jet colour printer. Of special interest is the use of the package to produce part of the graphics for membrane panel switches. These can be completed using special transfers, rub-down lettering, etc. (see page 56).

This chapter has introduced a range of techniques for communicating ideas on paper. Four main areas of presentation can be identified as follows:

1 Preliminary sketches.
2 Development sketches.
3 Working drawings.
4 Presentation drawings.

These stages will enable the whole design process, from the first thoughts and ideas about a problem to the final 'rendered' solution, to be illustrated clearly.

1 PRELIMINARY SKETCHES

This first step in the presentation of design includes a simple investigation of the problem, research notes and sketches, and a series of annotated sketches (sketches and notes) outlining first thoughts and ideas.

Annotated sketches are used because this is the most efficient way of getting information and ideas down on paper. Sketches are used to convey information related to shape, form and overall appearance. Notes are added as the quickest way of indicating possible details such as fixing methods, manufacture, materials, etc., in addition to general points which may be of use later. As many ideas as possible should be collected before one or two are chosen for further development.

2 DEVELOPMENT SKETCHES

These are used to transform the rather vague ideas brought forward from the preliminary sketches into workable solutions ready for drawing up to scale.

To achieve this aim, each individual detail has to be developed (there may be many possible solutions to each) to fit within the whole scheme or design. Study the example given carefully.

3 WORKING DRAWINGS

These can include quite a varied selection of sketches or drawings, depending on the type of problem and the level of design required. A scale drawing will in itself help to finalise the dimensions and proportions brought forward from the development sketch stage.

However, the main purpose of working drawings is to provide all the information needed to make the artefact. This information can be displayed in a number of ways:

(a) **Orthographic projections** give specific information about dimensions and materials to be used and usually take the form of either:
    (i) assembly drawings, or
    (ii) parts drawings.

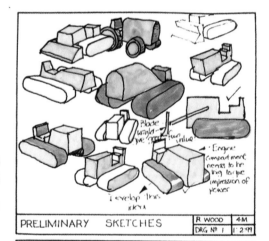

PRELIMINARY SKETCHES — R WOOD 4·M — DRG Nº 1

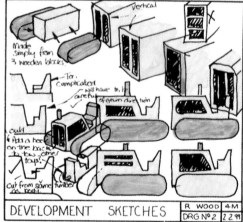

DEVELOPMENT SKETCHES — R WOOD 4·M — DRG Nº 2

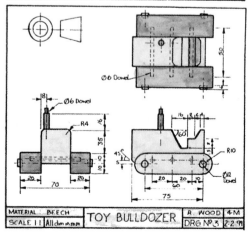

MATERIAL: BEECH — TOY BULLDOZER — R WOOD 4·M — SCALE 1:1 All dim in mm — DRG Nº 3

(b) **Pictorial views** are more commonly used to give instructions for assembly, but can be used as an alternative to (a). They may include:

(i) dimensions,
(ii) sections,
(iii) detail views,
(iv) exploded views.

Of course, the number of drawings that may be necessary depends upon the nature of the design solution. As a check to see if you have provided sufficient information ask yourself the question, 'Could a complete stranger understand and make the artefact illustrated on the drawings?'

4 PRESENTATION DRAWINGS

Not all design solutions require presentation drawings, many being manufactured directly from the information given in working drawings. However others, especially those that must have an attractive appearance, are far better drawn up and rendered to look like the made-up object. Once the techniques involved have been learned it will not take long before quick presentation views are possible. In this way, any modifications to the design can be made easily on the presentation drawing, and hence save time and expense by avoiding the same modifications having to be made to the actual artefact.

Good presentation drawings show your intentions and can suggest suitable materials, colours and finishes. They can even illustrate the object in use. You are, in a way, selling the idea to yourself and to others.

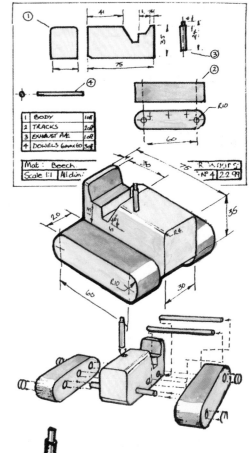

Many examples have been used to explain the presentation techniques used in this chapter. You should be able to learn them with practice and develop your own distinctive style of working.

More examples of presentation graphics are given here — including an example of packaging, and one showing how presentation of an idea in electronics can be made visually stimulating and interesting.

The first presentation drawing is a colour rendering of the hand-held thermometer shown in its design stage on pages 100–101.

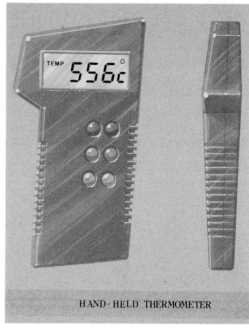

HAND-HELD THERMOMETER

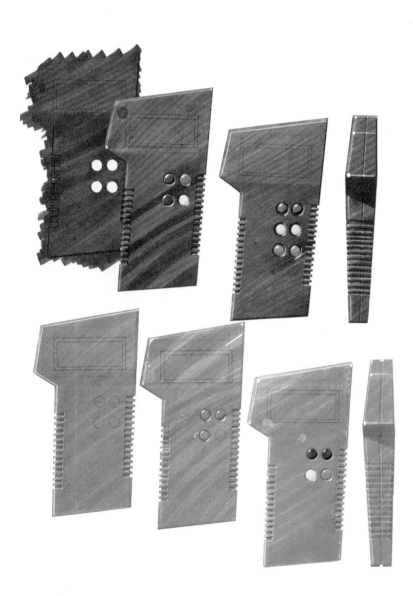

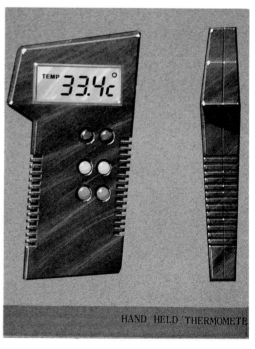

HAND HELD THERMOMETE

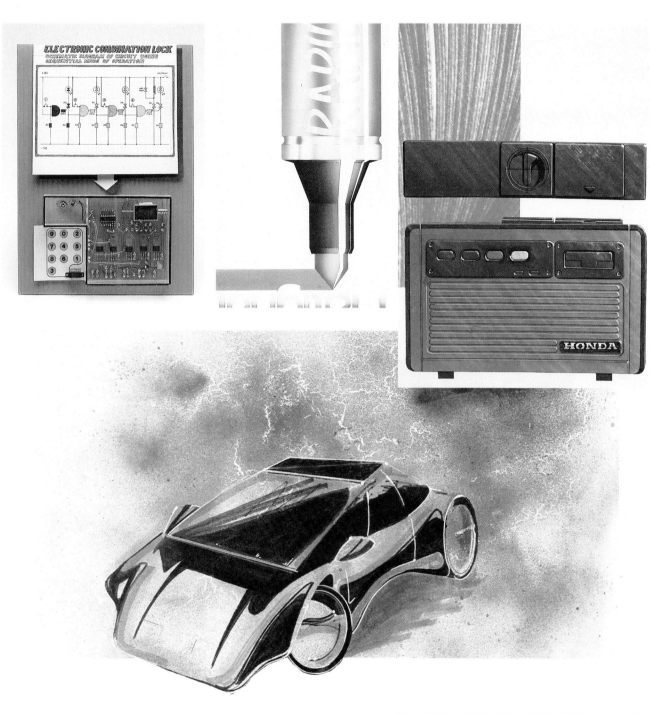

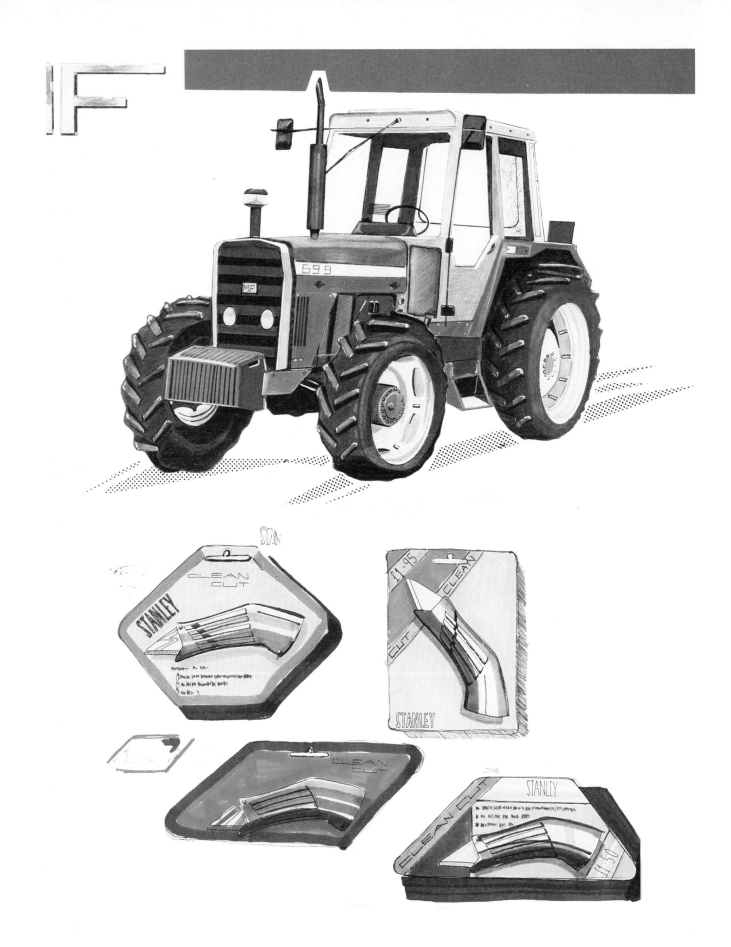

3 Communicating through models

Turning ideas into three-dimensional models is a way of developing design thinking and communicating it to other people. Professional designers are interested in models for many different reasons. Those designing large chemical plants, for example, build huge scale models of pipework that can cost anything up to a million pounds. These models, however, can save many more millions by showing up possible mistakes before building starts on the real thing.

To an engineer designing car body shells, the word 'model' sometimes means a computer-generated image on a screen. Computer modelling is now an important part of car design, ensuring — among other things — maximum safety in the event of a collision. Full-size three-dimensional models of cars are also made before final design decisions are taken.

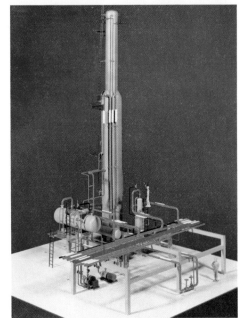

(a)

Product designers rely on models both to work out ideas and to show their clients precisely how a product will look, and sometimes how it will work, before it is mass produced. Product modelling is the name given to the creation of models for the whole range of consumer products, ranging in size from calculators to washing machines.

(b)

(c)

(d)

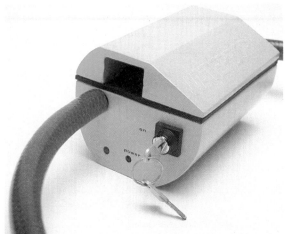

Working product models:

(a) torch (with thyristor switch circuit)   (b) electronic timer   (c) electroplating unit   (d) alarm unit

Some models can be compared to rough sketches and others to finished drawings. If you want to develop and express ideas, it is important to be able to 'sketch' and 'draw' in model form.

Paper and card models

These are commonly used materials because of the range of sheet thicknesses, colours and finishes available, in addition to their comparative cheapness, their ease of working and because most glues will stick them.

However, if a good standard of work is to be maintained certain procedures must be observed.

(i) **Technical drawing.** Accurate models can only result if precise drawings are made of the surface development of a three-dimensional solid object.

(ii) **Developments.** By using drawing instruments and adhering to correct drawing techniques, it is possible to draw the sides of almost any solid object on a sheet of paper or card so that they can be folded to make the form of the required object. Developments should be drawn so that they are made up of as few separate pieces as possible and in one piece if practical.

(iii) **Geometric forms.** As we observed earlier, most artefacts around us are made up of geometric forms. Therefore, it follows that the best way to learn to make developments is to practise on gradually more difficult geometric solids.

(iv) **Detailing.** One of the great advantages of using paper and card to make models is that the addition of small intricate details can be done very simply by drawing them onto the flat development and colouring them before it is even cut out. In this way quite simple but realistic models can be made.

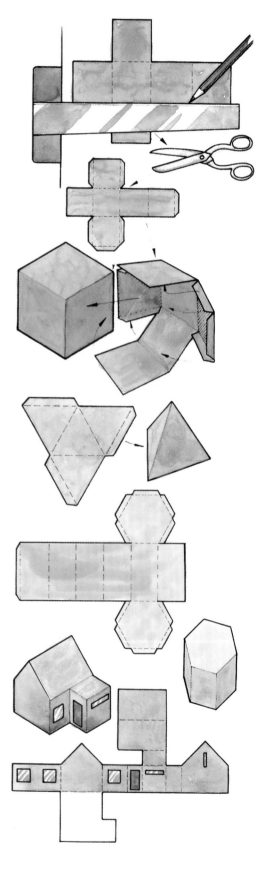

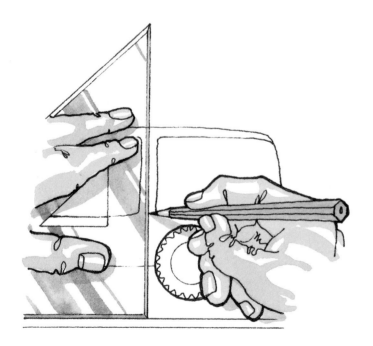

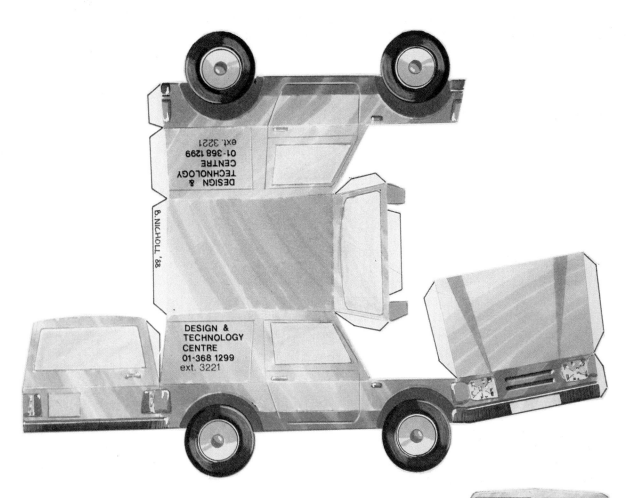

B. NICHOLL '88

DESIGN &
TECHNOLOGY
CENTRE
01-368 1299
ext. 3221

CUTTING AND SCORING PAPER AND CARD

Although for many simple tasks scissors can be used to cut paper, and some card, accurately, for more detailed work a modelling knife should be used. However, remember that if knife blades are to cut efficiently they must be very sharp and so are **very dangerous**!!! Also remember that the edge of paper can cut quite deeply into a careless finger.

To make straight line cuts use a steel straight edge if possible. Make sure that bevel edges are not used and that hands are always kept well behind the cutting edge of the blade.

Carefully and lightly score down the line you have previously made in pencil. This score line will act as a guide for your next cut which should go right through the card. Repeat this process several times if thicker materials are being used.

Always cut on scrap materials or special boards to protect furniture, etc.

TO MAKE CURVED CUTS

Where possible use a graphic-type compass and a cylindrical modelling knife. With this method, accurate arcs and circles can be cut. If irregular curves are to be cut follow the pencil lines freehand very slowly, making a light score line at first and then a heavier cut as described above. Scissors should be used where possible!

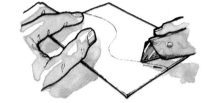

TO MAKE BENDS IN CARD

Paper will of course bend quite easily to any required curve, but because thicker card is more rigid other methods have to be found.

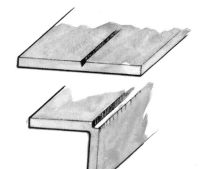

To make a bend along a straight line

Merely score along the previously drawn pencil line and bend downwards. This method will give you a very strong, sharp, accurate bend which will be better than any attempts to join two separate pieces of card to achieve the same bend. However, when using this method be careful not to cut too deeply as this may result in the bend coming apart as you try to bend it to the required angle.

To make a radiused bend

Divide the section to be bent into a series of lines going across the bend. Score along these lines as above. Manipulate the bend to the required curve.

To make a cylinder

To make a cylinder from card which is too thick to bend on its own, draw out the flat development on the card. Then mask and score equally spaced, parallel lines along the length of the cylinder and simply bend into the cylindrical form required. Finally, fix the ends together. If calculated correctly, good accurate cylinders can be formed, although to be precise these forms are really multi-sided polygons.

TO JOIN PAPER AND CARD

To do this either tape the back of the joints or add gluing tabs to the model **at the drawing-out stage.**

PAPER AND CARD MOCK-UPS

Paper and card can be used, instead of the more expensive and harder-to-work materials which will eventually be used to make the product, when we are uncertain about what the shapes should be. When the shape has been finalised these mock-up parts can often be used as templates to mark out the real pieces.

Scale models

Many models are created full size, but in the case of buildings or some larger products this is not possible. Instead, scaled-down models are built, often using materials and parts specially made for the purpose. Many things, such as furniture, can be constructed quickly and cheaply in model form and then realistically enlarged using photography or video before a full-size prototype is built.

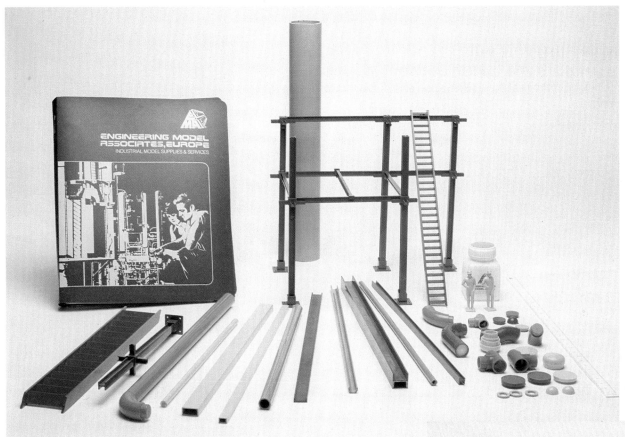

Scale models can be divided into three categories:

- systems models.
- architectural models.
- furniture/interior design models.

SYSTEMS MODELS

A huge range of specialised scale model components are available to the professional modeller for building up systems involving pipework, electrical ducting, mechanical conveying, etc. In fact, the same inexpensive components used for modelling oil refineries and chemical plants can be put to use in design and technology for working out and showing smaller systems. A project on domestic solar heating, for example, might require a good scale model. In the example shown, the basic materials are polystyrene sheet (2.5 mm thick) covered with brick and tile modelling papers. All the parts are held together with self-adhesive Velcro tape, which means that the model can be broken down easily for modification — and for storage.

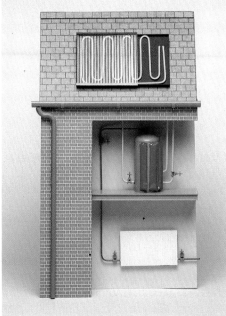

The colour-coded pipework is made from butyrate tubing (with a wire core) over which scale-model valves are clipped. The radiators are small sections of embossed polystyrene sheet fastened onto the walls using double-sided tape pads.

Corrugated plastic sheet in miniature represents the covering of the solar collector on the roof, and to give extra realism even the guttering and downpipe can be added using quick-fit components.

All the parts can be purchased cheaply, or some can be made up from scrap materials. The golden rule is that the scale dictates how much detail is needed. The smaller the scale, the less the detail that will suffice.

FURNITURE/INTERIOR MODELS

A good scale model of a piece of furniture or an interior is one that is difficult to tell from the real thing when seen as a video image or as a photograph.

In this example, a storage unit has been assembled using butyrate tubing and fittings to represent steel tubing. The surfaces are perforated plastic sheet — representing punched steel sheet. This is an inexpensive and effective way of communicating an idea, and it is very much easier to modify and adapt the model than to re-make an expensive full-size prototype.

Using either video or photography, the model can be looked at from many different angles and even the effects of different lighting can be assessed. Almost all furniture can (and should be) modelled in this way before any full-size construction takes place.

ARCHITECTURAL MODELS

In putting forward the idea for a building, the furthest an architect normally goes prior to building is a good scale model. This is a very specialised branch of model making and involves many skills — not the least of which is the selection of materials and finish to suit different scales of model.

To fully exploit such a model in making decisions about the real thing, photography and video can be used to look at different parts of it. In a group of models, even periscopes are used to get a view from the street!

Architectural modellers rely on specialised materials and fittings for their work, but these can easily be obtained for use in Design and Technology project work.

The part-architectural model of a solar heating installation (page 41) is designed to show a technical system. Architectural modelling is not the main part of this project, but presenting a realistic model is a far more effective and professional way of selling an idea to a client — or an examiner!

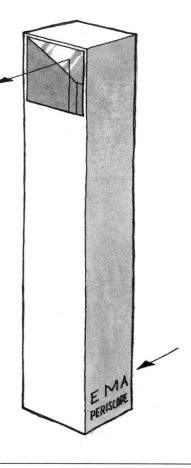

Foam models

Shaping high density polystyrene foam is a fast way of creating solid models to work out shape and proportion, and sometimes to provide an exactly detailed form.

The foam is supplied in rectangular blocks that can be cut and worked using hand tools and (approved) power tools. It gives off a fine dust and should be worked only when using a face mask, and preferably close to an extractor/filter unit.

■ **Step 1: Cutting.** The model profile is first drawn onto the polystyrene block with a soft pencil or felt-tip pen. This profile is best cut out with a small vibrasaw or bandsaw. (If a disc is to be cut, the block can be rotated on a drawing pin Sellotaped upside-down to the table of the saw.)

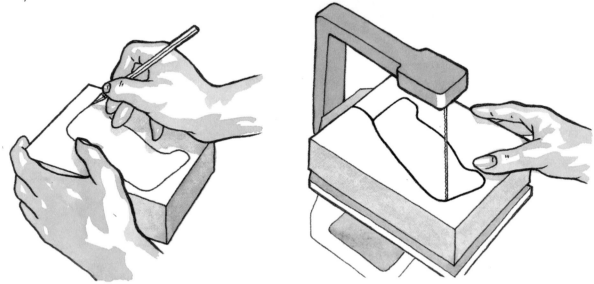

■ **Step 2: Shaping.** Any odd larger pieces of material are sawn off, and the block is shaped by rasps, files and abrasive papers. Most work, and certainly the fine finishing, is done with abrasive paper. This can be wrapped around or glued to sticks of different sections.

■ **Step 3: Finishing.** If the model is the equivalent of a very rough 'sketch', no further work may be required before the model is handled and examined. The handle model shown, for example, can have its ergonomic qualities judged without fine detailing — although it may help to colour the model for a final presentation. (Use acrylic or emulsion paints, or spirit ink.)

Where a finer finish is required and/or when surface details are to be added, the model can be coated with emulsion paint mixed with plaster. When dry, this leaves a hard shell that can be further rubbed down and given additional layers if necessary. Additional painted detail can be added at this stage, together with applied reliefs (see page 51).

Exact product models

Exact product models resemble the intended commercial product and, if well made, can be mistaken for the real thing. Model making of this sort is really about creating illusions using simple materials and 'tricks of the trade'.

Most consumer products, ranging in size from calculators to typewriters, are largely injection moulded (see chapter 19) and would appear very difficult to model. In fact, modelling these things can be both easy and very convincing, as the torch shown here illustrates. It was made simply using scraps of polystyrene sprayed over with car touch-up paint, to give it an injection-moulded appearance.

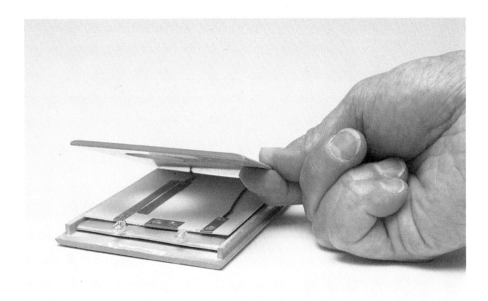

MATERIALS

Practically any materials can be used in exact product model making, providing that they can be worked easily, joined precisely and well finished for painting. Ordinary materials such as wood can be completely transformed as the hot-melt glue gun model shows. It is nothing more than a shaped piece of jelutong that has been very carefully finished with several coats of paint.

The table below lists five materials used in exact product model making, and points out their advantages and disadvantages in design and technology.

Material	Advantages	Disadvantages
Wood: jelutong or lime	Relatively cheap and easily worked with bandsaw, disk sander and common hand tools. Useful for structural work — especially in larger models. Bonds well.	Difficult to create very fine details. Requires many coats of paint to get a good surface. Not as stable as metal and plastics. Can dent easily.
Acrylic	Easily worked with hand tools. Can be machined by turning and milling. Very fine details can be produced. Can be heat formed. Bonds well.	Can be expensive, especially in thicker sections. Does not vacuum form well. Prone to fracture during machining.
Polystyrene	Easily worked with hand tools. Can be cut by scoring and cracking. Can be vacuum formed. Bonds extremely well. Can be fabricated easily.	Very sensitive to heat: machining can be a problem. Cellulose paint must be left for a long period after spraying.
Aluminium	Easily machined by turning or milling. Very fine details can be produced. Great strength in thin-walled shells. Adhesive bonding possible.	Normally requires use of machine tools. Much material might have to be removed to achieve a realistic weight. Fabrication can be very difficult.
ABS	ABS offers **all** the advantages of the above materials.	A relatively expensive material for model making.

Probably the easiest to work as well as the cheapest of the above materials is polystyrene. This has the advantage, too, that it can be vacuum formed as well as fabricated from smaller pieces. The remainder of this section will look at polystyrene as the main modelling material, but the surface detailing techniques apply to the other materials equally well.

Many exact product models are not intended to work in any way, and are simply solid blocks given realistic styling and details (e.g. the hot-melt glue gun, page 45). If a model has to work, it can be made as hollow shell so that, for example, it can contain electronic circuitry, battery, bulb, etc.

Most simple injection moulded goods are in two parts, and it is a good idea to make your first models so that they open up in a similar way. It is advisable to study a range of commercial products to see how they come apart and how they are held together — and what sort of details appear on their surfaces.

FABRICATING MODELS

Fabrication means assembling from a number of parts. The most straightforward type of hollow shell is made up, or fabricated, as a rectangular box that sits on a flat back. Many commercial products are actually produced like this, and injection moulded in two parts.

Making the shell for the simple timer model shown is accomplished in a few easy steps.

STEP 1

Mark out the sizes of the individual pieces required for the box and flat back. Two-millimetre thick polystyrene will suffice for the front of the model, but 3 mm material should be used for the sides to give extra strength and a wider gluing surface when the front is bonded on. The back should also be 3 mm thick.

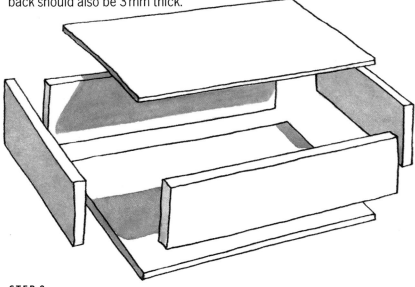

STEP 2

Do not use a saw to cut the polystyrene! Score it deeply with a hook-nosed scoring tool or sharp scriber and then bend it so that the material fractures. If a very thin strip is being cut off thick material, it is scored and then cracked off along its length using pliers.

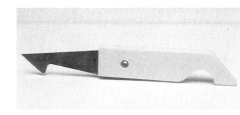

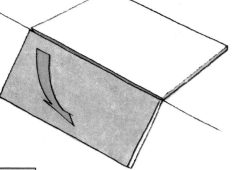

STEP 3

All the fractured edges are rubbed down on wet and dry paper placed on a flat surface such as a piece of acrylic. Wooden blocks and simple made-up wooden jigs are used to ensure accuracy. (**Note:** All good model makers spend time making these jigs, however skillful they are.)

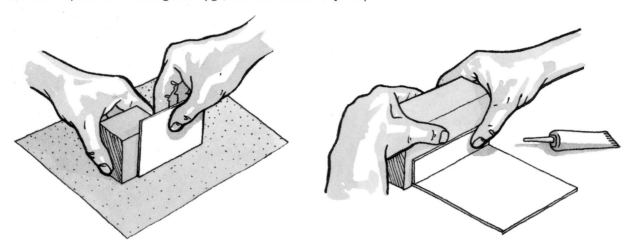

STEP 4

The polystyrene pieces are bonded together either with polystyrene adhesive from a tube (used in plastic model kits) or with a solvent cement. The adhesive in a tube is easy to use, and simply involves coating the 3 mm edges and assembling accurately against blocks to ensure 90° corners.

Professional model makers often assemble pieces first and then apply solvent cement to the edges, where it is drawn into the joint by capillary action. This is a much cleaner method of 'welding' plastics because there is no squeeze-out of adhesive, but it can be difficult with smaller surface areas.

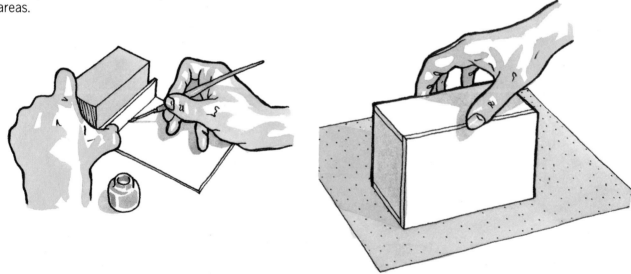

STEP 5

When the solvent or adhesive has set, all faces of the shell are rubbed down on fine wet and dry paper (400 grit) to trim off excess material.

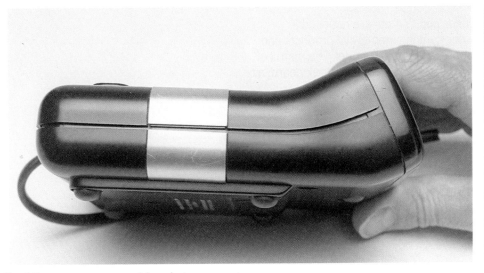

Break lines seen on commercial products

STEP 6

The back of the model is rubbed down on wet and dry paper so that it fits exactly over the back of the shell. Using a file or wet and dry paper, a small chamfer can be created along the edges of one face. The purpose of this is to form a break line or shadow line when the back is placed onto the shell. This is a very common feature of commercially produced products and, as well as giving visual interest, sometimes disguises the fact that the two injection moulded parts will not match perfectly! An alternative to chamfering the back is to form a square shoulder by bonding a smaller and thinner piece of polystyrene to the back. This could be attached, for example, using 'Spraymount' or with solvent adhesive drawn in by capillary action (see Step 4).

STEP 7

The back can be fitted to the shell in several ways. Small strips of polystyrene can be glued across the shell to accept self-tapping screws through the back. Alternatively, small patches of double-sided adhesive tape can be used in place of screws — remembering that the tape must be used sparingly so that the back can be taken off when necessary.

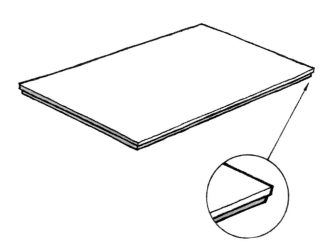

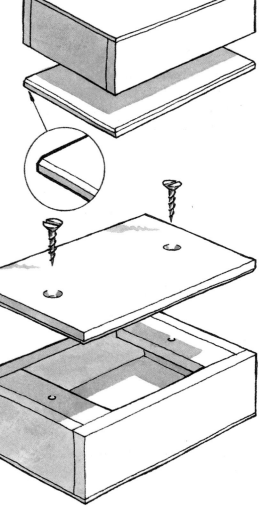

STEP 8

To complete the basic shell, the edges and corners are radiused as appropriate. This kind of detail is important in commercial products and can make a big difference to the appearance of the model. The matrix of small sound holes is drilled using a form of circuit board (matrix board) as a drill jig, held on temporarily with Sellotape.

The model is now ready for surface detailing and finishing (see pages 51 and 54).

stick faced with wet and dry paper

VACUUM FORMING MODELS

The timer model could also have been vacuum formed (see chapter 18). This method of manufacture is the obvious alternative when the model is rounded or curvilinear. However, it must be stressed that most of the effort must go into making a good mould: the process of vacuum forming itself is over in seconds but the result is only as good as the mould.

To withstand the loading of even a fraction of atmospheric pressure over a large area calls for strength, and most moulds are therefore solid. They are frequently made of wood such as jelutong, but it is now very common to use MDF (medium density fibreboard), which is hard and gives a good surface finish. Plastics and metals can also be used as part of a mould.

The mould should have a slight draught or taper to enable its withdrawal from the forming, and it should be slightly deeper than needed to allow waste to be trimmed off. If at all possible, avoid deep moulds: these can lead to excessive thinning of material and problems with webbing.

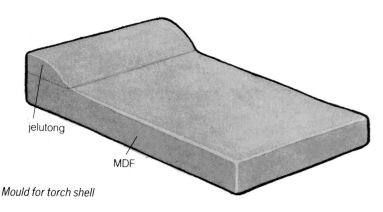

jelutong

MDF

Mould for torch shell

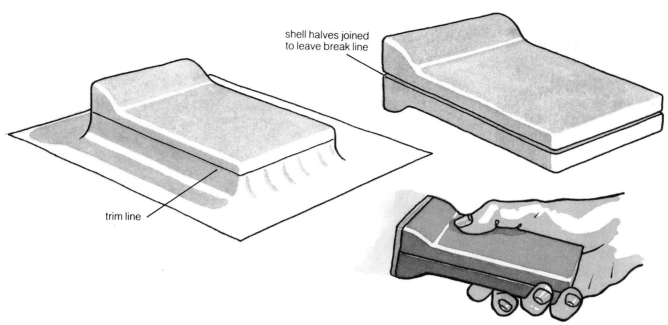

shell halves joined
to leave break line

trim line

Models are best formed from thicker material to give a feel of solidity. If
this is not available, one layer of thinner material can be vacuum formed
over another and bonded by the capillary action method to give a
laminated shell (see chapter 18).

SURFACE DETAILING

Most injection moulded products include details that stand up from the
surface in relief. These details, such as textures and lettering, can be
represented on models by adding other materials. When the model is
finally sprayed, they acquire a moulded-in look.

A sampler board shows the kind of 'before and after' effects that are
possible by adding a variety of materials to a surface. For textures,
practically any material that is itself textured can be applied to a surface
using, for example, Spraymount. This includes coarse wet and dry paper,
embossed polystyrene sheet and EMA self-adhesive reflector sheet.
Self-adhesive paper stickers and labels are also excellent sources of
textures and surface details. Even though it is very thin, paper shows up
in relief when sprayed over, and layers can be put one on top of the other
for additional thickness.

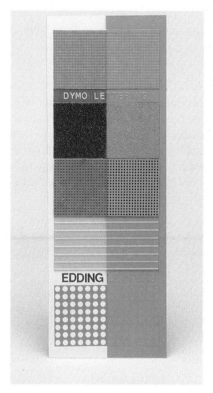

One popular label system comprises a number of small dot stickers. If the grid from which they are stamped is carefully peeled away from the wax paper backing, it makes an interesting and realistic texture on a model. Alternatively, the remaining dots can be lifted off the wax paper with Frisk film (a low-tack adhesive film) and transferred to the model. It is important to note, however, that any self-adhesive paper must be burnished hard onto the model surface (e.g. with the back of a spoon) otherwise it will lift when sprayed.

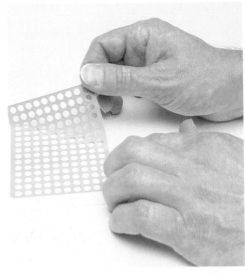

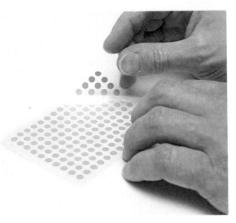

Self-adhesive paper address labels can be cut with a sharp scalpel to make low relief logos. They can also be given a textured surface by heavy lining with an empty ballpoint pen.

Relief lettering on a model can be achieved in many ways. Letters are available, for example, as complete injection moulded alphabets. These are best handled by lightly stabbing them with a pin or scalpel. Their backs are either wetted with solvent adhesive and applied to the model, or they are held against the surface dry and a small amount of solvent is applied with a brush. (Polystyrene adhesive from a tube should not be used because it will squeeze out between the letters.)

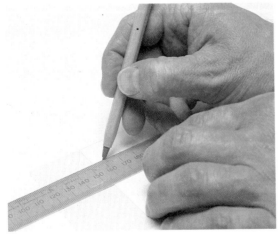

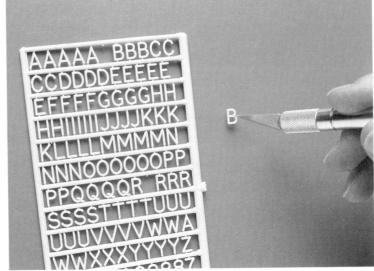

The Eddings range of vinyl die-cut letters will also stand out in sharp relief when sprayed over. Dymo tape can be very effective too, but it normally needs to be recessed to disguise the edge of the tape.

FALSE DETAILS

Commercial products often have small moving parts such as the opening lid of a battery compartment. Unless it is absolutely necessary, working details of this sort are not included in models. Instead, false details are created so that it looks as if a battery cover is in place and will open. Details like this can be built up using paper, or lines can be carefully incised into the surface of the model.

Creation of a false battery compartment lid by incised-line and stick-on paper details

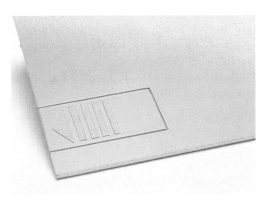

False battery compartment lid after spraying

FINISHING THE MODEL

Before painting, any deep scratches should be filled with cellulose putty, which is rubbed down when dry with the finest wet and dry paper.

Exact product models should be sprayed rather than brush painted. If spray equipment is not available, aerosol spray paints can be used. The easiest to use is cellulose paint, available in a wide variety of colours — including metallic finishes. It does not adhere well to polystyrene without a special primer, but it is successful if left to harden off for at least 24 hours.

Spraying must be done in a spray booth or very well-ventilated place. The paint is built up in very thin coats with the can held at least 300 mm from the work. Spraying from a greater distance uses more paint, but the result is a matt and slightly granular finish of the type usually seen on injection moulded goods.

Finally, graphics in the form of rub-down lettering can be applied to the painted surface after it is fully hardened. This does not need fixing or lacquering after application.

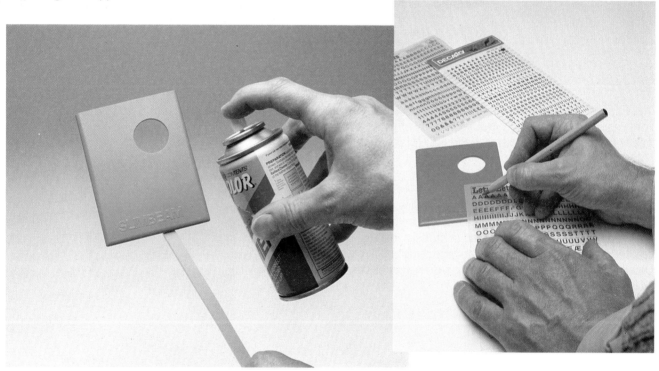

SWITCHES FOR WORKING MODELS

Switches are very important details of electrical or electronic products. These can be made very easily as working features of a model. Instead of relying on the limited range that can be bought, you can design and produce your own. This is important when the switch (or switches) is the main focus of interest — as on the Slimbeam torch.

The simplest type of switch is made using two short lengths of springy brass which just overlap. When one is pushed, it comes into contact with the second, and the switch is closed. This can be mounted directly onto the underside of the model shell or it can be made up as a sub-assembly, i.e. constructed on a separate piece of plastic which is fastened to the underside of the shell. The brass strips can be bonded using Araldite or double-sided adhesive tape.

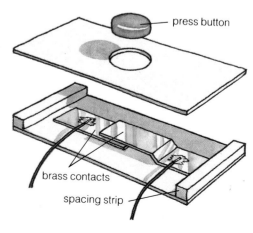

press button

brass contacts

spacing strip

The switch is completed by gluing on a button that might be turned from a scrap of rod and then sprayed. As the photograph shows, switches made in this way look surprisingly convincing.

This type of switch is described as push-to-make, and only stays on when pressure is applied. If a latching action is required, e.g. push one button for 'on' and another button for 'off', a thyristor can be used (see chapter 7).

MEMBRANE PANEL SWITCHES

Membrane panel switches have revolutionised the way designers think about product design. Despite their high technology looks, they can be modelled realistically — and can be made to work without difficulty.

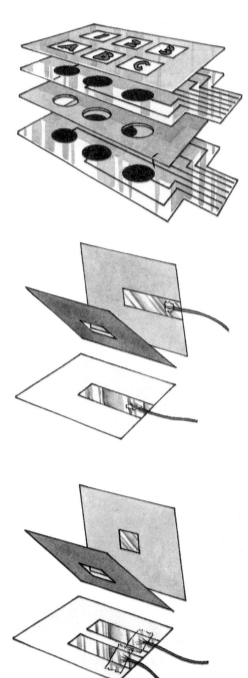

A typical membrane panel comprises three thin plastic laminates. Conductive tracks printed on the top and bottom layers are held apart by a centre layer whose windows correspond to the position of the track ends on the top and bottom. When a position over a window is pressed, the two track ends come together to make a contact.

Membrane panels are constructed easily using thick paper or card. The tracks can be made of self-adhesive copper or aluminium tape — or kitchen foil bonded with Spraymount. PVA glue or an adhesive like PrittStick can also be used. Wires to the foil tracks are soldered using normal solder for copper or multicore aluminium solder. Stranded wire can be fastened well using just Sellotape.

In an alternative form of membrane panel, two strips of aluminium or copper foil are laid close together (e.g. 1 mm apart) and a paper 'window' is glued over the top. A patch of foil glued to the underside of another piece of paper is then glued over this. When the top paper is pressed, its foil patch dips through the window and makes contact across the strips.

The thickness of the centre layer of either type of membrane panel, together with the window size, determines the sensitivity. If thicker paper is used and the windows are small, more pressure has to be applied to make the top layer dip through to make contact on the bottom. On the other hand, if the middle layer of paper is too thin and the window too large, the top and bottom layers might come together by chance. A typical circular window size for cartridge paper is 10 mm in diameter.

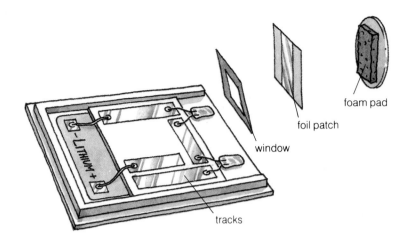

foam pad

foil patch

window

tracks

If a solid button is to be put onto the top of the switch, a small foam pad (preferably double-sided self-adhesive) is placed between it and the top membrane layer to ensure that the foil deflects through the window.

The Slimbeam torch illustrated on page 37 uses a membrane panel with a push-button top. The torch was designed around an ultra-thin lithium battery so that it could be slipped into a pocket like a wallet, and this necessitated a switch with hardly any thickness.

Many electronic devices, such as the digital temperature module seen here, require a number of momentary-action press switches for their programming. The membrane panel is an ideal solution to this problem.

From the design and modelling point of view, perhaps the most important feature of a membrane is its top. There is enormous scope here to give a product an identity by creating bright graphics, instructions, etc. Any variety of graphics media can be used, ranging from felt-tip pens to airbrushing. Computer graphics packages such as AMX SuperArt can also be used in creating an interesting top surface.

To add realism and resilience to the membrane, the top graphics panel should be covered with a self-adhesive transparent covering which has a matt surface (e.g. Transpaseal). This can also be used to bond the membrane onto the surface of a model, but it is usually better to set it into a shallow recess first.

Surprisingly, excellent use can be made of old colour supplements and magazines in making up professional-looking membranes. Large or small areas of bright colour can be cut out and pasted onto the top layer as a montage. Rub-down lettering, for example, can also be applied on top.

The working models seen below show parts of a modular instrument system for use in a laboratory. The models are constructed in polystyrene and incorporate all the techniques discussed in this section. The membrane panel switches use paper and foil and have been found to work reliably for many months.

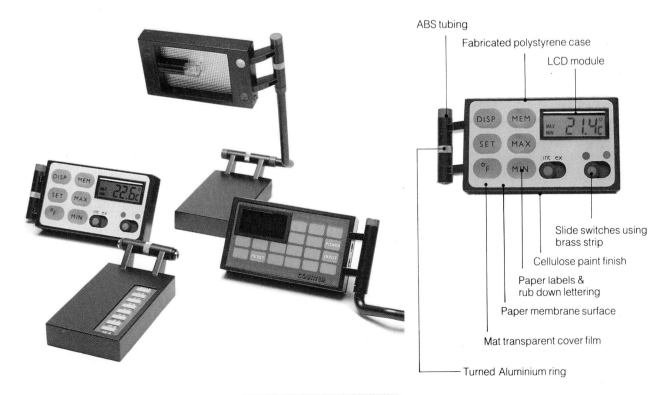

ABS tubing

Fabricated polystyrene case

LCD module

Slide switches using brass strip

Cellulose paint finish

Paper labels & rub down lettering

Paper membrane surface

Mat transparent cover film

Turned Aluminium ring

Appendix

RESISTOR COLOUR CHART

For the purposes of identification, resistors are given a code in the form of coloured bands. This code can be 'read' with the help of a colour chart and the resistance value can be determined (see page 112).

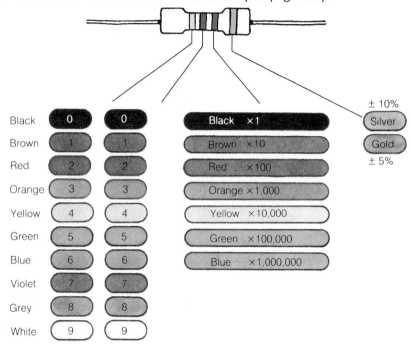

Black	0	0	Black ×1	± 10% Silver
Brown	1	1	Brown ×10	Gold
Red	2	2	Red ×100	± 5%
Orange	3	3	Orange ×1,000	
Yellow	4	4	Yellow ×10,000	
Green	5	5	Green ×100,000	
Blue	6	6	Blue ×1,000,000	
Violet	7	7		
Grey	8	8		
White	9	9		

Resistor colour coding. To read off the value of a resistor, look for the colour of the first band in column one and note the number. Do the same for the second band. For the third band, look up the number in the multiplier column and use to multiply the first two digits. The example shown is yellow (4), violet (7), red (× 100), i.e. 47 × 100 = 4700 ohms.

To avoid lots of zeros in writing down values, the prefix 'k' is used to stand for 1000 and 'M' for 1 000 000. In our example, 4 700 Ω can be written as 4.7 kΩ. Similarly, 10 MΩ would stand for 10 000 000 Ω. To avoid any confusion, 'k' and 'M' are now used instead of decimal points. For example, 4.7 kΩ is written as 4k7 Ω.

The fourth (metallic) band of the resistor states its accuracy. If it is gold, the resistor is within plus or minus 5% of the coded value. A 1 k resistor, for example, might be found to be as high as 1050 Ω or as low as 950 Ω.

Thermographic picture of a house

THERMOGRAPH

A special form of photograph—a thermograph—shows temperatures as a range of colours. This thermograph of a house shows marked differences in temperature on the outside, and indicates that much heat is being lost from 'hot spots' such as windows. Correct insulation at such places can save energy (see page 179).

The different colours in this special photograph represent different amounts of heat coming from the building. The colour scale is:
white   hot
yellow
red
green
blue   cold

4 A vocabulary for design

Function

The most important consideration when designing a product is that it should perform its intended job correctly, and a careful analysis of what the product has to do will provide many starting points for design.

Visual judgements

The second most important consideration is the appearance of the product, and the **key questions** here should seek to investigate the **aesthetic requirements** of the design, such as its appearance, finish and the environment in which it will be used.

In the same way that we have to learn to recognise and understand words, in order to be able to read, we must learn to recognise and understand the words used when talking about aesthetic principles, in order to be able to discuss the visual judgements which we must make when designing. Some of these words have different meanings in general conversation and we must therefore be careful to use them accurately.

As well as making design understandable and definable by isolating and considering some of the basic units of design, this vocabulary provides many sources of design ideas, and we have shown examples of projects and everyday objects based on them.

Line

Lines can be used in many ways.

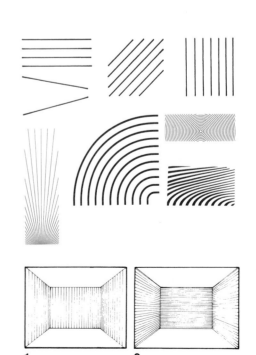

DIRECTION
Lines can be used to indicate directions. For example, they can be vertical, horizontal, inclined (sloping), converging, diverging, radiating or curving.

The way in which lines are applied to shapes or forms can create significantly different visual effects. For example, the dimensions of a room can appear to be altered by the use of wallpapers which have strong lines of direction:

1 Vertical pattern lines will tend to make a room appear higher, but smaller in other directions.
2 Horizontal lines will tend to make the walls look longer, but the ceiling lower, etc.

MOVEMENT
Lines can be used to indicate movement in a particular direction.

1   2

RHYTHM

Lines can also be used in ways which will create a visual rhythm (flow). Functional objects, which may be rather dull, can be transformed by the application of more interesting linear detailing. For example, the appearance of cars is often completely changed by the addition of patterns of lines.

TEXTURE

Various combinations of lines can give the impression of textured surfaces and create interesting effects.

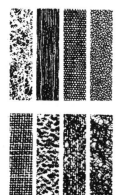

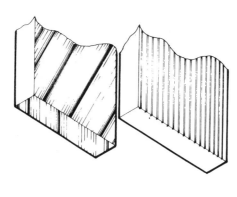

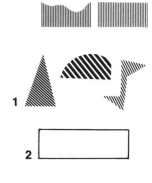

SHAPE

This is simply a two-dimensional area defined by lines, and lines can be used to do this in two ways:

1 By using a series of measured lines which will cover a specific area and suggest an outline.
2 By joining lines together to enclose a space.

FREE FORM DESIGN

This can be used when objects are to be created for their appearance, but when you have no particular shape in mind. A limitless number of ideas and shapes can stem from using this method. Here are some ways of producing a variety of shapes:

1 Shapes can be created by drawing random curved lines which cross each other. Suitable shapes can be outlined boldly and the best ones can be developed as required (diagram 1).
2 Straight lines can be used in the same way. In diagram 2 they are used to create suitable outlines for a door number plate.
3 Curved and straight lines can also be used together. In diagram 3, for example, they are used to design decorative panels on a container top.

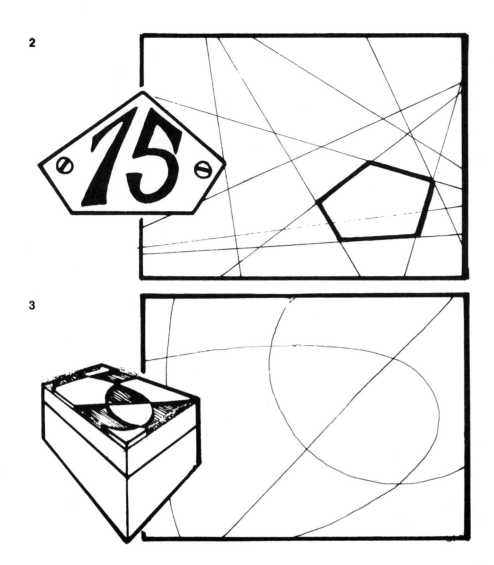

2

3

Planes

The word 'plane' usually refers to a flat, smooth surface. A table top is considered to be a horizontal plane, a door front is a vertical plane and many roofs are inclined planes.

One can use a plane as a base in which to work and we can add further planes by overlapping, penetrating, joining and so on. In this way, many interesting compositions can be created, and two-dimensional shapes can be built-up into three-dimensional constructions.

PLANE GEOMETRIC SHAPES

Look very carefully around you and you will see that most of our man-made environment and some of our natural environment is based on geometric shapes (e.g. honeycombs are hexagonal).

Many of these geometric shapes can be developed into grids for use in basic pattern design work. (See the next section.)

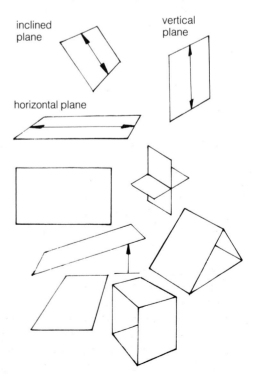

inclined plane

vertical plane

horizontal plane

The circle

circle

semi-circle

1/3 circle

quadrant

ellipse

Triangles

isoceles

equilateral

right-angled

scalene

Quadrilaterals

square

rectangle

rhombus

parallelogram

trapezium

trapezoid

Polygons

octagon (8)

heptagon (7)

hexagon (6)

pentagon (5)

irregular polygon

Units and grids

By using grids developed from tessellating (interlocking) geometric shapes such as rectangles, equilateral triangles, hexagons, etc., we can develop new pattern designs which may be difficult to produce in any other way.

The first drawing shows how a square grid is built up. From this simple grid quite complex designs can be produced by:

1 Drawing any shape into the sub-unit.
2 Copying this shape into all four sub-units within the larger unit. (Here the sub-units have each been rotated through a quarter turn.)
3 Repeating the unit design onto the large grid or super-unit.

Notice how this shape is repeated throughout the grid so that both positive and negative shapes are identical, i.e. the shape itself also tessellates as well as the units.

Here are some patterns developed from one sub-unit design. To create the full effect, the shapes have to be drawn out carefully before they can be inked or coloured in.

With the use of drawing instruments a straightforward pattern can be drawn accurately and quickly. However, difficulty arises when the sub-unit becomes complex, or is a random shape, or has to be rotated frequently. Therefore, you may find the stencil, template or tracing methods easier to use.

Below are examples of designs produced from the same unit using a template. These are just some methods of varying the original shape, but there are many more.

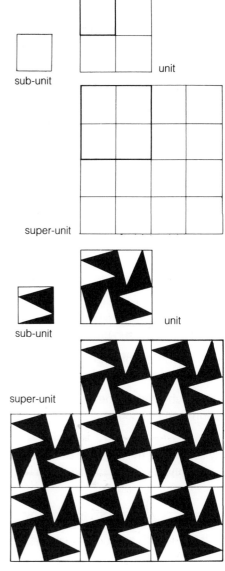

sub-unit

unit

super-unit

sub-unit

unit

super-unit

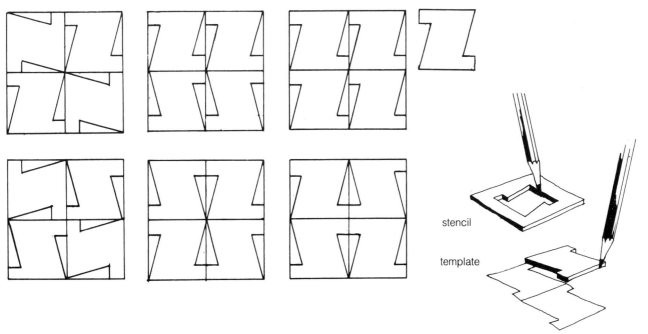

stencil

template

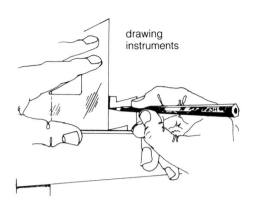

drawing instruments

tracing paper

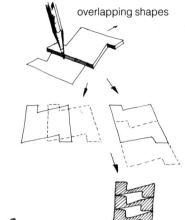

overlapping shapes

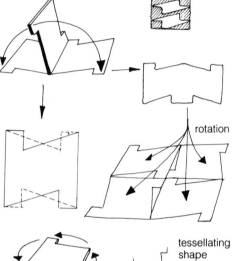

rotation

tessellating shape

SYMMETRY

Symmetrical shapes are those which can be halved equally, resulting in two identical parts, with one part reversed.

Hence, by flipping over the stencil shown, symmetrical shapes can be produced either by extending the design over the grid or by repeating it within the same sub-unit.

With a good use of **negative** and **positive**, the sub-units can be made to join onto each other to form new shapes.

Some sub-units can be developed to form many different shapes which in turn can be used as units. The equilateral triangle is a good example of this.

By separating the negative and positive shapes, and colouring both in the same way, we can rearrange them to create new shapes.

HINTS ON DESIGNING A SUB-UNIT

1 If the shapes are to tessellate well the design on the sub-units must touch the edges of each sub-unit grid.
2 It is advisable to limit yourself to two colours when designing units and grids.

The above methods of pattern designing can often form the basis of both two- and three-dimensional work.

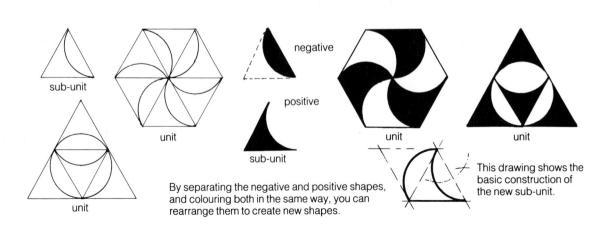

sub-unit

unit

unit

negative

positive

sub-unit

unit

unit

By separating the negative and positive shapes, and colouring both in the same way, you can rearrange them to create new shapes.

This drawing shows the basic construction of the new sub-unit.

Form

When we give flat two-dimensional planes or shapes a third dimension, we refer to the three-dimensional solids which we have made as forms. Many objects around us are developed from geometric forms.

To fully describe a form we must give details of all its characteristics: shape, size, proportion, weight, opacity, colour and texture. The design language which we have learnt in this chapter will help us to do this.

SIZE

This is a relative concept in which we rely upon comparisons to help describe the magnitude of an object. For example, we only consider someone to be particularly small (or tall) because they are below (or above) the height of most people of the same age and sex.

SHAPE

As shown earlier, two-dimensional shapes define specific areas. When shape is used in connection with a three-dimensional form it defines the overall outline of the object.

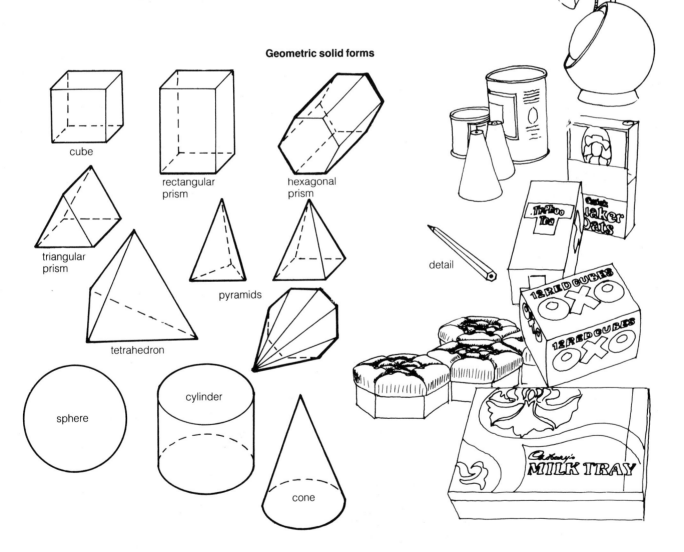

Geometric solid forms

cube

rectangular prism

hexagonal prism

triangular prism

pyramids

tetrahedron

detail

sphere

cylinder

cone

Natural forms

The study of natural forms such as leaves, flowers, insects, fish, fruit, pieces of wood and stones provides an endless source of shapes for design. The usual approach is to make analytical drawings of these forms, often using some form of magnification to obtain detailed knowledge of the internal and external structure of them, and then to develop the shapes which have been suggested into designs for jewellery, decorative panels, ceramics, etc. Alternatively, the objects can be used as models for sculpture, work in clay, etc., as patterns for the casting of exact replicas, or as subjects for embedding.

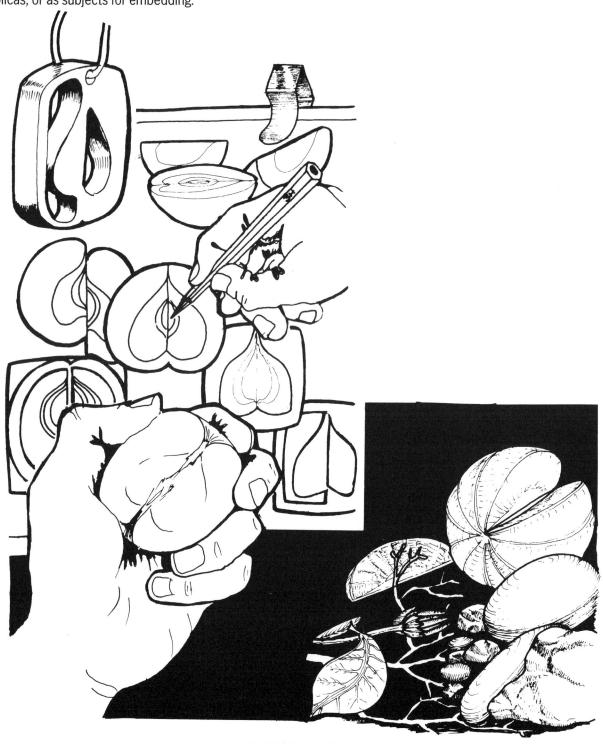

Visual properties of materials

When we think about the materials available to us as designers we must look at their properties. In addition to those such as strength, hardness and weight discussed in the sections on materials, we must consider the following.

1 OPACITY

If we can see through the material, it is **transparent**. If we cannot see through it, but light shines through, it is **translucent**. If we cannot see light through the material at all, it is **opaque**.

2 TEXTURE AND FINISH

This is the physical surface condition of a material, which may range from rough to smooth in an infinite number of ways, and any finish which we might apply to it.

3 COLOUR

This is made up of three basic elements:

(a) Hue, which is the actual colour or complexion, i.e. whether it is red, yellow, orange, etc.
(b) Chroma, which is the brilliance of colour (intensity).
(c) Tone, which is the amount of black or white in a colour. The maximum contrast one can gain is by the use of black and white alongside each other.

Primary colours are the basic pigments from which other colours (secondary colours, etc.) can be mixed.

Complementary colours are those colours which are opposite each other on the colour wheel (spectrum). They give maximum contrast.

Harmony comes from using colours which are close to each other around the colour wheel. Harmony can also be gained when using complementary colours, by toning down both colours with equal amounts of black or white.

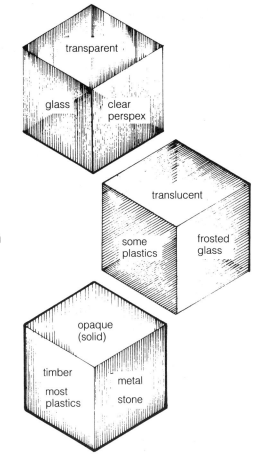

transparent

glass

clear perspex

translucent

some plastics

frosted glass

opaque (solid)

timber

most plastics

metal

stone

r = red
y = yellow
b = blue
o = orange
g = green
v = violet
t = tertiary

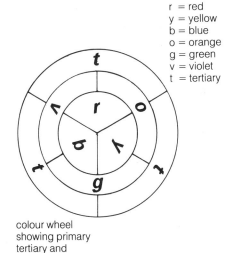

colour wheel showing primary tertiary and infinite colour ranges

Proportion

This refers to the relationship of one part of a form to another and gives an object its particular composition. A good composition is one in which all the characteristics of an object are visually correct. This gives agreeable proportions. Too much or too little of any characteristic gives bad proportions.

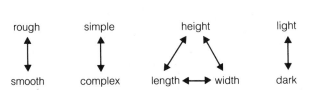

rough

smooth

simple

complex

height

length ⟷ width

light

dark

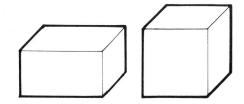

Using units and grids

EXAMPLE 1

DESIGN BRIEF

'To design an interlocking shape.'

As you can see the design brief is very short, leaving much interpretation to the individual. Not all design problems necessarily result in the making of a particular product with a definite function. Some can be quite open ended.

SOLUTION

This type of open-ended design problem can be a good source of ideas for other work. Here the original two-dimensional interlocking shape has developed into interlocking candle holders.

Resin is cast into moulds, vacuum formed from wooden patterns which have a draw angle for easy release.

The holes are drilled and polished aluminium sleeves inserted to hold the candles. The candles could be bought or special candles made.

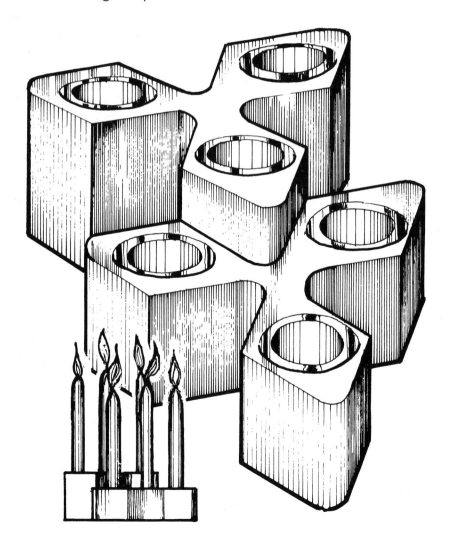

To design an interlocking shape'

INTERLOCKING SHAPES | TIM WATTS | 4S

This type of basic work is often used to create schemes for wall coverings, upholstery, textiles, tiles, paving, etc.

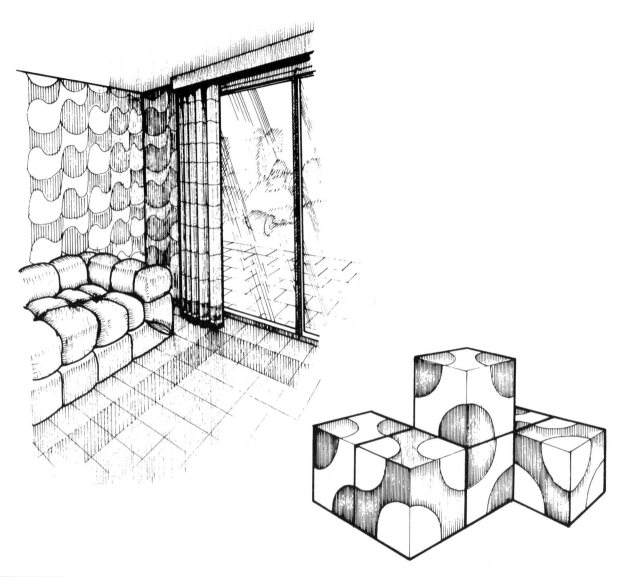

EXAMPLE 2

DESIGN BRIEF
To design a pattern for a tile that is to be used on a coffee table top. There must be no more than two different patterns. (See Units and grids.)

One pattern should be selected for futher development after preliminary investigation of several alternatives (as shown in Example 1).

SOLUTION
This simple example shows the build up towards a final solution. The solution satisfies the requirements stated in the design brief and need go no further.

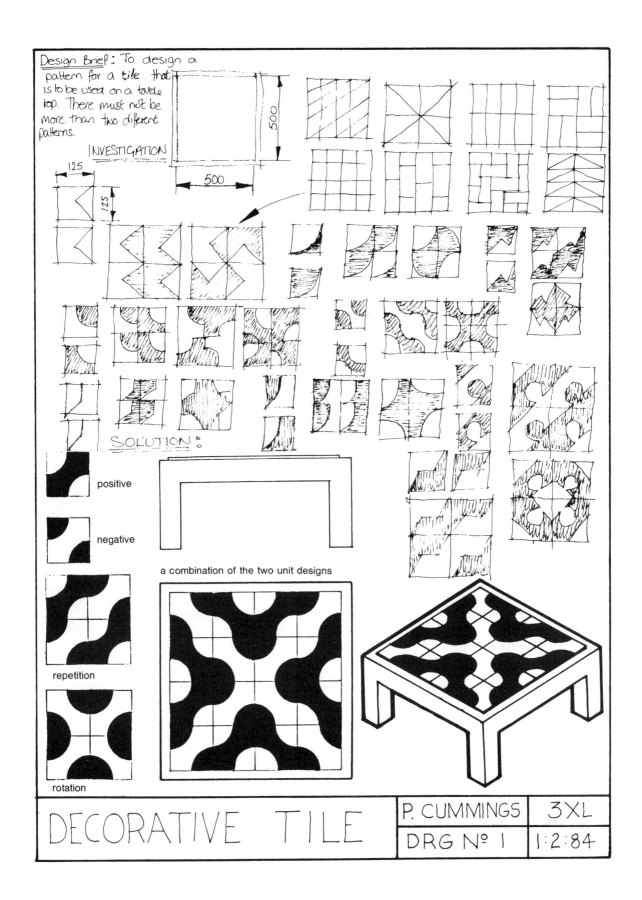

Design Brief: To design a pattern for a tile that is to be used on a table top. There must not be more than two different patterns.

INVESTIGATION

SOLUTION:

positive

negative

a combination of the two unit designs

repetition

rotation

DECORATIVE TILE | P. CUMMINGS | 3XL
DRG Nº 1 | 1:2:84

5 Design method

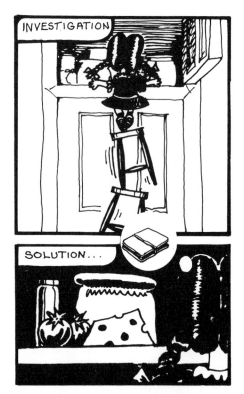

It is not possible to produce solutions to design problems like rabbits from a magician's hat. If asked without warning to solve a design problem, most people would not know where to start. The purpose of this chapter, therefore, is to overcome the obstacles which most people think they are faced with when asked to solve design problems.

In chapter 1 we saw that the word 'design' can have many different meanings but that for our purpose it should be defined as problem solving. We then saw examples of how we can find solutions to simple design problems by developing ideas suggested by the many sources available to us.

When tackling these simple problems we can successfully record and develop our ideas entirely by sketching, and this is how we start to design. However, when we are faced with more complicated problems a lot more thought and preparation are needed before we can even begin to get ideas to provide starting points for our designing.

We therefore need a design method which we can follow stage-by-stage to ensure that no part of a problem is overlooked and no opportunities missed.

This chapter provides details of such a design method and then shows how it can be developed further to deal with advanced projects.

A simple design method

The cartoons opposite show the stages which we subconsciously follow when we seek to satisfy a **need**, and in doing so we are following a simple design process. By consciously approaching every problem with which we are faced in the same step-by-step way, we can develop our ability to solve gradually more difficult and wide ranging problems.

STAGE 1 SITUATIONS FOR DESIGN

The problems you are required to solve will usually arise from normal everyday situations or **context**. Some of them will be set by your teacher, but many others will occur to you as a result of your own and other people's interests and experiences.

For example:

(a) Visitors to your home have difficulty in finding the correct house as there is no identification on the outside.

(b) Having made hot drinks in your kitchen you find you have to make several trips before your family are served in the lounge. This routine often results in messy spillages.

(c) You have difficulty doing work on your desk in the evening because your back is to the light which is in the centre of the room. As a result, an irritating shadow is cast over the work surface.

(d) You have nowhere to keep your pens and pencils which always seem to be lost or broken when you need them.

All of these are examples of a context suggesting a problem.

STAGE 2 THE DESIGN BRIEF

This is a short statement of the **need** you have identified from the contexts or situations as described above.

For example: If you decide that the lack of proper storage for your pens and pencils in example (d) is a suitable design problem, you should begin to tackle it by trying to state clearly what you need to do to solve the problem.

This could be **to design and make a unit to hold pens and pencils.** This statement then is the **design brief** for the given problem. This must be worded in such a way that preconceived ideas of what the solution might be are avoided.

Such a short statement clearly does not give sufficient information for design solutions to be found. Therefore, a full **investigation** into the problem is necessary.

STAGE 3 INVESTIGATION

The nature of the investigation will vary considerably, depending on the type of design problem being tackled. Basically it consists of asking yourself a series of questions about the problem and finding the answers to them. Let us continue with the example specified by the design brief.

Below are examples of the type of questions which you might ask yourself:

Key questions
- How many pens and pencils have to be held?
- Should other items such as rubbers, sharpeners, etc., be included?
- What are the sizes of the items to be held?
- Where is the unit to be used?
- Will the unit have to be carried at any time?
- Could the pens, pencils, or other items be dangerous in any way?
- What materials are available?
- Which of these are suitable?
- How much will the unit cost?
- How much time have you got to make the unit? etc.

All of these questions are important. The answers to them will dictate the starting points from which design ideas can be found. When you first begin to tackle design problems you may be given these **key questions** to ensure that you isolate and research all the important factors, but experience will enable you to prepare your own.

STAGE 4 SOLUTION

From the information gathered by this investigation you can begin to make **ideas sketches** which investigate visually the possible answers to the problem. The best idea(s) are then chosen from these ideas sketches and **developed** further in sketch form to give one or more **partial solutions**.

One or more of these partial solutions are then chosen and put together to give the **final solution**. It is worked out in detail, and presented in a way which gives all the information needed to realise (make) it. (See Working drawings.)

These working drawings should include:

(a) dimensions,
(b) materials,
(c) processes (e.g. joints),
(d) fittings,
(e) finishes.

The best way to present this information is in the form of annotated flat views, plus a pictorial presentation view showing what the finished product should look like and a cutting list if needed.

1. SITUATION FOR DESIGN.

2. DESIGN BRIEF
TO DESIGN AND MAKE A UNIT TO HOLD PENS AND PENCILS

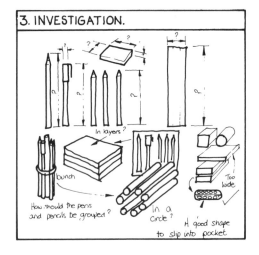

3. INVESTIGATION.

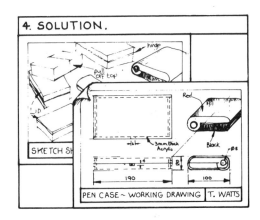

4. SOLUTION.

STAGE 5 REALISATION

This is the actual making of the solution from the working drawings described above.

STAGE 6 TESTING

The finished artefact must be tested to find out whether it satisfies the original design brief. This can only be done by using it and if necessary making modifications to it.

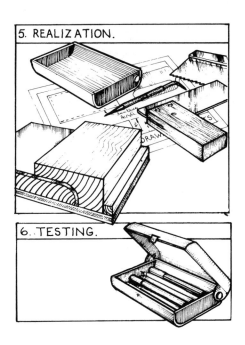

5. REALIZATION.

6. TESTING.

Tackling more advanced problems

While the design method which we have just described is adequate for fairly straightforward problems, we need to add additional detail to these basic stages in order to make a thorough examination of more advanced problems. These additional detailed stages can best be explained by going through the design process stage-by-stage again.

STAGE 1 THE CONTEXT

This should be expanded to ensure that all possible sources of information and all parts of the problem have been identified.

STAGE 2 DESIGN BRIEF

With more advanced projects the design brief needs to be as concise as possible, yet fully specify the requirements of the prospective artefact without leading to preconceived ideas.

For example, if the words 'to design a torch' were included in a design brief, it could be criticised for vagueness and for suggesting a preconceived solution. These criticisms are overcome by changing the wording to something like, 'to design a battery-powered light source . . .' It would then be necessary to specify the nature of the problem in more detail.

There are many different ways of directing light, but the word 'torch' suggests something that is held and simply shone at a target. If we consider the problem of a service engineer needing to illuminate the inside of typewriters or a locksmith examining a lock through the keyhole, an ordinary 'torch' would not necessarily be the best solution. Faced with such problems, an open-minded designer might consider the technology now cheaply available and think about piping light into the lock or typewriter using a lightguide — a thin glass or plastic fibre that allows very little light directed into it to escape.

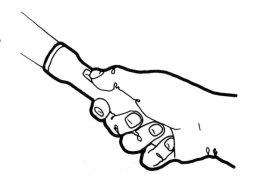

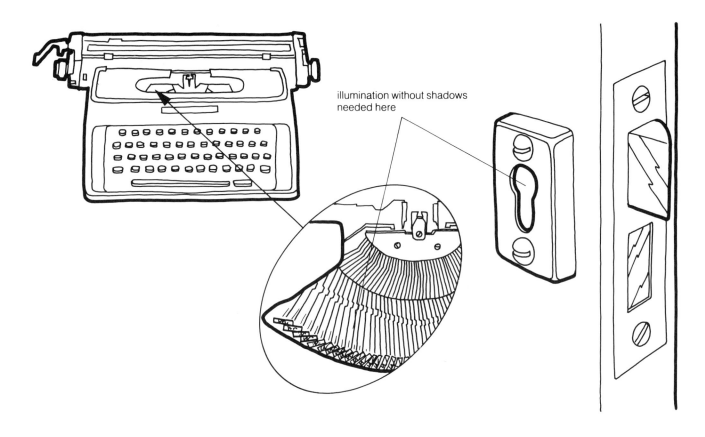

illumination without shadows needed here

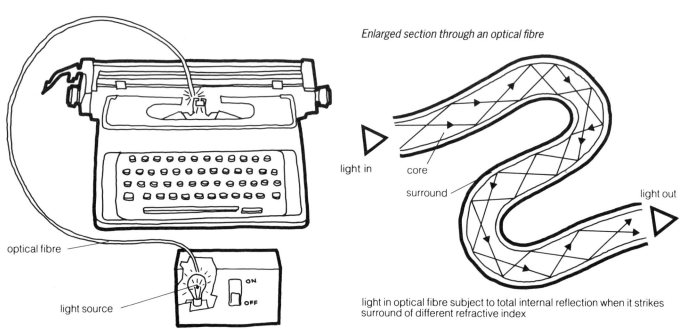

Enlarged section through an optical fibre

light in

core

surround

light out

light in optical fibre subject to total internal reflection when it strikes surround of different refractive index

optical fibre

light source

ON

OFF

STAGE 3 INVESTIGATION

This can be broken down into two main areas:

(a) **Research:** the accumulation of useful data.
(b) **Analysis:** the consideration of all the factors which may have an influence on the final design.

We will now look more closely at each of these areas.

RESEARCH

We have already seen that even the simplest design problems usually involve some research, for example the measurement of objects to be stored, and one of the main distinguishing features of more advanced projects is that they involve much more research. This information is often needed before designing can even begin.

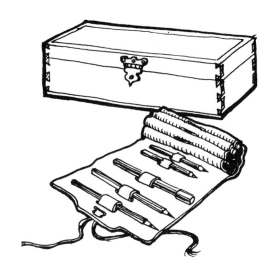

Most of the information needed to design comes under the following headings:

(i) Collection of technological information.
(ii) Measurements of the person(s) for whom an artefact is intended (anthropometrics).
(iii) Study of the environment for which the artefact is intended (ergonomics).
(iv) Finding out about the range of existing products, evaluating them, assessing their popularity and examining how they are made.
(v) Market research.

FACTOR ANALYSIS

Once you have become used to asking yourself the type of key questions shown earlier, you will soon become aware that many of them are the same for most design problems. It is important that we understand how these common **design factors** can interact with each other. **Factor analysis** is the study of the relationship between all the factors involved in solving a problem so that a **compromise** can be found.

Here are some common design factors:

(i) **Function**. This is the job which the artefact will have to do (specified by the design brief). The main job an artefact has to do is called its **primary function**, and any others are called the **secondary functions.**

For example, the primary function of a chair is to support people safely in a sitting position. However, depending on exactly where it is to be used, the chair may also have to look attractive, be easy to clean, match other furniture in the room, support people at the correct height for sitting at a table, etc.

(ii) **Safety.** There are many safety considerations which may affect the solution of a design problem. These might include for example:

- ■ **Toxicity.** Avoid using toxic materials where they are likely to cause danger (e.g. do not use lead-based paints on toys).

- ■ **Sharp corners and edges.** Design smooth rounded shapes whenever possible so that, for example, you cannot hurt yourself when brushing past furniture and so that small items will not scratch furniture which they might be stood on.

■ **Stability.** Make sure that things cannot easily be knocked over. For example, a chair should not tip over even if someone rocks it back on two legs, and the base of a desk lamp must be large enough and heavy enough to prevent it from being knocked over.

■ **Fire hazards.** You must not use materials which are likely to catch fire easily, give off dangerous fumes, or melt during normal use.

■ **Electrical safety.** Any mains-operated appliance must conform to the specifications set out in the appropriate British Standards.

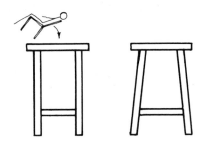

(iii) **Materials.** These must be suitable for the job they have to do and should also be appropriate to the environment in which they are used.

Each of the materials available to us has its own properties and limitations, which you should study carefully to make sure that your choice is appropriate. This can prove difficult at times when you consider, for example, how many different alloys and plastics there are. Manufacturers of raw plastics material, such as ICI, will often be able to supply useful information.

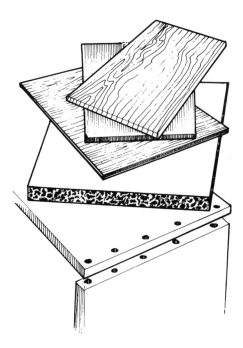

(iv) **Cost.** The cost of a product does not simply depend on the cost of the raw materials. You must also take into account production costs. In either a small craft workshop or a large factory the production costs would have to include:

■ labour (designing, prototyping, making time),
■ overheads (cost of equipment, rent, rates).

These factors explain why profit margins can appear quite high — especially when production output is small. It is difficult to make an allowance for these factors **but** you must show that you are aware they exist.

(v) **Manufacture.** This will depend on whether the product is to be produced in volume (mass production), or if just a few are to be made. In general, for mass production, the capital costs are high and the unit cost of the product low. An injection moulding tool, for example, is very expensive but is capable of turning out many thousands of identical products.

In contrast, the capital cost of making a pair of chairs by hand can be low — the cost of the hand tools — but the cost of each chair is likely to be high.

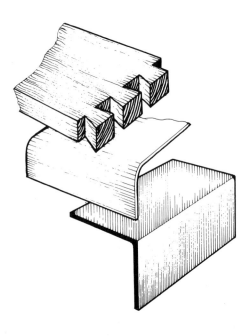

(vi) **Size and weight.** These are important factors when designing many jobs and their effect on the following should be considered:

■ portability
■ storage
■ environment
■ materials used

(vii) **Maintenance.** It is not enough merely to make an artefact which works for a short time. We must make sure that it will work for the maximum length of time without any problems, and that when maintenance or repairs are needed they can be carried out easily and economically.

(viii) **Appearance.** This is usually a very important factor because there are few situations in which we do not consider the appearance of a design and its effect on its environment. Appearance is also the first characteristic of an artefact which most people notice. We should therefore remember that:

(a) The appearance should suit the nature of the job an artefact has to do.
(b) The appearance should suit the environment in which the artefact will be used.
(c) The overall appearance will depend on the materials which are used and the finishes which have been applied to them.
(d) Safety considerations may affect appearance, for example when rounding off edges as mentioned earlier.
(e) Colour and texture can play a very important role in the overall effect of an artefact.
(f) An aesthetically pleasing overall effect will enhance the quality of an artefact.

(ix) Ergonomic and anthropometric data.

(a) **Ergonomics.** This is the study of man in relation to his work and his environment.
(b) **Anthropometrics.** This is the study of the development of man.

Since the purpose of design is to make life better in some way for human beings, it is reasonable to expect that many design investigations will involve the study and measurement of man and his movements.

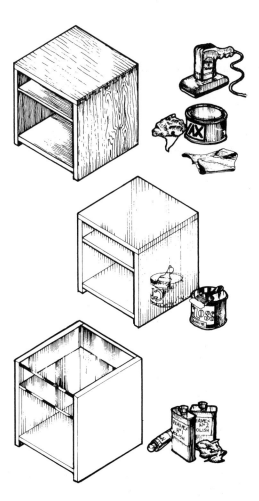

For example, when designing a chair we need to know where the users back, arms and legs should be supported to provide comfort in different sitting positions, and the range of measurements of the different people likely to use the chair (see Chair design example).

Once a compromise has been reached between the conflicting requirements of the many design factors, and the possibilities have been narrowed down to specific ranges of materials, approximate sizes and proportions, and the general character aimed at for the product, a visual investigation can begin. In other words, the purpose of the investigation stage in an advanced project is to provide the designer with everything he or she needs to know before starting to make the preliminary design sketches, to resolve conflicts between the design factors and reduce the problem to manageable proportions.

STAGE 4 SOLUTION

From the information provided by the investigation above, a visual investigation is begun leading to the **synthesis** of a solution to the problem. (The word 'synthesis' means the building up of a solution from the many, separate parts of a problem.)

The synthesis can be divided into five stages:

(i) **Preliminary ideas** recorded in notes and sketches.
(ii) **Development sketches** presented as annotated sketches, models and mock-ups.

(iii) **Working drawings** giving all the information needed to make the design.

(iv) **Presentation drawings** and models showing what the completed artefact would look like.

(v) **The final design compared with the original design brief** to make sure that it fulfills the original need.

Some aspects of this synthesis need to be explained further.

(i) **Preliminary ideas.** You should try to produce the largest possible number and range of ideas. All ideas, however unconventional they may seem, should be recorded by sketches (these sometimes turn out to be very good original solutions). Use sketching to think aloud. Your first sketches will probably be rather simple geometric forms. However, these will at least have given you a starting point on which to build new ideas. Be spontaneous!

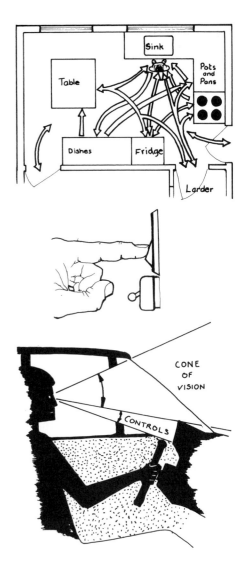

(ii) **Development sketches.** From your preliminary sketches you should take the best idea or ideas and begin to produce **partial solutions** from which a final solution can evolve. Partly developed ideas can usually only be finalised when they are drawn or modelled to scale so that the composition can be checked for proportions, etc. Mock-ups can be used at this stage so that accurate measurements can be worked out. From these sketches and models working drawings can be made.

(iii) **Working drawings.** Remember that working drawings can be in many different forms, but their purpose is always to ensure that all the information needed to make the artefact is given (see chapter 4).

At this point a cutting list should be made of all the materials needed (see Making a cutting list).

(iv) **Presentation drawings or models.** These are used to communicate a realistic impression of what the final artefact will look like well before it is actually made. In this way aesthetic and functional judgements can be made and any mistakes corrected before the prototype is started.

In industry several **visuals** and/or exact product models may be presented to a client so that he may choose the most appropriate one for production.

(v) **Realisation.** This is the making of the artefact. Again in industry the **prototype** is made individually by skilled technicians. Modifications are made as required and if it is given a good evaluation the go-ahead is given for production.

Other products may be designed on a one-off basis. It is important that the final prototype is correct in every way and this can only be ensured by rigorous testing.

(vi) **Testing.** The artefact should be tested under the conditions under which the product will eventually be used. With one-off artefacts this will probably simply mean using it in its intended position. The artefact should be observed carefully under normal use for an initial period. If modifications are needed they should become apparent fairly early in its use.

In large-scale production situations, protypes are sometimes tested to destruction to identify trouble areas needing particular attention or modifications, or to indicate the potential spares back-up required.

MAKING A CUTTING LIST OR PARTS LIST

Having designed a piece of work and made working drawings of it, a list of all the parts should be made showing the length, width and thickness of each. These will be the finished sizes of each piece.

Making a cutting list is very important because it allows you to check that you have all the materials needed to complete the job and that you have worked out the sizes correctly, making use of readily available standard sizes wherever possible, thus avoiding mistakes, waste and extra work.

SOLID WOOD

Where the surfaces have a rough 'as sawn' finish we must allow extra material on all sides for planing, filing or machining the surfaces smooth and square. However, where the width and thickness are already finished exactly to size and have a smooth surface, we need only allow extra on the length where we have sawn it from a larger piece.

The allowances made depend on the materials being used.

The allowances on a board are: 3 mm extra on the thickness, 6 mm extra on the width, 12 mm extra on the length.

The allowances on square wood are 3 mm extra on the sides and 12 mm extra on the length.

Where a mortise is to be chopped out near the end of a piece of wood, the allowance on the length is increased to 25 mm so that enough wood can be left at the end to prevent the end-grain from splitting.

MAN-MADE BOARDS, METALS AND PLASTICS

The cutting list for these is simpler. It is necessary only to allow 3 mm for finishing any sides which have been left as-sawn and have to be smoothed.

On metal and plastic rods, squares, flats, etc., allowances are usually needed only on the length.

On sheet materials of all kinds, allowances are required for smoothing the edges.

The following examples show a convenient way of making out a cutting list.

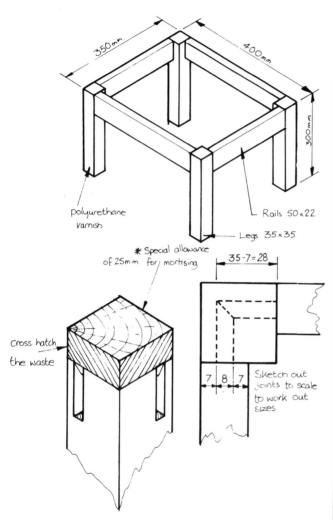

Rails 50×22

Legs 35×35

polyurethane Varnish

* Special allowance of 25mm for mortising

Cross hatch the waste

35 - 7 = 28

7 | 8 | 7

Sketch out joints to scale to work out sizes.

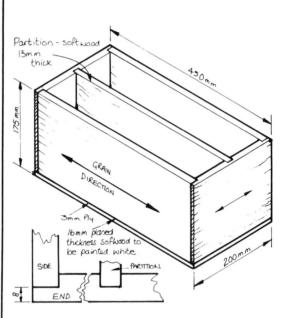

Partition - softwood 13mm thick

450mm

175 mm

GRAIN DIRECTION

3mm Ply

16mm planed thickness softwood to be painted white.

SIDE

8

END

PARTITION

200mm

PART	No. Req'd	MATERIAL	FINISHED SIZES			SAWN SIZES		
			L	W	Th.	L.	W.	Th.
ENDS	2	P.B.S. SOFT WOOD	200	175	16	212	181	✕
SIDES	2	"	434	175	16	446	181	✕
PARTITION	1	"	434	175	13	446	181	✕
BOTTOM	1	"	450	200	3	453	203	✕

PART	No. Req'd	MATERIAL	FINISHED SIZES			SAWN SIZES		
			L.	W.	Th.	L.	W.	Th.
LEGS	4	IROKO	300	35	35	325*	38	38
LONG RAILS	2	IROKO	386	50	22	398	56	25
SHORT RAILS	2	IROKO	336	50	22	348	56	25

Design method in action

At the heart of Design and Technology is the activity of actually
identifying problems and solving them. The following pages show
examples of how different people have tackled different problems.

Example 1

SITUATION

You have a number of paperback books which are used frequently and
are difficult to keep tidy, as they have no set place where they are to be
stored.

DESIGN BRIEF

To design a holder to store paperback books neatly in a convenient
position near your desk.

INVESTIGATION

■ How many paperback books are to be stored?
■ How big are they?
■ What is the best way of grouping the books?
■ Which materials are most suitable? (Look at the room where it will be
used.)
■ Is the unit to be free standing or wall mounted?
■ If wall mounted, how will it be fixed?

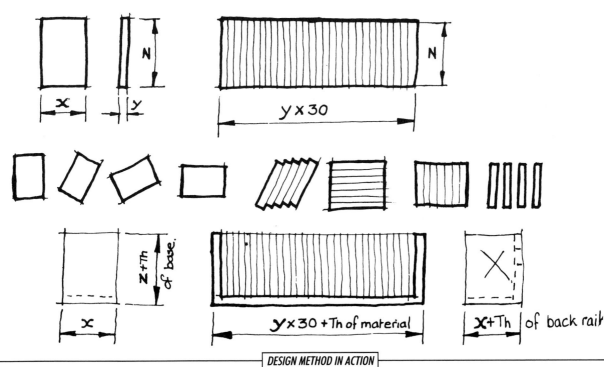

From the investigation a partial solution has been found which now
needs to be developed so that the details can be finalised:

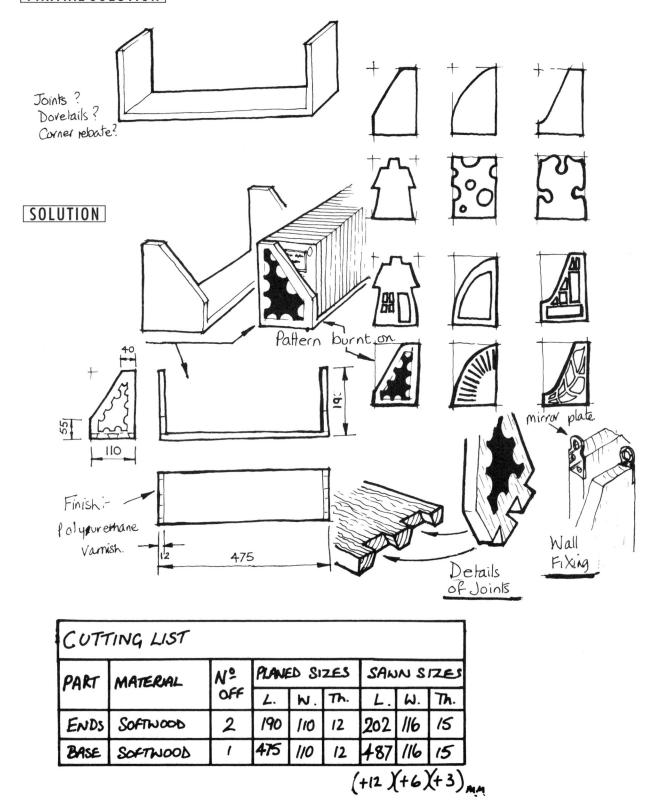

Joints ?
Dovetails ?
Corner rebate?

SOLUTION

Pattern burnt on.

40

55

110

190

Finish :-
Polyurethane
Varnish.

12   475

mirror plate

Wall
Fixing

Details
of Joints

CUTTING LIST								
PART	MATERIAL	Nº OFF	PLANED SIZES			SAWN SIZES		
			L.	W.	Th.	L.	W.	Th.
ENDS	SOFTWOOD	2	190	110	12	202	116	15
BASE	SOFTWOOD	1	475	110	12	487	116	15

(+12)(+6)(+3)mm

See the sections on commonly available forms of hardwood and
softwood, and making a cutting list.

Example 2 Noughts and crosses game

Situation for design — Most of the games I own are quite large and cumbersome, and have parts that are easily lost or damaged. This makes them difficult to carry around and impossible to play when travelling.

Identification of problem :- A small compact game that can be easily carried.

Design Brief — To design a simple pocket game which can be used when travelling.

Investigation —
① Which game(s) do I prefer ? ✓
② Which game do my brother + sister prefer? ✓
③ How big are the pockets I am likely to ✓
carry the game inside? ✓
④ What material would be suitable/available? ✓
⑤ Are there any safety factors I should be aware of? ✓
⑥ Where is the game likely to be played ? ✓
⑦ How many people should be able to play the game ✓
at one time?
⑧ How many parts does the chosen game include?

Monopoly X too complicated
Ludo ✓ possible — a bit complex for a small game.
Draughts X too many parts.
Chess X — Sister + brother cannot play.
Noughts + crosses ✓ — All prefer.

Nine pieces — 4 Noughts. 5 crosses.

Two players — rear passenger seats of car.
room for two people. — sometimes at home.

Square game would leave plenty of room for fingers.

About 100 m.m.

Will have to be careful of sharp corners.

180

Game has to be kept small and compact — but can be brightly coloured — must not wear off inside pocket or by constant touch by hand — Acrylic would be suitable — there are plenty of small pieces in school!

| POCKET   GAME | J Topp | 11:12:82 |

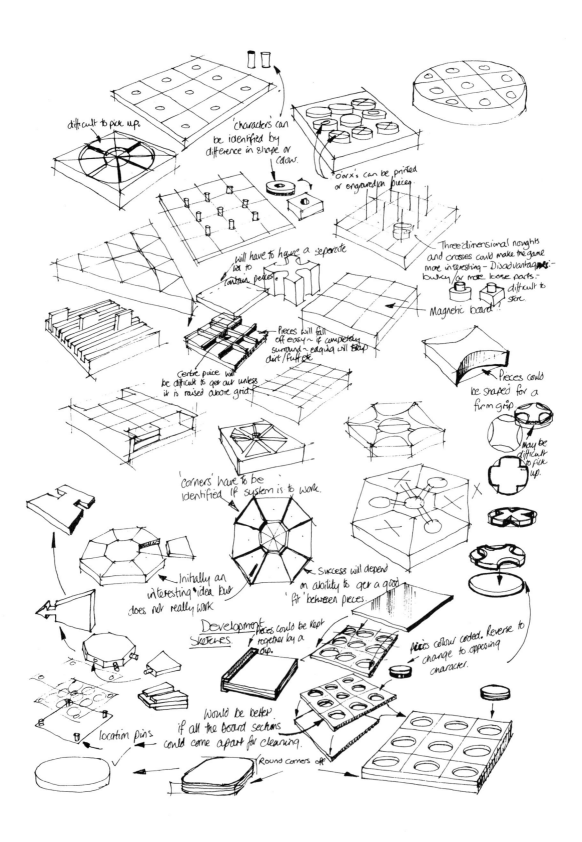

difficult to pick up.

'characters' can be identified by difference in shape or colour.

'O'orx's can be printed or engraved on pieces.

Three dimensional noughts and crosses could make the game more interesting – Disadvantages:- bulky/or more loose parts:- difficult to store.

Magnetic board?

Will have to have a separate lid to contain pieces.

Pieces will fall off easy - if completely surround - edging will trap dirt/fluff etc.

Centre piece will be difficult to get out unless it is raised above grid.

Pieces could be shaped for a firm grip.

May be difficult to pick up.

'corners' have to be identified if system is to work.

Initially an interesting idea but does not really work.

Success will depend on ability to get a good 'fit' between pieces.

Development Sketches.

Pieces could be kept together by a clip.

Pieces colour coded. Reverse to change to opposing character.

location pins

Would be better if all the board sections could come apart for cleaning.

Round corners off.

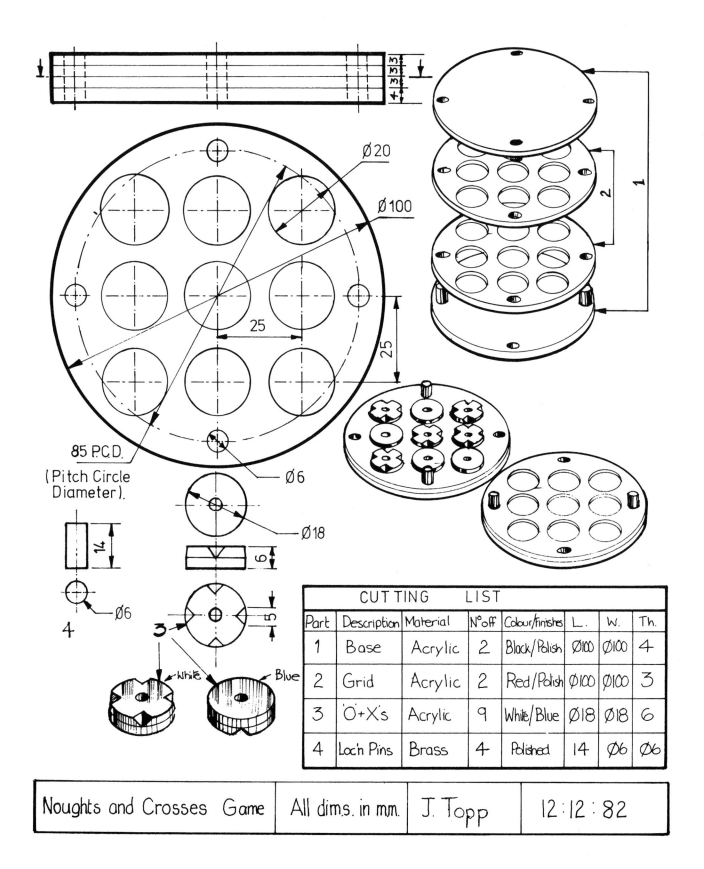

Ø20

Ø100

25

25

85 P.C.D.
(Pitch Circle
Diameter).

Ø6

Ø18

14

6

5

Ø6

4

3

White

Blue

CUTTING		LIST					
Part	Description	Material	Nºoff	Colour/finishes	L.	W.	Th.
1	Base	Acrylic	2	Black/Polish	Ø100	Ø100	4
2	Grid	Acrylic	2	Red/Polish	Ø100	Ø100	3
3	'O'+X's	Acrylic	9	White/Blue	Ø18	Ø18	6
4	Loc'n Pins	Brass	4	Polished	14	Ø6	Ø6

Noughts and Crosses Game	All dims. in m.m.	J. Topp	12 : 12 : 82

Example 3

A three-movement robot arm modelled in fluted plastic and using syringes as hydraulic rams.

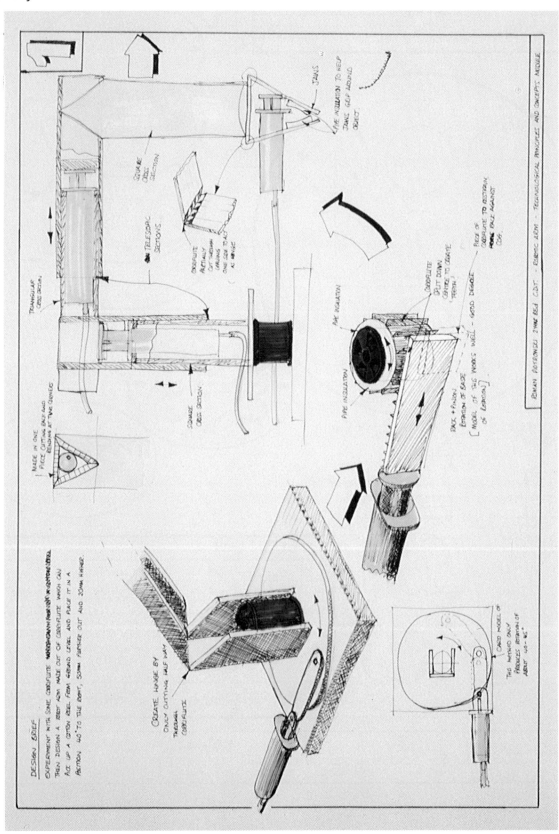

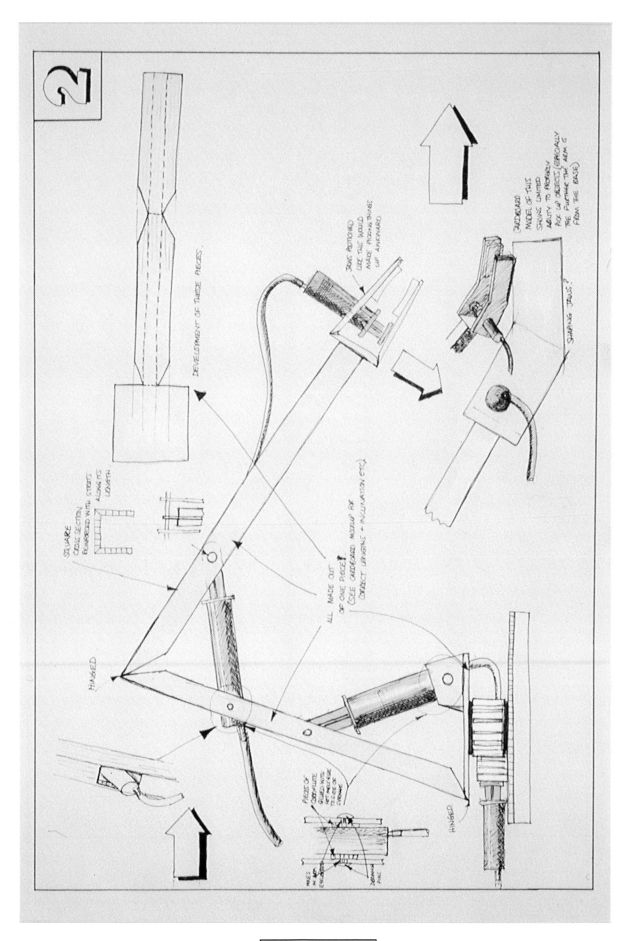

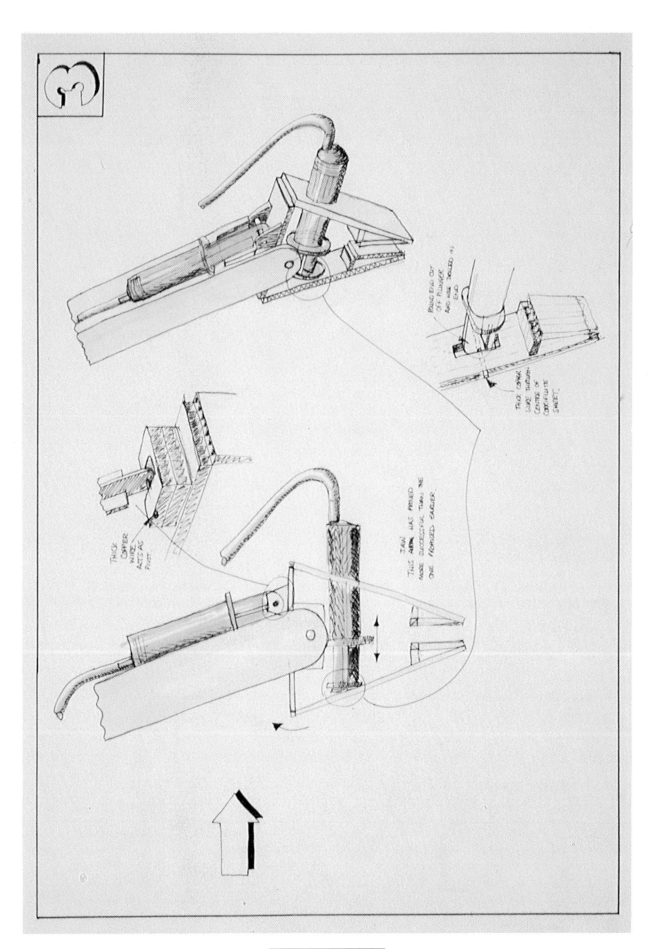

ROUND END CUT OFF PLUNGER AND HAS PUSHED IN

THICK COPPER WIRE THROUGH CENTRE OF CORIFLUTE SHEET.

THICK COPPER WIRE ACTS AS PIVOT

JAW

THIS ARM HAS PINNED MORE SUCCESSFUL THAN THE ONE PROPOSED EARLIER.

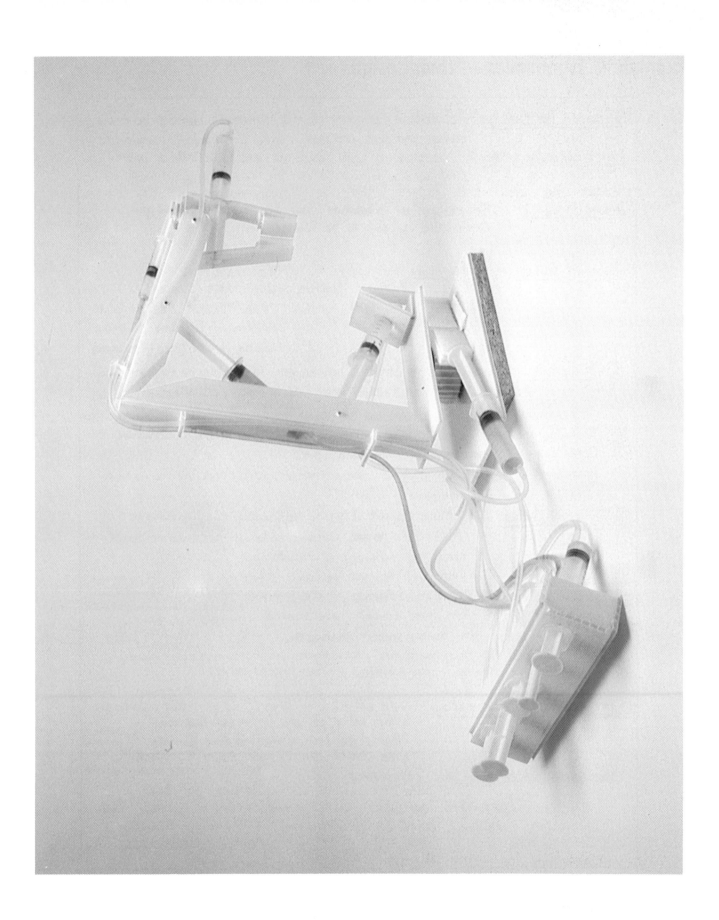

Example 4 Ergonomics — chair design

<u>Situation for Design</u> :- Existing seating in my lounge at home is becoming tatty and does not really give the comfort I would like

<u>Identification of problem</u> :- Need for a unit which will give comfortable support to those using it , and which will enhance the environment in which it will be used

<u>Design Brief</u> :- To design an attractive, low cost, unit which will give comfortable support to the human body.

<u>Design factors</u> — ① <u>Function</u> —

                   Primary function — To give comfortable support

                   Secondary function — Complete relaxation - allow comfortable watching of TV - listening to music. eating from a tray — reading

② <u>Materials</u> — Specifications — Strong , light weight - (if unit is to be moved regularly) Availability ! cheap - safe, comfortable to touch , durable, Aluminium, Steel , Plastics will depend on environment — Timber, Textiles — should allow simple construction yet give good appearance - suit other furniture

③ <u>Manufacture</u> — quick, simple, cheap methods , but strong construction

④ <u>Cost</u> — Inexpensive in money and time.

⑤ <u>Appearance</u> — suit environment , be attractive in colour and finishes - should look inviting ↗ room

⑥ <u>Strength/Weight</u> — Must support 1 person efficiently but fairly lightweight.

⑦ <u>Durability</u> — Must last many years - materials / construction - should need the minimum of maintenance.

⑧ <u>Environment</u> — Where will the unit be used? — LOUNGE
          Where is it relative to other furniture — BY window — for reading and near stereo music centre.
          What colour schemes have been used — CHROME - BROWNS.
          How much space is available. — Not enough space for a low, lying posture.

⑨ <u>Safety</u> — Non toxic materials , No sharp edges, — strong, stable, easily cleaned — non corrosive. — Fire proof as possible

⑩ <u>Ergonomics / Anthropometrics</u> — Who will use the unit ? ↗ whole family + visitors — So base sizes on averages
          What will it be used for ? — see functions?
          What is the best position for these functions ? — Semi upright
          Where should the human body be supported ? ↗ Draw out to scale - ergonome

Other factors to be aware of : (Brainstorm)

Efficiency	Appropriateness	Size	Balance	Style
Suspension	Posture	Texture	Structure	trends - Taste
Compatability		Frame / Carcase Construction	Washable	Flexibility
Stain Proof		Water proof	Appeal	Reliability
		Quality	Wear	
				etc.

INVESTIGATION - ANALYSIS

	I MOULD	5M
	DRG No 1	1 : 6 : 84

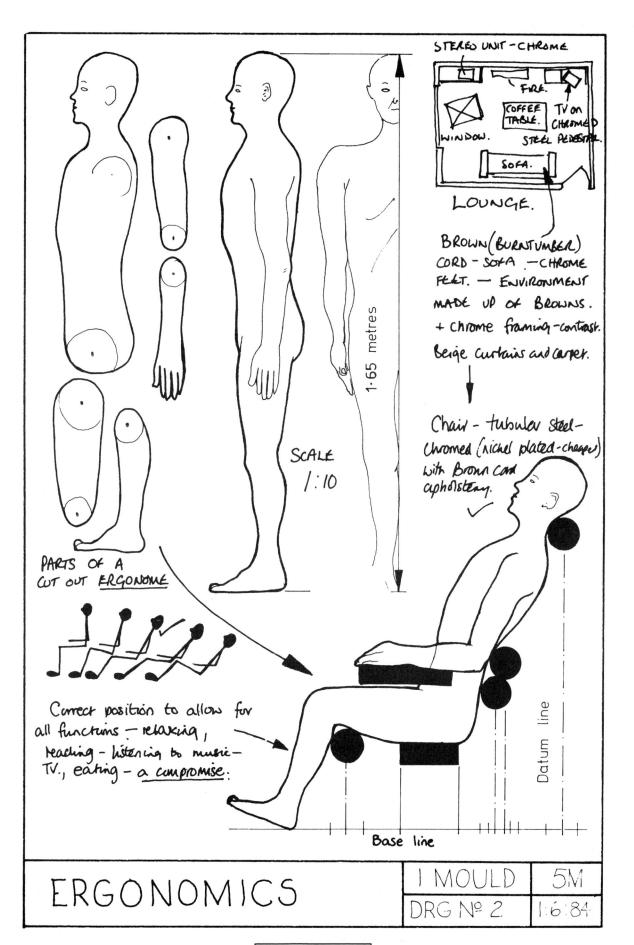

STEREO UNIT - CHROME

FIRE.

COFFEE TABLE.

TV on CHROMED STEEL PEDESTAL.

WINDOW.

SOFA.

LOUNGE.

BROWN (BURNT UMBER) CORD - SOFA. - CHROME FEET. — ENVIRONMENT MADE UP OF BROWNS. + chrome framing - contrast. Beige curtains and carpet.

Chair - tubular steel - chromed (nickel plated - cheaper) with Brown cord upholstery.

1·65 metres

SCALE 1:10

PARTS OF A CUT OUT ERGONOME

Correct position to allow for all functions - relaxing, reaching - listening to music - TV., eating - a compromise.

Datum line

Base line

ERGONOMICS

I MOULD	5M
DRG Nº 2	1·6·84

Design Specifications

The unit is to be made from tubular steel – chromed.

The upholstery is to include brown Cord if possible or similar material.

Due to the weight of tubular steel – the frame work should be kept to a minimum yet provide a rigid structure.

The frame work is to be designed to support the pressure points of the human body determined from the ergonome.

√ Develop further :-
– The basic concept on which further ideas can be centred.

SUPPORT REQUIREMENTS.

✓

Too unstable.

SUPPORT FRAME	I MOULD	5M
	DRG N° 3	2·6·84

Tube / bar sections

Some of
the ideas are
becoming a little
too complicated!

must be careful not
to make the unit too
heavy

Although an
interesting idea
tubing may
get in the way
of elbows

I like the way in
which the seat is
slung from the
frame.

could panel side
piece!

PRELIMINARY SKETCHES	SEATING UNIT	I. MOULD	5M
		DRG Nº 4	3.6.84

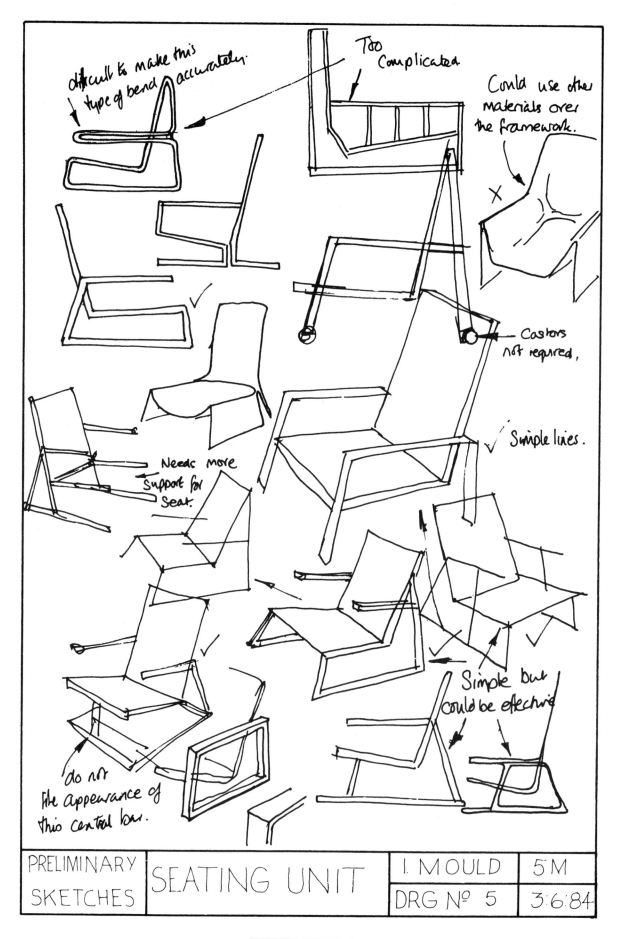

difficult to make this type of bend accurately.

Too complicated.

Could use other materials over the framework.

Castors not required.

Simple lines.

Needs more support for seat.

Simple but could be effective.

do not like the appearance of this central bar.

PRELIMINARY SKETCHES	SEATING UNIT	I. MOULD	5 M
		DRG Nº 5	3·6·84

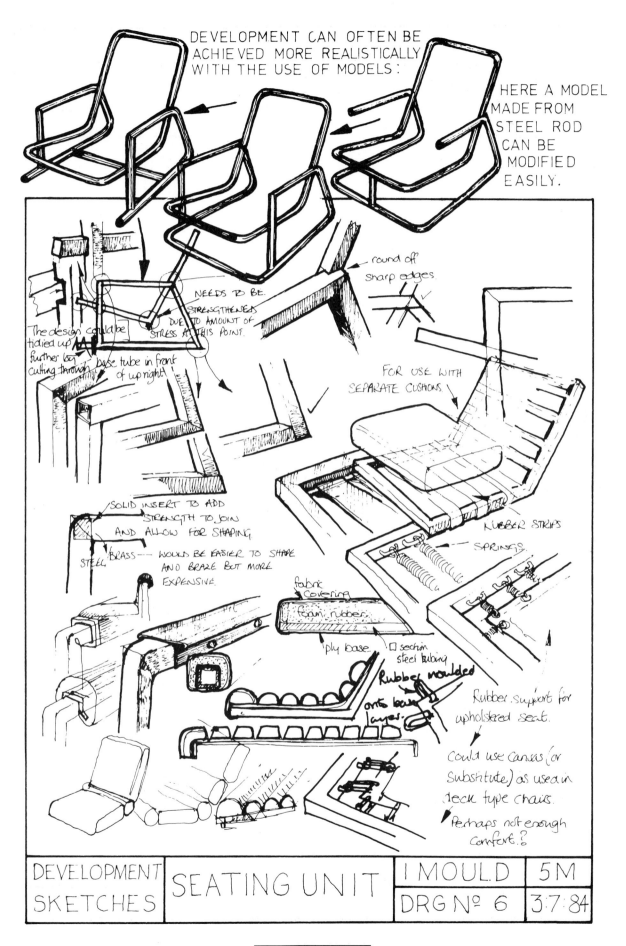

DEVELOPMENT CAN OFTEN BE ACHIEVED MORE REALISTICALLY WITH THE USE OF MODELS:

HERE A MODEL MADE FROM STEEL ROD CAN BE MODIFIED EASILY.

round off sharp edges.

NEEDS TO BE STRENGTHENED DUE TO AMOUNT OF STRESS AT THIS POINT.

The design could be tidied up further by cutting through base tube in front of upright.

FOR USE WITH SEPARATE CUSHIONS.

SOLID INSERT TO ADD STRENGTH TO JOIN AND ALLOW FOR SHAPING.

STEEL

BRASS — WOULD BE EASIER TO SHAPE AND BRAZE BUT MORE EXPENSIVE.

RUBBER STRIPS

SPRINGS.

fabric covering

foam rubber.

ply base

□ section steel tubing

Rubber moulded onto base layer.

Rubber support for upholstered seat.

Could use canvas (or substitute) as used in deck type chairs.

Perhaps not enough comfort.?

DEVELOPMENT SKETCHES	SEATING UNIT	I MOULD	5M
		DRG Nº 6	3.7.84

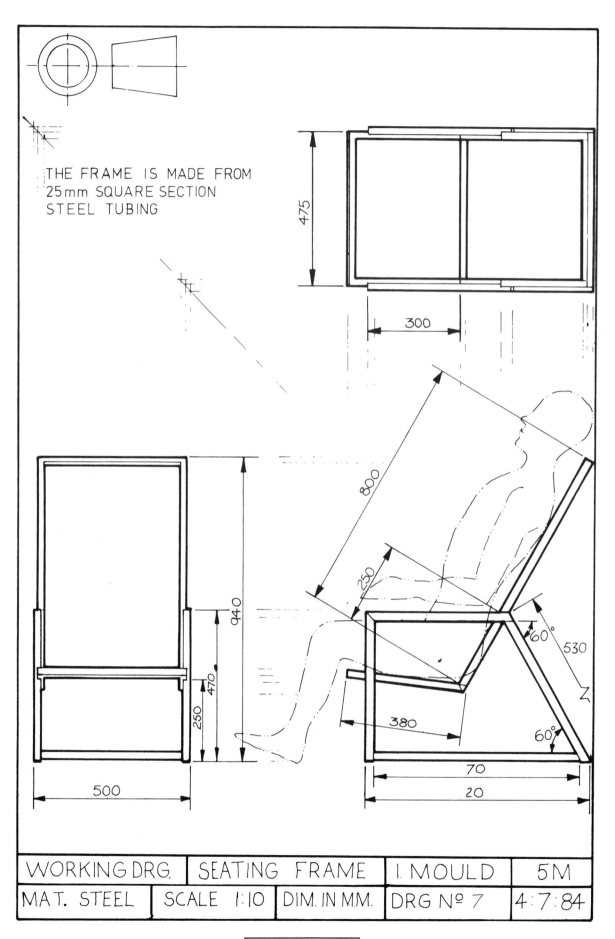

THE FRAME IS MADE FROM
25mm SQUARE SECTION
STEEL TUBING

475

300

800

250

940

470

250

500

60°

530

60°

380

70

20

WORKING DRG.	SEATING FRAME	I. MOULD	5M
MAT. STEEL	SCALE 1:10	DIM. IN M.M.	DRG Nº 7	4:7:84

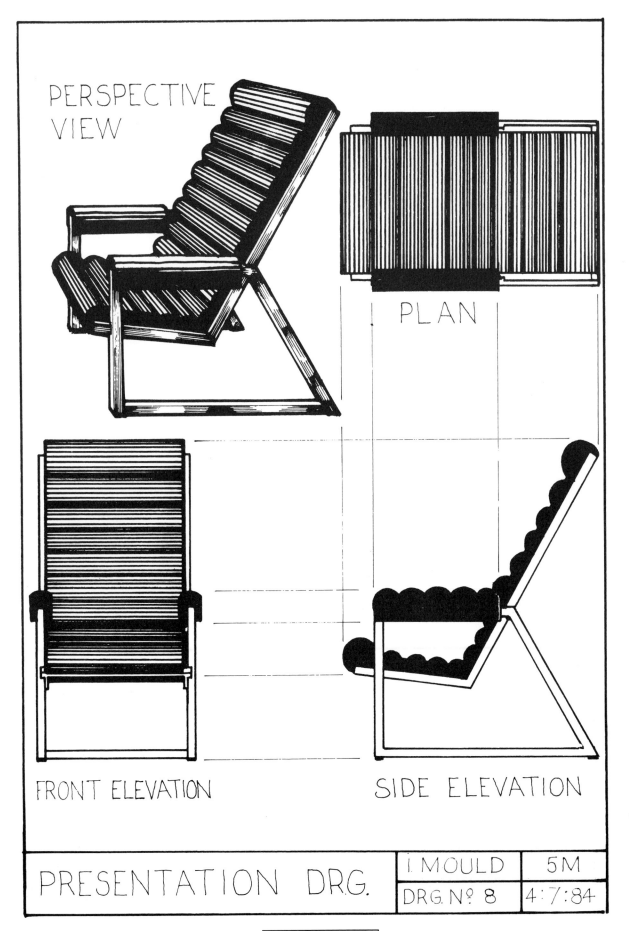

PERSPECTIVE
VIEW

PLAN

FRONT ELEVATION

SIDE ELEVATION

PRESENTATION DRG.

| I. MOULD | 5M |
| DRG. Nº 8 | 4:7:84 |

Example 5

Product design for a hand-held electronic thermometer using an electronic module with LCD display (see page 34 for final colour renderings).

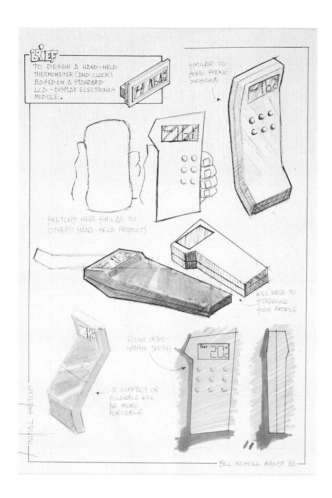

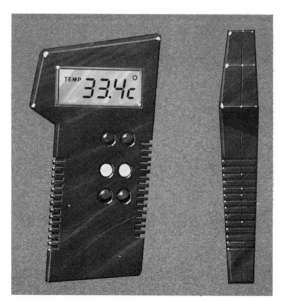

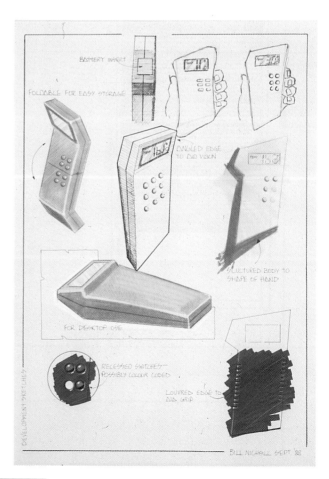

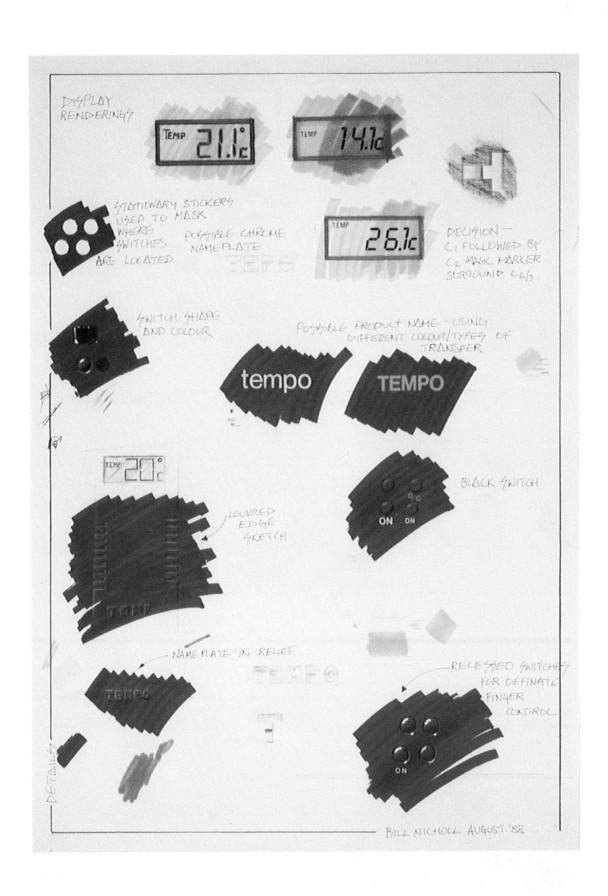

DISPLAY RENDERINGS

TEMP. 21.1°c

TEMP 14.1c

TEMP 26.1c

STATIONARY STICKERS USED TO MASK WHERE SWITCHES ARE LOCATED.

POSSIBLE CHROME NAMEPLATE

DECISION — C₁ FOLLOWED BY C₂ ANAC MARKER SURROUND C6/7

SWITCH SHAPE AND COLOUR

POSSIBLE PRODUCT NAME - USING DIFFERENT COLOUR/TYPES OF TRANSFER

tempo

TEMPO

TEMP 20°c

LOUVRED EDGE SKETCH

ON   ON

BLACK SWITCH

NAMEPLATE IN RELIEF

TEMPO

RECESSED SWITCHES FOR DEFINATE FINGER CONTROL

ON

DETAILS

BILL NICHOLL AUGUST '88

Example 6

The design of a robot toy having a programmable memory.

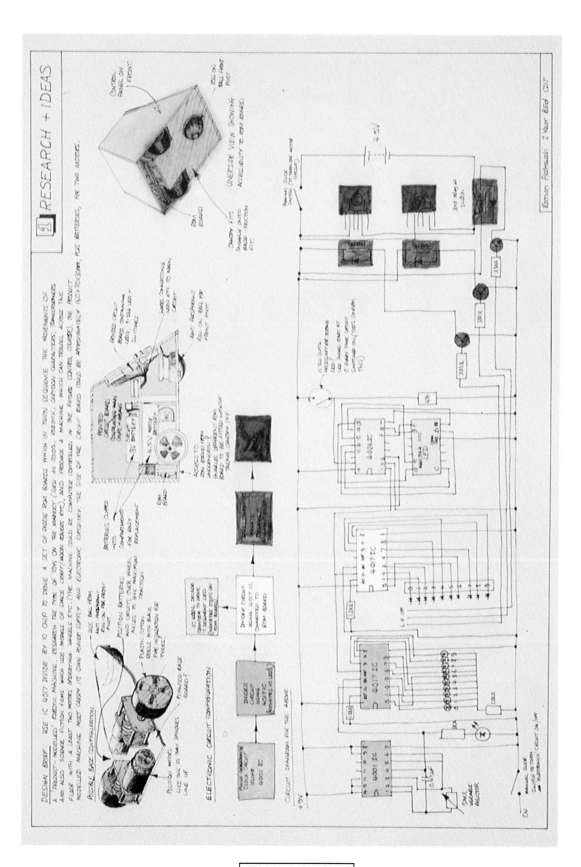

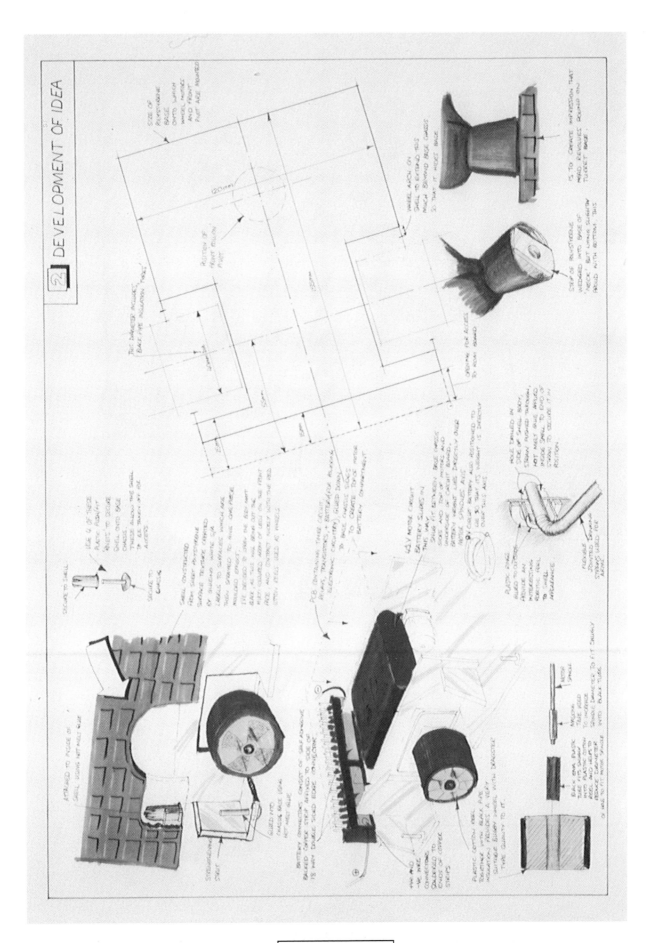

DEVELOPMENT OF IDEA

POSSIBLE COLOUR SCHEMES

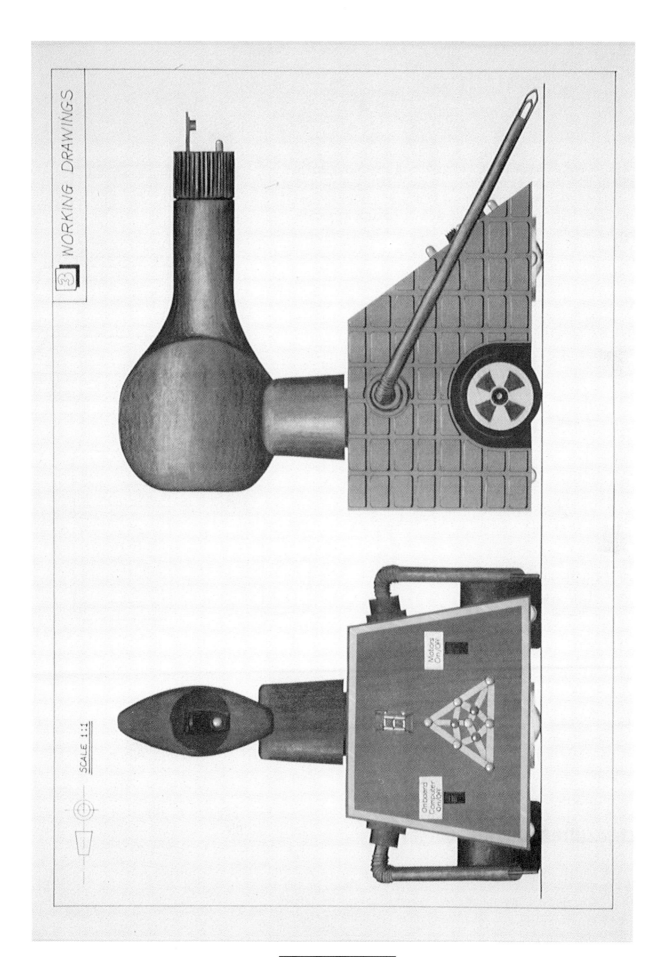

SCALE 1:1

Motors
On/Off

Onboard
Computer
On/Off

7 Technology for design: Electronics

Electronics is one of the fastest growing areas of technology and has probably had the greatest impact on our lives. The development of the integrated circuit — the 'chip' — in just 3 decades has revolutionised electronics, and we now take for granted cheap calculators, video recorders and computers. All of these would have staggered engineers just 10 years ago.

Understanding electronics and using it creatively in design and technology is not difficult. This section looks first at individual or discrete electronic components, and shows how they can be combined into useful circuits. The second part of the section shows how integrated circuits can be used to solve problems.

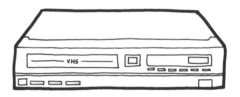

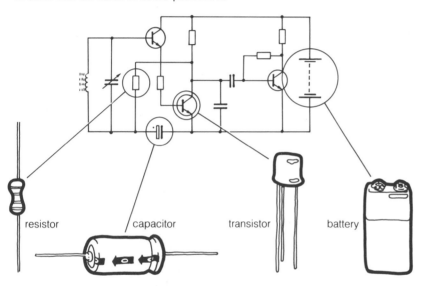

resistor   capacitor   transistor   battery

The circuit

An electronic circuit consists of a number of components connected so that current can flow. The components are shown as symbols in a circuit diagram. In a circuit diagram, straight lines represent conductors, and are drawn in parallel or at 90° to each other. Lines crossing over are **not** taken as connected. Only a dot on the junction means there is a connection. (Page 130 explains how circuits can be made up from components.)

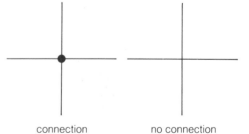

connection   no connection

Electric current and its sources

In the early days of physics, scientists thought that electricity was a kind of fluid like water, and they called it electric current — a term we still use. They also thought it flowed from +ve (positive) to −ve (negative). We now know that electricity is the movement of electrons that actually travel from −ve to +ve in a circuit.

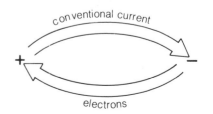

conventional current

+   −

electrons

Despite this knowledge, circuits are still described as if electricity is something that flows from +ve to −ve. This is known as **conventional current** flow.

There are several sources of electric current used in electronics and it is sometimes useful to think of these as pumps for driving current around — like the water pump in a central heating system.

DRY CELLS

A single dry cell is the proper name given to the chemical package that most people call a 1.5 volt (1.5 V) 'battery'. They are available in various sizes, but each has a voltage (pressure, if you think of water) of about 1.5 V. Chemical change within the cell produces electric current.

BATTERIES

A battery is a number of chemical cells connected together in series — normally in a sealed package. The total voltage of a battery is the sum of all its cells. A small PP3 radio battery, for example, is made up of six small rectangular cells giving a total of 9 V (6 × 1.5 V). Two PP3 batteries connected in series would give a total of 18 V. The cells that make up a battery can be small or large, and it is their actual physical size that determines how much current they can supply. Small batteries, whatever their voltage, must not be used for something requiring a large current. A PP3 battery, for example, will go flat quickly if used to run even a small electric motor. Cells and batteries vary in their uses (and cost) according to the chemical processes inside that produce the current.

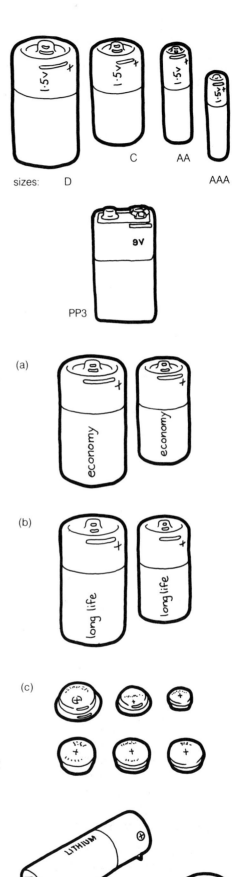

(a) **Zinc chloride** cells and batteries are the cheapest in general use but have a limited life.
(b) **Alkaline cells** and batteries are the most expensive for normal use, but can supply far more current over a period of time than zinc chloride equivalents.
(c) **Mercury cells** are small (and expensive), but are used only for small devices like hearing aids where current consumption is low.
(d) **Lithium cells** and batteries give high current output for their size and have an exceptionally long life — many years if only used occasionally. They are commonly found in all-electric cameras, calculators and computers (to back up memories).

(e) **Nickel cadmium** (NiCad) cells and batteries are rechargeable — up to 1000 times. These are used in cordless appliances, and their availability has given designers many new opportunities. NiCads should only be charged with a special constant-current charger and must never be short circuited.

The amount of current a battery is able to provide is measured in **ampere hours**, i.e. the number of amps (A) per hour that can be drawn. If a battery is rated at 1 ampere hour, it should be possible to draw from it 1 A for the duration of 1 hour, or 0.5 A for 2 hours, or 0.25 A for 4 hours.

The performance of a battery can be examined by drawing current from it with a resistor and measuring its voltage over a period of time. The performance of a typical PP3 9 V battery is shown. The current passing through the 600 ohm resistor (see page 113) is about the same as that needed to power a small radio. At the end of its useful life, the voltage of the battery drops quickly, and it is said to go 'flat'. (**Note:** In order to measure the condition of a battery, it is no good just measuring its voltage. It has to be made to 'pump' current at the same time, and this is normally achieved by connecting a resistor across it.)

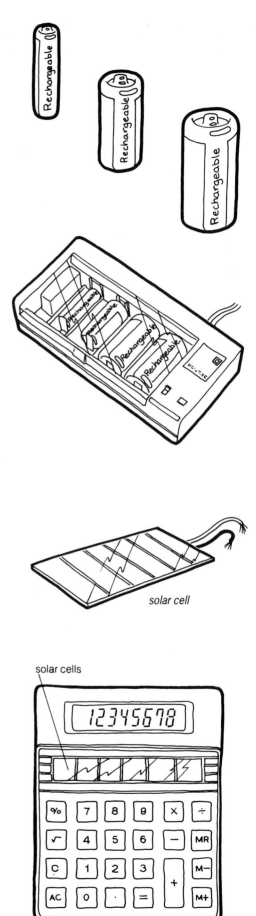

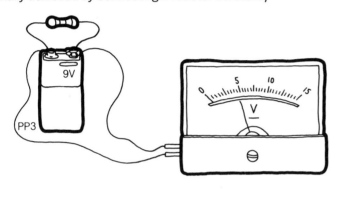

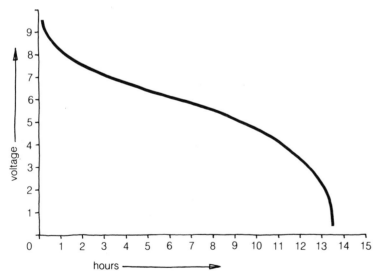

PHOTOVOLTAIC CELLS

Photovoltaic cells, commonly known as solar cells, convert energy from light directly into electrical current. The voltage of a typical cell is about 0.4 V, but like chemical cells they can be connected in series to give higher voltages. Solar cells are gradually getting cheaper and are used, for example, in calculators (no more flat batteries!), and in telephone systems where normal supplies are not available.

solar cell

solar cells

LOW-VOLTAGE POWER SUPPLY UNITS

A low-voltage power supply unit (PSU) draws current from the mains and converts it from high voltage a.c. to low voltage d.c. — like the supply from a battery. Many PSUs do not give a smooth d.c. supply: the voltage moves up and down, producing a hum in a loudspeaker. A good PSU for electronics work has a voltage regulator built in that gets rid of this problem. Only this type of PSU should be used with integrated circuits.

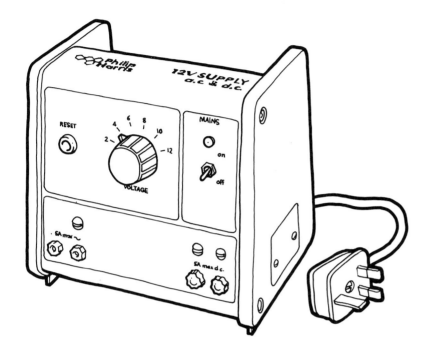

Components used in electronics

FILAMENT BULBS

A filament bulb is a glass envelope (almost empty of gas) containing a fine coiled wire (filament) of tungsten. The filament has a certain resistance, and when current passes through it, heating takes place and it becomes white hot — giving out light as well as a lot of heat. In fact, the filament gets hotter than molten steel, and most of the electrical energy is converted into heat.

Filament bulbs are largely being replaced by LEDs (see page 116) as indicators. (**Beware:** Small bulbs that look the same size can consume very different amounts of current.)

symbol for bulb

SWITCHES

Switches are used to control current flow in circuits, and there are many different types to suit different applications.

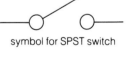

symbol for SPST switch

(a) TOGGLE SWITCH

In the simplest type of toggle switch a moving part (pole) comes together with a fixed contact when the switch is closed. This is described as a single-pole single-throw (SPST) switch. Like other types of switch (e.g. rocker and slider), toggle switches may have more than one throw position and more than one pole.

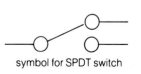

symbol for SPDT switch

SPDT switches (also having an 'off' position) are often found in products such as torches, so that the user can, for example, switch on either the main beam or a warning flashing light. Some small torches double as personal attack alarms: in one position the SPDT switch completes a bulb circuit and in the other position a loud buzzer is energised.

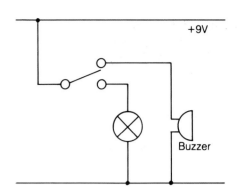

(b) ROCKER SWITCH
Rocker switches are similar in operation to the above, but they have a different (rocking) mechanical action.

(c) SLIDE SWITCH
This type of switch has a metal slider (or sliders) that slips over and connects fixed contact points. It is commonly available as a DPDT type and is often used to reverse current flow to electric motors to change their direction.

Note: *In most circuit diagrams the battery or power supply is not normally shown. It is assumed that it is connected to the bottom and top supply rails—the top marked with the supply voltage*

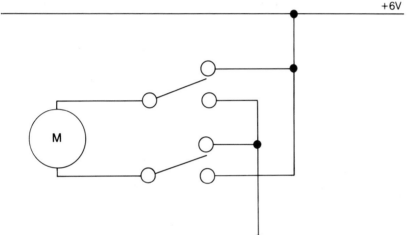

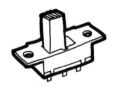

(d) REED SWITCH
This switch comprises a pair of small contact reeds sealed in a glass tube. When a magnet is brought near, the reeds come together and make contact to complete a circuit. Reed switches are often used in burglar alarm systems because they can be concealed, e.g. in door or window frames. Small magnets buried in the doors and windows affect the switches when a door or window is opened.

(e) TILT SWITCHES
Mercury tilt switch
This form of switch has two closely spaced contacts in the end of a plastic tube containing a blob of mercury. When the tube is tilted, the mercury runs to one end and bridges across the two contacts to complete a circuit.

Pendulum tilt switch

Pendulum switches take many forms, but usually consist of a small pendulum weight (one contact) suspended on a metal ribbon near a second fixed contact. When the switch is tilted, the pendulum touches the fixed contact to complete a circuit.

This type of switch is commonly used in car alarms, and can be used, for example, in warning systems where a buzzer sounds if there is a dangerous angle of tilt on a ladder or farm vehicle.

Pendulum switches can be made up using shim brass or wire to hang a small weight inside a metal tube, or other fixed contact. If possible, the weight and fixed contact should be solder coated to reduce contact resistance. In commerical switches, the contacts are usually electroplated to prevent any oxide film spoiling the contact.

(f) PUSH-BUTTON SWITCH

A momentary-action push-button switch is one that closes to complete a circuit only for as long as it is pressed. Some push-button switches have a toggle action and latch 'on' when pressed once and 'off' when pressed a second time.

Push-button switches can be made using overlapping brass strip (see page 54)

(g) MEMBRANE PANEL SWITCH

Membrane panel switches are quite new but have already replaced some of the switches described above in products such as video recorders, photocopiers and calculators. Because they are so cheap and reliable and give designers new opportunities, they may become the most important type of switch during the next decade.

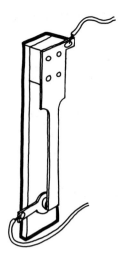

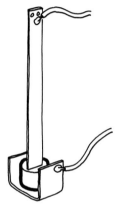

switch symbol

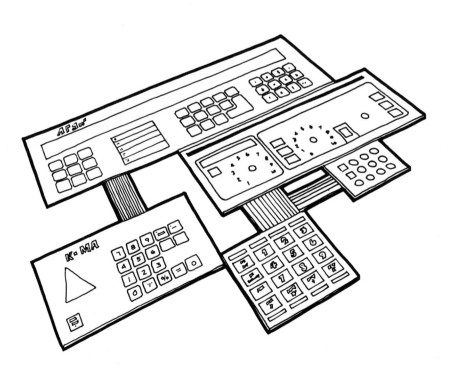

In principle, a membrane panel is very simple, and in practice they are easily made. They normally consist of a three-layer sandwich of plastic films — two of which are printed with tracks using a special conductive ink. The third (insulating) layer is placed between these two, and has small windows cut out at the switch positions. When pressure is applied to the sandwich over one of the windows, the top layer dips through the window and its conductor track makes contact with a corresponding one on the bottom layer. The tracks lead to a thin ribbon cable that is connected to any electronics behind the switch.

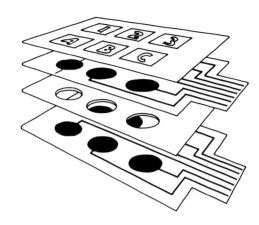

The membrane panel is a momentary contact switch, but if latching is required this is done by electronics (see page 121). The section on modelling (page 55) shows how to make working membrane panels that look realistic.

RESISTORS

A resistor restricts or resists current flow rather like a kink in a hosepipe restricts water flow. The most common type of resistor used in electronics consists of a small ceramic tube covered in a film of carbon — each end of which is connected to a wire leg. The composition of the carbon determines the value or amount of resistance measured in ohms (Ω). The higher the value in ohms, the more resistance there is. For example, a resistor of 10 ohms in the bulb circuit shown will dim the light slightly; a resistor of 50 ohms will restrict the current so that it just glows red. A 1000 ohm resistor will not let enough current pass to light the bulb at all.

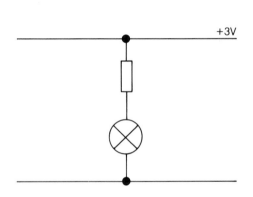

resistor symbol

Resistors are colour coded with coloured bands so their value can be read (see page 58 and refer to the colour chart).

Like a lightbulb filament or electric fire element, resistors warm up when they resist the flow of current. In most electronics work this is hardly noticeable because the currents are small, but where larger currents are passing larger or higher wattage resistors must be used. For most purposes, the 0.25 watt resistor will do.

Resistors are available in a limited range of values known as preferred values. These can be combined to give other values.

RESISTORS IN SERIES

For resistors connected in series, the total value is the sum of the individual resistances. It is given by

$$R = R_1 + R_2$$

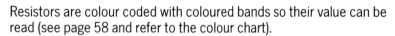

For example, the total value of a 1 k and 10 k resistor in series is

$$R = 1k + 10k$$
$$R = 11k$$

Note: k is used to mean $\times 1000$.

RESISTORS IN PARALLEL

If resistors are connected in parallel, their total resistance is less than any of the individual resistors because the current has two or more paths to take. The total is given by

$$\frac{1}{R} = \frac{1}{R_1} + \frac{1}{R_2}$$

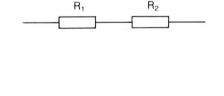

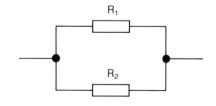

For example, the total value of two 10k resistors in parallel is

$$\frac{1}{R} = \frac{1}{10k} + \frac{1}{10k}$$

$$R = 5k$$

RESISTORS AND OHM'S LAW

Ohms Law describes the relationship between resistance (R), voltage (V), and current (I). If we know two of these things, the third can be worked out. (Ohms' Law is really the only maths needed for basic electronics work.)

Ohm's Law states $V = I \times R$ or $R = \dfrac{V}{I}$ or $I = \dfrac{V}{R}$

Ohm's Law is best remembered by thinking of a triangle:

$$\begin{array}{c} V \\ I \quad R \end{array}$$

When the unknown is removed from the triangle, the position of the two remaining known quantities tells us whether to multiply or divide.

Some examples will help:
If we have a 9V battery and want only 0.25A to flow in a circuit, e.g. to control the speed of a motor or the brightness of a bulb, Ohm's Law states

$$R = \frac{V}{I} = \frac{9V}{0.25A} = 36 \text{ ohms}$$

(**Note:** In electronics a more convenient unit of current is the milliamp

$$= \frac{1}{1000} \text{ amp; } 0.25A = 250mA)$$

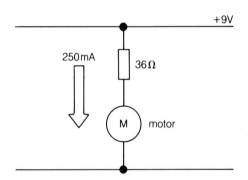

if a resistance of 1k is connected across a 9V battery, the current flowing would be

$$I = \frac{V}{R} = \frac{9V}{1k} = 9.0 \text{ mA}$$

POTENTIAL DIVIDERS

As well as controlling current flow in a circuit, resistors can be used to 'divide' a voltage. This is useful, for example, where different voltages are needed at different places in a circuit working from one battery.

If a pair of resistors is connected in series across a supply, and the voltage measured where they join, this will be in proportion to the values of the two resistors. Some examples are given overleaf.

If the value of the lower resistor is less than that at the top, the voltage measured at the middle will be less than half the supply voltage, and vice versa. It may help you to think of water being pumped through two valves with an outlet between them (see p. 115). If the lower valve is almost fully closed (high resistance) and the top one almost fully open (low resistance, water comes from the outlet under some pressure (higher voltage). If the top valve is almost fully closed (high resistance) and the bottom one almost fully open (low resistance), there will be little water pressure at the outlet (lower voltage).

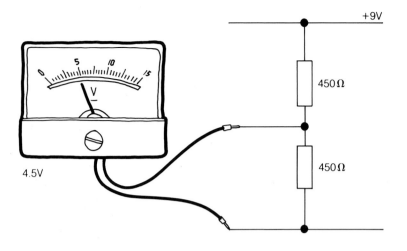

4.5V

450 Ω

450 Ω

+9V

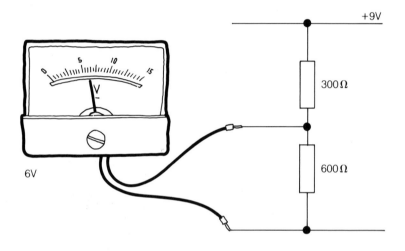

6V

300 Ω

600 Ω

+9V

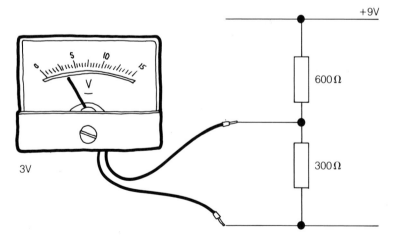

3V

600 Ω

300 Ω

+9V

It should be remembered that current is always flowing through a potential divider, and higher value resistors are used if possible. Only a small current can be drawn from the middle of a potential divider, and this is further reduced as the resistance values increase.

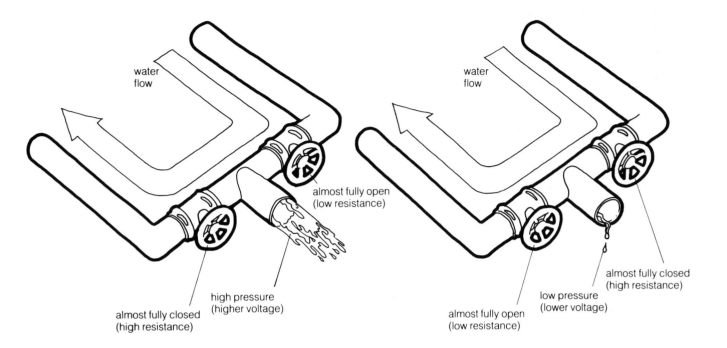

water flow

water flow

almost fully open
(low resistance)

almost fully closed
(high resistance)

high pressure
(higher voltage)

almost fully closed
(high resistance)

low pressure
(lower voltage)

almost fully open
(low resistance)

VARIABLE RESISTORS

The most common form of variable resistor is the rotary type which has an almost circular track of carbon. This track is broken and the two ends of the track connected to tags. In between these two, a third tag is connected to a wiper in contact with the track. The wiper is moved by a spindle, and the length of carbon track between the wiper and one of the outside tags determines the resistance. The variable resistor can be used as a potential divider to give a variable voltage at its centre tag.

A smaller version of the variable resistor is the pre-set resistor. As its name implies, it is normally pre-set (with a screwdriver) and then left at that value.

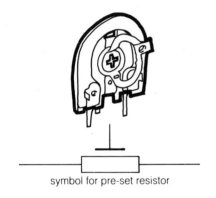

symbol for pre-set resistor

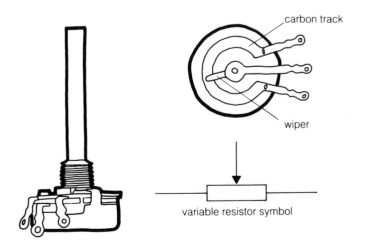

carbon track

wiper

variable resistor symbol

LIGHT-DEPENDENT RESISTOR (LDR)

An LDR is a resistor whose value alters according to the amount of light falling on it. A common LDR, the ORP12, has a resistance of more than 100k in the dark, but this drops to less than 100 Ω in bright light.

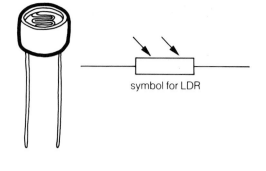

symbol for LDR

THERMISTOR

This is a form of resistor whose value depends on its temperature.

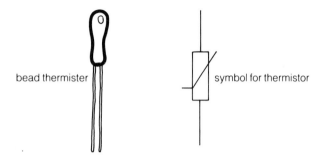

bead thermister

symbol for thermistor

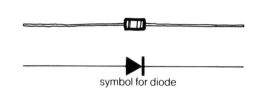

symbol for diode

THE LIGHT-EMITTING DIODE (LED)

A diode permits current to flow through it only in one direction — from anode to cathode, if you think of conventional current flow. A light-emitting diode (LED) is a special form of diode that gives out light when connected the correct way around. The cathode leg (connected to −ve) is next to a small flat edge on the bottom of the plastic case. This leg is usually shorter as well, but not always.

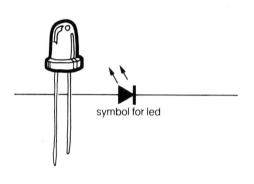

symbol for led

LEDs normally need to be connected in series with a resistor to prevent them drawing too much current and burning out. The value of this resistor depends on the voltage. It can be worked out very accurately, but a good rule of thumb (a rough rule) is that the resistance should be 50 ohms per volt of supply voltage. A LED placed across a 9 V battery would therefore require a resistor of 9 V × 50 ohms = 450 (the nearest preferred value is 470 ohms).

A circuit employing only a battery, LED and resistor has a surprising number of uses, and many products can be designed (and modelled) around it. Some possibilities are shown below.

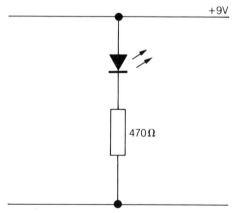

+9V

470 Ω

1 CONTINUITY TEST CIRCUIT

A fuse or filament bulb placed to complete the circuit will show whether the bulb or fuse is good.

In complicated wiring systems such as those in a car, it is not always clear if the end of a wire coming out in one place is the end of the same wire emerging somewhere else. If the wire is continuous, connecting the two ends into the circuit will cause the LED to light up. (**Warning:** Under no circumstances must a car battery or any other supply be connected while such a test is made.)

Printed circuit boards often need to be tested to find out if there are unseen breaks in the tracks (see page 130). The LED circuit can be used to find breaks by seeing if all lengths of the track will complete the circuit.

2 MOISTURE INDICATOR

If flying leads are connected from the circuit to a pair of wire probes about 15 mm apart, there will be sufficient conduction through damp soil to energise the LED. A product incorporating this circuit could be used to give a rapid indication of moisture levels in plant pots. (A 9 V battery should be used here.)

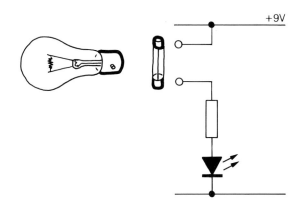

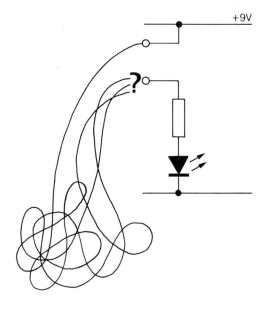

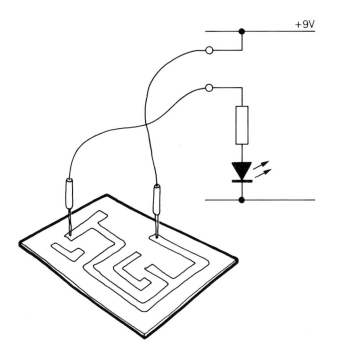

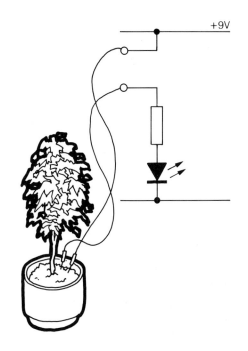

THE CAPACITOR

A capacitor can store and then release current: it can be charged and discharged. The unit of capacitance is the Farad, but this is too large for electronics and the capacitors actually used are measured in microfarads ($\frac{1}{1000000}$ Farad, abbreviated to μF), or in even smaller units.

An electrolytic capacitor has a special make-up to give it greater storage capacity for its size, but it must be connected into a circuit the correct way round. Most capacitors over about 1 μF are electrolytic.

A capacitor is fully charged when the voltage measured across its legs is the same as the supply voltage. A 2000 μF capacitor offered to a 9V PP3 battery will charge up almost instantly, and retain some of this charge for several hours (the charge gradually 'leaks' away). A 2000 μF capacitor charged from a PP3 battery will provide enough current to energise a LED for about 3 seconds in normal daylight.

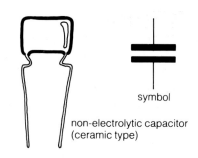

symbol

non-electrolytic capacitor
(ceramic type)

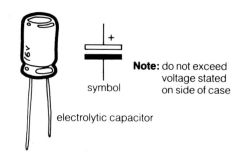

symbol

electrolytic capacitor

Note: do not exceed voltage stated on side of case

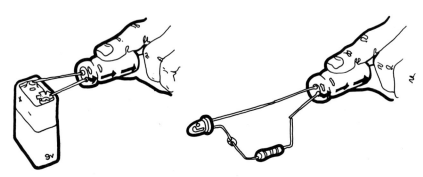

A graph will show that the capacitor discharges quickly at first, but slows down as the voltage drops. If the experiment with the 2000 μF capacitor and LED is carried out in a dark room, the LED glows brightly for about 3 seconds as before, but it can then be seen continuing to glow faintly as the capacitor reaches the bottom of its discharge curve.

If a large capacitor is placed across a LED and its resistor in a circuit, it has the effect of keeping the LED energised after the battery has been disconnected. When the switch is closed, the capacitor charges up (almost instantly) and the LED lights up. When the switch is opened again, the charged capacitor keeps the LED supplied with current for a few seconds. This circuit is useful in giving an extended signal (the LED glowing), after a very rapid contact is made. It can be used, for example, in wire loop continuity games to show when momentary contact is made between two conductors.

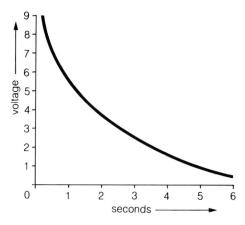

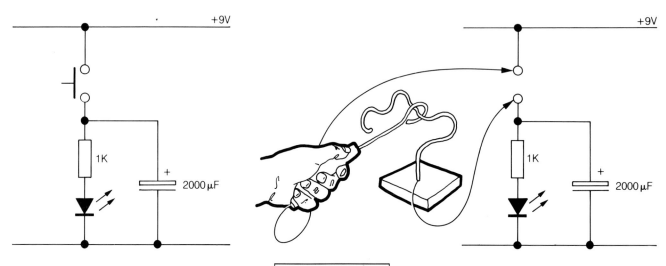

THE TRANSISTOR

Transistors can be divided into two main families: bipolar and field effect. This section will concentrate on the bipolar family. Bipolar transistors can be further divided into two types: NPN and PNP. These are similar in operation except for the way the current flows. Because they are already commonly used in design and technology, this section will look only at NPN transistors.

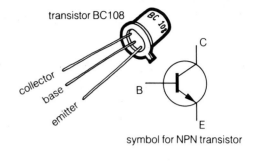

transistor BC108

symbol for NPN transistor

There are many NPN transistors to choose from, but they all operate in the same way. A small current flowing to the base of the transistor enables a large current to flow between the collector and emitter.

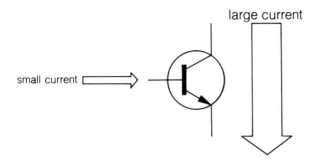

large current

small current

BC108 is the name given to a very cheap and common NPN transistor which is ideal for experiments. If BC108 is connected into a circuit with a LED and resistor, nothing happens. The transistor does not allow current to flow collector to emitter, and is like a switch turned 'off'. If, however, a tiny current is made to flow to the base, the transistor starts to switch 'on' and the LED lights up as current flows between the collector and emitter. The tiny current flowing from the positive side of the supply through the skin of a hand to the base is enough to do this!

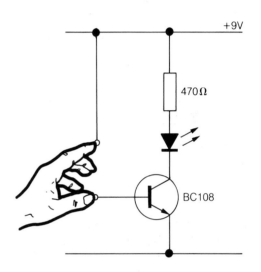

+9V

470 Ω

BC108

The simple transistor circuit can be used as a sensitive moisture detector if flying leads are taken from the transistor base and supply to a sensor — which might be a piece of blotting paper separating the ends of the leads. Moisture absorbed by the blotting paper would conduct base current and cause the transistor to begin switching on. (The resistor shown here connected to the base limits the base current to a safe value.)

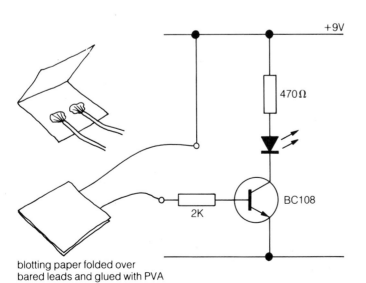

+9V

470 Ω

2K

BC108

blotting paper folded over
bared leads and glued with PVA

Amazingly, a graphite line on paper will also conduct enough base current to switch on the transistor. The lines should be drawn using a soft pencil (e.g. 4B) and pencilled over several times. Stranded wire leads should be Sellotaped over the lines.

The collector/emitter current flowing is dependent on the amount of base current. The relationship between the two is called the gain of the transistor, and for BC108 this is roughly 100:1, i.e. a base current of 1 mA will cause a collector/emitter current of 100 mA to flow.

It is important to note that the transistor will not do anything until the voltage measured at the base exceeds about 0.6 V, and sometimes a potential divider is put into a circuit to provide this 'starting' voltage. This is called biasing the transistor. The potential divider can be made up using a LDR or thermistor to create a light- or temperature-controlled switch.

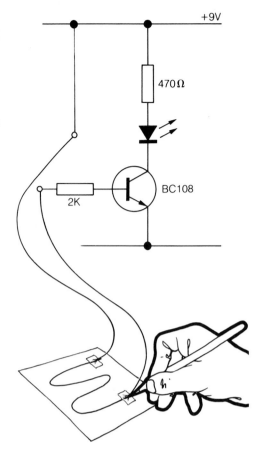

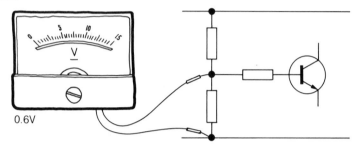

In the example shown, when no light falls on the LDR its resistance is high and there is no base current for the transistor. The buzzer (in place of the LED and resistor) does not sound. When light falls on the LDR, its resistance drops and base current starts to flow causing current to flow collector to emitter, and energising the buzzer. If the second resistor of the potential divider is variable, its setting will control the sensitivity of the transistor switch to light. (A diode has been added across the buzzer to protect the transistor against potentially damaging voltages that might be produced. This is known as a clamping diode, and any device connected to a transistor and containing a coil must be 'clamped'.) If the LDR is placed in circuit as the bottom resistor, the opposite will happen and the buzzer will sound when the LDR is shielded from light.

A more useful light-operated switch uses a second transistor whose base current is provided by the first. BFY51 is a larger NPN transistor with a maximum collector to emitter current of 1 A — ten times that of BC108. This means that a larger device or load can be substituted for the buzzer.

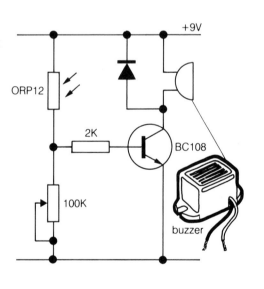

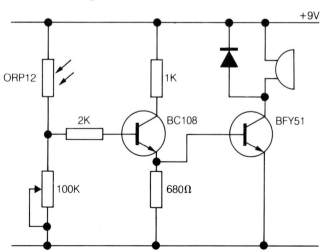

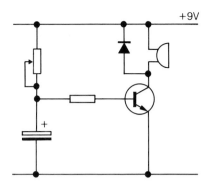

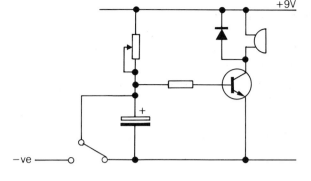

A capacitor can be used with the transistor to produce a timing circuit. In the circuit shown, base current will only be available after the capacitor has charged up through the variable resistor. The time this takes can be increased either by using a larger capacitor or by increasing the value of the resistor.

When the capacitor has charged sufficiently, base current will flow to the transistor, causing current to flow collector to emitter and energising the buzzer.

The capacitor in this timing circuit may remain charged for some time, and it is therefore normal to switch such a circuit 'on' and 'off' using a SPDT switch. In the 'off' position the switch discharges the capacitor so that it is ready for the next timing run.

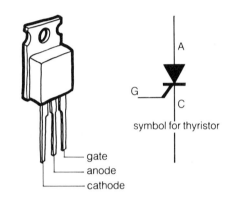

symbol for thyristor

gate
anode
cathode

THE THYRISTOR

In some ways the thyristor appears similar in its operation to a transistor. The thyristor also has three legs, and when a small current is applied to the gate it causes a large current to flow between anode and cathode. The important difference is that the thyristor will continue passing anode/cathode current even when the small gate current has ceased. This condition is called latching.

Unlike the transistor, whose collector/emitter current is proportional to base current, the thyristor will pass its maximum anode/cathode current when triggered with just a small momentary gate current.

106 is a cheap thyristor that can pass up to 3A between anode and cathode, and it can form the basis of many useful alarm circuits where a switch closing only briefly produces a continuous warning signal. The trigger switch could be a membrane panel (e.g. under a carpet), a reed switch, a tilt switch — or several of these wired in parallel so that any one closing, even for a split second, triggers the thyristor into conduction. Water or moisture bridging across two probes will also conduct enough gate current to trigger the thyristor.

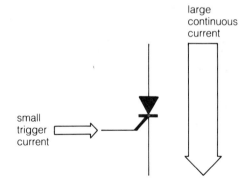

large continuous current

small trigger current

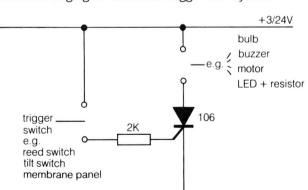

+3/24V

bulb
buzzer
e.g. motor
LED + resistor

trigger switch
e.g.
reed switch
tilt switch
membrane panel

2K

106

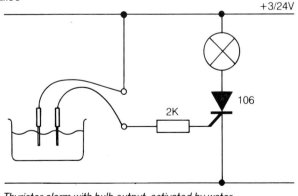

2K

106

Thyristor alarm with bulb output, activated by water rising between probes

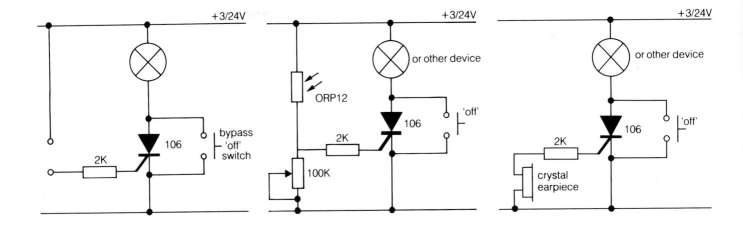

The thyristor ceases to conduct only when its supply of current is interrupted. In a practical circuit, this is achieved either by briefly opening a switch between the thyristor and its supply, or by briefly closing a switch connected between anode and cathode. In the second of these two options, current bypasses the thyristor by flowing through the switch, and this has the same effect as cutting off the supply. (If the switch was held closed, of course, current would continue to flow through it and keep something like a bulb on.)

There are other useful methods of triggering a thyristor. It can be connected, for example, to a potential divider containing a LDR. This makes it light activated.

If a crystal earpiece is connected to the gate, a knock or vibration will cause the earpiece to generate a small voltage — sufficient to trigger the thyristor!

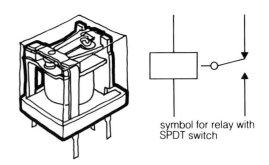

symbol for relay with SPDT switch

RELAYS AND SOLENOIDS

A relay is an electrically operated switch. It has two main parts: an electromagnet and a switch. When current is supplied to the coil of the electromagnet, it becomes magnetic and attracts a plate whose movement operates the switch. There is a mechanical, but no electrical, connection between the electromagnet and the switch. The switch itself can be of any type, but SPDT and DPDT types are the most common (see page 109).

The purpose of a relay is to make it possible to switch large currents (sometimes at a high voltage) when only a small control current is available from a circuit. For example, if a large pump needs to be switched on automatically when the water level rises in a cellar, a relay can be used as part of a transistor circuit (see page 123). Water rising between the two probes causes base current to flow, and thus a larger collector/emitter current flows to energise the relay and switch on the pump — possibly operated by mains current.

A solenoid is similar in its operation to an electromagnet, but the coil is wound around a hollow tube rather than a metal core. When current flows through the coil, it becomes magnetic and pulls a metal rod into the tube. This rod is connected to something that needs a mechanical movement. The bolts of some locks, for example, are moved by the action of a solenoid.

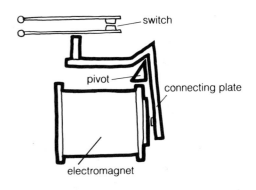

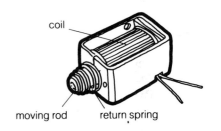

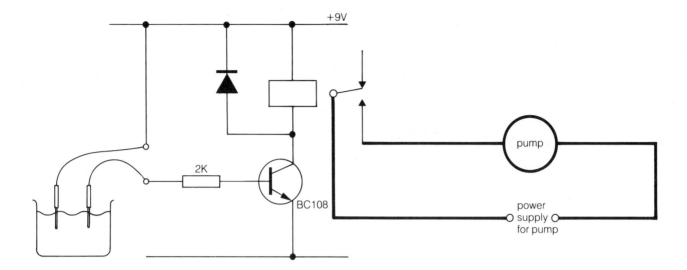

The wire used to wind relay and solenoid coils is usually very fine and very long. Its total resistance is normally marked on the device, and using Ohm's Law the current consumption can be worked out.

If, for example, a relay coil has a resistance of 120 Ω, and a 9 V battery is used to energise it, the current is given as:

$$I = \frac{V}{R} = \frac{9\,V}{120\,\Omega} = 75\,mA$$

This current would be at the maximum limit for BC108 (maximum collector emitter current 100 mA), but well within the range of BFY51 — or thyristor 106 if a latching action is required.

When using a relay or solenoid in this type of circuit, it is essential to add a protective clamping diode (page 120).

ELECTRIC MOTORS

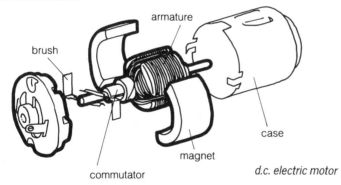

d.c. electric motor

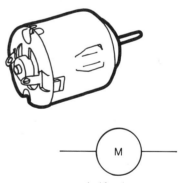

symbol for d.c. motor

MINIATURE D.C. MOTORS

Very small direct current motors are the most common type used in design and technology, and are usually cylindrical in form. These motors contain two permanent magnets either side of a rotating armature. This has a number of coils that get current from two brushes pressed against the commutator. Current flowing in the armature coils sets up a magnetic field opposed to that of the permanent magnets — and the armature rotates. The development of special permanent magnets with a very strong magnetic field has now given us small motors that are extremely powerful for their size and weight.

The direction of a d.c. motor is reversed by changing the polarity of the supply current (see page 110). Because of the inertia of the rotating armature, d.c. electric motors do not stop spinning the instant that the current is switched off. They can be stopped very quickly, though, by a method known as shunt switching. When the switch shown in the diagram is thrown into the 'off' position, a connection is made across the motor, and it behaves as if a strong brake has been applied.

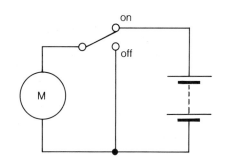

Small d.c. motors are at their most efficient when running fast, and they are normally used to drive a load through gears or pulleys. If the load is increased, the motor has to do more work and current consumption rises — and it gets hotter. If it is stopped altogether and current continues to flow, the coils of the armature will heat up and may burn out.

STEPPER MOTORS

Instead of an armature, stepper motors have a rotor consisting of several permanent magnets. This is surrounded by fixed coils that, when switched on and off in the right combination, cause the rotor to move through a small angle or step. If the coils are switched on and off in a particular sequence, the rotor steps around continuously. Unlike d.c. motors, stepper motors can be started, run and stopped with great precision. They are normally controlled by electronic circuitry and are used in CNC machine tools, robotic arms, computer printers/plotters — and in many other applications where very accurate control of movement is needed.

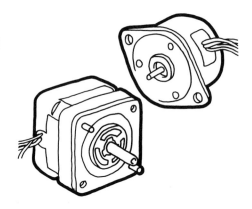

Stepper motors

Microelectronics

An integrated circuit consists of components such as capacitors, resistors and transistors and their interconnections fabricated or 'grown' in a single tiny structure. The basic material of this structure is commonly silicon — hence the term silicon chip. The chip of silicon itself is minute and when magnified reveals a maze of conductor tracks and components. Some larger chips contain hundreds of thousands of components, yet can be made quite cheaply. As a result many pocket calculators are more powerful than large computers of the 1950s — and cost a tiny fraction of the price. The use of integrated circuits in products such as cameras, typewriters and sewing machines has enabled them to do many more things and at the same time reduce the number of mechanical moving parts.

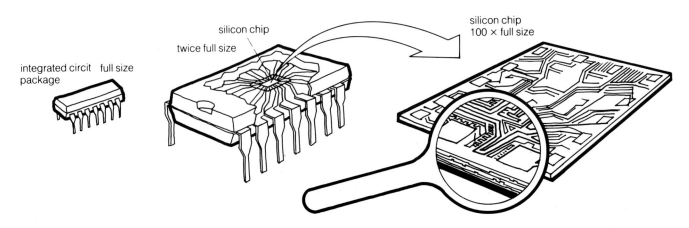

integrated circit   full size
package

silicon chip
twice full size

silicon chip
100 × full size

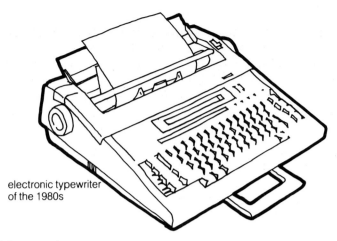

typewriter of 1900

electronic typewriter of the 1980s

In design and technology work, integrated circuits (ICs) can make electronics much easier because complicated circuits can be bought almost complete — often requiring the addition of just a few external components. ICs have revolutionised the way designers think about product design, and knowing something about them will probably make you think differently as well. What follows will look at two integrated circuits and consider some of their uses.

1. LED FLASHER — LM3909

LM3909 is probably the easiest IC to use because it needs so few parts added to get it working. It is designed to supply regular pulses of current to a LED so that this emits light in brief flashes like a flash gun.

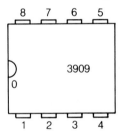

The IC comes as a small rectangular package having two rows of four pins. This is called a dual-in-line package — abbreviated to 'dil'. The pins on this sort of package are numbered as shown.

The diagram shows how to connect the IC to a LED, battery and capacitor: in this instance no series resistor is needed for the LED.

In use, the IC performs a sequence of switching operations:

1 The capacitor is connected across the battery and charges up.
2 The charged capacitor is switched in series with the battery.
3 The capacitor and battery in series are connected across the LED which lights up briefly until the capacitor has discharged.

The whole sequence then begins again.

The supply for this IC can be as low as 1.5 V, and an alkaline battery will last for several months of continuous running! The flashing rate is determined by the capacitor size, and will speed up when the capacitor value is reduced.

In practice, LM3909 is used in products to provide a warning signal. For example, it is used in modern alarm systems to show that an alarm in a house or car has been set. It is often built into fake alarm boxes to fool would be burglars.

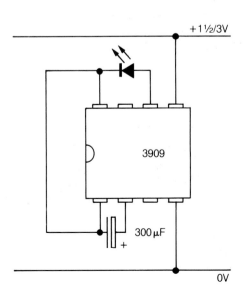

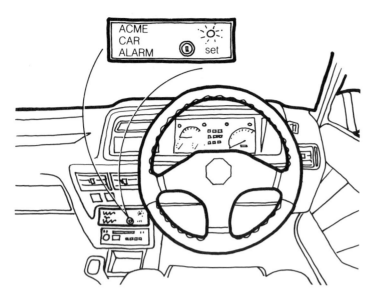

It can also be built into portable units to warn of dangerous situations at night-time — for example, overhanging scaffold tubing or a hole in the footpath.

2 THE 555 TIMER

The 555 timer is a cheap and widely used IC that can be employed to do a surprising variety of timing jobs. Just a few external components are needed to complete the basic timing circuit. When the 'start' switch is closed momentarily, the LED lights up for the duration of the time interval and then goes off.

The length of the timed interval depends on the values of R_1 and C_1. The higher the values of each of these components, the longer the duration of the timed interval. R_1 is normally a variable resistor so that the interval can be adjusted easily.

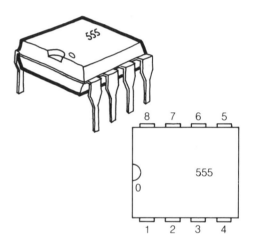

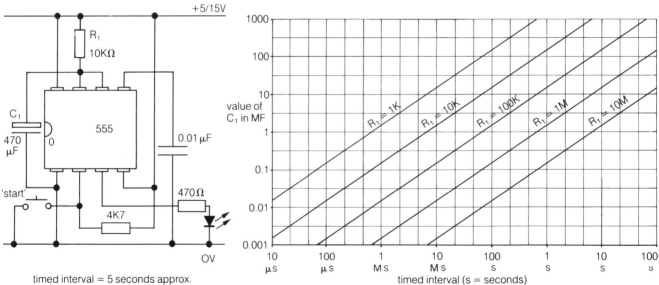

timed interval = 5 seconds approx.

timed interval (s = seconds)

When the 'start' switch is momentarily closed, the LED lights up and C_1 starts to charge up via R_1. When it has charged to a certain voltage, the 555 switches causing the LED to go off. The timing cycle can then be started again by closing the switch.

The length of the timed interval is given by

time = 1.1 × Resistance (ohms) × capacitance (F)

For example, the 10k resistor and 470 µF capacitor shown would give a timed interval of

$$1.1 \times \frac{10\,000\,\Omega}{1} \times \frac{470}{1\,000\,000}\,\mu F = 5.17 \text{ seconds}$$

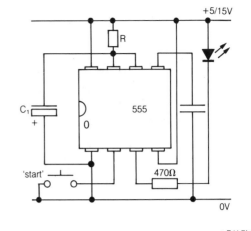

In many timing applications such as photographic developing or cooking it is preferable to have a LED lighting up (or a buzzer sounding) at the end of the timed period rather than the other way round. This can be achieved by re-connecting the LED between pin 3 of the 555 and the + ve side of the supply. The LED now lights up as soon as the supply is connected. It goes out when the 'start' switch is closed, and lights up again at the end of the timed interval.

In terms of conventional current flow, the output pin (3) will either source current (current coming out) or sink current (current going in). In the first circuit the output is sourcing current to energise the LED and in the second circuit it is sinking it. The 555 timer can source or sink up to 200 mA at its output, and it may therefore be connected directly to a buzzer or small relay (remembering to use clamping diodes).

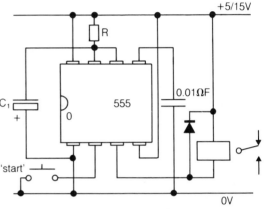

The 555 timer can also be used to switch a LED (or other device) on and off at regular intervals and at different speeds. Unlike the LM3909 flasher, a LED controlled by the 555 remains on for a period and then off for a period. This can be shown on a graph, and such a plot is called a square wave.

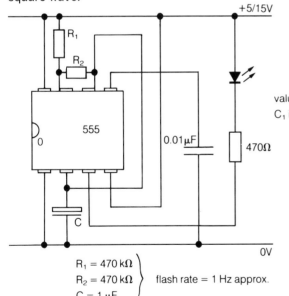

R₁ = 470 kΩ
R₂ = 470 kΩ } flash rate = 1 Hz approx.
C = 1 µF

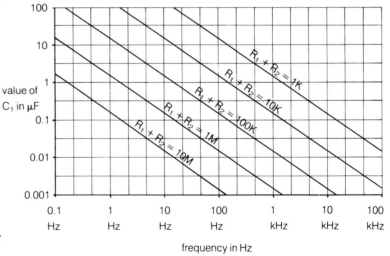

frequency in Hz

Note: *The length of the 'on' periods and the length of the 'off' periods depend on the values of R_1 and R_2. If they are the same, the output is said to have an equal mark/space ratio*

The on/off frequency is controlled by the values of $R_1 + R_2$ and C. The values shown give a flash rate of about 1 hertz (Hz). (1 Hz equals 1 cycle per second.) The value of the two resistors combined controls the length of the 'on' period, and the value of R_2 controls the length of the 'off' period.

This circuit is useful for pulsing a LED as a warning light, and is sometimes used as an oscillator or clock for driving certain other ICs.

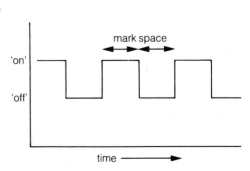

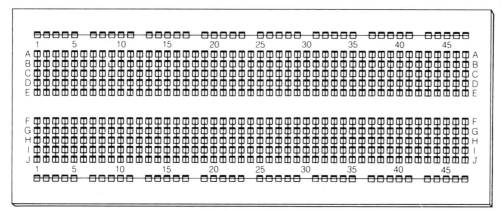

connections between sockets on board

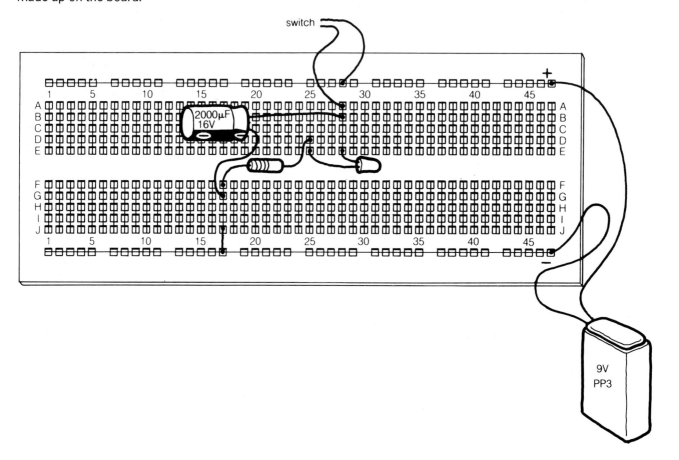

prototyping board

Experimenting with circuits

Electronic components can be assembled quickly into trial circuits using a prototyping board. These contain groups of sockets which are interconnected under the board, as shown in the illustration. Components are plugged into these sockets together with additional wire links as needed to complete a circuit. The two rows of sockets running the length of the board are normally used as supply rails. Examples are given of the capacitor-delay circuit (page 118) and the LM3909 circuit made up on the board.

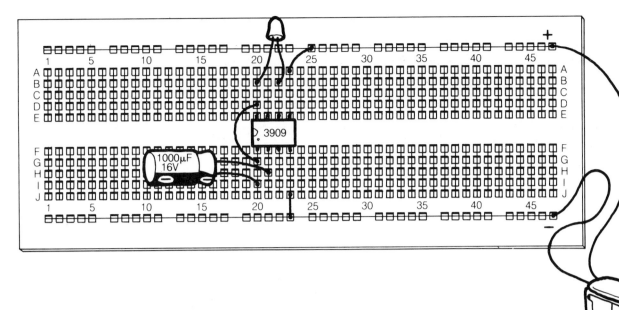

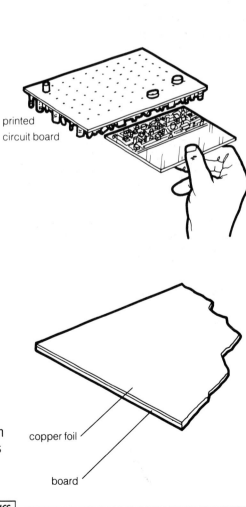

printed
circuit board

MAKING PRINTED CIRCUIT BOARDS

The original method of connecting components in a circuit was by means of many individual connecting wires. The printed circuit board (PCB) was developed during the war as a more economical and space-saving alternative.

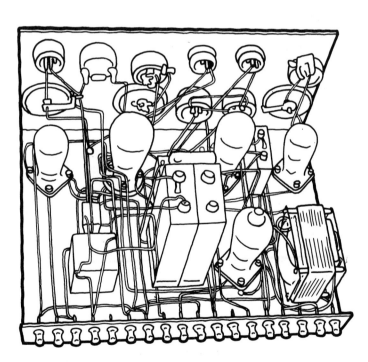

War-time circuit using valves and wire interconnections

A PCB begins as a copper-clad board — a very thin layer of copper foil bonded onto a plastic sheet. After some of the copper has been protected by an acid-resist medium (defining the pattern of conductors), the board is etched to remove unwanted copper.

On a conventional PCB the component legs or pins pass through holes in the board and are soldered to copper tracks beneath. Sometimes tracks run across both sides of a board to complete all the interconnections needed.

copper foil

board

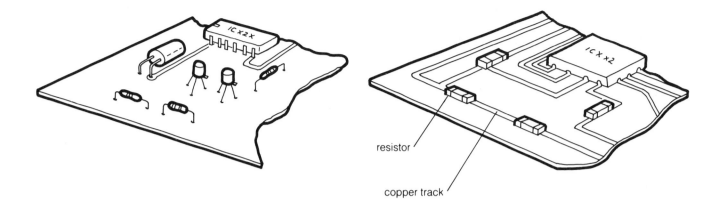

resistor

copper track

The latest generation of PCBs are now designed for surface mounting (SM). Here, the components — many redesigned for the purpose — are soldered directly to the copper tracks, and there are no holes.

MAKING A CONVENTIONAL PCB

A conventional PCB can be produced either by stopping out areas of copper using ink or transfers, or by photoetching (see page 132). The LED flasher circuit is used as an example to explain the first method:

1 Thoroughly clean the copper surface of the board using abrasive powder, or plastic-coated steel wool if it is heavily oxidised.
2 Draw out the circuit diagram on tracing paper, and use this as a guide to designing a layout of tracks and pads on paper. The connections under the board are a mirror image of the top, and it helps to look through the tracing paper to see connections on the diagram as a mirror image.

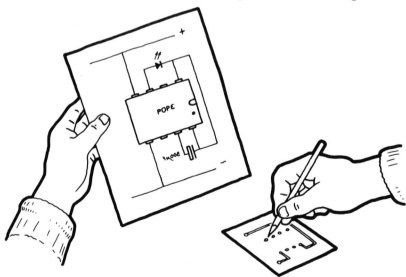

3 Using either etch-resist transfers or spirit pen (or both), mark out the tracks and pads onto the copper surface. The spacing of the pads for the IC pins is very important and must be carefully marked out if the special transfers are not available. (Put your name on the board at this stage so that it comes out as copper lines.)
4 Suspend the board in a warm solution of ferric chloride until the excess copper has been etched away. **Note:** Wear protective clothing and goggles during this operation.

5 Wash the board in water and remove the stop-out medium from the copper tracks. If a tinning solution is available, the board should be dipped to give all the copper a tin film. If not, the points on the board to be soldered should be lightly tinned using solder to prevent oxidisation at these points.

6 Holes are drilled as required through the board and the components soldered in position (see page 290). To avoid heat damage to the IC, a small socket is soldered to the board into which the IC is plugged.

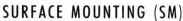

SURFACE MOUNTING (SM)

Surface mounting is the most important recent development in PCB design and manufacture. It has meant economy in production (e.g. no holes to drill) and a revolutionary reduction in the size of PCBs. All common electronic components are now available in an SM version.

Special equipment has been developed for handling the tiny SM components and soldering them to boards. Although they can be soldered by hand, this is extremely difficult when many components are only 3 mm long!

It is possible to surface mount conventional wire-ended components and ICs, and this is already widely done in prototype work because it is so much quicker. The layout of the tracks is no longer a mirror image of the diagram connections, and any errors can be easily spotted.

surface mounting resistor

actual size

The 3909 flasher circuit can be surface mounted as shown. The track layout is very similar to the diagram and the pins of the IC socket are bent outwards to sit flat on the surface. The other mounting pads are slightly larger than normal (ϕ 4mm) to reduce the risk of the copper pulling off the board. Larger components, e.g. larger capacitors, should also be secured mechanically using hot-melt glue or cable ties.

Soldering to the board is very straightforward. Both the mounting pads and the component legs and pins are tinned with solder. It is then just a matter of placing the two together and reheating with the soldering iron.

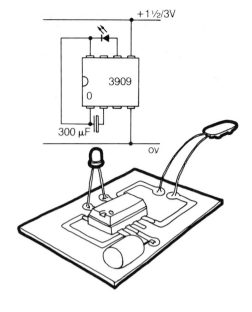

PHOTOETCHING

Whether the PCB uses conventional or surface mounting, photoetching can be used to produce the pattern of copper tracks. In this process, the copper-clad board has an additional coating of light-sensitive resist medium. This is resistant to ferric chloride, but if exposed to ultraviolet light (UV) will dissolve off in a developer to expose the copper.

A transparent mask containing a dense black image of the track pattern is placed between the board and a UV source. The exposed resist will then dissolve in the developer leaving a pattern that precisely matches the image on the mask. The board is finally etched in the normal way.

In Design and Technology, masks can be made in several ways:

1 Rub-down transfers on acetate sheet.
2 Black ink (or transfers) on tracing paper.
3 Ink on thin paper made translucent with a transparentiser (sometimes WD40 is used as a transparentiser).
4 A photocopier image on tracing paper.
5 Computer print-out treated with transparentiser. (The mask image can be generated using one of several cheap computer programmes.)

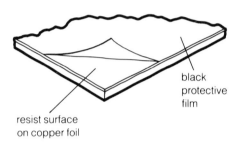

resist surface
on copper foil

black
protective
film

A special UV lightbox can be used for exposure, but *most photoetch boards can also be exposed face down on an overhead projector.* Each type of mask requires a different exposure time that can be found by trial and error.

The developer is commonly a weak caustic soda solution. Protective clothing, including goggles, should always be worn when using this.

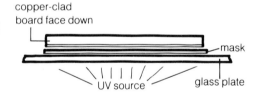

copper-clad
board face down

mask

UV source

glass plate

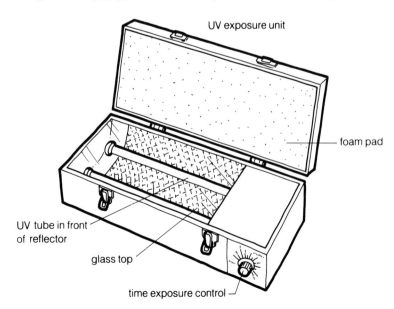

UV exposure unit

foam pad

UV tube in front
of reflector

glass top

time exposure control

1 What is the total voltage of six 1.5V cells connected in series?

2 Two mercury button cells connected in series to give 3V will not drive a 3V electric motor. Why?

3 What is a membrane panel switch? Explain its main advantages over other types.

4 Calculate the total value of these resistors connected in series: 2k2; 1k2; 470 Ω.

5 Calculate the total value of these resistors connected in parallel: 1k2; 4k7.

6 When the two resistors are connected across a supply as shown on the right, what should the voltage reading be?

7 How much current flows through a 1k2 Ω resistor connected across a 9V PP3 battery?

8 How does a LDR differ from an ordinary fixed resistor?

9 What is the difference between a LDR and solar cell?

10 What happens to (a) an electric motor and (b) the battery supplying it with current, if the motor is overloaded?

11 Explain the purpose of a relay in a circuit. What component could be connected across the relay coil to keep it energised briefly after the current is cut off?

12 Why is a LED normally connected in a circuit in series with a resistor?

13 What is the most obvious difference in operation between a transistor and thyristor?

14 Why is a thyristor commonly found in alarm circuits?

15 A 2000 μF capacitor charged from a PP3 battery will light up a LED (with series resistor) for several seconds when connected. If connected to a buzzer or small motor, it will hardly have any effect. Why?

16 In a basic 555 timer circuit, a timed interval of 20 seconds is needed. What value resistor is needed if the capacitor is 1000 μF?

17 Design a simple alarm circuit for use in a camera equipment case. Sketch the type of trigger switch(es) you would use and a suitable circuit in diagram form.

18 Design a photographic timer with an adjustment for timing an interval between 1 and 30 seconds. The timer should include a switch to give the option of either a red LED lighting up at the end of the timed interval, or a green LED staying lit during the timed interval.

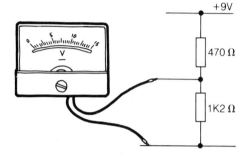

+9V

470 Ω

1K2 Ω

8 Technology for design: Mechanisms and control

Mechanisms are used by people every day in driving cars, riding bicycles — or even just doing up clothing. Like the humble zip fastener, most mechanisms go unnoticed. The zip is in fact a most important mechanical invention, and one that has revolutionised clothing design and fashion.

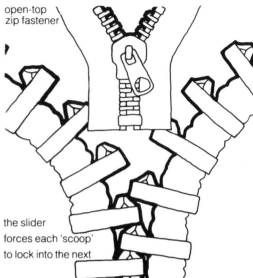

open-top zip fastener

the slider forces each 'scoop' to lock into the next

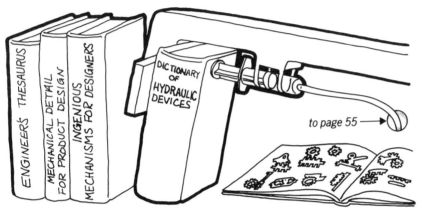

ENGINEER'S THESAURUS

MECHANICAL DETAIL FOR PRODUCT DESIGN

INGENIOUS MECHANISMS FOR DESIGNERS

DICTIONARY OF HYDRAULIC DEVICES

to page 55 →

Designing anything having moving parts from zips to car engines requires a knowledge of different mechanisms. Dictionaries containing pictures of mechanisms instead of words have been published to help designers find solutions to problems. These show that most mechanisms are a clever combination of a few simple mechanical parts or elements.

This chapter provides you with a dictionary of simple mechanical elements, and shows how to construct and use them in design work. Most of these mechanical elements are found on a bicycle and you will probably be familiar with using them.

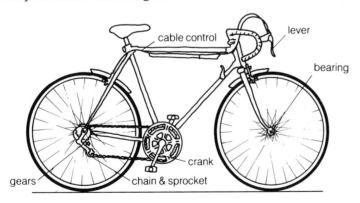

cable control

lever

bearing

gears

crank

chain & sprocket

The lever

A lever is a rigid beam that pivots about a fulcrum. An effort applied to one end will cause a load to be moved at the other. Levers are normally used to obtain a mechanical advantage (MA) where the effort put in needs to be 'magnified'. The effort applied to a cycle brake lever is 'magnified' to force the rubber blocks tightly against the wheel rim.

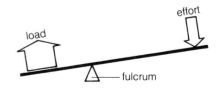

load

effort

fulcrum

A load, otherwise impossible to move, can be raised with the help of a lever. The mechanical advantage of the lever is given by

$$\text{mechanical advantage (MA)} = \frac{\text{load}}{\text{effort}}$$

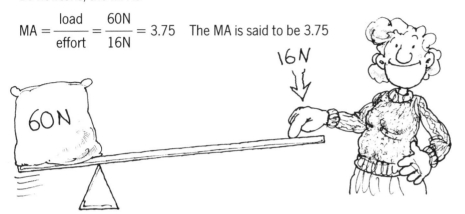

For example, if a load of 60 newtons can be raised using an effort of just 16 newtons, the MA is

$$\text{MA} = \frac{\text{load}}{\text{effort}} = \frac{60N}{16N} = 3.75 \quad \text{The MA is said to be 3.75}$$

However, the distance moved at the effort end of the lever is greater than the distance moved by the load. This is the price paid for being able to raise it. The ratio between these two movements is called the movement ratio or velocity ratio. It is given by

$$\text{velocity ratio} = \frac{\text{distance moved by effort}}{\text{distance moved by load}}$$

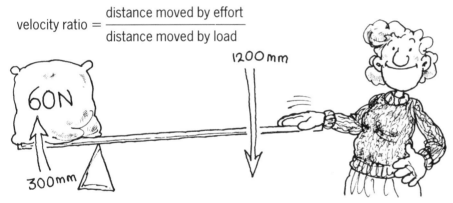

In the example, if the effort moves through 300 mm and the load through 1200 mm, the VR is

$$\text{VR} = \frac{\text{distance moved by effort}}{\text{distance moved by load}} = \frac{1200\,mm}{300\,mm} = 4$$

In practice, the lever does not work perfectly because of friction at the fulcrum. Friction is the resistance of one surface moving in contact with another. In trying to cut paper with stiff or rusty scissors, more effort can actually go into making the scissors move than into the cut.

The same is true of any lever or mechanical system. In the cycle brake, much effort is wasted in pulling the cable through its outer sleeve.

If all the effort went into lifting the load, our lever would be 100% efficient. Because of friction, some effort is always lost, and efficiency is given by

$$\text{efficiency} = \frac{\text{MA}}{\text{VR}}$$

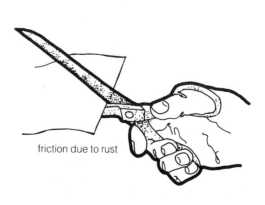

friction due to rust

Note: MA depends on friction; VR does not.

In our example, the efficiency of the lever is

$$\text{efficiency} = \frac{MA}{VR} = \frac{3.75}{4} \times \frac{100}{1}\% = 93.75\%$$

Levers are divided into three categories, depending upon the position of the fulcrum: Class 1, Class 2 and Class 3 levers.

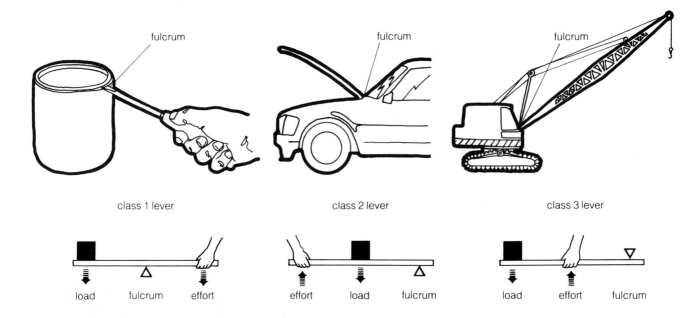

class 1 lever

load fulcrum effort

class 2 lever

effort load fulcrum

class 3 lever

load effort fulcrum

QUESTIONS

1 In a bicycle braking system, an effort of 5N applied to the brake lever results in a force of 45N acting on the brake blocks. The brake lever moves through 50 mm and the brake blocks through 5 mm. Calculate MA, VR and efficiency for this system.

2 Why are the figures for MA and VR slightly different?

3 What would you do to the brake to improve its efficiency?

4 Name the class of lever used in the following:
   (a) scissors,
   (b) wheelbarrow,
   (c) fishing rod.

The linkage

A linkage is something that transmits force and movement in a mechanical system. It is useful to talk about linkages having an **input** and **output** so that what happens in between can be clearly described.

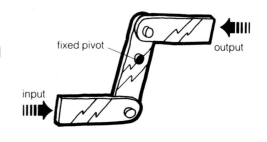

fixed pivot

input

output

The output movement of a simple lever is opposite to the input. The addition of a linkage rod and second lever will reverse this. The input movement can be turned through 90° using a **bell crank**. Linkages can be used to divide an input movement along two or more paths.

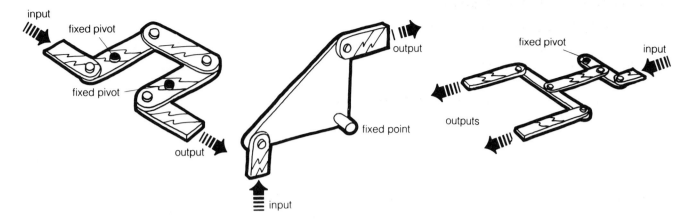

In practice, linkages are used and applied in many different ways:

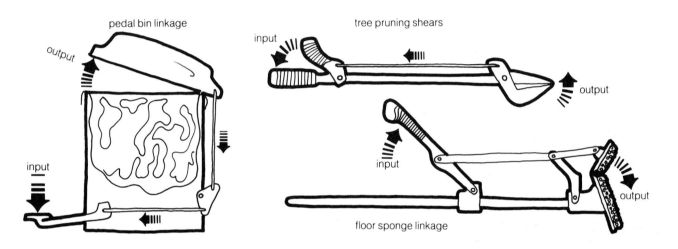

pedal bin linkage

tree pruning shears

floor sponge linkage

A considerable mechanical advantage can be obtained through the levers in a linkage system. Linkages are therefore used for applying pressure and for clamping. The **toggle clamp**, for example, and many pram brakes use the principle of **geometrical locking**. The linkage moves so far, and then gets 'stuck' or locks up.

The crank

The crank will probably be most familiar to you as part of a bicycle. Here it converts the straight line or linear movement of your legs into rotary motion to turn the rear wheel.

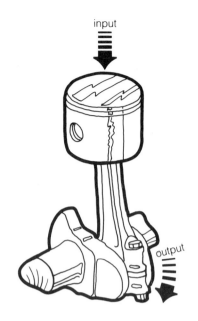

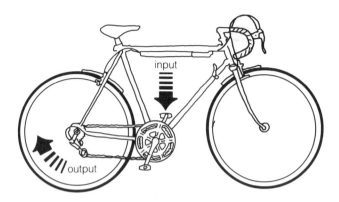

A car engine uses the same principle to turn the up and down reciprocating movement of pistons driven by expanding gases into rotary motion of the crankshaft.

The crank principle can also be used to convert rotary into linear movement. Many cassette deck cleaners use the rotary drive from the deck itself to wipe a cleaning pad backwards and forwards over the playback/recording head.

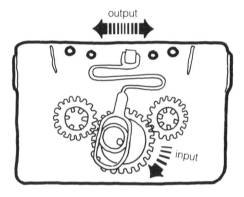

The robot toy shown moves its legs backwards and forwards and appears to walk. A look inside shows that a steel rod driven by gears is bent to form a crank at each end. These cranks connect to linkage rods driving the legs.

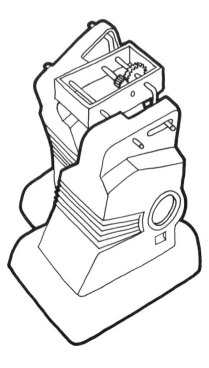

The pulley

Pulleys are an important means of transmitting forces in machines. A simple pulley system consists of two grooved wheels rotating on shafts and connected by a belt. When the driver (effort) pulley turns, the driven pulley (load) turns in the same direction — unless the belt is crossed over.

The speed of rotation of the driven pulley depends on its diameter and that of the driver. If the driven pulley is larger than the driver, it will run slower; if it is smaller, it will run faster.

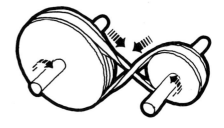

This is explained by the different distances the belt has to travel around the edge or circumference of each pulley. If we know the distance moved for one revolution of each pulley, the velocity ratio (VR) for the system can be worked out. From the lever, we know that:

$$VR = \frac{\text{distance moved by effort}}{\text{distance moved by load}}$$

For the pulley systems this means

$$VR = \frac{\text{distance moved by driver pulley}}{\text{distance moved by driven pulley}}$$

This is the same as saying

$$VR = \frac{\text{circumference of driven pulley}}{\text{circumference of driver pulley}}$$

or

$$VR = \frac{\text{diameter of driven pulley}}{\text{diameter of driver pulley}}$$

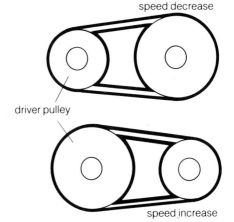

speed decrease

driver pulley

speed increase

For example, if pulley A drives pulley B, the VR is given by

$$VR = \frac{\text{diameter B}}{\text{diameter A}} = \frac{30\,\text{cm}}{10\,\text{cm}} = 3$$

This means that pulley A turns 3 times for 1 revolution of pulley B.

If there was no friction in the system, 3 would also be the figure for mechanical advantage. In practice, much input effort is lost as the belt continually flexes around the pulleys. This loss is converted to heat and the belt warms up. (*If you rapidly flex an elastic band, it will warm up.*)

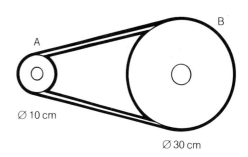

Ø 10 cm

Ø 30 cm

The workshop pillar drill provides a good example of pulleys at work. When the rubber belt is on the top pair of pulleys, the driven pulley runs very fast, but its shaft has low **torque** or **'turning power'**. When the belt is on the lower set of pulleys, the driven pulley rotates very slowly but its shaft has high torque and is difficult to stop.

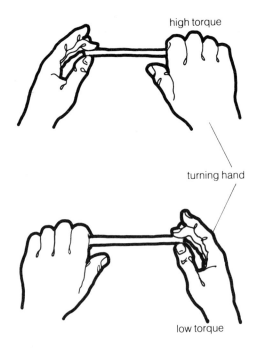

high torque

turning hand

low torque

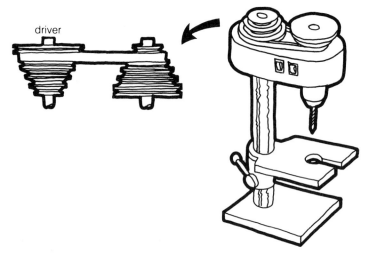

driver

The difference between high and low torque can be demonstrated if you think of a pen or pencil as the shaft. The pen has high torque or turning power if it is gripped heavily in one hand and slowly turned. A finger and thumb cannot stop it. The pen has low torque if it is spun between finger and thumb. Another finger and thumb can stop it easily.

Small electric motors are found in many domestic appliances. These normally run at high speeds but have low torque. Pulleys are one solution to reducing their speed and providing the output torque needed.

Speed of rotation is measured in revolutions per minute (r.p.m.). If the speed of one pulley is unknown, it can be worked out if we know both the speed of the other pulley and the two pulley diameters:

$$\text{speed of unknown pulley} = \frac{\text{speed of known pulley} \times \text{diameter}}{\text{diameter of unknown pulley}}$$

If the Hoover brush cylinder is fitted with a 30 mm diameter pulley and is driven by a 90 mm diameter pulley on a 1000 r.p.m. motor, the cylinder speed is

$$\text{speed} = \frac{1000 \text{ r.p.m.} \times 90 \text{ mm}}{30 \text{ mm}} = \frac{90000}{30} = 3000 \text{ r.p.m.}$$

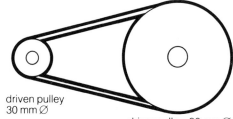

driven pulley
30 mm Ø

driver pulley: 90 mm Ø
speed = 1000 r.p.m.

The bicycle chain and its sprocket wheels are a form of pulley system in which there is no possibility of the 'belt' slipping. The same pulley calculations apply. (Assume the pedal sprocket to be 200 mm in diameter and the rear wheel sprocket 80 mm.)

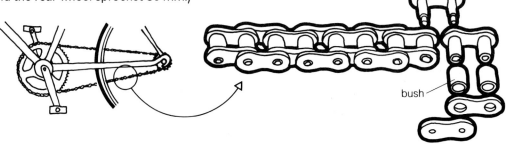

bush

If, for example, the driver sprocket is turned at 50 r.p.m., the speed of the rear wheel sprocket is given as

$$\text{speed of driven sprocket} = \frac{50 \text{ r.p.m.} \times 200\,\text{mm}}{80\,\text{mm}} = \frac{10\,000}{80} = 125 \text{ r.p.m.}$$

If the circumference of the rear wheel (including tyre) is 2 m, the distance travelled by the cycle in 1 minute would be

$$125 \text{ r.p.m.} \times 2\,\text{m} = 250\,\text{m}$$

PULLEY BELTS

In smaller systems, pulley belts are typically square, circular or rectangular in section. In larger machines, 'V'-section belts are used. Under tension, these wedge tightly into their pulley wheels to avoid slipping.

In many applications toothed belts and pulley wheels are now used. These have replaced the conventional chain and sprocket system on some bicycles and are used in computer plotters and on drawing boards where slipping of the belt cannot be tolerated.

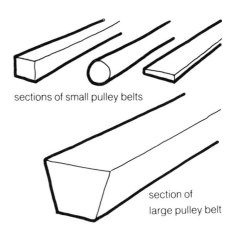

sections of small pulley belts

section of large pulley belt

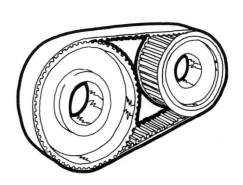

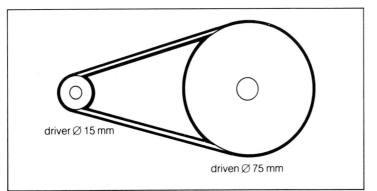

QUESTIONS

1 Calculate the VR of the pulley system shown below.

driver ∅ 15 mm

driven ∅ 75 mm

2 If pulley A rotates at 50 r.p.m., what is the speed of pulley B?

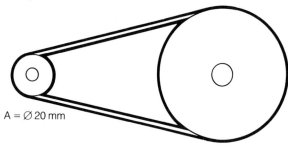

A = Ø 20 mm

B = Ø 80 mm

3 The pulley system of an X/Y plotter is shown below. How many revolutions of the driving motor would it take to make the arm move along 100 mm? The driving motor spindle is connected directly to the pulley.

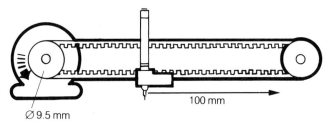

100 mm

Ø 9.5 mm

4 How would the belt be located on the pulleys in a pillar drill if a large diameter hole is being drilled? Why?

The Gear

A gear is a toothed wheel having a special tooth shape or profile enabling it to connect or mesh smoothly with other gears. These are used to transmit forces in machines ranging in size from watches to car gearboxes.

gear wheel

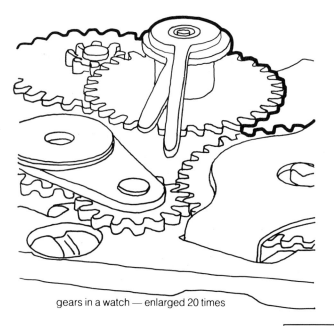

gears in a watch — enlarged 20 times

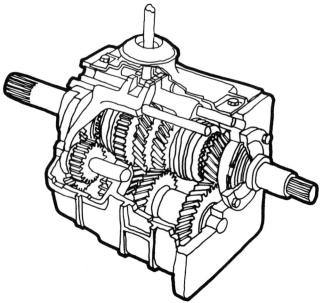

Unlike a pair of pulleys, one gear driving a second causes the direction of rotation to be reversed. This has to be taken into account when many gears are added together.

The velocity ratio for gear systems is worked out in the same way as for pulleys:

$$VR = \frac{\text{distance moved by driven gear}}{\text{distance moved by driver gear}}$$

Gears meshing

In the case of gears, however, we can use the number of teeth on each gear. In the example shown, VR is given by

$$VR = \frac{\text{number of teeth on driven gear}}{\text{number of teeth on driver gear}} = \frac{24 \text{ teeth}}{12 \text{ teeth}} = 2$$

For every 2 revolutions of the driver gear, the driven gear turns once. In gear systems, it is more usual to call the VR the gear ratio. In the above example, the gear ratio is said to be 2:1.

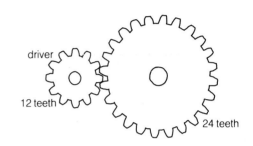

THE GEARBOX

A gearbox is an assembly of gears that connect input and output shafts. In a typical gearbox, pairs of gears are fixed together on rotating shafts, and these pairs mesh together to form a gear train.

In the example shown, the gear ratio between the first driver gear and its driven gear is 2:1 (i.e. $\frac{20}{10}$ teeth). The smaller gear on the first shaft then drives a larger gear on the second. In turn, the smaller gear on the second shaft drives a larger gear on the output shaft. The ratio for this gearbox between input and output is the sum total of the ratios of gears in mesh. In this example, it is $2{:}1 \times 2{:}1 \times 2{:}1 = 8{:}1$

If many such pairs of gears are meshed together in a gearbox, a high speed (low torque) input is transformed into a low speed (high torque) output.

Some gearboxes, such as those in cars, allow gears to be slipped in and out of mesh to give different ratios (and a change of direction).

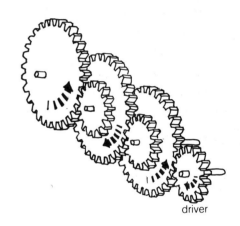

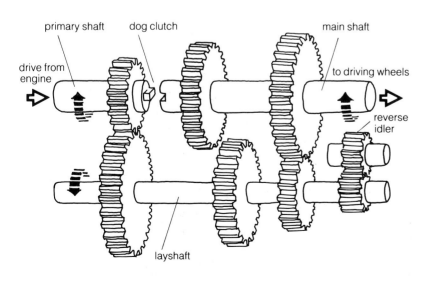

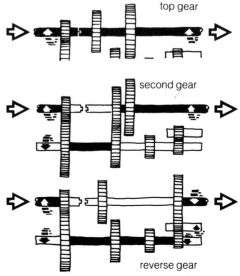

SPECIAL GEAR TYPES

1 RACK AND PINION

Rack and pinion gearing is used to convert rotary to linear movement and vice versa. Car steering systems commonly use rack and pinion gears. Electrically operated windows in cars and buildings also use this principle.

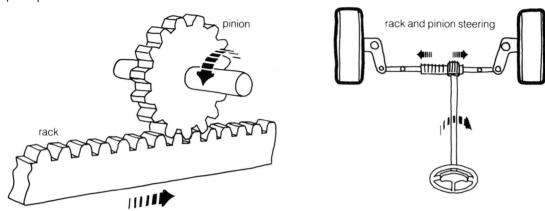

2 BEVEL GEARING

Bevel gears are used to turn the movement of a shaft through 90°. The gear teeth are specially formed to mesh on 45° sloping faces. This type of gearing is commonly seen in hand drills and electrically powered toys.

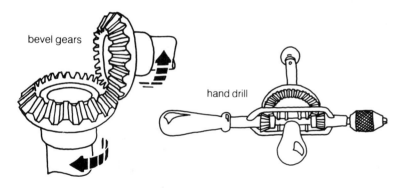

3 WORM GEARING

A worm and wormwheel are typically used to obtain a large reduction in speed and high output torque. Each complete revolution of the worm causes the meshing wheel to turn by only one tooth.

Hand-held electric food mixers often use worm gearing. Note that the beaters turn in opposite directions.

worm gearing

QUESTIONS

1 **In what direction is gear C rotating?**

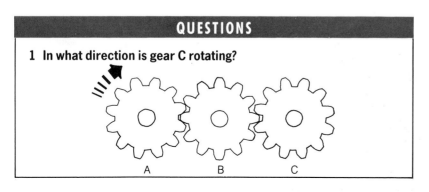

2 Calculate the VR or gear ratio for the pair of gears shown below.

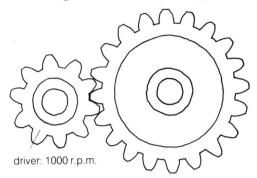

driver: 1000 r.p.m.

3 If the input shaft is rotating at 1000 r.p.m., what is the speed of the output shaft?

The Cam

A cam can be thought of as a wheel having an irregular outline or profile. Cams are used to convert rotary motion into special types of linear motion. A very commonly used cam has a profile like a pear, and when it rotates a follower in contact is given an up and down reciprocating motion.

During one half of its rotation, this cam does not lift the follower. There is a dwell period.

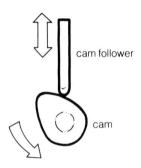

cam follower

cam

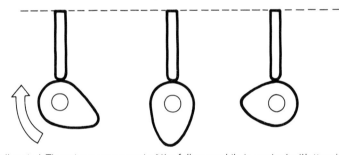

Dwell period. There is no movement of the follower while in contact with the circular side of the cam

Car engines use this form of cam to open and close valves. These need to remain closed for a time (the dwell period) during each revolution of the cam.

Some cam profiles, often used in toys, provide a slowly rising movement — followed by a sudden drop.

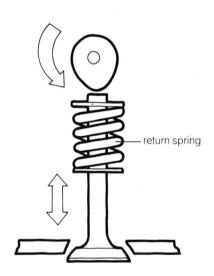

return spring

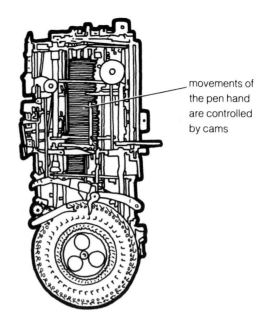

movements of
the pen hand
are controlled
by cams

French automaton figure capable of writing on paper

Slow turning cams having a very complex profile control the lifelike movements of old automation figures.

The screw

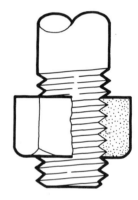

The screw can be broadly defined as a threaded rod that engages in a similar internal thread. Screw threads vary in their shape or profile for different applications.

Most of the important applications can be dealt with under three headings.

metric thread   square thread

Screw profiles

1 CONVERSION OF ROTARY TO LINEAR MOTION

Most machine tools use long screw threads to move and control the parts that slide. The motor driven leadscrew of a lathe, for example, engages in a nut on the carriage to move it along. The top slide on a lathe is similarly controlled by a smaller screw turned by a handwheel.

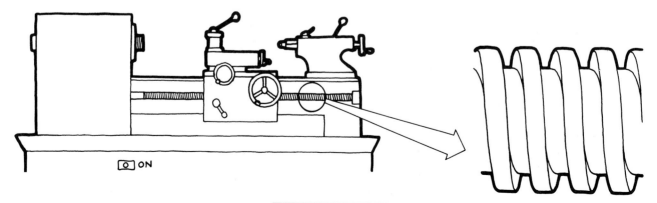

[O] ON

2 OBTAINING A MECHANICAL ADVANTAGE

An enormous mechanical advantage can be obtained using a screw, especially when it is turned with a lever.

In using a screwjack to raise a car, the effort moves through a far greater distance than the load. A typical VR is 500:1 when the end of the lever travels 1000 mm and the car rises 2 mm. Even if the system is only 25% efficient because of frictional loss, an effort of 5 N at the end of the lever will raise a load of 1875N. In a similar way, a cramp can exert great pressure on a piece of work.

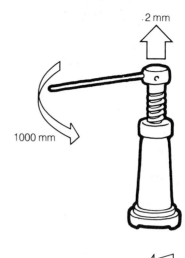

.2 mm

1000 mm

3 FASTENINGS

The nut and bolt is a very common mechanical fastening device. Tightened with a spanner (a lever giving extra MA) the nut is forced towards the head of the bolt, trapping anything in between. Friction between the mating threads keeps the nut and bolt rigidly locked together.

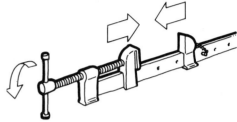

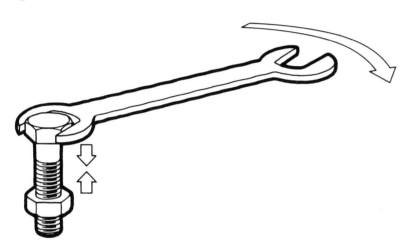

Screw fastenings are used for permanent fixtures, and in a wide range of applications where temporary locking (e.g. for adjustment) is needed.

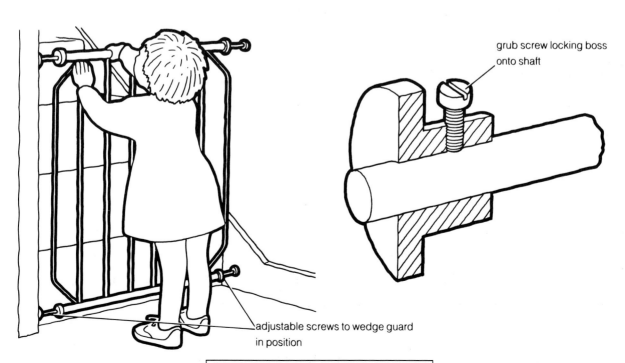

grub screw locking boss onto shaft

adjustable screws to wedge guard in position

Cable control

Cables can be regarded as a totally flexible form of linkage for transmitting force and movement. The most common form is the **Bowden cable**, consisting of a strong flexible sleeve enclosing a stranded steel cable.

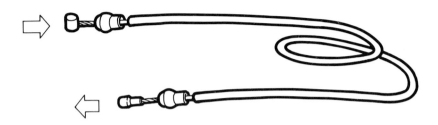

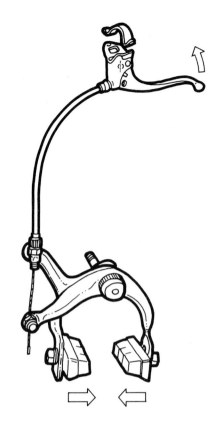

In a bicycle brake, for example, a lever pulled against the handlebars pulls the cable through the sleeve to close the pincers holding the brake blocks. This principle is sometimes used to operate the shutter release of cameras, and even finds its way into people's stomachs in the form of the endoscope. This is a tube that, as well as allowing a surgeon to see down inside the body, can carry a Bowden cable to operate small tools.

Pneumatic control

In many situations it is clumsy or uneconomic to use linkages — or even cables. An alternative method of getting a control movement from A to B is by compressed air.

In the foot-operated switch shown here, air is compressed by flattening a small plastic bellows. The rise in pressure causes a flexible diaphragm in a chamber at the other end of the tube to deflect and operate the switch. This is known as a closed system, because the air is not allowed to escape. It has replaced linkages in many small machines, and is now even used as a cable replacement for gear changing on a bicycle.

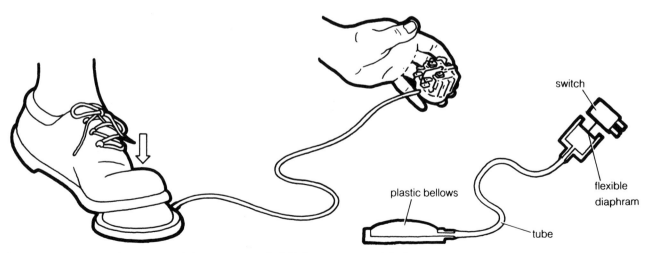

In an open pneumatic system, air is compressed at high pressure and fed via a valve to piston/cylinder units. The air is used to drive a piston(s) and then released into the atmosphere.

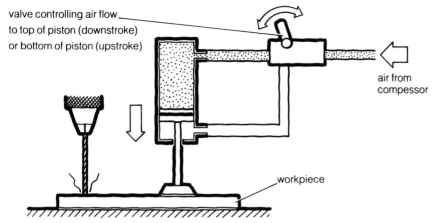

valve controlling air flow to top of piston (downstroke) or bottom of piston (upstroke)

air from compessor

workpiece

A workpiece can be clamped and unclamped, for example, using a valve and piston/cylinder unit. By arranging for the piston to operate a valve when it reaches the end of its travel, the whole cycle of opening and closing can be achieved automatically — perhaps as a small part of a larger operation.

Hydraulic control

Air behaves like a spring when it is compressed (think about using a cycle pump). This makes it unsuitable for many control uses. Liquids such as oil and water, on the other hand, are virtually incompressible and are used in hydraulic control systems.

A simple closed hydraulic system consists of two piston/cylinder units filled with liquid and connected by tubing. When effort is applied to one piston, fluid moves through the system to lift the load on the second piston. It is possible to demonstrate hydraulic systems using disposable plastic syringes and PVC tubing. **Note:** It is dangerous to handle a syringe if it has a needle.

The great advantage of hydraulic systems is that one master piston/cylinder unit can be connected to two or more slave units. This enables a control movement to be transmitted to several places with little friction. This is the system used for car braking.

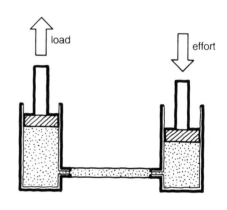

load

effort

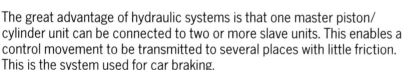

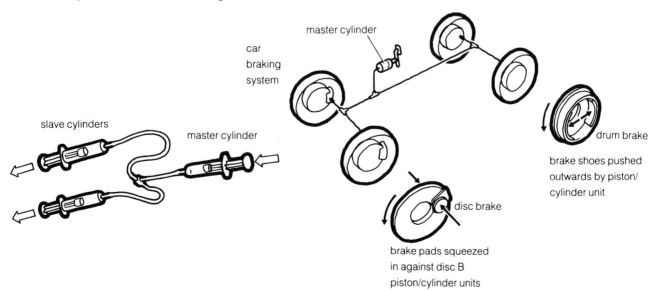

slave cylinders

master cylinder

car braking system

master cylinder

drum brake

brake shoes pushed outwards by piston/cylinder unit

disc brake

brake pads squeezed in against disc B piston/cylinder units

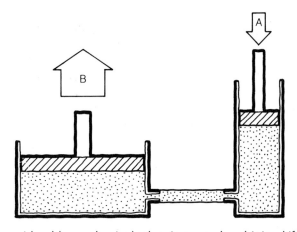
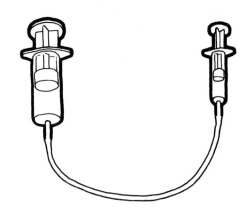

A considerable mechanical advantage can be obtained if two different diameter piston/cylinder units are connected. Ignoring any friction, if an effort of 1 N is applied to piston A, it will support a load of 3 N at B. This is because the pressure produced by piston A is acting on three times the area at B. Piston B, though, will move only one third of the distance of A.

Hydraulic jacks use this principle. The driving piston is made very small in relation to the driven piston, and the mechanical advantage is increased further by using a lever.

hydraulic car jack

As the Eiffel Tower was being constructed, massive hydraulic jacks containing water were used at the base of its columns to keep it jacked upright

Bearings

Wherever a moving surface is in contact with a fixed one, a form of bearing is needed to reduce friction and wear. To support rotating shafts, two types of bearing are common.

1 PLAIN BEARINGS

A plain journal bearing consists of a bush fitted into a housing. The bush is often just tightly pressed into the housing, and can be replaced if worn. Alternatively, a bearing bush can be fitted into the centre of a gear or pulley rotating on a fixed axle.

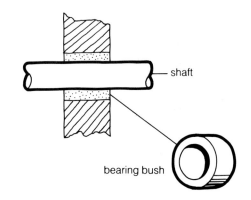

shaft

bearing bush

Bearing bushes are made from a number of materials including bronze alloys (basically a mixture of copper and tin). Most are now made by a process called sintering where fine metal granules are pressed together in a mould and then heated to fuse them. This enables other good lubricating materials such as lead and graphite to be added to the mixture. Sintered bearings can also be made porous enough to soak up and retain oil. Such bearings are common in power drills and electric motors, and their bearings are often said to be 'lubricated for life'.

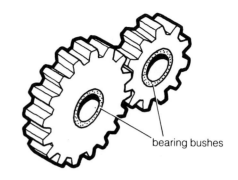
bearing bushes

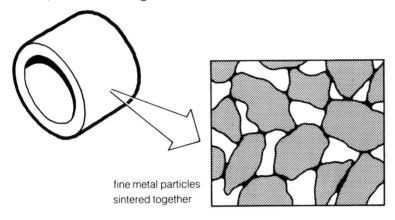
fine metal particles sintered together

Lubrication is essential for most plain bearings, and consists of a film of lubricating medium (usually oil) that partially or fully separates the surfaces in contact.

Bearing bushes are also made from some plastics such as PTFE. This is a naturally 'slippery' material and does not require lubrication. It can only be used, however, for small bearings operating at low speeds.

2 BALL BEARING RACES

An important family of bearings uses steel balls (or rollers) trapped in a cage between inner and outer rotating shells. A ball bearing race takes a fixed axle or rotating shaft through its inner shell. When either the inner or outer shell rotates, it does so supported by the free-running bearing balls, and there is consequently very little friction.

Ball bearing races are used for bicycle wheels, and in a large number of machines where shafts are subjected to heavy loading. If the loading is very severe, rollers are used in place of balls to provide additional support.

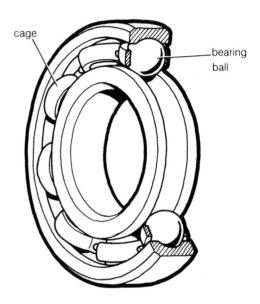
cage
bearing ball

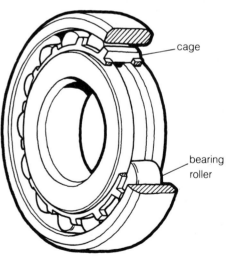
cage
bearing roller

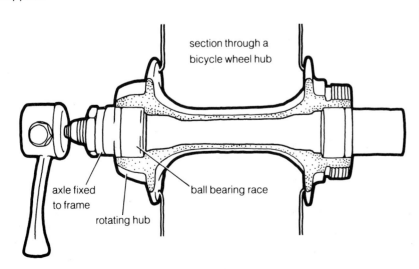
section through a bicycle wheel hub

axle fixed to frame
ball bearing race
rotating hub

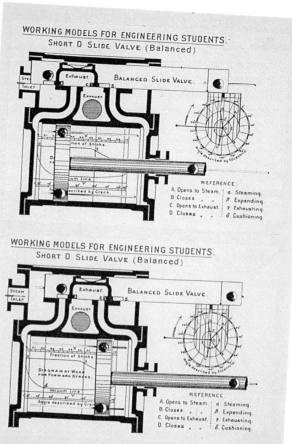

WORKING MODELS FOR ENGINEERING STUDENTS.
SHORT D SLIDE VALVE (Balanced)

Mechanical models and prototypes

Edward Heath Robinson was a cartoonist who drew odd-looking
mechanical contraptions. The machines in his cartoons (e.g. the one
above) were easy to understand, but in most cases would not have
worked. What follows are some methods for making mechanical models
and prototypes that actually work. (If you study Heath Robinson, you can
learn what not to do!)

1 TWO DIMENSIONAL MECHANICAL MODELS

'Cardboard engineering' is the name given recently to working models
that use cardboard parts made to pivot together or slide using paper
fastener type fixings. This technique is in fact very old, as the 1897 card
model (above right) of a steam engine shows.

Cardboard is still useful for modelling linkages, etc., but a more accurate
method involves the use of polystyrene sheet and eyelets — a kind of
hollow rivet normally used for reinforcing holes in paper and card.

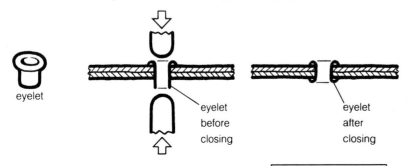

eyelet

eyelet
before
closing

eyelet
after
closing

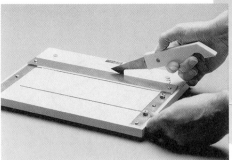

(a) Scoring polystyrene strips

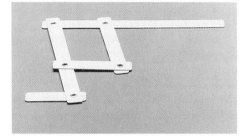

(b) Punching holes using Philip Harris punch tool

(c) Closing eyelet with punch pliers

The polystyrene sheet is cut by scoring and cracking. The eyelet holes are then punched through or drilled to a diameter of 4 mm. After insertion, the eyelets are opened out at the back with an eyeletting tool or with a ball-nosed punch (made from scrap steel). Stages in making a pantograph drawing aid are shown here using the Philip Harris construction kit.

For guides to produce linear movements, lengths of polystyrene are bonded to a baseplate and bridged over with smaller pieces. Polystyrene cement or double-sided adhesive tape is used for this. **Note:** Elastic bands are used for springs where necessary.

(d) Complete pantograph

2 GEARS AND PULLEYS

Small gears and pulleys can now be obtained quite cheaply as injection mouldings. A gearbox can be constructed by laying out the train of gears as required on paper and marking through their centres. (Ensuring that the teeth mesh at the correct depth at this point is known as 'depthing'.)

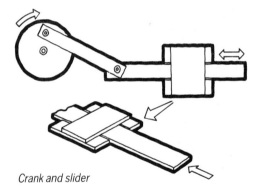

Crank and slider

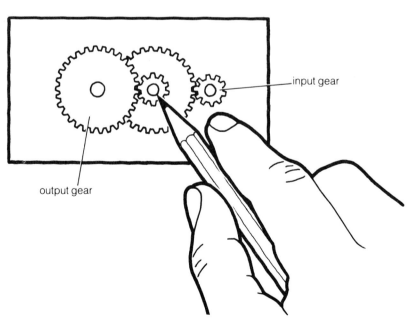

input gear

output gear

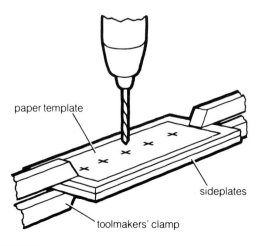

paper template

sideplates

toolmakers' clamp

The paper template is used as a guide for drilling through a pair of plates of plastic sheet, wood, metal — or even foam plastic. At least two holes for spacing bars are also drilled. The gears are then force-fitted onto their shafts and assembled between the plates. Spacing washers (or short lengths of tubing) can be slipped over the shafts to prevent cross movement of the gears between the plates. In the example shown, the spacing bars could be EMA precision tubing.

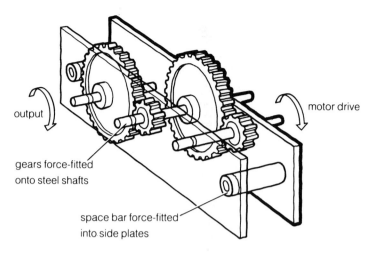

output

motor drive

gears force-fitted
onto steel shafts

space bar force-fitted
into side plates

Plastic cotton reels serve well as pulleys, and offer an easy means of getting useful work out of a small motor. In the example shown above, a cotton reel acts both as a pulley and a wheel in a small vehicle.

3 BEARINGS

The availability of precision plastic rod, tubing and other sections means that many mechanisms can now be modelled or prototyped entirely in plastics. For low speeds and light loads, there is no need for special bearings. EMA tubing, for example, will run well simply in a drilled hole, providing that this is lubricated with silicon grease. (This is available from builders' merchants and makes a remarkable difference to bearing performance and wherever plastic rubs on plastic.)

For plain metal bearings, brass is normally an adequate substitute for bronze. If at all possible, silver steel should be used for the rotating shaft or axle.

To make a bearing bush, drill the brass in a lathe slightly under the size of the silver steel, and then run through a reamer made from the same silver steel. The reamer is easy to make: simply file a flat across the end of the silver steel, as shown. When this is run through the hole, it cuts into the brass and produces a perfect bearing fit. Plenty of lubrication is needed during the reaming process.

4 HYDRAULIC AND PNEUMATIC SYSTEMS

Simple pneumatic systems can be made up from squeezy bottles and balloons. It is an advantage to sandwich the balloon between two plates to contain it.

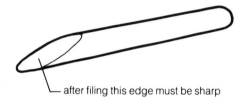

after filing this edge must be sharp

Simple reamer

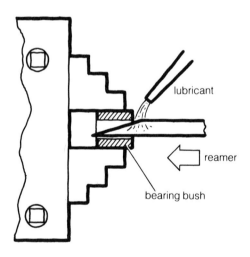

lubricant

reamer

bearing bush

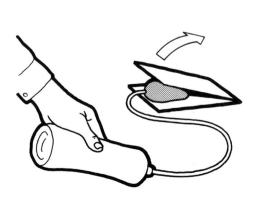

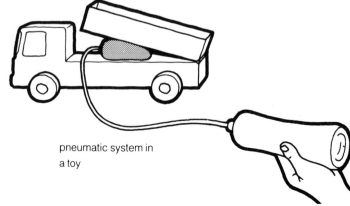

pneumatic system in
a toy

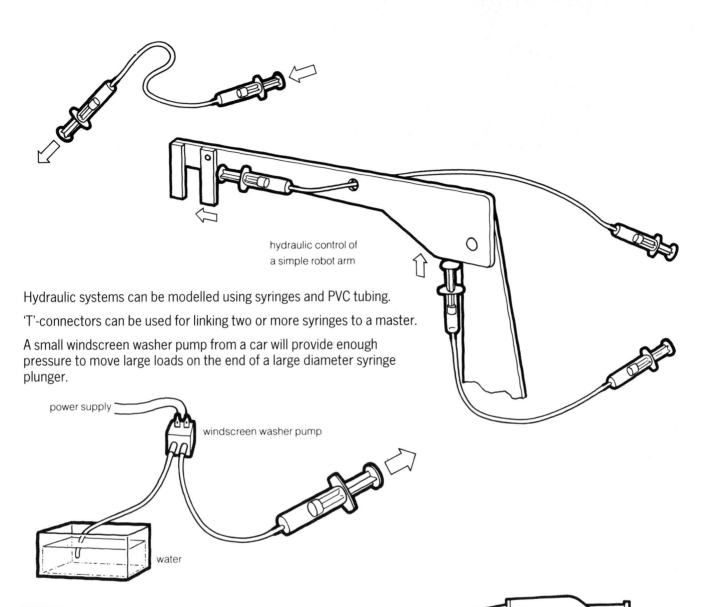

hydraulic control of
a simple robot arm

Hydraulic systems can be modelled using syringes and PVC tubing.

'T'-connectors can be used for linking two or more syringes to a master.

A small windscreen washer pump from a car will provide enough pressure to move large loads on the end of a large diameter syringe plunger.

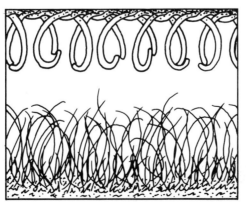

power supply

windscreen washer pump

water

5 FAST ASSEMBLY TECHNIQUES

If models are to be taken apart, self-adhesive Velcro tapes can be used for joining parts together. Double-sided adhesive tapes work well on smooth surfaces, as do double-sided adhesive foam pads. Above all, the hot-melt glue gun is probably now the most useful fast assembly tool. It will join practically any material to any other, but it must be used with caution.

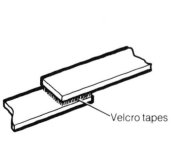

Velcro tapes

Velcro tapes seen under the microscope – the hook of one tape becomes entangled in the fine mesh of the opposite tape

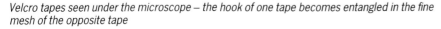

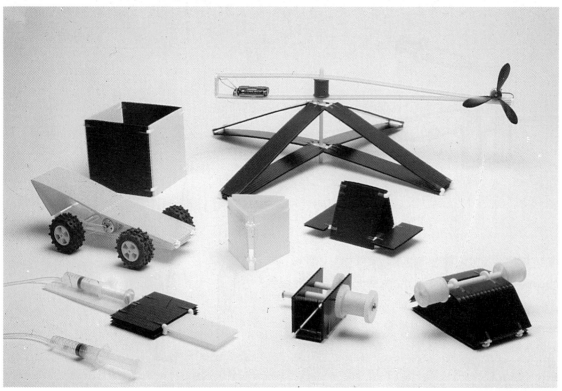

EMA Corrijoiners in action

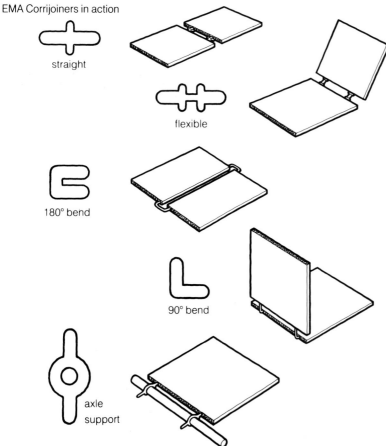

straight

flexible

180° bend

90° bend

axle
support

Among commercial joining systems, EMA's 'corrijoiners' enable rapid
construction in fluted plastics. They can also be used to join other
materials very rapidly if force-fit diameter holes (approx 5.25 mm φ) are
drilled first.

9 Technology for design: Structures

A structure is something that has evolved in nature or has been designed by man to resist loads or forces. Natural and man-made structures surround us, and because these 'work' without problems for most of the time we tend to take them for granted.

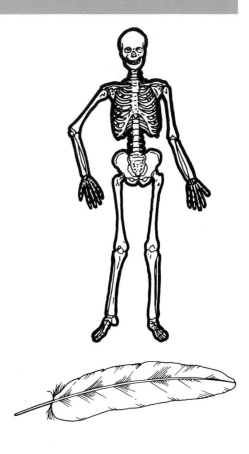

The human skeleton, for example, is an amazing structure. It supports the mass of our body as a static load (sitting or lying down) or as a dynamic load (moving about). Even when subjected to the dynamic loading given to it by an athlete, the skeleton seldom breaks except in accidents.

The expression 'light as a feather' is a common one, but few people realise how complicated feathers are as structures. The quill or rachis of a feather is in fact a long rectangular section box with a foam core, and its construction resists the forces in flight that would otherwise snap it.

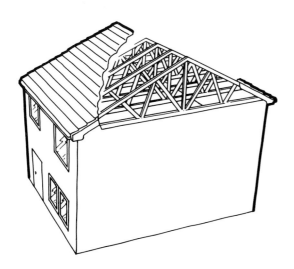

The roof of a typical modern house weighs many tons with its heavy concrete roofing tiles. The amount of wood used for the supporting framework has been reduced in recent years as designs have improved. Many other man-made structures have also become more efficient in terms of the amount of material they use.

Understanding how and why all these structures work so well is the key to knowing how to design your own.

How simple structures work

In placing a plank of wood between two ladders, a decorator has created a simple beam structure. Its behaviour in use tells us a lot about all structures and how to design them.

The decorator's plank is a beam that deflects under load. Ideally for the decorator (and in most structures that use beams), the beam should be able to span a wide gap and support its load without deflection.

To improve the decorator's beam, we need to understand how simple beams behave under load. Much can be learnt about beam behaviour by making a model with a length of foam plastic and painting a grid on it. When the foam beam is loaded, it deflects like the plank, but the movement is exaggerated.

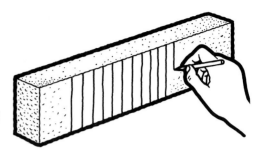

Under load, the top of the beam is compressed and the bottom is stretched or put into tension. The grid spacing along the centre remains roughly the same. An imaginary line running along the centre of the beam is described as the **neutral axis**: it maintains its length when the material above is compressed and the material below is stretched.

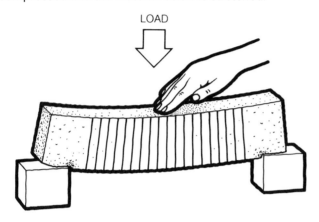

We could improve the performance of the beam by preventing it stretching at the bottom. A length of Sellotape running the length of the beam on the bottom will do this because the tape will not stretch as easily as the foam. Actual scaffold boards used by decorators sometimes have a steel strap running along the underside to make them stiffer.

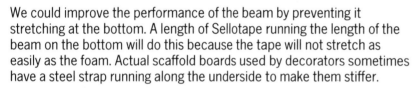

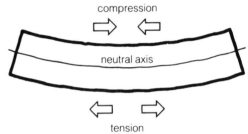

Concrete beams in buildings are usually reinforced by steel rods cast in the concrete. In horizontal beams these are set mainly below the neutral axis. Concrete is very strong in compression (top of beam) but weak in tension (bottom of beam). Knowing about how the beam behaves, and the properties of the material (see page 168) tells us where to put the reinforcement.

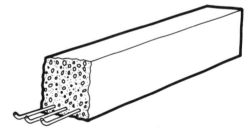

The Greeks used stone, usually supported on columns, for horizontal beams in their buildings. Because of the weakness of stone in tension, the beams had to be kept short and the columns quite closely spaced.

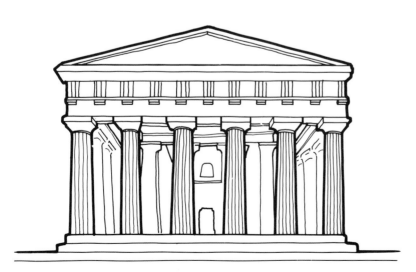

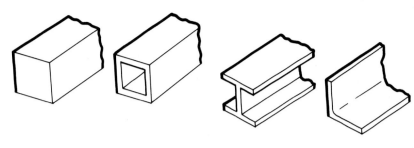
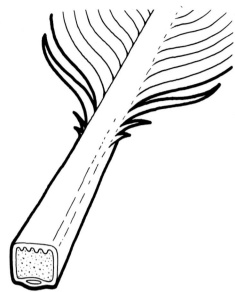

Beams used in larger structures take many different forms. Some are simple solids, some are hollow, and others are given a special cross-section for strength and rigidity.

In nature, the quill of a bird's feather is a good example of a box-section beam. The top of the box is made stronger with ribs so that as the feather bends upwards in flight it will not crumple in compression.

Designing a simple structure

One approach to understanding and designing structures is to create models, test them to the point of failure, and work out why failure took place. A simple beam, for example, can be designed and constructed from a weak material such as paper if models are tested and their weaknesses noticed and corrected.

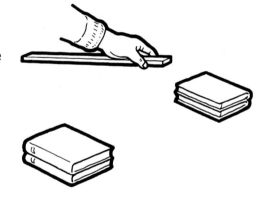

Using a strip of paper or thin card (400 mm × 40 mm) you should be able to take part in solving the following problem:

Problem: Using a single strip of paper or thin card (and paper adhesive if needed), design a beam spanning a gap of 300 mm to support a load of 100 g at its centre. (Place the beam between two books and let one end of a rod of suitable weight represent the load.)

Solution 1:   Place the strip flat across the gap.

Conclusion: This beam sags badly.
Solution 2: Turn the strip through 90°.
Conclusion: This beam is **unstable**: it simply collapses sideways. Can this movement be prevented?
Solution 3: Fold the strip along its length to form an inverted 'V'.
Conclusion: Some success! The beam supports the load, but it tends to flatten out. Can this be prevented?
Solution 4: ????????

Practical structures

Many of the solutions to the problem above are seen at work in the real world. Steel sheet, for example, is folded into sections to create lintels for supporting brickwork. The roof-support pillars of cars are folded into a complex profile to give maximum strength for what is usually a small cross-sectional area. Entire bridges are built using box-section decking to provide strength and stiffness without excessive weight.

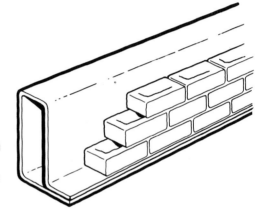

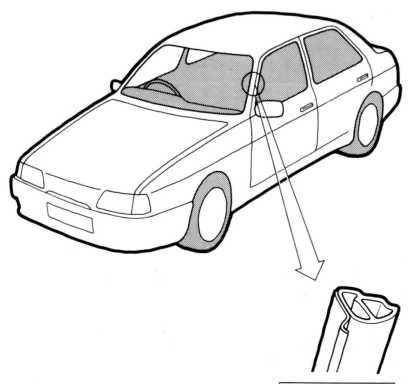

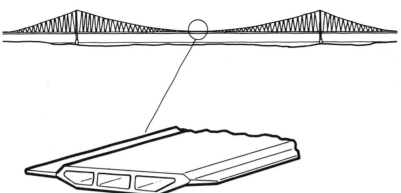

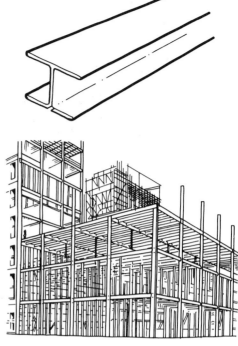

If the paper/card strip used in the problem was carefully folded along its length and glued, it would work in the same way as girders in steel-framed buildings. In an 'I'-section girder, the centre 'strip' prevents the top and bottom 'strips' moving up and down, and they in turn prevent the centre strip moving sideways — a sort of stalemate. A similar principle is demonstrated in large plastic mouldings that use these familiar strong sections. Many ordinary looking mouldings are, in fact, complex structures.

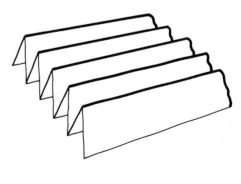

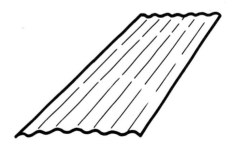

If, instead of a single beam, we wanted a stiff platform to span across a gap, the most obvious solution (knowing about the beam) would be to fold a wider strip into a concertina. In effect, this is a series of triangular beams each supporting the next.

This structural principle is used in many ways to stiffen sheet material such as corrugated plastic and corrugated 'iron'. An experiment with concertinered paper will show, however, that such a platform quickly fails

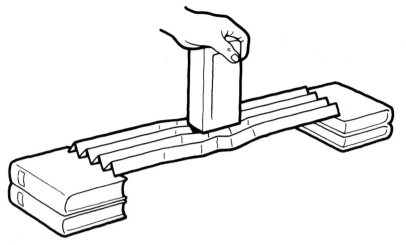

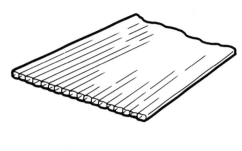

in compression to the top when it is heavily loaded. The paper folds simply collapse sideways. Gluing a sheet of paper over the top and bottom of the concertina will prevent this happening and provide a much stronger structure. Corrugated cardboard works in this way — as does its newer counterpart, fluted plastic sheet, which is used universally for packages, cases, estate agents' notice boards, etc.

The space between two thin flat plates can be divided up in other ways to create a very strong sheet structure. Interior doors, for example, now commonly use divisions of thin cardboard glued between two skins. Interior division panels in aircraft often consist of an aluminium honeycomb bonded between two thin aluminium skins. This type of structure is sometimes known as a **torsion box**, and can be applied in making furniture that is very light but strong. It is said to have a high **stiffness-to-weight ratio**.

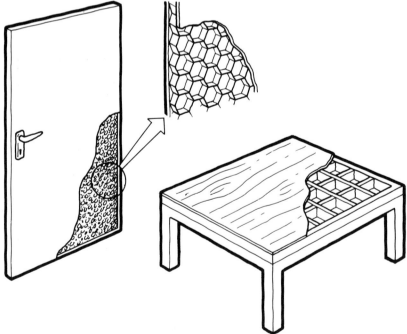

Different types of foam (e.g. polyurethane) sandwiched between two plates have the same stiffening effect. Instead of individual division pieces, there are thousands of interlocking cells that support one another. In fact, polyurethane foam can now be moulded into complete products so that in the moulding process a thin continuous skin of this material is formed around the outside.

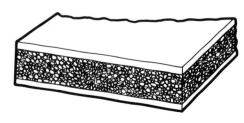

THE TRUSS

The truss is a framed structure that is very familiar in roof construction, and is typically used to span across wide gaps. The Crystal Palace in London, built for the Great Exhibition of 1851, was one of the first buildings to use metal trusses extensively for roof support. Their use is now common in modern buildings to provide large unsupported roof spans.

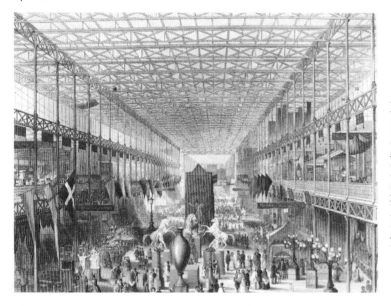

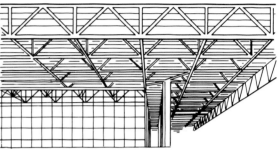

The way a truss works can be understood from a very simple example. If a load is suspended from the first truss, it will deflect easily; the three vertical parts do not have any structural purpose apart from tying the horizontals together.

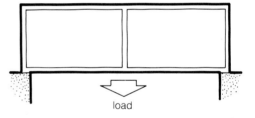

If diagonals are added, they prevent the movement that was previously possible, and the truss tends to remain rigid. When a load is applied, some parts of the truss are put into compression and others into tension. This happens throughout a more complex truss.

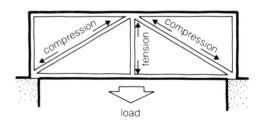

Designers of trusses attempt to produce better and more **efficient** structures. Efficiency, here, means being able to do a job using the least amount of material. Roof trusses in modern houses are more efficient in using less timber. Most loft space, though, is taken up with the latticework of a modern roofing truss.

Common truss designs used in bridge building are the Warren truss and Howe truss, but over the years many other types have been designed.

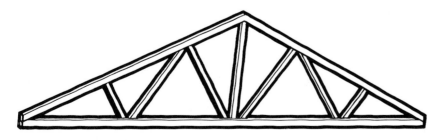

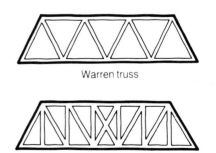

Warren truss

Howe truss

STRUCTURES IN THE HOME

The home is full of structures that work in the ways described above. Shelves are simple beams that deflect under load. Most will spring back to the horizontal when the load is taken off, but some — especially those made from chipboard — may remain distorted (see page 169). Thin metal sheet can be turned into shelving by folding its edges to give a rigid section. Similarly, the treads in metal stepladders are often found to be folded sheet metal.

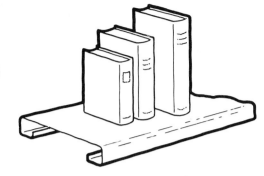

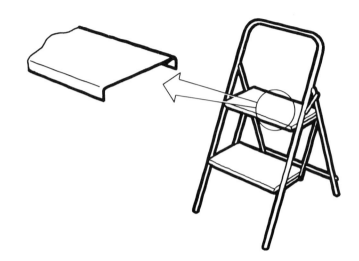

Probably the most familiar examples of structures in the home are pieces of furniture. Good designers of furniture have always understood how basic structures work, but this is especially important now as new materials and fastening techniques (see page 306) offer so many opportunities to experiment with new forms.

It is no longer uncommon, for example, to find pieces of furniture using tensioned wires as part of the overall structure. A typical bookshelf unit braced in this way might otherwise be very unstable and move like a parallelogram. Such instability is often a problem with furniture that comes ready to be assembled in a flat pack. Much of it relies on the addition of a thin hardboard skin lightly pinned to the back to give rigidity. If this is not securely fitted or comes loose, the piece of furniture will continue to move.

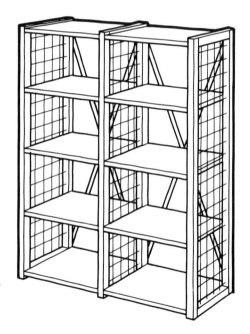

Many plastics products used in the home are carefully designed as structures to combine strength with light weight. Plastic storage boxes, for example, have a moulded rim that provides stiffness and strength — especially around the handles. Similar design features are also common in plastic garden furniture and children's toys.

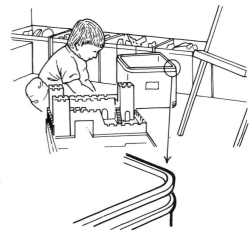

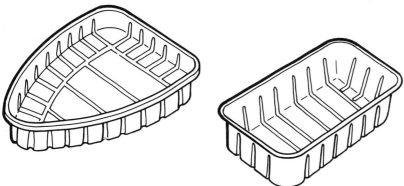

Most throw-away products, especially packages, are very carefully designed as structures. A typical food tray, for example, vacuum formed from very thin sheet material, derives most of its strength from its geometry or shape. Such packages rarely have large flat surfaces: they are formed with ribs to act as stiffeners. Paper and card are still widely used to make packaging structures that protect their contents from breakage. Egg boxes and lightbulb containers are two good examples. Both eggs and lightbulbs can themselves resist enormous loads if applied gently, but neither can offer much resistance to **impacts**. One of the functions of a good container is therefore to absorb impacts or any sharp blows.

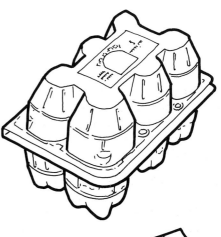

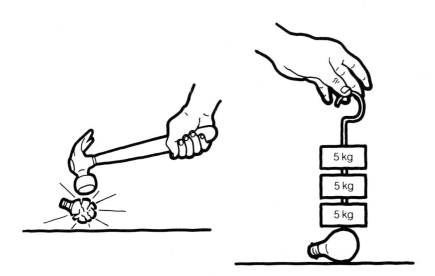

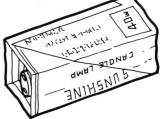

How structures can fail

Structures can fail in use for many different reasons, including poor design, overloading and faulty manufacture. Many problems in the design of structures can be avoided by choosing appropriate materials and ensuring that jointing techniques are adequate.

Materials can never be classified as simply 'strong' or 'weak': they are strong or weak in many different ways (see page 168). A material like acrylic, for example, is less than ideal for suitcases and other portable containers likely to be knocked, because — like eggs and lightbulbs — it has low impact resistance. It must be used very carefully if it is to be subjected to any loading.

In any structure, it is important that materials are held together properly. The use of melamine-faced chipboard, for example, is now common in furniture construction, but many problems arise when conventional wood screws and fittings are used to join it. Special coarse-threaded screws are available that will not easily pull out of the material and will not tend to burst it apart when driven in. Hinges for melamine-faced chipboard doors are of a special mechanical form and have a large plastic plug that forces into a shallow hole in the door to secure them.

Even where materials and fastenings are correctly selected for a structure, problems can still arise. For example, the danger of **stress concentrations** is recognised by designers in all fields. It is a problem best demonstrated by attempting to pull apart a strip of paper about 300 mm × 25 mm. This is in fact very difficult. If, however, a small nick is cut in one edge and the paper pulled again, it breaks easily as a tear develops from the nick across the strip. The stress in pulling the strip apart has been concentrated on the few fibres of paper at the bottom of the nick and, as these will break easily, the tear quickly moves through

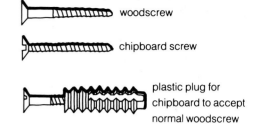

woodscrew

chipboard screw

plastic plug for chipboard to accept normal woodscrew

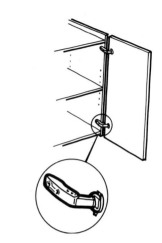

the paper. (This also explains why it is easy to tear up paper but not to pull it apart!) A strip of polystyrene scored across its centre will break easily as stress set up by bending is concentrated there. This principle is used for 'cutting' polystyrene and other materials, including glass.

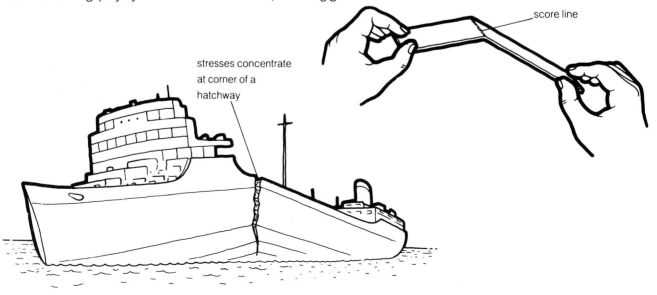

score line

stresses concentrate at corner of a hatchway

Large oil tankers have been known to break in half because of stresses caused by heavy seas becoming concentrated at weak points such as hatchway corners — so the steel skin actually starts to tear like paper. High-performance car engine parts such as connecting rods are brightly polished so that stresses are not concentrated in surface imperfections — causing cracks to develop.

On a more mundane level, it is found that acrylic, for example, may suddenly crack while being worked, or when in use as part of a product. This usually results from stresses being concentrated at the tip of a small crack or a sharp corner. Great care must therefore be taken in working acrylic — especially when drilling holes. Anything designed in this material and likely to be subjected to loading should have smooth polished edges and rounded details. (Remember: even a simple folded acrylic picture frame is heavily loaded at the bend when it is sprung apart to insert a picture.)

The same principle applies to other materials. A steel 'G'-cramp, for instance, should not have sharp corners where stresses can become concentrated in use. The actual removal of material from a badly designed cramp to give it rounded corners improves its strength!

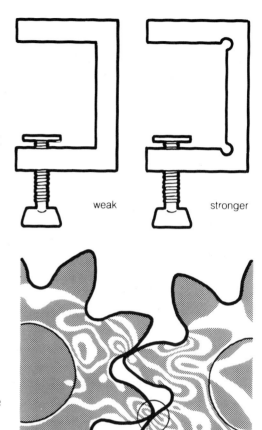

weak   stronger

Modelling and testing structures

Professional engineers frequently create models in order to examine behaviour. Often, special plastic models are made up that when viewed between polaroid filters show up the pattern of stresses as the model is loaded. This technique is called **photoelastic stress analysis**. (You can demonstrate the principle for yourself by crumpling a piece of cellophane between the two lenses of some old polaroid sunglasses. One lens is removed and turned at 90° to the second.)

Testing models to give useful results is very complicated, but models of structures can be examined in very simple ways to give an indication about performance. Models of trusses, for instance, can be made up on a flat surface by 'spot welding' the joints between taped-down artstraws with PVA adhesive. Obvious points of weakness can be identified when these models are put under load. Failure will tend to occur in compression at the top, so in improving performance the top must be given special attention.

points of contact between teeth are revealed as high stress regions

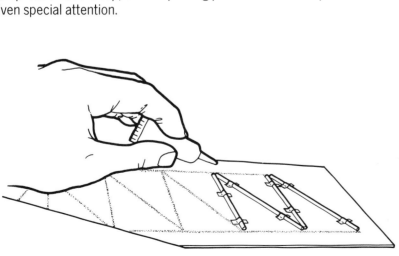

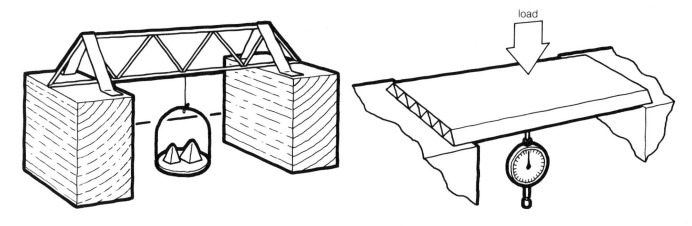

Other structures such as box sections or torsion boxes can be made up in card, paper or polystyrene as models and loaded with weights to give an indication of where failure is likely to occur. At the same time, the amount of deflection for a given load can be measured using an instrument like a clock gauge.

Some important properties of materials used in structures (see also page 331)

TENSILE STRENGTH

This is the resistance a material has to being pulled apart. Steel rod has high tensile strength, but concrete, for example, is very weak in tension.

Tensile strength is given by dividing the load or force in newtons by the cross-sectional area in square metres. Engineers use the unit MN/m^2 (meganewtons per square metre) because they are usually dealing with very large figures.

Tensile strength of common materials (MN/m^2)	
Human muscle	0.1
Wood (across grain)	3.5
Wood (along grain)	110
Glass	35–170
Cast aluminium	70
Copper	140
Mild steel	400
Fibreglass-reinforced plastics	350–1000
Nylon thread	1050
High tensile steel	1550

COMPRESSIVE STRENGTH

This is the resistance of a material to being squashed or compressed. Concrete has a very high compressive strength — the opposite of its strength in tension! Glass, too, is very strong in compression, for example, in the form of building blocks.

This is the resistance a material has to sudden impacts such as hammer blows. Glass has a very poor impact resistance but polypropylene has very high resistance to impacts and is used, for example, in school chairs.

The behaviour of materials

When a material is loaded in tension or compression, it first behaves like a spring — though without so much movement. Up to a certain load, the material will return to its original length when the load is removed. However, if the load is further increased, the material becomes permanently deformed. This can be shown on a graph.

For a piece of steel under tension, the straight line part of the graph shows it behaving like a spring. The steel obeys **Hooke's Law**, and if the load is removed anywhere along the straight line it returns to its original length. If loaded and stretched beyond the **elastic limit**, the steel springs back, but not to its original length. It remains permanently distorted, and has undergone **plastic deformation**.

A simple experiment with a paper clip shows the difference between elastic and plastic deformation. If gently pulled apart, a paper clip springs back to its original condition. If it is prised open beyond the elastic limit of the steel wire, it springs back only partially and shows permanent distortion.

It is essential in structures of any kind that materials are not loaded beyond their elastic limit. Normally, a very wide margin of safety is allowed for. Sometimes, even when a material is loaded within its elastic limit, it starts to behave plastically over a period of time (depending upon the material and environmental conditions). This is known as creep and affects chipboard, for example. Creep is responsible for chipboard bookshelves sagging over a period of time and not returning to the horizontal when the books are removed.

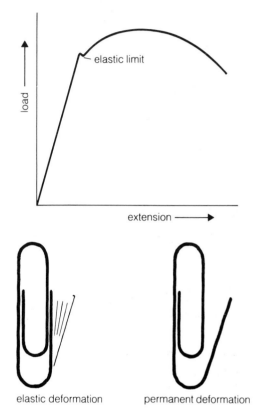

elastic deformation   permanent deformation

10 Technology for design: Energy

Energy cannot be seen like a structure, a mechanism or an electronic circuit — but all these things depend on it. Understanding where energy comes from and how to apply it is the key to understanding much of our technology.

Energy is defined in dictionaries as the **capacity for doing work**. This means that whenever any kind of work is done — for example, when you lift a weight or even just move around — energy is needed to do it.

Work is measured in joules, and 1 joule is the amount of work done when a force of 1 newton moves through 1 metre. For example, the work needed to move a table through a distance of 2 metres using a force of 6 newtons is given as:

work done = force × distance moved = 6 N × 2 m = 12 joules (J)

The energy needed for doing this work would have come from chemical energy in the form of the person's food intake. Twelve joules of chemical energy would have been converted into mechanical energy through the muscles used. (Much of our food is also converted into heat to keep our bodies at their required temperature.)

Energy exists in many different forms, and can be converted from one form into others.

potential energy

kinetic energy

Forms of energy

MECHANICAL ENERGY
This is the energy of movement, and takes two forms: potential and kinetic energy. **Potential energy** is stored energy. Any mass of material can be given potential energy by raising it up. When an elastic band or spring is stretched, energy is stored. (**Note:** Engineers call the potential energy locked up in springs **strain energy**.)

When the elastic band or spring is allowed to spring back to its original length, the stored or potential energy is released as **kinetic energy**. A single brick falling from a height has sufficient kinetic energy to do very real damage.

ELECTRICAL ENERGY

Electricity is used to transmit energy over long and short distances, and modern technology would be unthinkable without it. It is called a **flexible** form of energy because electric current flowing in a conductor can be converted easily into the forms of energy that are needed.

CHEMICAL ENERGY

Chemical energy is available in a variety of substances such as coal, gas, oil — and the food we eat. When chemical reactions take place, energy appears in other forms — for example, heat from a burning gas fire, electric current from a torch battery, sound and light from an exploding firework.

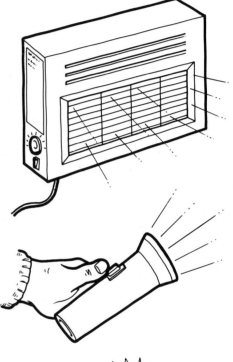

HEAT ENERGY

This is the energy of movement of the atoms or molecules in materials. All things we come into contact with possess a certain amount of heat energy, and this can be increased or decreased in many ways. Heat is transferred by **conduction**, **radiation** or **convection**.

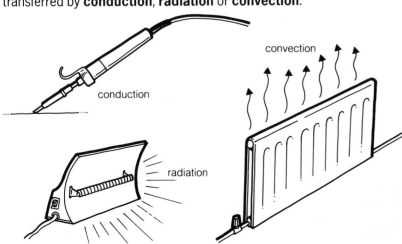

conduction

convection

radiation

SOUND ENERGY

Sound is a form of energy produced by movement of our own vocal chords, by loudspeakers and in many other ways. Very little sound energy is actually needed for hearing: most of the energy that comes from a radio or television is absorbed by objects such as curtains or books in a room.

LIGHT ENERGY

Light is the source of energy for plants and, indirectly, for most living things. Plants convert light energy by a process known as photosynthesis, and this gives us most of the food we eat. Light itself can also be produced from other forms of energy. In the form of lasers, for example, we can use this energy for communications, cutting materials, and even in surgery.

Conversion of energy

Energy can be converted from one form into others, and much of our technology is about designing and making things to do this. Here are some familiar examples of energy conversion.

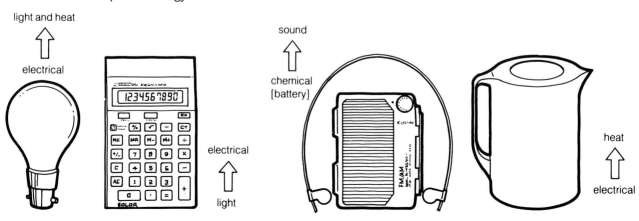

The law of conservation of energy states that energy can never be created or destroyed. Whenever energy is converted, it must all reappear again in different forms. This does not mean, however, that energy is never wasted. In an ordinary lightbulb, for example, only a tiny fraction of the electrical energy is converted into light: the rest is 'lost' as unwanted heat. In a car engine only a small amount of the chemical energy in the fuel is converted into mechanical energy to move the car.

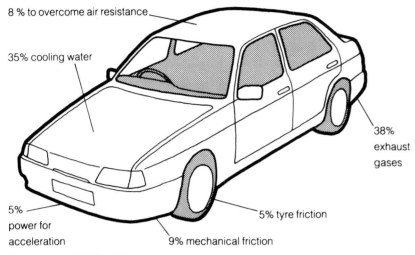

8 % to overcome air resistance

35% cooling water

38% exhaust gases

5% power for acceleration

9% mechanical friction

5% tyre friction

Where energy goes in a car

Ideally, domestic appliances such as food mixers, vacuum cleaners and electric drills should convert all their electrical energy into mechanical energy. The electric motors in each of these examples, however, convert much of the energy into heat, and this has to be got rid of by blowing air over it. (The more work a motor is made to do, the hotter it gets: if too much load is put on, it will overheat and burn out.)

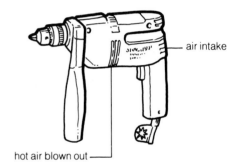

air intake

hot air blown out

We describe as efficient those things that convert most of the energy input into the kind of energy we want to get out. The energy output is measured as a percentage of what went in. The car engine is a good example of a device whose efficiency has recently improved.

Designers are always striving to make things more efficient, but there will always be some loss of energy. No machine will ever be 100 % efficient. For hundreds of years, though, inventors have believed (and continue to believe) that perpetual motion machines can be built that will power themselves and do useful work!

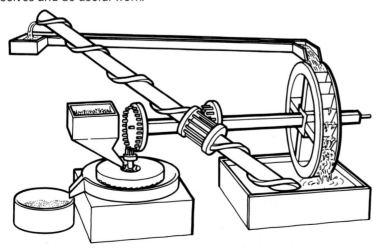

A seventeenth century perpetual motion machine for corn grinding

Friction between moving parts in machinery is a serious cause of energy loss, but the science of tribology — the study of moving surfaces in contact — has done much to improve performance and efficiency. You, as a designer, must ensure, for example, that rotating shafts run smoothly in lubricated bearings (see page 151). Any chatter or noise coming from something like a gearbox means that energy is being lost in the form of sound and as heat through friction.

tip: use silicon grease on plastic gears

Sources of energy

Because energy can be converted from one form into others, it is not always obvious where the energy we actually use came from in the first place. After some thought, it is possible to draw up an energy map or chain.

The energy chain here shows that there are several sources for the electrical energy consumed in the home.

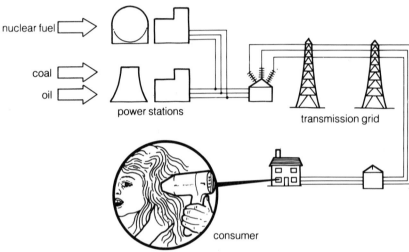

nuclear fuel

coal

oil

power stations

transmission grid

consumer

THE SUN

If the energy chain is pushed back another step, we see that much of the energy we now enjoy came from the sun — locked up for millions of years in fossil fuels.

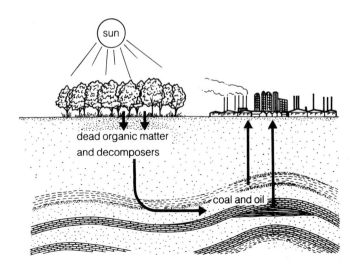

sun

dead organic matter and decomposers

coal and oil

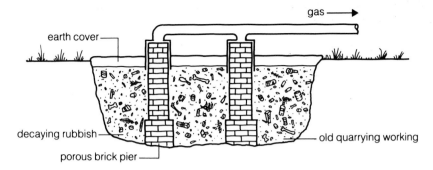

earth cover

gas →

decaying rubbish

porous brick pier

old quarrying working

All kinds of more recently formed organic matter, such as wood, animal waste and much household rubbish, can be converted into useful energy. When organic materials in rubbish dumps decay, methane gas is given off, and can seep out from older dumps over many years. If the dump is properly constructed, however, the gas can be drawn off and used for heating or to generate electricity.

The sun and moon are ultimately responsible for the movement of water in the atmosphere and on the earth's surface. The energy of moving water is converted into electricity by hydroelectric power plants that channel the water through large turbines. Hydroelectric power plants that channel the water through large turbines. Hydroelectric power plants are found where water naturally falls through a distance, or where a dam can be built to increase the water level behind it.

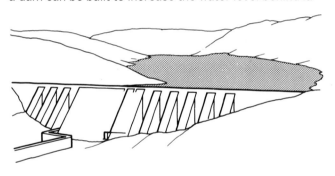

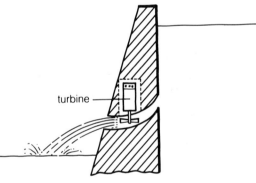

turbine

The sun is also indirectly the source of energy for electricity generated by windmills. It is responsible for the huge currents of air in the atmosphere that are experienced as wind. Although making only a tiny contribution to our total energy needs, windmills are beginning to be built in large numbers and are now found grouped together in 'parks'.

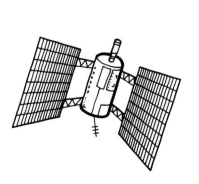

Light from the sun can be converted directly into electricity using the kind of solar cells found on many calculators. At the moment, these are too expensive to use on a very large scale on earth, but most satellites in space get their electrical energy from large arrays of solar cells.

Many experiments have been tried to harness energy from the sun's radiation by focussing it to a small point using mirrors. Some of these experiments were carried out quite a long time ago, e.g. the steam printing press shown. More recently, very large arrays of mirrors have been constructed to capture energy directly from the sun.

Anyone who has felt the temperature of roofing tiles on a hot day will know that a lot of energy is absorbed from the sun. A few years ago this was largely wasted, but many households are now installing solar panels on roofs to collect some of it. A typical solar panel consists of a glass-fronted box containing a length of coiled piping. The interior of the box and the piping are coloured black for maximum absorption.

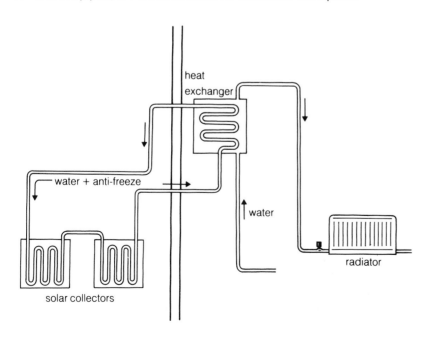

Radiation from the sun raises the surface temperature of the coiled piping, and heat builds up in the box as it does in a greenhouse. Water, or any other fluid flowing through the piping, is heated and passes its heat to a storage tank supplying the house with hot water. The problem with solar heating tends to be that less sunlight is available in the winter when it is most needed. However, a useful amount of energy can be collected even at this time of the year.

TIDAL POWER

As the tides rise and fall, massive amounts of water are moved in and out of natural estuaries. Tidal barriers, containing turbines to generate electricity, have already been built across some estuaries to harness this energy. The turbines are driven as the rising water flows into the estuary, and they are driven again as the tide falls and the water flows out.

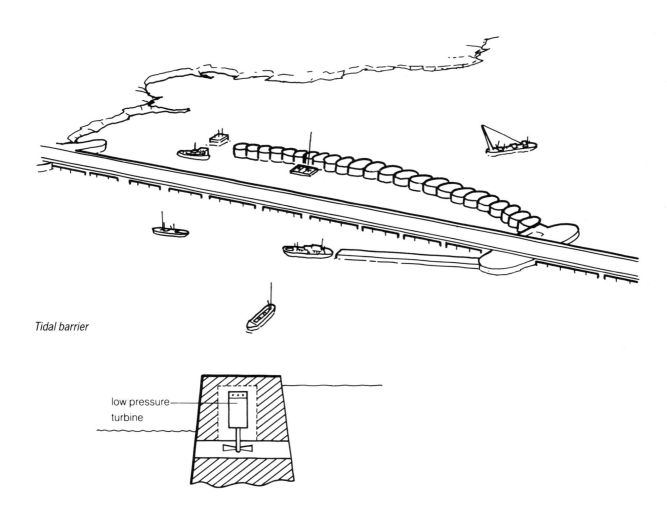

Tidal barrier

low pressure turbine

NUCLEAR ENERGY

Energy in the form of heat can be obtained from nuclear reactions that break down matter itself. A very small mass of material can be made to yield an enormous amount of energy for conversion into electricity. At present, nuclear energy accounts for only a small percentage of our total energy needs. Nuclear power stations are expensive to build (and to demolish), and their safety is being questioned following serious accidents and leaks of radioactive materials.

It is hoped that we shall be able to exploit the process known as nuclear fusion in the future. This promises abundant nuclear energy without many of the problems of current nuclear power stations.

HEAT PUMPS

A heat pump works like a refrigerator in reverse. When a refrigerator is running, heat is removed from inside and 'dumped' into the room. The heat exchanger on the back gets very warm and gives off a surprising amount of heat.

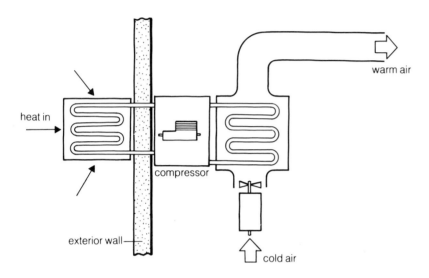

Installed in a house, a heat pump takes heat from the air outside and this heat re-appears inside the house as the heat exchanger warms up. It might help you to think of a refrigerator built into the wall of a house with its door open to the outside air.

GEOTHERMAL ENERGY

Erupting volcanoes tell us that just below its surface the earth remains very hot indeed. This heat can be exploited by boring very deep holes into hot rock and pumping in water. This is turned into steam that can be used for driving electricity-generating turbines. At present, only a handful of **geothermal** power stations are in operation.

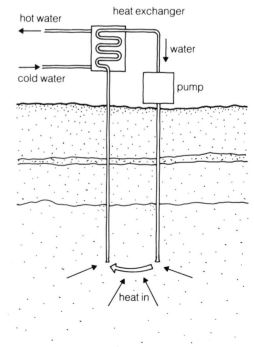

Energy conservation

Energy, in whatever form, costs money. Since the oil crisis of the 1970s when the price of oil rose steeply, there has been particular concern about conserving energy resources and using them wisely.

Oil is not a renewable resource, and will eventually run out — some predict that this will happen in a few years time. Careful conservation will give us more time to develop economic alternatives to oil.

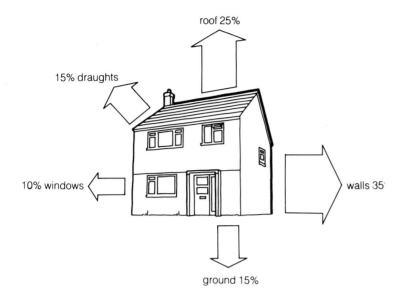

roof 25%

15% draughts

10% windows

walls 35

ground 15%

It is possible to cut down on energy consumption by good design. In cars, for example, this is achieved by reducing drag (resistance to moving through air), decreasing weight and improving the efficiency of the engine.

Most energy used in the home is for heating. Again, good design can prevent heat loss and assist in energy conservation. In a typical house, it can be shown where heat losses occur and where savings can be made. Insulation can be provided to eliminate much of this waste. The heat lost can actually be photographed (see page 58).

QUESTIONS

1 How can heat loss be prevented in a typical house? Give four methods.

2 Why is it wasteful of energy to throw away an aluminium drinks can (see page 170)?

3 Why is electricity described as a flexible form of energy?

Energy and power

Power is defined as the rate of doing work, or the rate at which energy is converted into other forms. Work done is measured in joules (see page 173) and power is measured in joules per second or **watts**.

1 watt = 1 joule/second
1 kilowatt (kW) = 1000 watts

(**Note:** 1 horsepower = approximately 750 watts.)

All the electrical appliances we use in the home have a power rating indicating how much energy will be used in a given time. For example, if an electric fire has a power rating of 2 kilowatts, it produces 2000 joules of heat per second. Some electric kettles have the same power rating and will raise the temperature of their contents to boiling point in less than a minute. A portable electric drill with a power rating of 1000 watts develops $\frac{1}{50}$ of the power of an average car.

The cost of running these appliances is easy to work out. Electricity is sold in energy units called kilowatt-hours:

1 kW-hour = 1 kW × 1 hour

In an electrical circuit, current (I), voltage (V) and power (P) are related:

$$P = I \times V \qquad V = \frac{P}{I} \qquad I = \frac{P}{V}$$

Normally, we can assume that mains voltage is in the region of 240 V (although it does vary slightly around the UK). Since power rating is given on the appliance, we can work out current consumption. For example, for a 3 kW electric kettle the current consumption is given as:

$$I = \frac{P}{V} \qquad I = \frac{3000\,W}{240\,V} \qquad I = 12.5\,A$$

The current consumption of an appliance indicates what size fuse should be used to protect it. In the example of the kettle, we would use a 13 A fuse (the nearest in value to 12.5 A). A television, however, with a power rating of only a few hundred watts has a lower fuse rating and the fuse size would normally be 3 A.

In some appliances using one or more electric motors, there can be a high current surge when the appliance starts up, and these may need larger fuses. **Note:** In the case of any appliance, the manufacturers' instructions must be followed.

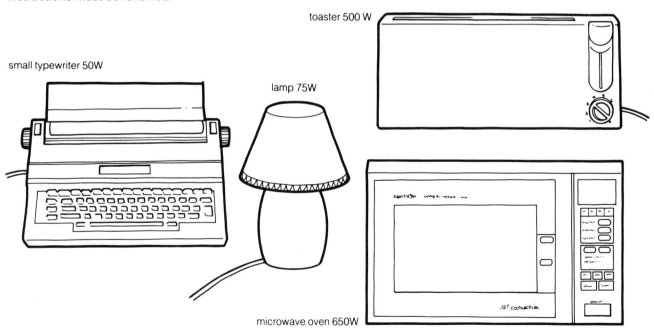

toaster 500 W

small typewriter 50W

lamp 75W

microwave oven 650W

11 Introduction to tools, processes and materials

In the past, skills and processes associated with different trades and materials were often passed on as if each was completely different from any other. We now know that this is not true, and that there are many similarities between the tools and processes used with different materials. First, a close look at how we work materials will show that the basic principles are the same for them all. Secondly, the tools used share many common features, and they can be more easily grouped together according to the work they do than by the materials they are used with. In fact it would be impossible to decide which material many of them should be listed under. Thirdly, new tools, processes and materials are being invented every year, and new uses are continually being found for old ones. These often cut across traditional boundaries. For example, the injection moulding of plastics can be thought of as a development of the die casting of metals, and the blow-moulding of plastics as a development of glass blowing.

We have, therefore, begun this section of the book by explaining the way in which we group together the tools we use and the principles upon which all the ways of working materials are based.

The classification of common hand tools

All the tools used to work materials can be grouped under one of four headings.

1 **Marking-out, measuring and testing tools** such as rules, try-squares, dividers, gauges and calipers.
2 **Holding tools** such as vices, cramps and jigs.
3 **Driving tools** such as hammers, screwdrivers and spanners.
4 **Cutting tools** such as saws, planes and files.

By arranging all the tools we know in this way we are able to see the similarities between tools used for working different materials. Where there are differences we should ask ourselves why they are necessary. This analysis of tool design should help us to choose the best tools to use in a new situation, and to see what is wrong when a tool is not working efficiently.

The principles of working materials

There are three main reasons why it is necessary for us to work materials. These are:
1 To change the **function** of the material.
2 To change the **properties** of the material.
3 To change the **appearance** of the material.

There are four distinct ways in which we can shape materials.

1 **Wasting.** This is where we change the shape of the material by cutting bits off it. Sawing, planing, filing and drilling are good examples.

2 **Deformation.** This is where we change the shape by bending and forming. Forging hot metal, vacuum forming thermoplastics and bending wood veneers are good examples.

3 **Moulding and casting.** This is where we change the shape by changing the state of the material. For example, when casting metals or plastics resins we change them from liquid to solid.

4 **Fabrication.** This is where we change the shape by joining two or more pieces together by such processes as nailing, screwing, gluing and rivetting.

All the processes used in school and in industry are examples of at least one of these ways of working, and many involve two or more. For example, the blow moulding of plastics bottles consists of moulding (extruding the parison) and deformation (blowing this to shape). Making a simple wooden box is a combination of wasting (cutting the pieces to shape) and fabrication (joining them together). Laminating and bending wood veneers involves fabrication (gluing) and deformation (bending). Making a wrought iron gate involves wasting (sawing up the metal), deformation (forging to shape) and fabrication (assembling the parts).

It is important that as we learn new skills and processes we analyse them, and understand both how and why they work. This analysis will help us to see the similarities and the differences between different situations and materials, so that when faced with a new problem we can draw upon our experience of related ones. It is not sufficient to learn to use tools and materials parrot fashion, without thinking about what we are doing.

Safety

Attention to safety is the most important thing in any workshop, and everyone must learn the following simple safety rules before beginning any practical work.

1 **Dress safely** to avoid getting caught in machines or on the many snags around workshops. The best way to prepare for a practical lesson is to take off your jacket, roll up your sleeves and put on an apron. Long sleeves are very dangerous. Long hair must be tied up so that it cannot fall forward and get caught, jewellery must be removed and ties must be safely tucked in.

Always wear the correct protective clothing. Take special care to protect hands, eyes and feet. Soft shoes must not be worn in a workshop. Broken toes are one of the commonest industrial injuries.

2 **Move safely** to avoid bumping into people and things or tripping up. Never run or play in a workshop and do not play tricks on people. Carry tools and materials safely. Sharp tools must be held so that they cannot cut anybody, hot materials should not be carried about and long lengths of material must be handled carefully to avoid poking them into anyone.

3 **Act safely.** Never work alone or without permission in a workshop. If you had an accident there would be no one there to help you. Never misuse tools or improvise. Always read instructions carefully and follow them. Never put down anything hot except in a clearly labelled hot area. Take special care to guard against heat, dangerous liquids, fumes, dust and electric arc flashes.

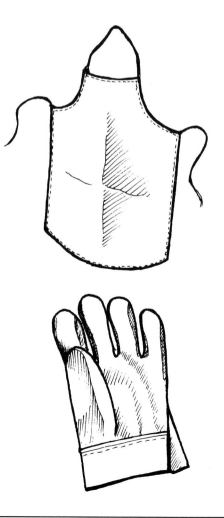

4 **Machine safety.** There must only be one operator on a machine at a time. Never use a machine without permission and correct training. Use all guards and safety equipment provided. Never reach across or go behind a machine. Never leave chuck keys in. Never machine work held in your fingers. Never adjust or clean a machine without switching it off at the isolator. Never remove swarf with a cloth or your bare hands.

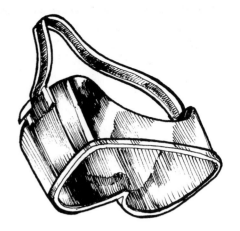

5 **Report all accidents, breakages and faults however small,** so that a qualified person can decide what action is needed. This applies equally to first aid for people and repairs to faulty or broken equipment which might become dangerous. For example, a loose or split hammer shaft could result in the head flying off.

6 **Keep yourself and the workshops clean and tidy.** Do not allow tools, materials or waste to litter benches, machines or the floor, as this bad habit causes accidents such as tripping-up, heavy items falling on your feet and things falling into moving machines. Always wash your hands thoroughly to avoid skin disease and avoid spilling oil, chemicals, etc. onto your clothes.

Never break a safety rule. If in doubt ask.

Safety pays. An accident could change your life by causing permanent injury to yourself or a lifetime of regret for injuries caused to someone else. There is no replacement for a lost hand or eye.

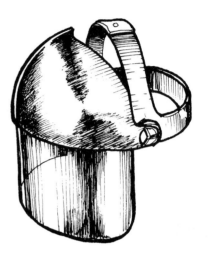

PLASTICS SAFETY
There are extra precautions to remember when using plastics, paint, acid pickles and any other chemicals.

1 RESPIRATORY HAZARDS
Never work without adequate ventilation. **Always switch on the extractor fans before starting any work causing fumes.**

Always switch on the dust extractor when machine sawing or sanding. Wear a face mask when sawing or sanding GRP.

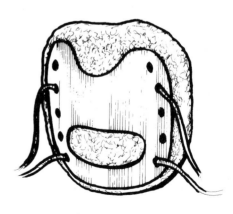

2 EYE HAZARDS
Protect your eyes from dust, particles of plastic waste and organic liquids. Always wear safety glasses. **The catalyst used for curing polyester resins is especially dangerous to the eyes** (e.g. when embedding or laying-up GRP). It must only be used under the supervision of a teacher and using a special dispenser to prevent squirting of the liquid.

If catalyst gets into your eyes, wash immediately with water or a 2% aqueous solution of sodium bicarbonate and see a doctor without delay, taking with you details of the catalyst.

3 SKIN HAZARDS
Catalysts and resins can cause dermatitis (a skin disease) and skin irritation. Protect your clothes. (Disposable plastic aprons are available.) Use barrier cream to protect your hands. For messy jobs wear disposable plastic gloves. After handling use only proper skin cleaning creams, not

brush cleaner, etc. Wash thoroughly immediately after using resins and catalysts. Glass fibre can irritate the skin so cover your hands and arms when handling it. **Do not** allow molten plastics to touch the skin — they stick and have a high heat capacity.

4 FIRE AND EXPLOSION HAZARDS

Many plastics materials are highly flammable — keep them away from naked flames. Catalysed resin produces heat and can cause fire if not handled safely. Do not throw containers or cloths with uncured catalysed resins on them into waste bins.

Catalyst and activator must never be mixed together — they might explode.

12

Classification of common hand tools
PART 1—Marking out, measuring and testing tools

The chart below names the common marking-out, measuring and testing tools usually found in the school workshop, and shows with which materials they are usually used. Where tools with different names fulfil the same function on different materials, they are shown on the same line. This is followed by sketches of these tools together with brief notes about them.

Wood	Plastics	Metal
Rule and straight edge ————————▶ ——————————▶		
Try-square ———————————————◀▶ —————— Engineer's try-square		
Mitre-square ———————————————▶		X
Sliding bevel ———————————————▶ —————————————▶		
Marking gauge ———————————————◀▶ —————— Odd-leg calipers		
Mortise gauge	X	X
Cutting gauge	X	X
Panel gauge	X	X
Marking knife	◀——————	Scriber
Pencil	Wax crayon/felt-nib pen	Pencil
Wing compasses ———————————————◀▶ —————— Spring dividers		
Dovetail template	X	X
Spirit level ———————————————▶ —————————————▶		
Winding strips	X	X
Trammels or beam compass ———————▶ —————————————▶		
X	◀——————	Centre punch
X	◀——————	Dot punch
◀————————————————	◀——————	Inside calipers
◀————————————————	◀——————	Outside calipers
◀————————————————	◀——————	Centre square
X	◀——————	Micrometers
X	◀——————	Surface plate
X	◀——————	Surface gauge
X	◀——————	Vee blocks
X	◀——————	Angle plate
X	◀——————	Radius gauges
◀————————————————	◀——————	Drill gauge
X	◀——————	Wire and sheet gauge

Use of symbols

The symbols above are used in the following chapters. They show which sections apply to which materials. This enables students studying one material at a time to choose the relevant sections within a chapter, while students following a combined materials course will easily see where tools and processes are relevant to more than one material.

Marking-out tools

STEEL RULE

This is used to measure length and, as a straight edge, to test for flatness. It is marked in millimetres and made in 150, 300, 500 and 1000 mm lengths.

MARKING KNIFE

This is used to mark lines on wood, usually across the grain. A knife cuts a thinner and more accurate line than a pencil. It is nearly always used with a try-square. To use the marking knife, hold it like a pencil and cut with the long point of the blade. The blade is of tool steel with a hardwood or plastic handle.

SCRIBER

This is used to mark lines on metal and plastics. Hold the scriber like a pencil. When using a scriber or marking knife make sure that the point is pressed into the angle between the try-square and the material. The point is made of tool steel and has a 30° point angle.

TRY-SQUARE

This is used to test that one surface is square (at 90°) to another, and for marking-out lines square to the face-side or face-edge. Woodworkers' try-squares have a carbon steel blade and a wooden stock, sometimes with a brass face, while engineers' try-squares have a carbon steel blade and stock.

USING THE TRY-SQUARE

For testing, hold the work up to the light, put the stock against a true face, and slide it down until the blade touches the edge being tested. If no light shows under the blade, and work is square.

For marking-out, place the marking tool on the mark first, slide the square along until it touches the marking tool, and then mark the line. In this way the line is marked exactly where it is wanted.

MARKING GAUGE

This is used to mark lines parallel to the face-side and face-edge along the grain.

A panel gauge is a large marking gauge.

A cutting gauge has a cutter instead of a spur for marking lines across the grain from accurately prepared end grain, and for cutting veneers.

SETTING THE GAUGE TO SIZE

Put the zero of the ruler against the stock, and slide the stock along the stem. When the spur is against the correct mark lightly tighten the thumbscrew. Check the setting, adjust if necessary, and tighten the thumbscrew.

USING THE GAUGE

Hold with the thumb and first finger round the stock, and the other three fingers round the stem. Press the stock firmly against the face-side or face-edge, and lower the spur point until it trails on the wood. It will then mark a line as it is moved. Try to mark one continuous line. To make gauging easier, hold the wood in the vice or against the bench hook.

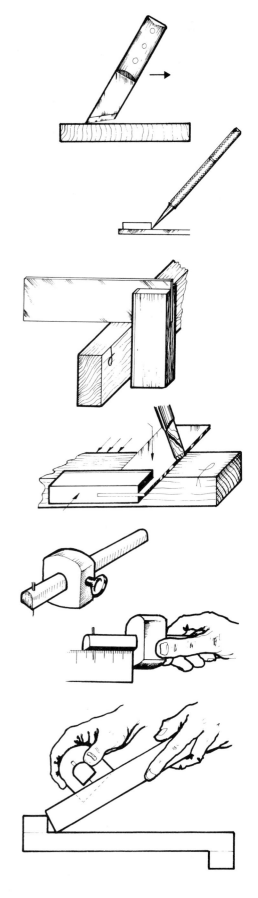

MORTISE GAUGE

This is used to mark double lines parallel to the face-side and face-edge. Its main use is to mark the thickness of mortises and tenons.

SETTING THE GAUGE TO SIZE

Set the spur points to the width of the chisel or cutter to be used (because chisels, etc., vary in size and should be chosen first). Set the stock and hold the gauge as for a marking gauge.

SETTING A MORTISE OR MARKING GAUGE TO THE MIDDLE OF A PIECE OF WOOD

Set the gauge as near as possible to the middle of the wood. Gauge a short line from each side of the wood. Adjust the gauge until the marks are exactly on top of each other. Gauge from face-side or face-edge.

THE THUMB OR PENCIL GAUGE

This is used to draw pencil lines parallel to a face-side or face-edge where a gauge line would show on the finished job. Cut out of scrap-wood as required.

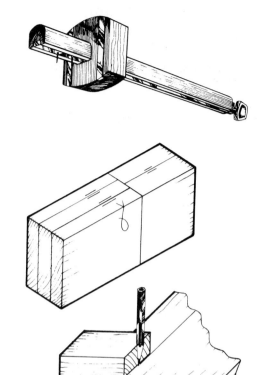

ODD-LEG CALIPERS

These are used to mark lines parallel to a true edge and to find the centre of a bar, mainly in metalwork.

SETTING THE CALIPERS TO SIZE

Put the stepped leg on the zero end of the ruler and adjust until the scriber point is against the correct mark.

USING THE CALIPERS TO MARK A LINE

Rest the stepped leg on the edge of the metal. Take care to keep the calipers square to the edge or the line will not be the correct distance from the edge.

TO FIND THE CENTRE OF A BAR

Set the calipers to the approximate centre and scribe arcs from several points around the edge. Adjust the calipers and repeat until the required accuracy has been obtained.

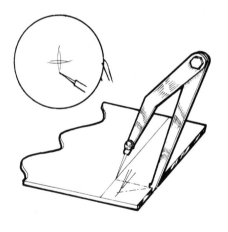

CENTRE PUNCH

This is used to mark the centres of holes to be drilled. It has a 90° point angle.

DOT PUNCH

This is used to locate the centres of circles, radii and arcs when marking out, and to witness mark scriber lines which are to be cut to. It has a 60° point angle.

WITNESS MARKING

Dot punch marks are very carefully made about 5 mm apart along the scriber line to prevent it from being rubbed off, and to act as a guide when filing. File until half of each witness mark has been removed. If more than half remains the work is oversize; if less than half remains you have filed off too much.

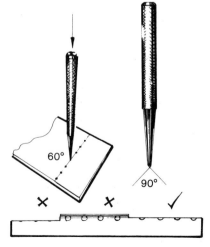

SPRING DIVIDERS AND WING COMPASSES

These are used to mark out circles and arcs, and to step off equal lengths along a line. Wing compasses are heavier and have a positive lock which makes them better for use on wood where divider points tend to try to follow the grain.

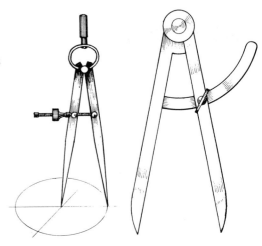

BEAM COMPASSES OR TRAMMEL HEADS

These are used to mark large circles.

MITRE SQUARE

This is used to mark out angles of 45° and 135° and for testing mitres. A mitre is a bevel which slopes at 45°. Use it as you would a try-square.

SLIDING BEVEL

This is used to mark out angles which are not at 90° to a true edge, and to test two flat surfaces meeting at any angle other than 90°. The bevel is set with a protractor and it is then used as for a try-square.

Carpenters' bevels have a hardwood stock and tool steel blade. Engineers' bevels are smaller and made entirely of tool steel.

WINDING STRIPS

These are used to test the face-side of a piece of wood for twist or winding. Because the face-side is the first part of the wood to be trued up, there are no accurate edges from which to test with a try-square, and so winding strips are used to show whether the wood is flat. To use, look along the top edges of the winding strips to see if they are parallel.

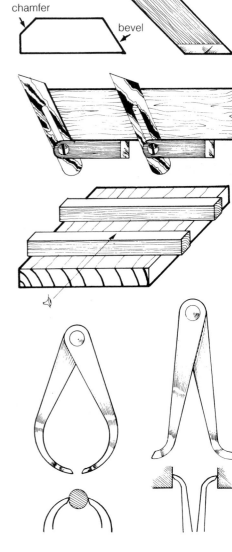

INSIDE AND OUTSIDE CALIPERS

Outside calipers are used to measure the outside diameters of tubes and round bars. Internal diameters are measured with inside calipers. Outside calipers can also be used to check the thickness of materials, for example the thickness of the walls of a tube.

CENTRE SQUARE

This is used to find the centre of round work. Draw two lines approximately at right angles to each other. The centre is where they cross.

RADIUS GAUGES

These are used like a try-square to test the accuracy of small radii and fillets. Each blade shows the exact internal and external curves for a given radius.

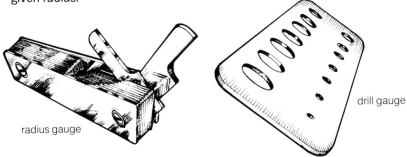

radius gauge

drill gauge

DRILL GAUGE

This is used to find the diameter of round rod and twist drills, usually from 1 mm to 13 mm in either 0.5 mm or 0.1 mm steps.

WIRE AND SHEET GAUGES

These are used to measure the thickness of wire and sheet metal.

Rules for marking-out wood, metal and plastics

1 On all materials we have ways of distinguishing between construction lines and lines which will be cut to.
On **wood**, we use a pencil for construction lines, and a marking knife for lines to be cut to.
On **metal** we use a scriber for construction lines and witness mark lines to be cut to.
On **plastics** we use a wax crayon or felt-nib pen for construction lines and a scriber for lines to be cut to.

2 We always work from a **true edge** when marking out to ensure accuracy.
On **wood**, always plane and mark a face-side and face-edge on each piece of wood, and mark out only from these.
On **metal and plastics** file and mark a first true edge and a second true edge and mark out only from these.

3 Use a try-square to mark lines across the grain at 90° to the true edges.

4 Use a marking gauge (on wood and plastics) or odd-leg calipers (on metal and plastics) to mark lines parallel to the true edges.

5 Mark out as clearly as possible to avoid mistakes. Use marking blue (a type of dye) to make scriber lines show up on bright metal. Use chalk rubbed onto the surface to make scriber lines show up on black mild steel and rough surfaces. Always shade the waste accurately and clearly. Chalk lines, witness marks and saw cuts will show up on red hot metal.

Stages in marking-out and preparing the edges of metal

(A similar procedure is suitable for plastics and wood sheet material of all sizes.)

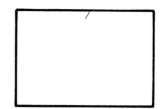

STAGE 1

File test and mark the first true edge on one long edge. Test for flatnesss with a straight edge and for squareness across the edge with an engineer's try-square. Finish by drawfiling. Mark with one straight line.

STAGE 2

File test and mark the second true edge on one short side, at right angles to the first true edge.

Test for squareness to the first true edge, flatness and squareness across the edge with an engineer's try-square. Finish by drawfiling.

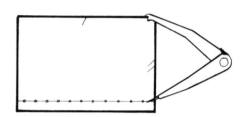

STAGE 3

Mark to width. Put the step of the odd-leg calipers against the first true edge and mark a line parallel to it. Witness mark the line. File down until half of each witness mark has gone. Test and drawfile.

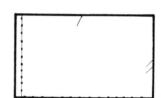

STAGE 4

Mark to length. Mark the required length with a ruler and then **either** put a try-square against the first true edge and scribe a line, **or** use odd-leg calipers against the second true edge. Witness mark, file, test and drawfile.

On thin metal, the waste would be removed with tin snips.

When using flat strip and square rod only stages 2 and 4 will be needed.

Stages in planing a piece of wood to size

For full details, see 'Planing' in chapter 16.

High accuracy marking-out, measuring and testing

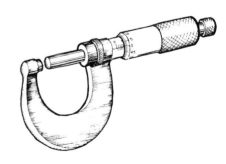

MICROMETERS

These are used to measure with great accuracy. The commonest type is the 0 to 25 mm external micrometer shown. It measures to an accuracy of 0.01 mm.

MARKING OUT ON THE SURFACE PLATE

This is a much more accurate way of marking out than those already described.

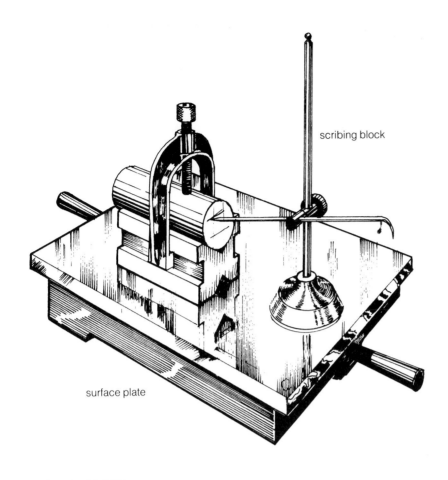

scribing block

surface plate

SURFACE PLATE

This consists of an iron casting with a very accurate flat top and a ribbed underframe to prevent distortion. The flat top provides a true surface from which measurements can be taken, parallel lines can be scribed and other flat surfaces can be tested. It is protected by a cover and light oiling when not in use.

SURFACE GAUGE

This is used to transfer measurements from the surface plate, to scribe lines parallel to the surface plate, and to test heights. The surface gauge has a fine adjustment screw and the spindle and scriber can be set to almost any angle.

A **scribing block** simply supports a scriber and has no fine adjustment (top picture).

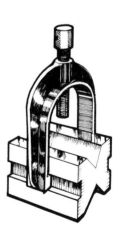

VEE BLOCKS

These are used to hold cylindrical work for marking out and while machining. They are made in sets consisting of two matched vee blocks and a clamp (see right).

ANGLE PLATE

This is a very accurately made 90° angle used to hold work at right angles to the surface plate. It is machined on the ends to enable work mounted on it to be marked both horizontally and vertically. Work with only one true face, such as a machined casting, can be mounted on an angle plate.

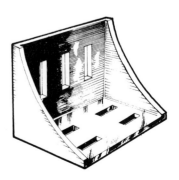

13

Classification of common hand tools
PART 2—holding tools

The chart names the common holding tools found in the school workshop and shows with which materials they are mainly used. This is followed by sketches of these tools, together with brief notes about them. Specialist tools used only for one type of work have been shown in the sections describing those processes.

Wood	Plastics	Metal
Carpenter's bench —————— ▸◂		┌ Engineer's bench
Bench vice —————————— ▸◂		┝ Engineer's vice
	◂——————	└ Vice jaw covers
Bench stop	X	X
Bench hook ————————— ▸		X
Bench holdfast ———————— ▸		X
Mitre box	X	X
G-cramp ————————————— ▸◂		
Dowelling jigs	X	X
Sash cramp ——————————— ▸◂		
X	◂——————	┌ Toolmaker's clamp
X	◂——————	┝ Hand vice
X	◂——————	└ Mole wrench
X	X	Smith's tongs
X	X	Brass tongs
X	X	Folding bars
X	X	Anvil and stand
X	X	Tinman's stakes
X	X	Silversmith's stakes

ENGINEER'S VICE

The vice is bolted to the bench top so that the back jaw is just forward of the bench edge. This allows long pieces of metal to reach down to the floor while held in the vice.

Soft metal or plastic vice jaw covers are used to protect work from the diamond-patterned gripping surfaces of the jaws when finish is more important than grip.

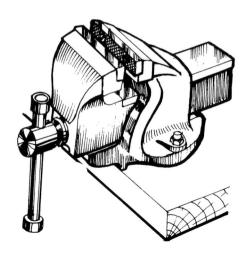

FOLDING BARS

These can be made to suit the job in hand from any rigid, straight material. The sketches show the common bought and home-made types. They are used when folding metal in order to obtain a straight, neat bend, and are usually held in the vice for small scale work.

TOOLMAKER'S CLAMP

These are used to hold parts together while marking out, shaping and drilling. The clamp is tightened with the centre screw until the jaws are parallel and grip the work lightly. A firm grip is then obtained by tightening the outer screw.

HAND VICE

This is used for holding small and especially irregularly shaped parts while drilling, rivetting, etc. It is especially useful when drilling sheetmetal.

MOLE WRENCH

The mole wrench can be firmly locked onto pieces of work to clamp them together, or to hold them while drilling, grinding or welding. It is now often used instead of the toolmaker's clamp and hand vice.

SMITH'S TONGS

There are many different shapes of tongs for picking up and holding hot metal of all sizes and shapes.

BRASS TONGS

Steel tongs must not be put into acid baths when handling beaten metalwork jobs. We therefore use brass pickling tongs, either of a closed mouth or scissor type.

WOODWORKER'S BENCH VICE

The vice is fixed to the bench so that the top of the wooden jaw facing is level with the bench top, and is used for holding work.

BENCH STOP

This is used to rest wood against while planing. The height is adjusted by unscrewing the wingnut and sliding the stop up and down.

This has been developed into a surface cramping system with adjustable dogs, and a tail vice to hold material of varying lengths and widths.

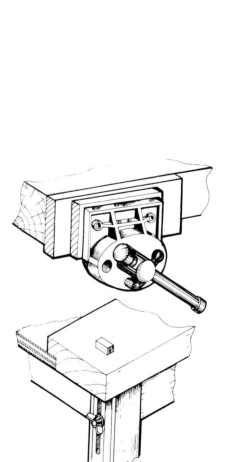

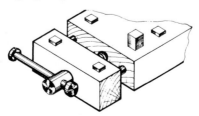

BENCH HOOK

This clips over the edge of the bench or in the vice, and is used to hold wood while sawing. The bench hook helps you to hold the work steady, prevents the wood from splitting by supporting it under the kerf and protects the bench top. Long pieces of wood should be rested across two or more bench hooks. Left- and right-handed bench hooks are needed to suit left- and right-handed users. Bench hooks are usually held in the vice.

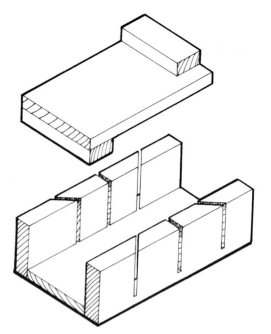

MITRE BOX

This is used to cut wood at 45° accurately. The 90° saw cut in the centre is for squaring wood accurately. Boxes can usually be made for cutting mitres at any angle, for example when making a hexagonal frame.

SASH CRAMP

This is used to hold frames, carcases and butt joints together while the glue sets and while welding large metal frames.

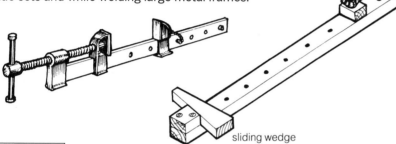

sliding wedge

G-CRAMP

This is used to hold work down onto the bench and to cramp small pieces of glued wood together. There are several different types, for example deep throat cramps to reach further in from the edge. The swivel shoe enables the cramp to grip angled pieces of wood. Common sizes go up from 50 mm to 350 mm in 50 mm steps. Protect the work with scrapwood.

BENCH HOLDFAST

This clamps work firmly down onto the bench top. The work must be protected by a piece of scrapwood.

The holdfast is particularly useful for holding down work while carving, mortising, rebating and ploughing.

A simple home-made cramp

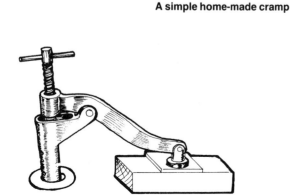

DOWELLING JIGS

These are used to ensure that the holes in the two halves of a dowelled joint line up with each other. It is possible to buy adjustable jigs, but these are often expensive and difficult to use. It is, therefore, often easier to make a simple jig from wood or metal to suit the job, and the design and manufacture of jigs is an interesting exercise in its own right. It is not advisable to attempt dowelled joints without using a jig.

Where legs and rails are of different thicknesses, make the jig to fit the thicker part and make a packing piece for use on the thinner one.

How to glue-up woodwork jobs

1 Always protect finished surfaces from metal cramps by using wooden cramping blocks.

Make any special cramping blocks you will need. For example, convex blocks are used to make sure that the middle of a long joint is pressed together and that warped wood is straightened. Cut-away blocks are used to allow pressure to be applied only in the right places, especially when cramping through dovetails and through mortise and tenon joints.

Cramping blocks must be strong enough to press the job into shape.
2 Always assemble the job without gluing, before gluing-up, to make sure that it fits together and to work out the best way of assembling and cramping it.
3 Break down the gluing of larger jobs into several easy stages.
4 Before starting, make sure that you are well organised. Lay out the parts of the job, apply glue to all parts which will touch and assemble them. If the right amount of glue has been used, a small amount will squeeze out of the joints when they are cramped up. This can be wiped off with a damp cloth while wet, or gently prised from polished surfaces with a chisel when dry.
5 Cramp up to your prepared plan and test for squareness and wind.

TESTING FOR SQUARENESS

Measure the diagonals using a long stick or rulers. If the diagonals are unequal move the cramps sideways as shown.

TESTING FOR WIND

Look along the top edges of the job or use winding strips to see that the job is flat. If the job is twisted move the cramps up and down as shown.

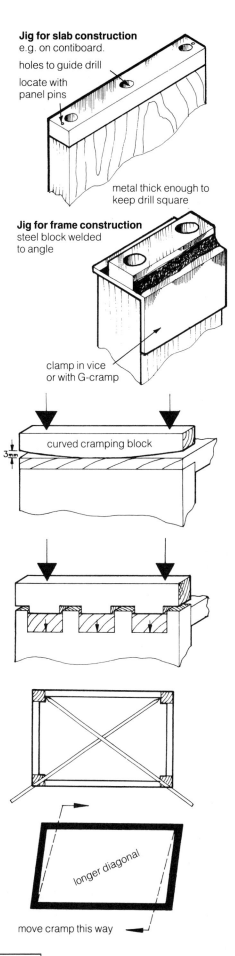

Jig for slab construction
e.g. on contiboard.

holes to guide drill

locate with
panel pins

metal thick enough to
keep drill square

Jig for frame construction
steel block welded
to angle

clamp in vice
or with G-cramp

curved cramping block

3mm

longer diagonal

move cramp this way

Methods of cramping

1 CRAMPING A FLAT FRAME

Lay the cramps on a flat surface. Make sure that they are along the centre lines of the rails, and press the job down onto the bars of the cramps. Test the diagonals for squareness and across the top edges for wind.

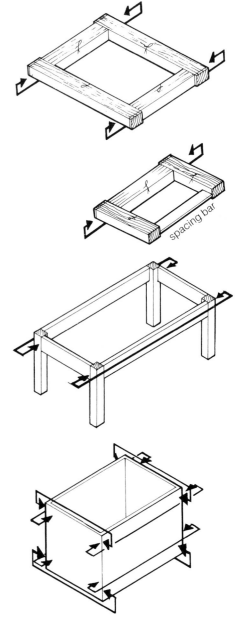

move cramp this way

2 CRAMPING A STOOL FRAME

STAGE 1

Assemble the short sides first as when cramping a flat frame. Test with a try-square for squareness and across the tops of the legs for wind. A spacing bar cut from scrapwood to exactly the length of the top rail may help to keep the legs parallel. Clean any surplus glue from the mortises, and leave the job to dry.

STAGE 2

When the short sides have set, assemble the long sides dry, and test. Glue-up as shown. Test the top frame for squareness and for wind, and take special care to test that the legs are in line and square. Use spacing bars if necessary.

spacing bar

3 CRAMPING A CARCASE

It is often necessary to cramp in two directions at once, and thought must be given to the positioning of cramps and the types of cramping blocks needed to do this. The thickness of the cramping block must be the same as the thickness of the carcase members so that the pressure is along the centre-lines of the members.

Alternatively, the cramping blocks can sometimes be placed alongside the joints as shown. Since this may cause the sides to bow inwards, a spacing bar should be used.

4 CRAMPING EDGE JOINTS

The cramps are placed alternately above and below the job to prevent bowing. Good cramping blocks are especially important to prevent bruising of the edges. Make sure that an even line of glue is squeezed out along the whole length of the joint. If necessary tap the joints flush with a hammer and wood block.

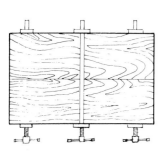

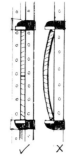

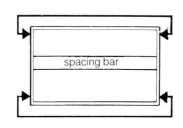

spacing bar

14 Classification of common hand tools
PART 3—driving tools

The chart names the common driving tools found in the school workshop and shows with which materials they are mainly used. This is followed by sketches of these tools together with brief notes about them. Specialist tools used only for one type of work have been shown in the sections describing those processes.

Wood	Plastics	Metal
Carpenter's mallet	◄	Tinman's mallet
X	◄	Rawhide mallet
◄	◄	Soft-faced hammer
X	X	Bossing mallet
Warrington pattern hammer	►◄	Engineer's ball-pein hammer
Claw hammer	X	X
X	X	Sledge hammer
Pin punch or nail set	X	X
Pincers	X	X
◄	◄	Pliers
Cabinet screwdriver	►◄	Engineer's screwdriver
London pattern screwdriver	X	X
◄	◄	Electrician's screwdriver
Pozidriv screwdriver	►◄	Phillips screwdriver
Ratchet screwdriver	►	►
Spiral ratchet screwdriver	X	X
Hand drill (wheel brace)	►	►
Carpenter's brace	►◄	Breast drill
Portable electric drill	►	►
X	X	Spanners
X	X	Wrenches
X	X	Rivetsnap
X	X	Rivet set or dolly
X	◄	Tap wrench
X	◄	Die holder
X	◄	Pop rivetting pliers
X	X	Tinman's hammers
X	X	Silversmith's hammers
X	X	Forging aids

Hammers

WARRINGTON PATTERN HAMMER

The Warrington or cross-pein hammer is used for light nailing and general work in cabinet-making. The cross-pein is used for starting small nails held between the fingers. The shaft fits into a shaped socket and is expanded by the wedge so that the head cannot fly off.

PIN HAMMER

This is a lightweight cross-pein hammer with a long shaft for driving small tacks, panel pins and thin nails.

USING A HAMMER

Grip the shaft near the end and watch the nail, not the hammer. After a few taps to start the nail, take larger swings from the elbow without bending the wrist. Hit the nail with the hammer head square to it.

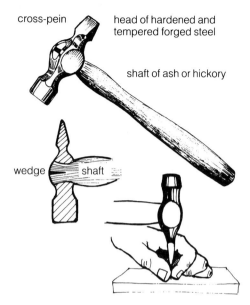

cross-pein

head of hardened and tempered forged steel

shaft of ash or hickory

wedge   shaft

scrapwood protects the job and increases leverage for long nails.

CLAW HAMMER

This is used for heavy nailing, and for removing larger nails.

BALL-PEIN HAMMER

Various sizes of ball-pein hammer are used for almost all general metalwork. Smaller sizes are used for dot and centre punching, rivetting and bending, while larger sizes are used for forging. The ball-pein is used for shaping rivets.

SLEDGE-HAMMER

This is used for heavy forging.

claw

ash, hickory, fibreglass or steel shaft

Mallets

CARPENTER'S MALLET

This is used in woodwork for striking chisels and when assembling jobs. The shaft and the mortise through the head are tapered so that the head cannot fly off. The striking faces are sloped so that they strike the chisel squarely when the mallet is swung from the elbow, while standing at a bench.

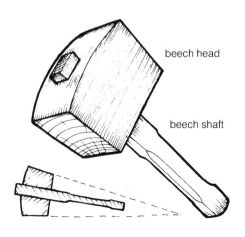

beech head

beech shaft

TINMAN'S MALLET

Wooden mallets are used for shaping sheet metal without damaging the surface. The faces can be shaped for special jobs.

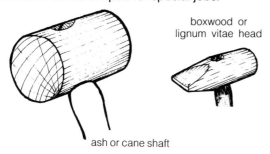

boxwood or lignum vitae head

ash or cane shaft

RAWHIDE MALLET

This is stronger, but more expensive, than a tinman's mallet.

SOFT-FACED HAMMER

A heavier blow can be struck, without damaging the material, by using a hammer having a cast-iron head, into which are fitted replaceable faces of soft materials such as rawhide, copper, nylon and rubber. This is useful for assembling large woodwork jobs, as well as for metalwork.

BOSSING MALLET

This has rounded faces of different sizes and is used for hollowing out sheet metal.

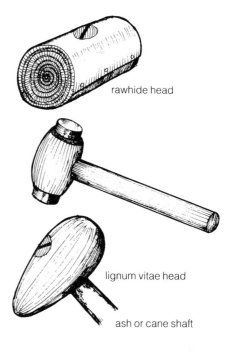

rawhide head

lignum vitae head

ash or cane shaft

Screwdrivers

There are many types, including cabinet, London pattern, engineer's, electrician's, stubby or midget, ratchet and spiral ratchet or Yankee.

It is important to keep the blades ground accurately to shape and to use the one which fits the screw exactly.

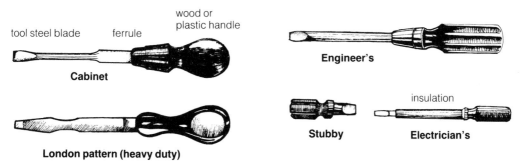

tool steel blade   ferrule

wood or plastic handle

Cabinet

Engineer's

London pattern (heavy duty)

Stubby

insulation

Electrician's

STRAIGHT BLADES

The blade should exactly fit the length and width of the slot in the screw head.

The following are common faults:

(a) A blade which is too narrow will need too much leverage to turn and will chew up the screw head.

(b) A blade which is too wide will damage the material around the screw head.

(c) A blade which is too thin may bend or break and will chew up the screw head.

(d) A blade which is too thick to touch the bottom of the slot will slip out damaging both the screw head and the surrounding material.

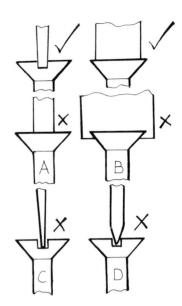

PHILLIPS AND POZIDRIV BLADES

The correct size of blade must be used as no other will fit. The sizes are identified by numbers. Most screws fit either numbers 1, 2 or 3, with number 2 being the most used size (see Screws).

Pozidriv   **Phillips**

Pincers

Pincers pull out nails which a claw hammer cannot grip, either because they are too small or have no head. The small thin claw on one handle of the pincers will fit under the heads of small nails and lever them out far enough for the pincers to grip. The ball on the other allows you to exert a lot of pressure comfortably. The rounded jaws roll to give leverage when pulled.

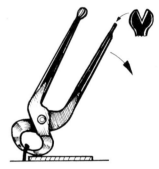

Pin punch or nail set

There are several sizes of pin punch to suit different sizes of nail. They are used to drive headless nails and panel pins below the surface, so that the hole can be hidden by filling, and so that the nails will not scratch anything. They are made from hardened and tempered tool steel, and have a hollow tip to fit over the nail head and prevent slipping.

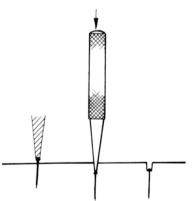

Drilling machines

HAND DRILL OR WHEEL BRACE

The hand drill is used to rotate twist drills up to 8mm diameter. The side handle can be unscrewed to allow the drill to work close against obstructions.

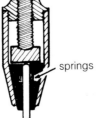

chuck casing   A   B   springs

The chuck has three self-centring jaws to grip the round shanks of twist drills. When the chuck casing is unscrewed the jaws spring back and allow the shank of the drill to enter (A). When the chuck casing is screwed back up, the jaws close and grip the drill (B).

BREAST DRILL

This is a large drilling machine which takes drills up to 13mm diameter and usually has two speeds. It is used against the chest to provide extra pressure.

PORTABLE ELECTRIC DRILLS

These are usually chosen for their chuck size and their number of speeds. Common chuck sizes are 6, 8 and 13mm maximum drill shank diameter, and drills usually have one or two speed drives. The safest portable tools are the **double-insulated** type.

CARPENTER'S RATCHET BRACE

Boring with a brace is best done horizontally because it is easier to apply pressure and to keep square. A brace holds only square-shank bits. The ratchet allows the brace to be used in corners where a full turn is not possible.

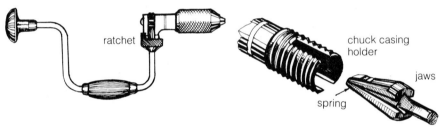

The chuck has two self-centring jaws with V-shaped slots into which the corners of the square tang of the bit fit. The spring end of the jaws fits into the slot in the chuck casing holder to give a positive drive from brace to bit. When the casing is screwed on, the taper inside it closes the jaws. The bit cannot slip round inside the chuck as can a twist drill in a three jaw chuck.

Pliers

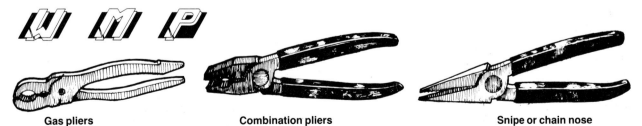

Gas pliers   **Combination pliers**   **Snipe or chain nose**

These are mainly used to grip small items. Combination pliers are also able to cut wire. There are many shapes and sizes, and only some of the most used are shown here.

Spanners

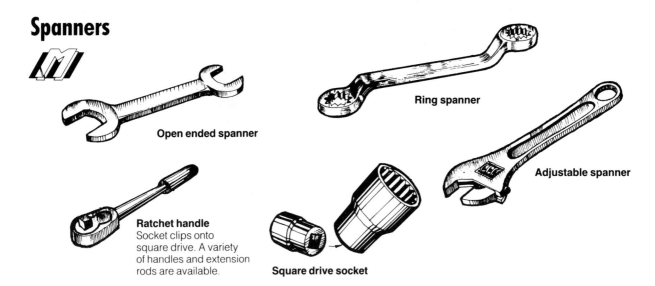

Open ended spanner

Ring spanner

Adjustable spanner

Ratchet handle
Socket clips onto
square drive. A variety
of handles and extension
rods are available.

Square drive socket

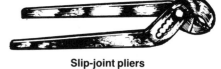

These are used to tighten or loosen nuts and bolts.

Wrenches

These are used to grip and turn pipes and round bars. Increased pressure
on the handles increases the grip of the jaws. Do not use them on nuts
and bolts.

**Stillson pattern
pipe wrench**

Slip-joint pliers

15 Classification of common hand tools
PART 4—cutting tools

The chart names the common hand-held cutting tools usually found in the school workshop and shows which materials each is used to cut. Where tools with different names fulfil the same function on different materials, they are shown on the same line. This is followed by sketches of these tools together with brief notes about them. Specialist tools used for only one type of work have been shown in the sections describing these processes.

		Wood	Plastics	Metal
Saws	Handsaws	— rip	X	X
		— crosscut	X	X
		— panel	X	X
	Backsaws	— tenon ──────	▸◂	────── Hacksaw
		— dovetail ───	▸◂	── Junior hacksaw
	For curves	— bow	X	X
		◂────────	◂──	── Abrafile saw
		— coping ─────	▸◂	── Piercing
		— pad ───────	▸◂	── Pad
Snips		X	◂──────	── Straight snips
		X	◂──────	── Curved snips
		X	◂──────	── Universal snips
		X	◂──────	── Jeweller's snips
		X	Scissors	X
		X	X	Bench shearing machine
		X	◂──────	── Nibblers
		X	X	Wire cutters
Knives etc.		◂────────	── Trimming knife	X
		X	Laminate and acrylic cutters	X
		X	Hot-wire machine	X
Files	Rasps ──────────		▸◂	── Engineer's files
		X	◂──	── Needle files
	General purpose files e.g. surform tools ──		▸◂	── General purpose files e.g. milled tooth files
Scrapers	Hand and cabinet scrapers		Scrapers for acrylics	Engineer's scrapers
Planes	Bench	— smoothing ──	──▸	X
		— jack ──────	──▸	X
		— try	X	X

continued overleaf

		Wood	Plastics	Metal
Planes	Special — plough		X	X
	— combination		X	X
	— rebate		X	X
	— router		X	X
	— block	→————→		X
	— shoulder		X	X
	— bull-nose		X	X
	— spokeshaves		X	X
Chisels	Firmer		X	Cold chisels
	Bevel-edge firmer		X	Sets and hardie
	Mortise		X	X
	Gouges-in-cannel		X	X
	-out-cannel		X	X
Drills	Twist drills	←————←————— Twist drills		
	Centre bit		X	X
	Jennings pattern auger bit		X	X
	Forstner pattern bit ————→			X
	Rose countersink bit ————→→			Rose countersink
	Flat bit		X	X
	Expansive bit		←————— Tank and washer cutter	
	Dowel sharpener		X	X
	Bradawl		X	X
	X		←————— Combination centre drill	
	Hole saw ————————→		————————→	
Taps and dies	X		←————— Taps	
	X		←————— Circular split dies	
Portable electric tools	Jigsaw ————————→		————————→	
	Circular saw ————————→		————————→	
	Belt sander ————————→		X	
	Orbital sander ————————→		X	
	Disc sander ————————→		————————→	
	Router ————————→		X	

Note: for fuller details of how to use the cutting tools shown in this chapter refer to chapter 16, Wasting-hand processes.

Saws

Saws are used for making straight and curved cuts in wood, metal and plastics.

SAWS FOR STRAIGHT CUTS
Handsaws are for straight cuts in large pieces of wood.

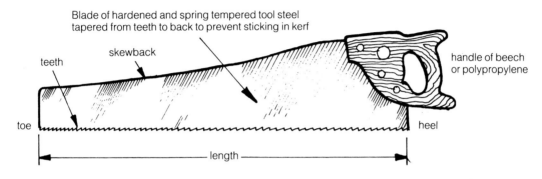

Blade of hardened and spring tempered tool steel tapered from teeth to back to prevent sticking in kerf

skewback

teeth

handle of beech or polypropylene

toe

heel

length

Name	Approx. length of blade	Approx. points per 25 mm	Uses
Rip-saw	700 mm	5	Sawing along the grain of large pieces of wood.
Cross-cut saw	600 mm	7	Sawing across the grain of large pieces of wood. Will also cut along the grain but not as quickly as a rip-saw.
Panel saw	500 mm	10	A fine toothed crosscut for sawing plywood, thin wood and large joints.

Backsaws are for accurate straight cuts in small pieces of wood. The back of the saw limits the depth of cut.

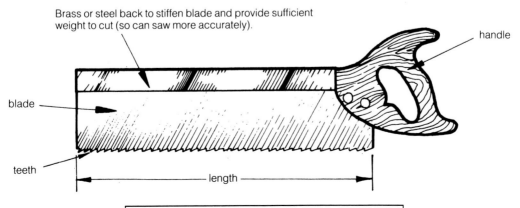

Brass or steel back to stiffen blade and provide sufficient weight to cut (so can saw more accurately).

handle

blade

teeth

length

Name	Approx. length of blade	Approx. points per 25 mm	Uses
Tenon saw	250, 300 and 350 mm	14	Sawing small pieces of wood and most joints. The most used backsaw.
Dovetail saw	200 mm	20	For the smallest and most accurate work, especially sawing small dovetail joints.

SAWS FOR CURVES
Bow saw

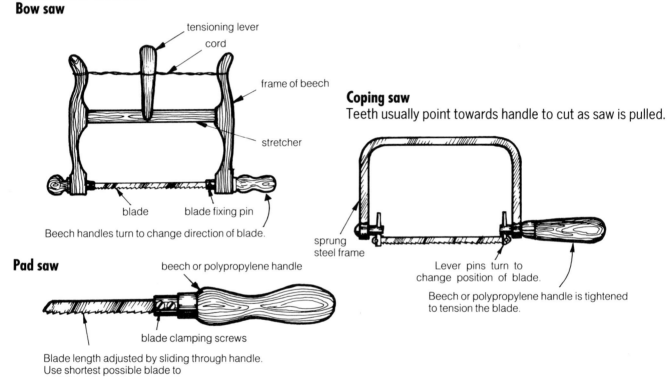

tensioning lever
cord
frame of beech
stretcher
blade   blade fixing pin
Beech handles turn to change direction of blade.

Coping saw
Teeth usually point towards handle to cut as saw is pulled.

sprung steel frame
Lever pins turn to change position of blade.
Beech or polypropylene handle is tightened to tension the blade.

Pad saw
beech or polypropylene handle
blade clamping screws
Blade length adjusted by sliding through handle.
Use shortest possible blade to avoid breakage.

Name	Approx. length of blade	Approx. points per 25 mm	Uses
Bow saw	300 mm	10	Sawing curves in thick wood.
Coping saw	150 mm	15	Sawing curves in thin wood and removing waste from joints.
Pad saw	150 mm	10	For straight and curved cuts in the middle of large sheets where other saws cannot reach.

When making internal cuts you first drill a hole to put the saw blade through.

SAWS FOR STRAIGHT CUTS

Hacksaws are for straight cuts in metal. The blade is held in tension in the frame **with the teeth facing forward**.

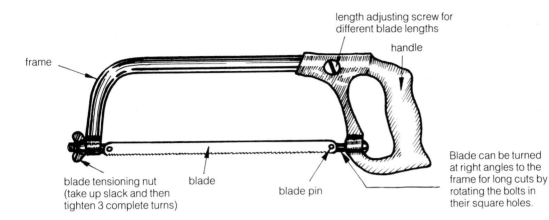

length adjusting screw for different blade lengths

handle

frame

blade tensioning nut (take up slack and then tighten 3 complete turns)

blade

blade pin

Blade can be turned at right angles to the frame for long cuts by rotating the bolts in their square holes.

The **junior hacksaw** is for straight cuts on small, light work. The blade is held in tension by the sprung steel frame.

Blade length: 150 mm   Number of teeth: 32 per 25 mm

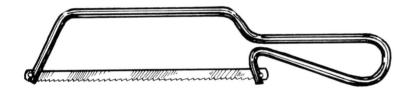

The **general purpose saw** is for sawing most materials including wood, non-ferrous metals and plastics.

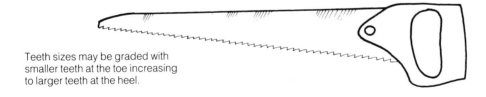

Teeth sizes may be graded with smaller teeth at the toe increasing to larger teeth at the heel.

Sheet saws are for sawing most materials including wood, sheet metal and plastics.

Blade lengths — 300 mm hacksaw blade
— 400 mm blades with six and ten teeth per 25 mm

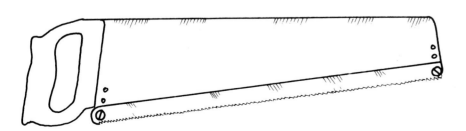

SAWS FOR CURVES

Name	Approx. length of blade	No. of teeth per 25 mm	Uses
Abrafile saw	225 mm	Coarse, medium and fine grades.	For cutting curves in sheet metal, ceramics, plastics and wood.
Piercing saw	100 mm	A range of very fine grades.	For cutting intricate curves in thin or soft metal and plastics.
Pad saw	Uses broken hacksaw blades.	32	For straight and curved cuts where other saws cannot reach.

Abrafile saw

Insert file into links with coloured end towards frame handle.

Links fit onto hacksaw blade pins.

Piercing saw

Teeth point towards handle to cut as saw is pulled. This keeps the blade taut.

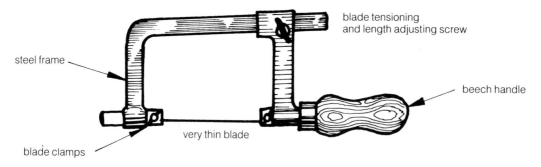

blade tensioning and length adjusting screw

steel frame

beech handle

very thin blade

blade clamps

Pad saw

Teeth point towards handle. Blade would bend if it cut when pushed.

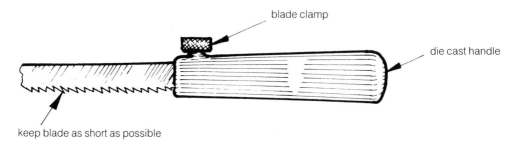

blade clamp

die cast handle

keep blade as short as possible

SAWS FOR STRAIGHT CUTS
- Back saws (tenon and dovetail).
- Hacksaws with 24 and 32 teeth per 25 mm blades.
- Junior hacksaws.
- General purpose saw.
- Sheet saws.

SAWS FOR CURVES
- Coping saw.
- Abrafile saw.
- Piercing saw (for intricate work).
- Pad saw with 32 teeth per 25 mm hacksaw blade.

Snips or shears

These are for cutting thin sheets of metal and soft plastics.

Name	Common sizes	Uses
Straight snips	150 to 350 mm long	For straight cuts and outside curves.
Curved snips	150 to 350 mm long	For inside curves only.
Universal snips	275 to 350 mm long	For straight and curved cuts in thicker material.
Jeweller's snips (straight and curved)	175 mm long	For small intricate work.

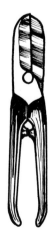

Straight and curved snips

Jeweller's snips

Universal snips

HAND-LEVER BENCH SHEARING MACHINE

This is used for cutting metal sheet, strip and rod. It consists of a large pair of shears on which a system of levers greatly increases the force which can be applied.

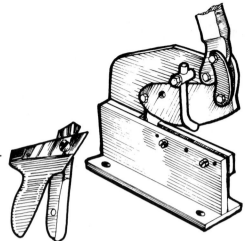

NIBBLERS

These are used for making straight or curved cuts in thin sheets without distorting the material being cut. Nibblers remove a thin strip of material. The operator's hands are kept clear of the cut and you can start a cut from inside the sheet, by first drilling a hole. For example:

Goscut. This has blades for cutting plastic laminates, hardboard, asbestos, aluminium, copper, thin mild steel, sheet, etc.
Monadex is for thin sheet metals.

WIRE-CUTTERS

Side-cutting, diagonal-cutting and end-cutting nippers are used for cutting wire. Snips must not be used to cut wire because the cutting edges will be damaged.

HOT WIRE CUTTER

This is used for cutting expanded polystyrene. It consists of either a heated wire held in a fixed framework for making straight, angled and curved cuts through blocks resting on a table, or a hand-held sculpting tool which melts its way through the material.

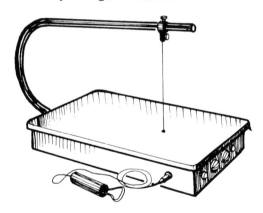

Knives

LAMINATE AND PLASTICS CUTTING TOOL

This is used for cutting plastic sheet up to 6 mm thick and plastic laminates.

First, score a line along the surface of the sheet (as in glass cutting). Then support the work with the line along the edge of the bench, and press on both sides of the line until the sheet breaks along the line.

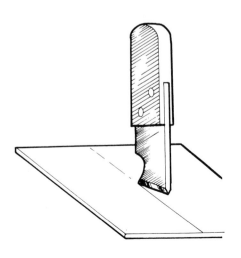

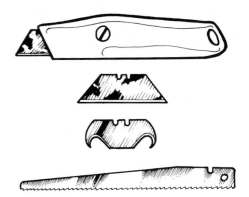

TRIMMING KNIFE

This is used for cutting thin sections of wood (e.g. when veneering and modelling), soft plastics, card, paper, floor coverings, etc., and for scoring plastic laminates.

It is available with standard, heavy duty, hooked, laminate scoring, and wood and metal cutting padsaw blades.

Files

Files are used for shaping and smoothing, mainly metal and hard plastics, but also wood.

Safety. Never use an engineer's file without a handle. The tang could stab your hand.

COMMON SHAPES

The thick lines in these diagrams show edges with teeth.

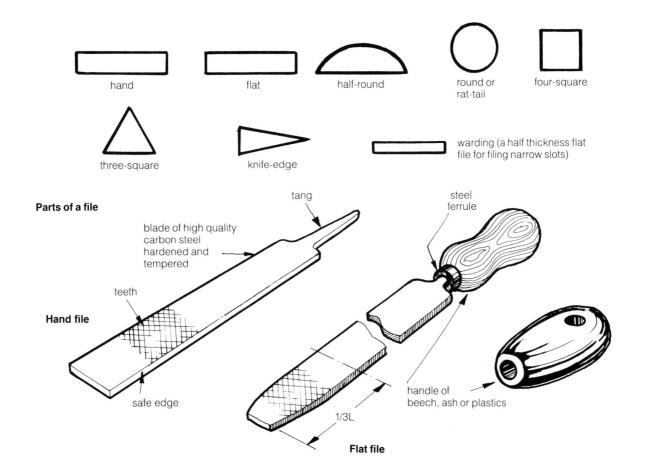

hand

flat

half-round

round or rat-tail

four-square

three-square

knife-edge

warding (a half thickness flat file for filing narrow slots)

Parts of a file

tang

blade of high quality carbon steel hardened and tempered

teeth

Hand file

safe edge

steel ferrule

1/3L

handle of beech, ash or plastics

Flat file

HAND FILE

The **hand file** has parallel sides and one safe edge (without teeth) for filing into corners where the vertical edges must not be touched. The **flat file** has the end of the blade tapered for one third of its length and teeth on both edges like most files, so that it can be used to enlarge small openings.

NEEDLE FILES

These are small precision files with round handles and fine cuts for intricate work. They have a length of 120 to 180 mm and are made in a wide variety of shapes. They must be used carefully because they are easily broken.

teeth   knurled handle

RASPS

These are for rough shaping of wood and other soft materials. The common sizes are 200 and 250 mm long and the common shape is half-round.

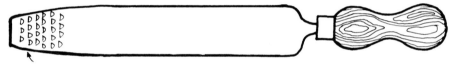

rows of individual teeth

GENERAL PURPOSE FILES

There are several types of general purpose file which will file almost any material including wood, metals and plastics. They are particularly useful for filing soft materials without clogging, e.g. milled-tooth files and surform tools.

1 MILLED-TOOTH FILES

These have fast-cutting teeth which do not clog easily. Common shapes are hand and half-round; common lengths are 300 and 350 mm; common grades are standard (nine teeth per 25 mm), fine (13) and extra fine (18).

Curved-tooth type (e.g. dreadnought files). The curve keeps more teeth in contact with the material when filing with large teeth.

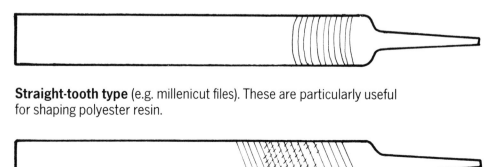

Straight-tooth type (e.g. millenicut files). These are particularly useful for shaping polyester resin.

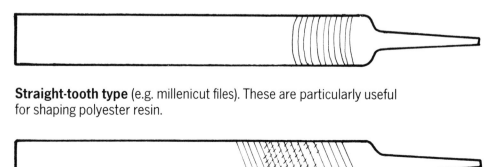

The Aven trimmatool is milled tooth. The blade has one curved-tooth side and one straight-tooth side, and can be adjusted to concave, straight or convex positions. The handle can be adjusted to file or plane positions.

2 SURFORM TOOLS

These have individual teeth, with each tooth having a hole through the blade to help clear the filings and reduce clogging. Blades are replaceable when blunt. Available with file or plane type handles.

Common shapes are flat, convex, curved and round; common lengths are 140 and 250 mm.

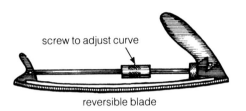
screw to adjust curve

reversible blade

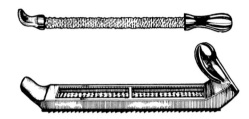

Scrapers

These are used for final smoothing of hardwood, metal and acrylic plastics.

SCRAPERS FOR WOOD

HAND SCRAPERS

These consist of a piece of hardened and tempered tool steel with the long corners burnished over to form cutting edges, which remove very fine shavings. They are used to obtain a smoother finish on hardwoods than is possible with a finely set smoothing plane, especially on cross-grained timber where a plane tears up the grain in both directions.

Rectangular scrapers are used for flat surfaces (common size is 125 mm × 60 mm) and **curved scrapers** for shaped work.

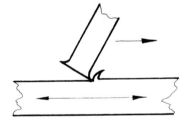

CABINET SCRAPER

This consists of a blade similar to a hand scraper held in a spokeshave-like body. It is easier and less tiring to use than a hand scraper.

SCRAPERS FOR ACRYLIC PLASTICS

A hand scraper as used for wood, or an old hacksaw blade with one edge ground, can be used to obtain a fine finish ready for polishing, after the acrylic has been filed and rubbed down with wet and dry paper.

SCRAPERS FOR METAL

These are used to remove very small amounts of metal in order to obtain very accurate flat and curved surfaces. Hand scraping has been largely replaced by surface grinding.

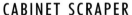

Planes

These are used for shaping and smoothing wood and acrylic plastics.

BENCH PLANES

Name	Approx. length	Uses
Smoothing plane	250 mm	For cleaning up work to remove all previous tool marks and leave the surface clean and smooth. For planing end grain. Because it is small and light, this plane is popular for all kinds of general planing jobs, but its short sole will not produce a flat surface.
Jack plane	350 mm	For planing wood to size. The general purpose plane. Its greater length produces a flatter surface.
Foreplane Jointer plane	450 mm 600 mm	For trueing-up large surfaces and long edges. The sole is longer for accurate long work.

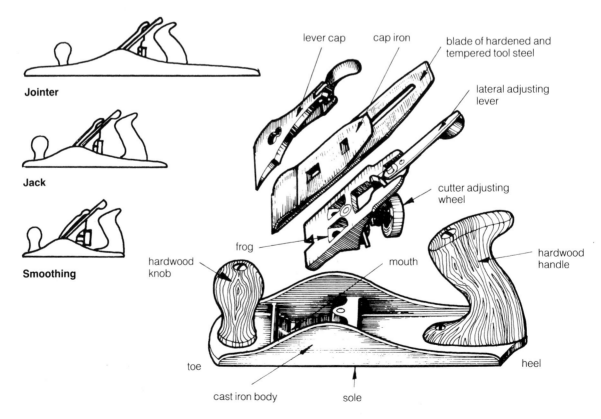

Jointer

Jack

Smoothing

lever cap

cap iron

blade of hardened and tempered tool steel

lateral adjusting lever

cutter adjusting wheel

frog

hardwood knob

mouth

hardwood handle

toe

heel

cast iron body

sole

Main parts of smoothing plane

PLOUGH PLANE

This is used to cut grooves and rebates.

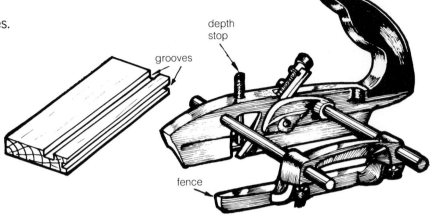

COMBINATION PLANE

This is similar to the plough plane, but has a wider range of cutters including beading cutters for curved shapes, and cutters for tongue and grooved joints.

REBATE OR FILLISTER PLANE

This is used to cut rebates. With the blade in the forward bed, stopped rebates can be cut.

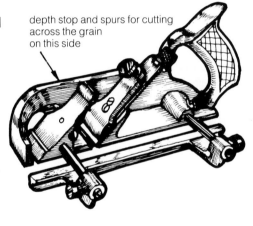

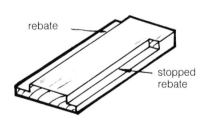

ROUTER PLANE

This is used to level the bottoms of housings, halvings or other depressions parallel to the surface of the work. Remove most of the waste by sawing and chiselling first.

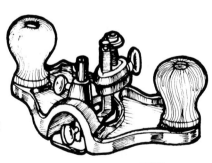

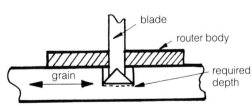

BLOCK PLANE

This is used for small work including planing end grain, trimming mitres and planing chamfers. It is a low-angle plane which is small enough to be used in one hand and has no cap iron.

SHOULDER PLANE

This is used for cleaning-up rebates, halvings and the shoulders of joints. It is a low-angle plane and the blade is the full width of the sole to cut into corners. It has no cap iron.

BULLNOSE PLANE

This is used to plane close up to an obstruction such as a stopped rebate. It is a shoulder plane with a very short nose which is removable to get right up to an obstruction. It has no cap iron.

SPOKESHAVES

These are used to smooth curves. There are two types

- flat faced spokeshave for outside (convex) curves;
- round faced spokeshave for inside (concave) curves.

They are sharpened and set in the same way as planes and special care should be taken to work always with the grain.

Chisels

CHISELS FOR WOOD

These are for cutting and shaping wood where planes cannot be used, and especially for cutting joints.

COMMON TYPES OF WOOD CHISEL

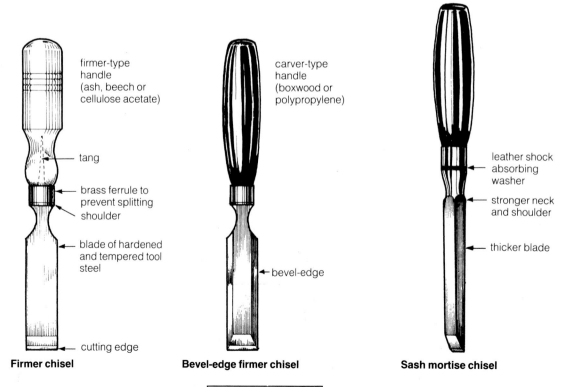

firmer-type handle (ash, beech or cellulose acetate)

tang

brass ferrule to prevent splitting shoulder

blade of hardened and tempered tool steel

cutting edge

Firmer chisel

carver-type handle (boxwood or polypropylene)

bevel-edge

Bevel-edge firmer chisel

leather shock absorbing washer

stronger neck and shoulder

thicker blade

Sash mortise chisel

Name	Common sizes	Uses
Firmer chisel	3 to 50 mm	General purpose chisel. Strong enough for cutting with hand pressure (called **paring**) or with light mallet blows.
Bevel-edge firmer chisel	3 to 50 mm	Similar to the square-edge firmer chisel except that the blade corners are bevelled for cutting into acute corners such as in dovetails. The blade is less strong than the square-edge blade and it must be used carefully.
Sash mortise chisel	6 to 13 mm	For heavy duty work such as cutting mortises. Made to withstand heavy mallet blows and the levering-out of waste. The thick blade also prevents twisting in the mortise.

GOUGES

Gouges-in-cannel are also called scribing or paring gouges. They are ground on the inside and are used for vertical paring of concave curves, cutting mouldings, channelling and other curved paring work.

Gouges-out-cannel are also called firmer gouges. They are ground on the outside and are used for scoooping-out, e.g. cutting out finger grips and carving the inside of bowls.

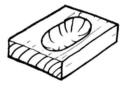

CHISELS FOR METAL

Cold chisels are used to cut, shear, and chip cold metal.

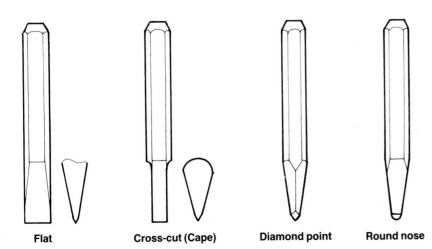

Flat   **Cross-cut (Cape)**   **Diamond point**   **Round nose**

Name	Common blade widths	Uses
Flat	6 to 25mm	General-purpose chisel for cutting sheet metal, cleaning castings and trimming metal to size.
Cross-cut	3 to 10mm	For cutting keyways and grooves.
Diamond point	3 to 10mm	Square-end with a cutting edge at one corner for cleaning out sharp corners.
Round nose	6 to 10mm	For cutting rounded grooves and cleaning out rounded corners.

Drills

These are used for cutting circular holes in most materials, including wood, metal and plastics.

TWIST DRILLS

Straight shank drills fit into the chucks of hand and electric drilling machines. Common sizes are 1mm to 13mm × 0.5mm steps, and 1mm to 10mm × 0.1mm steps.

Morse-taper shank drills fit directly into electric drilling machine spindles and lathe tailstock barrels. Common sizes are 10 to 20mm × 0.5mm steps, and 21 to 30mm × 1.0mm steps.

Twist drills are used for drilling wood, metal and plastics, and are the most used type of drill for hand and machine drilling. Made of carbon steel or high speed steel, hardened and tempered, the smaller sizes have straight shanks to fit into drill chucks, while larger sizes have a morse-taper shank to fit directly into drilling machine spindles and lathe tailstocks. They are usually used in wood only for sizes up to 8mm diameter, because the larger sizes leave a ragged hole. The flutes are too fast for adequate chip ejection, making frequent clearing necessary. Masonry drills are twist drills with hard cutting lips brazed onto the nose.

ROSE COUNTERSINKS

These are for countersinking holes in wood, metal and plastics for screw and rivet heads.

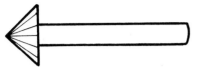

Light-duty pattern for hand drills

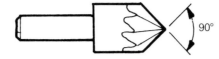

Heavy-duty machine countersink

COMBINATION CENTRE DRILL

This is used for starting holes on the lathe where centre punching is not possible and for drilling holes into which lathe centres will fit. The pilot drill makes a small hole to prevent the work resting on the point of the centre, because the friction caused would burn the point off.

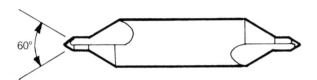

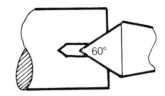

CUTTING LARGE HOLES IN METAL AND PLASTICS

TANK AND WASHER CUTTER

This is used in a brace and will cut holes of any diameter from 25 mm to 125 mm in metal, rubber and plastics. The pilot drill makes a small hole in the centre while the blade scrapes a circular groove until the waste is removed in the shape of a washer.

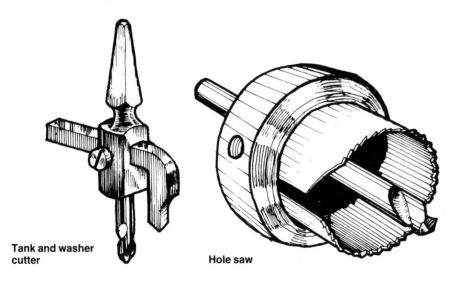

Tank and washer cutter

Hole saw

HOLE SAW

This is used in an electric drill and will cut holes from 19 mm to 75 mm diameter. It works in a similar way to the tank cutter and removes a washer. The hole saw can have interchangeable cutters which fit into one arbor (shown here), or separate cutters each with its own arbor and pilot drill.

COMMON TYPES OF WOODBORING BIT

Bits have a square tang to fit into a brace. (See Driving tools.)

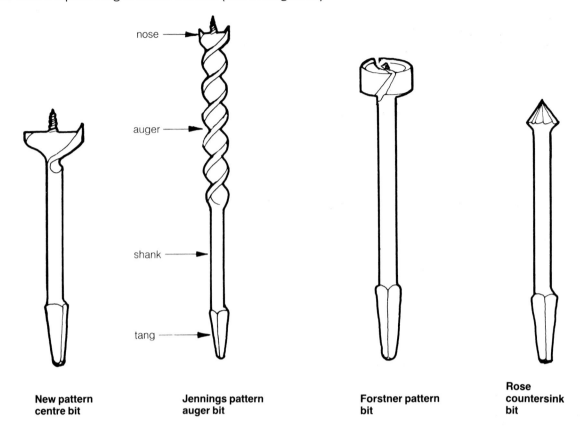

nose

auger

shank

tang

**New pattern
centre bit**

**Jennings pattern
auger bit**

**Forstner pattern
bit**

**Rose
countersink
bit**

Name	Approx. sizes	Uses
New pattern centre bit	6mm to 55mm	For boring shallow holes in wood. Not suitable for deep holes because: (a) it has no auger to carry away waste; and (b) it tends to wander off centre because it has no parallel sides to guide it in the hole.
Jennings pattern auger bit	6mm to 40mm	For boring deep holes in wood. It is one of several types of auger bit which work in the same say as a centre bit, but have a cylindrical auger to remove the waste and guide the bit in the hole.
Forstner pattern	10mm to 30mm	This bit is guided by its rim and not by a centre point. It will therefore bore clean, accurate, flat bottomed holes and overlapping holes in wood. It will also drill acrylic.
Rose countersink bit		Countersinking for screw heads in wood, plastics and non-ferrous metals.

EXPANSIVE BITS

These are used for drilling large-diameter shallow holes in softwood. Cutters are available to give adjustment from 12 mm to 150 mm diameter.

DOWEL SHARPENERS

These are used for chamfering the ends of dowels to make assembling dowel joints easier.

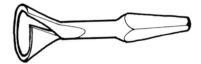

FLAT BITS

These are used in electric drills for fast, accurate drilling in hard and soft woods. They are used at the highest available speed and with only moderate pressure. Locate the point on the wood before switching on and wait for the drill to stop before withdrawing it from the hole. The usual sizes are 6 mm to 40 mm.

BRADAWL

This is used for making small holes in wood to start screws and nails. To use it press the blade into the wood with the cutting edge **across** the grain so that it cuts the fibres and does not split them. Then rotate it from side to side while continuing to push it into the wood until the hole is the required depth.

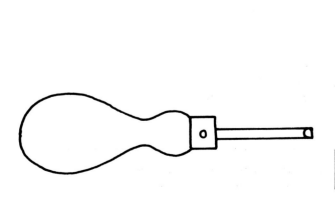

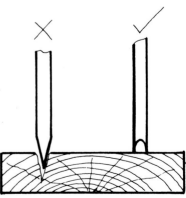

Taps and dies

These are for cutting threads in metals and acrylic plastics.

TAPS

These are for cutting internal threads. They are held in a tap wrench and are made from hardened and tempered carbon or high speed steel.

TAPER TAP

This is used to start the thread in the tapping size hole. It tapers from no thread to full thread over two-thirds of the thread length, with a short length of full thread at the top, and can be used to completely thread holes through thin material.

SECOND TAP

This is used to deepen threads started by the taper tap. It tapers for the first few threads only and can be used to finish threading holes drilled right through thicker material.

PLUG TAP

This is used to cut full threads to the bottom of blind holes and to thread right through thick material. It has no taper, but only a short chamfer to locate it in the hole.

The second tap is often left out of sets of taps and dies.

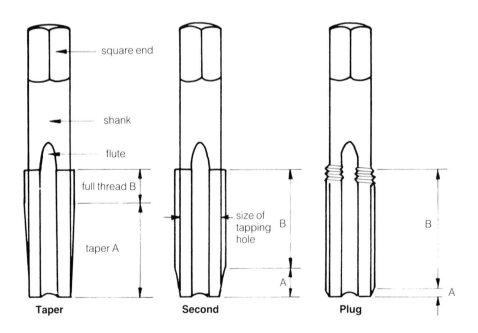

Taper   Second   Plug

TAP WRENCH

The jaws of the wrench grip the corners of the square on the tap. The correct size wrench must be used to avoid damage to the jaws.

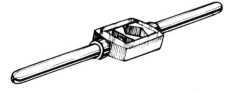

CIRCULAR SPLIT DIES

These are for cutting external threads. They are held in a die stock and are made from hardened and tempered carbon or high speed steel. The first few threads are tapered on the side of the die which has the size stamped on, to assist in starting to cut the thread. The split enables the die to be opened slightly when taking the first cut, and to be closed for a second cut if the thread is too tight when screwed into the internal thread.

DIE HOLDER OR STOCK

The circular split die fits into the die stock with the tapered side of the thread (shown by the writing on the die) on the open side is the stock, and the split in line with the centre screw. The centre screw is tightened to open the die to its full size and the side screws hold the die in the stock. To reduce the size of the die, slacken the centre screw and tighten the side screws.

This chapter explains how the most important cutting tools shown in chapter 15 work, and gives advice on their correct use. Each section should therefore be used together with the parallel section in chapter 15.

Sawing

PRINCIPLES OF SAWING

just enough pressure to make the saw cut

6 points per 25 mm

backwards and forwards movement (most saws cut on the forward stroke)

Notes.

1 It is important to select the correct shape and number of teeth per 25 mm for the type and section of material to be sawn.

2 Points per 25 mm are calculated by inclusive reckoning, so that on the example above there are six points per 25 mm although only five complete teeth are within the limit lines.

3 **Set**. Alternate teeth are bent to left and right to make the cutting edge slightly wider than the blade thickness. This prevents the saw blade from jamming in the cut or **kerf.**

SAWING WOOD

TOOTH SHAPES
Rip-saw teeth are for cutting along the grain.

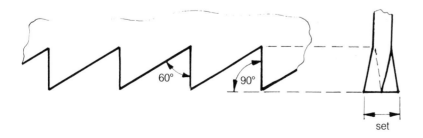

60°

90°

set

Cross-cut saw teeth are for cutting across the grain.

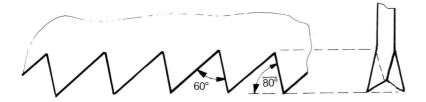

Rip-saw teeth are used only on the rip-saw, and have flat chisel-like cutting edges which remove small shavings. Rip-saw teeth cannot be used for cutting across the grain because they will tear the grain fibres instead of cutting them cleanly.

Cross-cut teeth are used on cross-cut, panel and back saws, and have knife-like cutting edges with needle points which cut the fibres at the sides of the kerf before crumbling the wood in the middle to sawdust. Cross-cut teeth will also cut along the grain, but more slowly than rip-saw teeth.

SAWING METAL

CHOICE OF CORRECT HACKSAW BLADE
You need to know the following:

1 **Length of blade**. The common sizes are 250 mm and 300 mm.

2 **Type of blade**. This can be made from either high-speed steel or low tungsten steel. High-speed steel blades are **all-hard** (hardened all over); low tungsten steel blades can be **all-hard** or **flexible** (hardened on the teeth only). Flexible blades do not break as easily as all-hard blades, but all-hard blades saw more accurately.

3 **Number of teeth**. At least three teeth must always touch the metal when sawing or teeth will be broken off.

COMMON NUMBERS
■ 32 teeth per 25 mm — for metal less than 3 mm thick.
■ 24 teeth per 25 mm — for metal 3–6 mm thick.
■ 18 teeth per 25 mm — for metal more than 6 mm thick. (This is the best blade for general purposes.)

Soft materials require blades with larger teeth to prevent clogging.

Notes.

1 The teeth point forward and cut on the forward stroke.
2 The blade is held in tension in the frame.
3 The depth of cut is limited by the distance between the blade and the frame — usually about 100 mm.

With the blade turned through 90°, long cuts can be made provided that they are within the frame depth of the edge of the metal.

SET

To make the cutting edge slightly wider than the blade thickness, in order to prevent jamming in the kerf: **either** the teeth are set alternately to left and right with one straight tooth between each bent tooth; **or** the teeth are set in a wavy line with several teeth bent one way and then several the other.

A new blade will not fit into a kerf started by an old blade which has lost some of its set. If a blade breaks, start a new cut from the other side with the new blade.

SAWING PLASTICS

Any fine-toothed saw can be used to saw soft or hard plastics provided that the work is well supported close to the kerf, and the minimum amount of pressure is applied. Take care not to let the saw slip and scratch the surface. For plastics, the teeth should be sharpened with the leading edges sloping farther backwards than for cutting wood.

HOW TO SAW

1 **Arrange** the work so that you always saw vertically.
2 **Support** the work firmly and as close as possible to the kerf.
3 **Stand** correctly and grip the saw correctly.

For straight cuts at the bench:

The **grip** — thumb and first finger of the right hand guide the saw (left hand for left-handed). The other three fingers grip the handle.
The **stance** — left foot in line with the saw, right foot slightly behind and apart to give a firm comfortable position.

The right arm should be in line with the saw (reverse for left-handed).

For curved cuts at the bench:

The **grip** — both hands grip the handle.
The **stance** — feet apart. Stand squarely in front of the job.
4 **When starting**, use the thumb to guide the blade as it is drawn back to start a small cut. Start cutting at a low angle on a corner with as many teeth as possible in contact (at least three).
5 **When sawing**, use the full length of the blade. Use long steady strokes (one per second) and release the pressure on the return stroke. The spare hand is used to grip the other end of the hacksaw frame (and occasionally the other end of the tenon saw back when sawing joints).
6 **When finishing a cut**, support any waste material to prevent it from breaking off before it is cut cleanly through.
7 **Sawing to the line.** Where a sawn finish is required, saw on the waste side of the line and leave the line just showing with no waste between the line and the kerf.

Where a planed or filed finish is required, leave 2 mm waste between the line and the kerf.

If you saw, plane or file off the line, you have made the piece too small. Once the line has gone you cannot judge how much smaller the piece is than was originally intended.

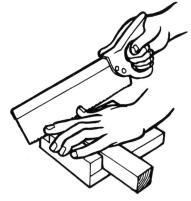

bench hook
gripped
in vice

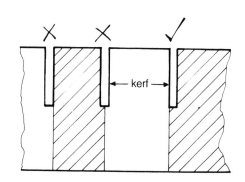

Planing

PRINCIPLES OF PLANING WOOD

The blade is a wedge which is driven into the wood. If the wedge angle is too great it will not cut, but if it is too small it will break. The wedge angle must therefore be a compromise between strength and sharpness.

The sole pressing on the wood prevents the blade from digging in too far and helps to prevent the wood from splitting.

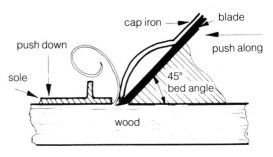

SHARPENING AND SETTING PLANES

GRINDING ANGLE

A plane blade is ground on one side only to an angle of 25°.

SHARPENING ANGLE

Because the tip of the grinding angle is weak and rough, it is honed down to an angle of 30° on an oilstone to give a smooth, strong cutting edge.

Sharpening leaves a small burr on the back of the blade which must be removed by rubbing the back flat on an oilstone. When the sharpening angle becomes too wide through repeated sharpening, or if the cutting edge is badly damaged, the blade must be reground.

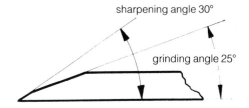

CUTTER SHAPES

The cutting edge of the **jack plane** is **slightly curved**, making the removal of waste wood a quicker and easier task, but leaving a slightly rippled surface.

Jointer and smoothing plane blades are straight across, with the corners rounded to prevent them scoring the work. They leave a flat surface.

Special planes have straight cutters with square corners, except for shaped moulding cutters.

CUTTER PITCH

This is the angle the blade makes with the sole. Bench planes, plough, combination and rebate planes have a 45° bed angle. Low-angle planes (block, bullnose and shoulder) have a 20° bed angle, but because on these planes the blade is used bevel up, the effective pitch is 50°. A 50° pitch is particularly suitable for planing across end grain and for planing small surfaces.

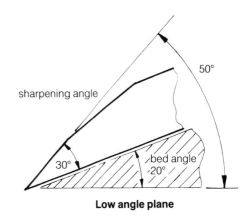

Low angle plane

THE CAP IRON

This serves three purposes:

1 It stiffens the blade to prevent **chatter.**
2 It lifts and breaks the shaving soon after it has been cut to prevent **tearing**.
3 It guides the shaving upwards and forwards to prevent **clogging** of the mouth.

ADJUSTING THE SET OF THE CAP IRON

The edge of the cap iron is set back from the cutting edge about 1.5 mm for general work. To plane cross-grained wood or to obtain a very smooth finish, the set is reduced to 1.0 or 0.5 mm to lift and break the shavings more quickly.

Always check that there are no gaps between the edge of the cap iron and the blade. If there are, shavings will jam between blade and badly fitting cap iron, and cause blocking of the plane mouth.

THE MOUTH

The width of the mouth can be adjusted by moving **the frog** forwards or backwards with the adjusting screw, after loosening the clamping screws.

A **wide mouth** allows a thick shaving to be taken, but the wood may split ahead of the cutting edge, causing a thick shaving to either break away or clog the mouth. In either case, the surface of the wood will be torn.

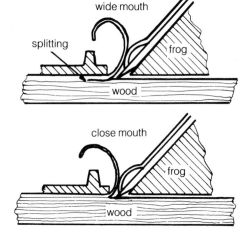

A **very close mouth** will allow the plane to take only a very fine shaving without clogging, but will leave a good surface on the wood by preventing splitting ahead of the cutting edge.

ADJUSTING THE BLADE

Before using a plane always look along the sole to check:

1 **The depth of cut.** The blade should stick out by a distance equal to the thickness of a sheet of paper. Adjust if necessary with the cutter adjusting wheel.
2 **Long cornering.** Make sure that the blade sticks out equally along the whole of its width. Adjust if necessary, by moving the lateral adjusting lever towards the long corner (the one sticking out furthest) to level the blade.

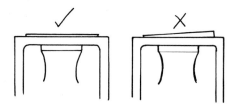

PLANING AWKWARD GRAIN

To obtain a good finish on wood that has an awkward grain you must:

1 Have a sharp blade.
2 Have a closely set and well-fitted cap iron.
3 Set a close mouth.
4 Set the protruding blade as finely as possible.
5 After planing, finish with a scraper if necessary.

HOW TO PLANE

1 BEFORE PLANING

Always *check which way the grain of the wood runs* and plane in the direction which smooths it down.

Always *look along the sole of the plane* and check that the blade is correctly set. (*See* Sharpening and setting.)

Support *the work firmly*, preferably flat on the bench top against the bench stop. Work held in the vice tends to slip.

2 WHEN PLANING

If the wood is twisted, plane off the high corners first. Press down on the toe of the plane at the start of the cut and on the heel at the end. Take special care not to slope the ends of the wood downwards, or to rock the plane.

Stand correctly and grip the plane correctly.

Stance
Stand in a position where you can plane without leaning over the bench; with the bench on your right if you are right-handed and on your left if you are left-handed.

Stand comfortably with your left foot parallel to the wood being planed (right foot if left-handed). Your weight should be on this foot at the end of the cut and your shoulder should be in line with the cut.

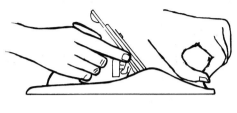

Grip
Thumb and first finger of right hand guide the plane; the other three fingers grip the handle (left hand for left-handed person). The other hand grips the knob.

When planing narrow edges, grip the toe of the plane instead of the knob and use the fingers as a fence.

Check frequently for flatness and squareness with straight edge and try-square or winding strips. It is easy to plane off too much. If necessary, use candle wax to lubricate the sole of the plane so that it slides over the wood more easily.

STAGES IN PLANING A PIECE OF WOOD TO SIZE

1 PLANE, TEST AND MARK THE FACE-SIDE
Test for flatness with a straight edge and for twist (or wind) with winding strips. Aim the face-side mark towards the face-edge.

2 PLANE, TEST AND MARK THE FACE-EDGE
Test for flatness with a straight edge and for squareness to the face-side with a try-square.

3 GAUGE TO WIDTH
Put the stock of the marking gauge against the face-edge. Shade the waste.

Plane to width, finishing when the gauge line is just visible all the way round.

4 GAUGE TO THICKNESS
Put the stock of the marking gauge against the face-side. Shade the waste.

Plane to thickness, finishing when the gauge line is just visible all the way round. This line will be removed later during cleaning-up.

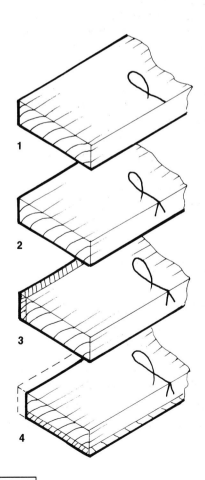

PLANING END GRAIN AND THE EDGES OF MAN-MADE BOARDS

Planing all the way across splits the wood. This can be overcome in four ways:

1 By planing to the centre from each side on a wide board.
2 By clamping or gluing a block of scrapwood to one edge and cutting off its corner. You can then plane all the way across.
3 By cutting off a corner where this will not spoil the finished job.
4 By using a shooting board.

PLANING PLASTICS

Some plastics, particularly the edges of polystyrene and acrylic sheet, may be planed **with a very sharp and finely set plane**. The procedure for this is the same as for planing the end grain of wood because planing all the way across can result in chipped corners. Because acrylics chip easily, set the cap iron and mouth as closely as possible.

Suitable planes are bench planes (smoothing, jack and jointer) and low angle planes (block, shoulder and bull-nosed). (See Planing end grain and man-made boards.)

Plastics can often be more readily filed to shape. (See Filing plastics.)

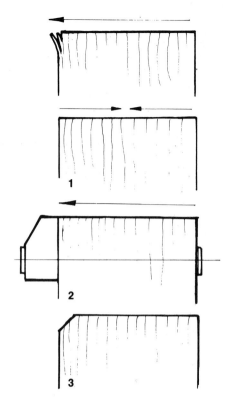

Filing

PRINCIPLES

Each tooth like a miniature cold chisel takes a separate cut and material is removed as fine particles (filings). The amount of material removed depends on the type and grade (or cut) of the teeth.

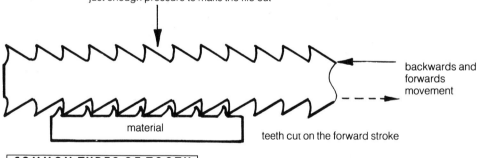

just enough pressure to make the file cut

backwards and forwards movement

material

teeth cut on the forward stroke

COMMON TYPES OF TOOTH

SINGLE-CUT FILES

These have one row of teeth cut at an angle of 80°. They are particularly good for soft materials which tend to choke (pin) double-cut teeth, and for getting a smooth finish.

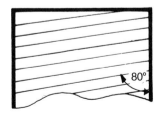

DOUBLE-CUT FILES

These have one row of teeth at 80° and a second row at 60°. They are general purpose files and are particularly good for medium and hard metals, and plastics.

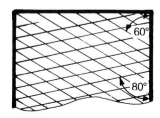

CURVED TOOTH FILES

Dreadnought files, for example, are used for rapid removal of soft metals, such as copper and aluminium, and fibrous materials, such as wood and glass fibre, without clogging.

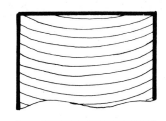

RASPS

These have individual teeth and are used for cutting wood and other soft materials. Rasps clog easily as there is no clearance to help remove waste.

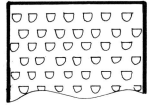

COMMON GRADES (OR CUTS) OF TEETH

Rough	approx. 20 teeth per 25 mm
Bastard	approx. 30 teeth per 25 mm
Second-cut	approx. 40 teeth per 25 mm
Smooth	approx. 60 teeth per 25 mm
Dead smooth	approx. 100 teeth per 25 mm

COMMON LENGTHS OF FILE

Measured from the shoulder to the end, these are: 100 mm, 150 mm, 200 mm, 250 mm and 300 mm.

Files are ordered by:

1 Length of blade.
2 Shape of blade.
3 Type of teeth.
4 Grade or cut of teeth.

HOW TO FILE

1 WAYS OF FILING

(a) **Crossfiling.** The file is moved across the work using the full length of the blade. This is used for rapid removal of waste material and for filing to a line, but does not leave a smooth surface.

(b) **Drawfiling.** The file is moved sideways along the work and is used to obtain a smooth finish after cross-filing, but it does not remove much material.

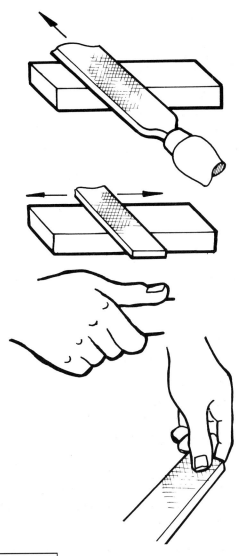

2 HOLDING THE FILE

(a) **Crossfiling** for a right-handed person (reverse for left-handed).

The **right hand** grips the handle with the thumb along the top. The **left hand**, for light filing, grips the end between the thumb and the first two fingers, but for heavy filing presses down on the end with the ball of the thumb. For accurate flat filing rest the thumb of the **left hand** on the middle of the blade, and the fingers on the end, to balance the file.

Stance. The left foot should be in line with the file, and the right foot slightly behind and apart, to give a firm comfortable position. The right arm must be in line with the file (reverse for left-handed). Rock the weight of the body from the back to the front foot as the file moves forward.

(b) **Drawfiling.** Grip across the blade, with one hand each side of the work as close to the work as possible, placing thumbs against one edge of the blade, first fingers on top to balance it, and the other fingers against the other edge.

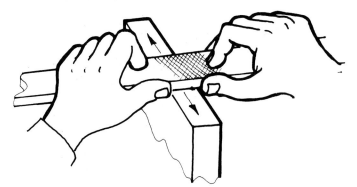
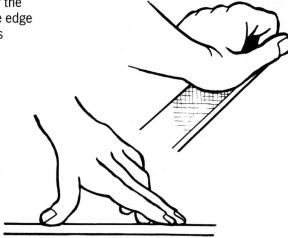

3 SUPPORT
Support the work as close as possible to where you are going to file, usually in the vice, with the minimum amount of metal projecting. Thin sheet can be held in a filing block or pinned to a wood block.

4 WHEN FILING
Use the full length of the blade. Press down on the file, push forward without rocking, and lift at the end of the stroke. Use just enough pressure to make the file cut. Work evenly across the whole surface. Use rough or bastard-cut files to remove waste almost to the line; finish with second-cut or smooth files. Test the surface for flatness and squareness frequently.

5 CLEANING THE FILE
Small pieces of material become trapped in the teeth of the file. This is called **pinning**. It causes bad scratch marks on the surface being filed.

- Remove these by brushing across the blade with a file card (a stiff short-bristled wire brush).
- Remove difficult pins with a file pick (a pointed piece of brass). Do not use a hard metal point.
- Finally, to reduce pinning when finishing a surface, rub chalk onto the file.

Snipping or shearing

PRINCIPLES

The cutting action is a **shearing action** and the cutting angle is 75°.

Check. Some snips are left- or right-hand cutting only. In one direction such snips will tend to cut over the line, in the other the waste will curl away easily.

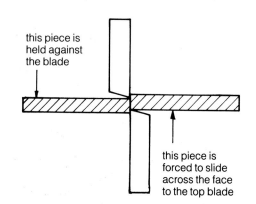

this piece is held against the blade

this piece is forced to slide across the face to the top blade

■ Hold the snips with the base of the thumb and the fingers round the handle, and squeeze.

■ Do not put any fingers between the handles. You could trap them.

■ To open the snips, push them forward into the work.

■ Do not close the snips completely except at a corner or at the end of a cut.

■ To stop accurately at a line, hold the nose of the snips level with the line before cutting. You cannot stop accurately enough with partly closed blades.

■ For accuracy in cutting complex shapes, first remove most of the waste, and then cut to the line.

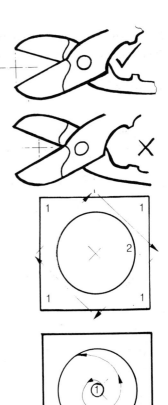

OUTSIDE CURVES

1 Remove waste to within 5 mm of the line.
2 Cut exactly to waste side of the line.

INSIDE CURVES

1 Drill a hole in the centre.
2 Work outwards in a spiral to the final line.

Cutting threads

PRINCIPLES

Threading means cutting external threads with a die. The diameter of the rod being threaded must be the same as the required screw diameter. The end of the rod is tapered to the core diameter for a length equal to the screw diameter to help start the die.

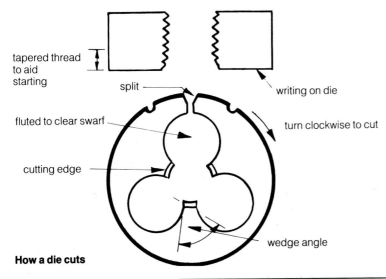

tapered thread to aid starting

split

writing on die

fluted to clear swarf

turn clockwise to cut

cutting edge

wedge angle

How a die cuts

Tapping is cutting internal threads with taper, second and plug taps.

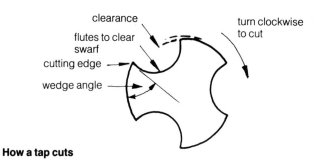

How a tap cuts

Cutting lubricants for threading	
mild steel	thread cutting grease
aluminium	paraffin
copper	paraffin
brass	none
cast iron	none
plastics	none or cold water

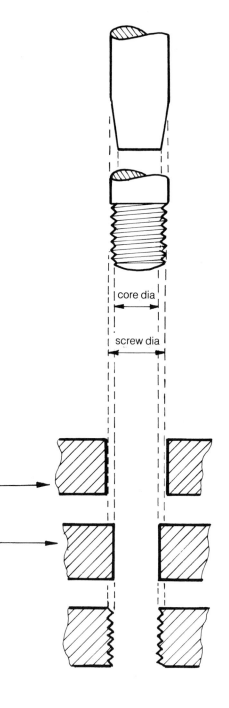

Tapping and clearance drill sizes		
Thread size	Tapping	Clearance
M2	1.6 mm	2.5 mm
M2.5	2.1 mm	3.0 mm
M3	2.5 mm	3.5 mm
M4	3.3 mm	4.5 mm
M5	4.2 mm	5.5 mm
M6	5.0 mm	6.5 mm
M8	6.8 mm	8.5 mm
M10	8.5 mm	10.5 mm
M12	10.2 mm	13.0 mm

Clearance size hole — to allow a plain or threaded rod to slide straight through, drill a hole slightly larger than the core diameter.

Tapping size hole — to prepare a hole for tapping, drill slightly larger than the core diameter. (Recommended clearance and tapping sizes are given in the tables.)

HOW TO CUT THREADS

GENERAL POINTS

1 Because the die is adjustable and taps are not, cut the internal thread first and then adjust the external thread, to give a good fit.
2 Use the correct cutting lubricant. (See the list above.)
3 When starting, press down on the tap or die to make it cut and keep it square to avoid a drunken thread.
4 Small taps and dies (smaller than 8 mm) are easily broken. Do not force them. Remove to clean out swarf frequently.

TAPPING

5 Drill the correct tapping size hole.
6 Use the correct taper tap, held in a tapwrench, followed if necessary by the second and plug taps.

THREADING

7 Taper the end of the rod.
8 Put the correct die in a die stock with the unwritten side of the die against the shoulder of the stock and the writing showing.
9 Place the die, written side down, onto the rod.
10 For the first cut, tighten the middle-die adjusting screw to open the die to its maximum size, before tightening the two outer screws to keep the die in place.
11 After cutting the thread, test the fit of the internal thread onto the previously cut external thread.
12 If it is too tight, slacken the middle screw and tighten the outer screws to close the die, before making the second cut.
13 When the thread is to size, turn the die over and screw it down, writing upwards, to complete the cutting of the final few turns which have only been partly cut by the tapered section of the die.

Drilling

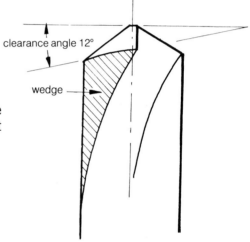

PRINCIPLES OF THE TWIST DRILL

The V-shaped **chisel edge** in the centre of the drill nose does not cut the material being drilled because the drill speed at the very centre is zero. It is simply forced into the material by the pressure put onto the drill.

The **cutting lips** should be seen as two chisel or plane blades which remove a shaving (known as swarf) as they revolve. They do all the cutting by a wedge action.

The **flutes** act as a conveyor to carry away the swarf from the lips. They do not cut at all.

The **land** or leading edge of each flute is made the exact diameter of the drill, while the rest of the flutes are made slightly smaller to reduce friction. The land helps to keep the drill straight in the hole.

CUTTING ANGLES

POINT ANGLE

- 118° for general purposes.
- 140° for plastics which can be cut with a knife (usually thermoplastics).
- 60° for plastics which cannot be cut with a knife (usually thermosetting plastics).

Note: To prevent thin sheets of any material breaking or bending when drilled, ensure that the whole length of the cutting lips is in contact with the sheet before the chisel edge breaks through. This often involves using a drill with a bigger point angle than that recommended for normal drilling of the material. Drills ground to a 140° point angle for thermoplastics are useful for all thin materials.

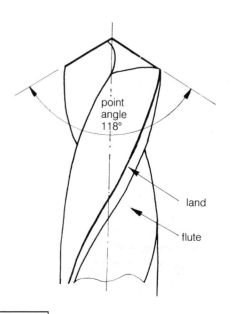

HOW TO DRILL

1 **Support** the work firmly and safely. Never hold work in your fingers when using any powered drilling machine. (See Holding tools.) Many plastics will crack unless well supported.

2 **Make sure** that you will not drill through into anything except scrap wood.

3 **Make sure** the drill is tight in the chuck. On a key-operated chuck, check with the key in at least two of the three holes. Never leave a chuck key in the chuck. Always close the safety chuck guard if fitted.

4 **Centre punch** metal before drilling, but not wood or plastics.

5 **Keep** drills sharp.

6 **Apply** just enough pressure to make the drill cut. Too much pressure can break drills; too little can cause rubbing which blunts them. Use a slow feed on plastics to avoid overheating. **Select the correct speed and cutting fluid** if needed.

7 **Withdraw** the drill frequently to remove swarf and prevent binding.

8 **Reduce** the pressure as the drill breaks through, or it may jam and break.

9 **If the drill starts off centre**, stop immediately and tap the centre over to the correct position with a centre punch or small round-nose chisel.

10 **When drilling a large hole** in metal or plastics, first drill a pilot hole larger than the chisel edge of the large drill.

When using wood bits, drill to the full size in one step because the screw point cannot centre the drill over an existing hole, or screw the bit into the wood.

11 **Do not** drill right through wood as this will leave a ragged exit hole;

either drill from one side with a bit until the screw point shows through, reverse, locate the point in the hole, and drill from the other side, **or** clamp scrap wood firmly against the exit hole side before drilling.

12 **When using a brace or hand drill** it is easier and more accurate to drill horizontally than vertically.

CLEARANCE ANGLE

There must be the correct clearance behind each cutting edge to allow the cutting lips to penetrate the material. This is 12° for general purposes and 15° to 20° for plastics.

CHISEL POINT ANGLE

The angle between the chisel point and the cutting lip is always 130°.

PRINCIPLES OF NEW PATTERN CENTRE BIT AND JENNINGS BIT

1 The **screw point** pulls the bit into the timber.
2 The **spurs** scribe the diameter of the hole. This cuts through the grain fibres in advance of the cutters to prevent splitting.
3 The **cutters** lift the chips and pass them up the **twist or auger**.

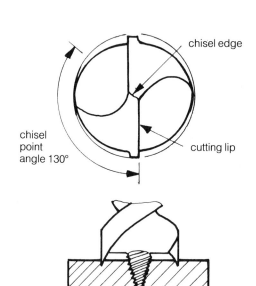

chisel edge

chisel point angle 130°

cutting lip

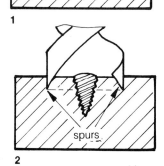

screw point

1

spurs

2

chips

cutters

3

Chiselling

CHISELLING WOOD. PART 1 — PARING

PRINCIPLES OF PARING

Paring is chiselling using hand pressure only. (Compare with principles of planing wood.) The wedge shape of the cutting edge is driven between the fibres of the grain.

Paring with the grain splits the wood instead of cutting it unless a very thin chip is taken, and it is difficult to control the thickness of the chip removed. Therefore, a plane should be used instead whenever possible.

Paring across the grain gives a clean cut because wood does not split across the grain, and the fibres separate and curl away easily, provided that the sides of the cut have been sawn first to prevent splintering.

Paring across the end grain also gives a clean cut.

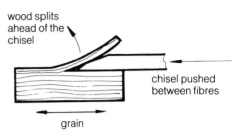

HOW TO PARE

HORIZONTAL PARING

Hold the chisel in the palm of the hand, rest the other hand against the bench if possible, and guide the blade through the clenched hand.

VERTICAL PARING

Hold the chisel like a dagger, rest the other clenched hand on the work, and guide the blade with the first finger and thumb. When chiselling vertically always work on a protective chiselling board.

USING A MALLET

If too much effort is needed to cut using hand pressure, use a mallet. When using a mallet, always clamp the work down and always position the chisel with both hands before striking it with the mallet.

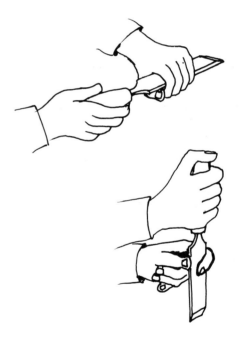

CHISELLING WOOD. PART 2 — MORTISING

PRINCIPLES OF MORTISING

Mortising is cutting rectangular holes in wood using mallet blows to drive the chisel into the wood.

Cuts are made across the grain. The wedge shape of the cutting edge moves the chip sideways as it cuts.

HOW TO MORTISE

GENERAL POINTS

1 Cut the mortise before the tenon, because it is easier to adjust the width of the tenon to fit the mortise than vice versa.

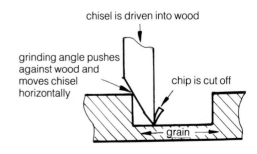

2 The width of the mortise and tenon should be chosen to match the available widths of mortise chisel — usually 6, 8, 10 and 12mm.

3 When mortising near the end of a piece of wood, leave extra waste on the end to help prevent splitting, and to enable the ends to be sawn off square after gluing.

4 When mortising thin wood, clamp scrapwood on each side to prevent splitting, or clamp it in the vice making sure that it is well supported underneath.

5 Use both hands to locate the chisel correctly before striking sharply with the mallet once only.

6 Always cut across the grain. Chiselling along the grain splits the wood and leaves the finished mortise with ragged sides and irregular width.

STARTING TO MORTISE

7 Press the chisel into the wood along the ends of the mortise to make a shallow cut. This helps to prevent accidental splitting beyond the line, especially when removing waste.

8 Start cutting in the middle of the mortise and take small bites, working to one end of the mortise, with the grinding angle facing in the direction of the cuts. (See Principles of mortising.)

9 Leave 5mm waste at the end so that the end of the mortise will not be damaged during cutting.

10 Repeat steps 8 and 9 from the centre to the other end.

11 Repeat as necessary to reach the required depth, levering out loose waste. Do **not** try to lever out partly loosened waste, as this splits the wood.

12 If mortising right through, cut halfway from each side.

FINISHING

13 Cut the waste at each end of the mortise back to the line, taking small bites.

GRINDING AND SHARPENING CHISELS

FIRMER CHISELS
- For general purposes the wedge angles are the same as for a plane.
- Grinding angle is 25°.
- Sharpening angle is 30°.

MORTISE CHISELS
- For heavier work the wedge angle can be increased to strengthen it.
- Grinding angle is 30°.
- Sharpening angle is 35°.

CHISELLING METAL

PRINCIPLES
The cutting edge is a wedge which is driven into the metal. The angle depends on the hardness of the metal being cut. For example, with mild steel use 60°, brass and copper use 45°, and aluminium use 30°.

SAFETY

The head is left soft where it is struck by the hammer because if two hard surfaces were struck together they might shatter, causing dangerous chips to break off and fly across the room.

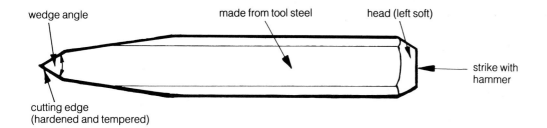

wedge angle

made from tool steel

head (left soft)

strike with hammer

cutting edge
(hardened and tempered)

This soft head will mushroom after repeated use, leaving a dangerous rough edge which might cut your hand or cause pieces to break off and fly across the room.
Therefore:

1 Keep the head ground to its correct shape.
2 **Protect your eyes**.

HOW TO CHISEL METAL

1 Always chisel on a soft metal block (e.g. cutting face of anvil, chiselling block).
2 Grip the chisel firmly in one hand with thumb and fingers clenched round it.
3 Place the cutting edge on the work, and strike with the hammer held in the other hand.
4 Watch the cutting edge **not** the head of the chisel or the hammer.

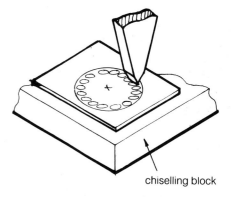

chiselling block

CUTTING

1 Place the cutting edge on the cutting line (leaving a small amount for filing to the finished size).
2 Cut lightly along the line to start the cut.
3 Repeat using heavier blows to complete the cut.
4 Cut from both sides if necessary.
5 When cutting internal shapes, drill a series of holes just inside the line, and cut through the waste between them to remove most of the waste quickly.

Finish by chiselling and filing.

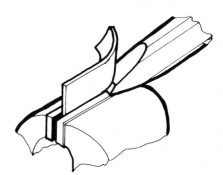

SHEARING

1 Clamp the metal in the vice with the cutting line just showing above the jaws.
2 Hold the chisel with the cutting edge at 30° to the cutting line and one side of the wedge angle resting on the top of the vice jaw.
3 Strike with the hammer to shear the metal just on the waste side of the line.

CHIPPING

This is the removal of waste metal from a surface, e.g. removing rivet and bolt heads, and cleaning up castings.

17 Ways of working materials
PART 1B—wasting machine processes

The principles of machining

A machine tool is any power-driven machine used to cut and shape materials. Industrial machines are basically the same as school machines, but they are usually larger and more complicated. Industry uses machine tools to produce smooth, accurate surfaces.

Machining is done by removing chips from the material, using either cutting tools or abrasives, mounted on a machine tool. The chips produced can range from fine dust when polishing or sanding to continuous thick swarf from a lathe tool which is cutting steel.

In the chart below we have arranged the most used types of machines into three groups according to the type of cutter used on each (single-point, multiple-point and abrasive). We have then explained briefly how each machine and each type of cutter works.

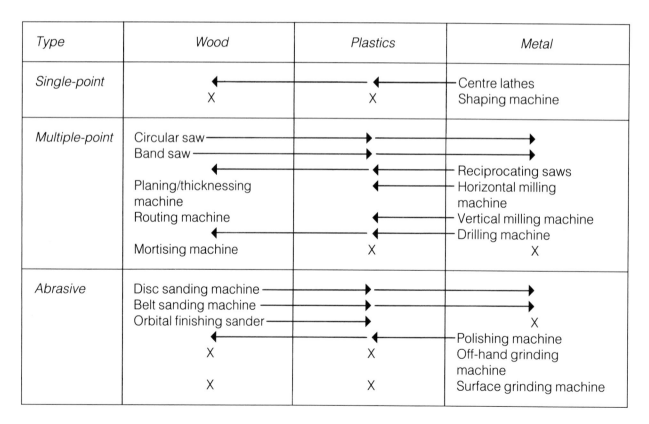

Type	Wood	Plastics	Metal
Single-point	X	X	Centre lathes Shaping machine
Multiple-point	Circular saw Band saw Planing/thicknessing machine Routing machine Mortising machine	X	Reciprocating saws Horizontal milling machine Vertical milling machine Drilling machine X
Abrasive	Disc sanding machine Belt sanding machine Orbital finishing sander X X	X X	X Polishing machine Off-hand grinding machine Surface grinding machine

The chart shows the similarities between machines used for different materials, even where names differ, and also those used for only one material.

Single-point cutting

1 TURNING — CENTRE LATHE (WOOD, METAL, PLASTICS)

A single-point cutting tool is moved against work revolving in a centre lathe. The tool is hand-held on a wood turning lathe, and mounted in a toolpost on a metal turning lathe. Plastics are turned on a metal turning lathe. A lathe produces cylindrical shapes.

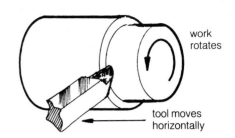

work rotates

tool moves horizontally

2 SHAPING — SHAPING MACHINE (METAL)

A single-point cutting tool moves in a straight line across a block of metal, cutting on the forward stroke, and sliding over the metal on the return stroke. The work is moved the width of one cut sideways after each forward stroke.

A shaper produces flat surfaces, vee-grooves, slots, keyways, etc., and is used only for one-off metal shaping jobs.

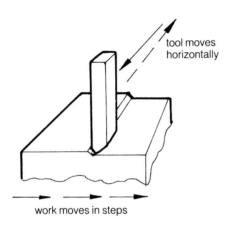

tool moves horizontally

work moves in steps

Multiple-point cutting

1 HORIZONTALLY ROTATING CUTTERS

- ■ Planing/thicknessing machine (wood)
- ■ Horizontal milling machine (metal, plastics)
- ■ Circular saw (wood, metal, plastics)

In all these machines, the work is moved against a horizontally rotating cutter with at least two cutting points. Circular saws cut material into strips and planers produce flat surfaces on wood, while horizontal millers do the same on metal and plastics, and in addition cut grooves, rebates and more complex shapes.

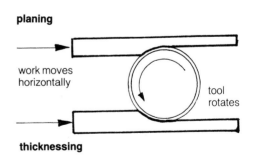

planing

work moves horizontally

tool rotates

thicknessing

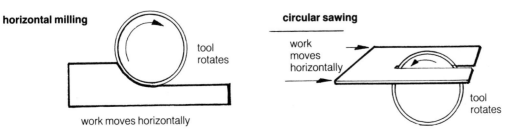

horizontal milling

tool rotates

work moves horizontally

circular sawing

work moves horizontally

tool rotates

2 VERTICALLY ROTATING CUTTERS

- Drilling machine (wood, metal, plastics)
- Routing machine (wood, plastics)
- Vertical milling machine (metal, plastics)
- Mortising machine (wood)

In all these machines, the cutter revolves vertically. In the drilling and mortising machines the revolving tool moves down against a stationary workpiece to make a hole. In the vertical milling machine the work moves against the revolving cutter, while the router is hand-held and is moved across the surface of the work as the cutter revolves. The miller and router both produce grooves, rebates, chamfers, etc. The vertical milling machine can also be used as an accurate drilling machine for cutting holes too large for drilling and to make flat surfaces.

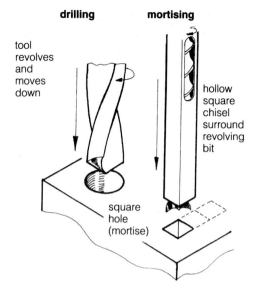

drilling   mortising

tool revolves and moves down

hollow square chisel surround revolving bit

square hole (mortise)

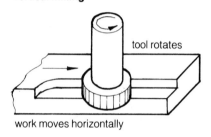

routing and vertical milling

tool rotates

work moves horizontally

3 BAND SAWS (WOOD, METAL, PLASTICS)

The work is pushed against a continuous band with teeth on one edge, which is rotating round two or more wheels. Band saws usually cut vertically, but for heavy metal cutting they sometimes cut horizontally. They are able to cut both straight lines and curves in most materials.

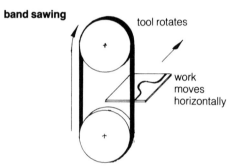

band sawing

tool rotates

work moves horizontally

4 RECIPROCATING SAWS

- Jig saw (wood, metal, plastics)
- Power hacksaw (metal, plastics)

A blade with teeth on one edge moves up and down or backwards and forwards, and is pushed against the work. The power hacksaw is mounted horizontally and makes straight cuts. It is mainly used for cutting lengths of metal to size. Jig saws can be hand-held or mounted on a stand, and are used mainly to cut shapes out of sheet material. Hand-held jig saws are especially useful for cutting large holes because they can be started in a small drilled hole at any point on a sheet, and for cutting sheets too large for the bandsaw.

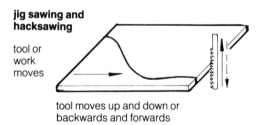

jig sawing and hacksawing

tool or work moves

tool moves up and down or backwards and forwards

Abrasive cutting

1 VERTICALLY ROTATING ABRASIVE WHEELS

- Disc sanders (wood, metal, plastics)
- Off-hand grinders (metal)
- Surface grinding machines (metal)
- Polishing machines (wood, metal, plastics)

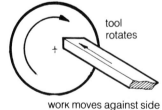

(a) Vertical disc sanding

tool rotates

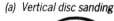

work moves against side

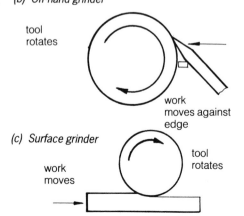

(b) Off-hand grinder

tool rotates

work moves against edge

(c) Surface grinder

work moves

tool rotates

Disc sanding machines use suitable abrasive sheets mounted on a backing disc or flexible pad. Polishing machines use abrasive compounds (polishes) applied to cloth mops. Grinding machines use wheels made from abrasive powders cemented together into discs. The workpiece is pressed against the abrasive cutter and a small amount of material is removed. These machines are mainly used for cleaning-up and finishing work. The surface grinding machine is a precision machine which grinds hard metals to an accurate smooth finish.

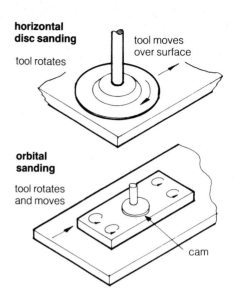

horizontal disc sanding

tool rotates

tool moves over surface

2 HORIZONTALLY ROTATING ABRASIVE WHEELS

- Disc sanders (wood, metal, plastics)
- Orbital finishing sanders (wood)

Horizontally rotating disc sanders are usually hand-held. They are moved across surfaces which are too large to press against a mounted vertical disc.

Orbital finishing sanders have an abrasive sheet mounted on a soft rectangular pad which is rotated by a cam. This rotates it in a way which has the same effect as lots of miniature sanding discs held perfectly level, and makes it possible to produce a very smooth surface.

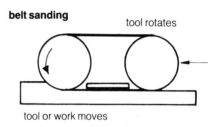

orbital sanding

tool rotates and moves

cam

3 BELT SANDING MACHINE

A continous abrasive band rotates over two rollers and is supported between the rollers by a pressure pad.

The machine can be hand-held for sanding large surfaces, or mounted either vertically or horizontally on a stand, so that small workpieces can be pressed against it.

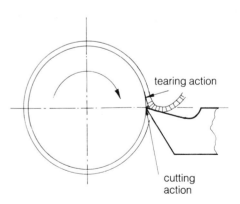

belt sanding

tool rotates

tool or work moves

The cutting action of machine tool cutters

SINGLE-POINT CUTTERS

Although we have shown the action of lathe tools here, the same rules apply to other machine tool cutters, regardless of whether the tool or the work moves, or whether we are machining a flat surface (as when shaping), or a rotating cylindrical surface (as when turning). Multiple-point tools should be seen as a series of single-point tools.

The cutting action consists of the cutting edge of the tool forcing its way into the material and tearing away a strip by a wedge action. If a heavy roughing cut is taken, most of the chip presses behind the cutting edge and is torn off before the cutting edge reaches it. This leaves a rough surface which is cleaned up by the extreme tip of the tool immediately afterwards.

On a light finishing cut only the second part of the action operates leaving a much smoother surface.

tearing action

cutting action

TOOL ANGLES

No cutting tool will work unless **clearance angles** are provided to allow the cutting edge to reach the work. Without them it will only rub against the surface.

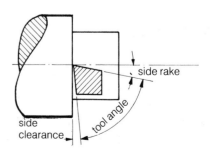

side rake

side clearance

tool angle

In addition the correct tool angle is needed for the material being cut, and this is obtained by varying the **rake angles.** These angles are shown below.

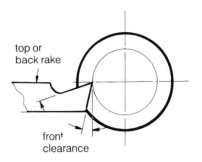

top or back rake

front clearance

	Rake angles	Clearance angles
Aluminium and nylon	30–40°	10°
Brass	0°	10°
Mild steel	15–20°	8°
Cast iron	0°	6°
Tool steel	10°	6°

- **Side clearance** allows the cutting edge to advance freely without the heel of the tool rubbing.
- **Front clearance** allows the tool to be fed freely into the work.
- **Top rake** is the backward slope from the cutting edge, and controls the cutting action and chip formation.
- **Side rake** increases the keenness of the cutting edge.

The **tool angle** or angle of keenness is the shape of the wedge which actually penetrates the metal. For example, this is approximately 62° for mild steel. This can be compared with the wedge angles of hand tools in chapter 16 where, for example, the angle for cutting mild steel with a cold chisel is 60°.

The softer the material being turned, the smaller the tool angle needed to prevent the tool from breaking. The smaller the tool angle, the more easily the tool will cut. The tool angle is therefore a compromise between strength and ease of cutting.

Materials (such as aluminium) which stick to the tool need increased rake to help prevent sticking. Materials (such as brass) which produce chips instead of swarf do not need any top rake and have a flat top, or even a slight negative rake.

MULTIPLE-POINT CUTTERS

Multiple-point cutters have each tooth carefully designed to give the correct clearance and rake angles, in the same way as single-point tools, and each tooth removes a separate chip. Details of the twist drill, which is an example of a two-point cutter, are given in chapter 16 and a milling cutter is shown below.

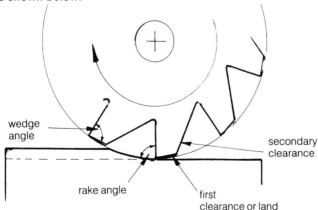

wedge angle

secondary clearance

rake angle

first clearance or land

Each tooth has a strong wedge angle, and a short land with just enough first clearance to prevent rubbing (about 3°), to give maximum support to the cutting edge. Each tooth would have a positive rake for milling steel or aluminium and a negative rake for brass, as on a lathe tool.

ABRASIVE CUTTERS

Most abrasive cutting is done with grinding wheels. These consist of millions of grains of very hard abrasive known as the grit, glued together in a bonding material known as the matrix and cast into the required shape. Both the size and the type of the abrasive grains, and the type and the strength of the matrix, can be varied to suit the materials being ground. A wheel with a soft matrix is used to grind hard materials, and vice versa.

The grit provides thousands of minute cutting points on the circumference of the wheel. When these become worn down and clogged with metal particles the wheel is **dressed** with either a diamond point, or a star wheel dressing tool which has several very hard toothed wheels. The dressing tool is pressed against the revolving wheel to true it up and expose sharp new abrasive grains.

SAFETY

When using the off-hand grinding machine, make sure that the tool rest is set to centre height, and that the gap between the wheel and the rest is as small as possible. Otherwise work could be carried down between the wheel and the rest, causing damage to the wheel and the work, and possible injury to the operator.

On most machines the rest can be set at any required angle for grinding tool shapes. Always wear safety glasses when grinding. Whenever possible grind on the circumference of the wheel because the wheel is less able to withstand side forces and the side of the wheel is difficult to dress.

Similar abrasive grits bonded to paper or cloth, or cast in a flexible matrix, are used to make the abrasive discs and pads used on hand-held sanding and grinding machines.

The centre lathe

The centre lathe is used to turn accurate cylindrical and conical shapes, to cut flat surfaces across the end of pieces of material and to bore holes.

PARTS OF THE LATHE

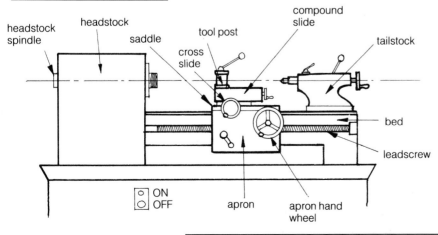

THREE-JAW SELF-CENTRING CHUCK

This is a quick and easy way of holding round and hexagonal shapes. Once removed, work can be put back in the chuck with reasonable (but **not** perfect) accuracy. Its main uses are, therefore, for one-setting operations and preliminary work such as centre drilling, before mounting between centres.

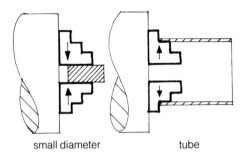
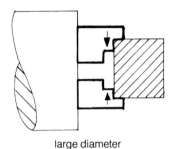

small diameter   tube   large diameter

The three jaws are moved together by a scroll, and the curve of the grooves on the back is different on each. Therefore, they are numbered and must always be replaced in order. There are two sets of jaws. One is for holding large-diameter work, and the other for small diameters and gripping the inside of hollow work.

Always clean and lightly oil the spindle and chuck threads before mounting the chuck. Tighten the chuck using hand pressure only.

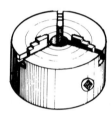

THE FOUR-JAW INDEPENDENT CHUCK

The four jaws are moved independently, one at a time. This allows a much stronger grip to be exerted on the work, and the jaws are reversible so that one set can be used for all sizes of internal and external gripping. Work can be set up very accurately, but cannot easily be put back once removed. It can be used to hold round, square or irregular shapes, and for drilling and boring off set holes.

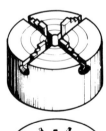

THE FACE-PLATE

The face of the plate has a series of holes and radial slots so that irregular shaped work, such as castings, can be bolted onto it.

CENTRES

Lathe centres can be put into the headstock spindle or tailstock barrel. (See Combination centre drill.)

The headstock centre turns with the work and is not subject to friction. It can therefore be left soft, and is known as the live or soft centre.

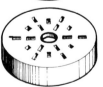

The **tailstock centre** remains stationary while the work rotates. This causes friction, and so the centre must be hardened and grease must be used to lubricate it. It is known as the dead or hard centre.

On a **revolving centre**, the centre is mounted in a bearing which allows it to rotate with the work to prevent friction.

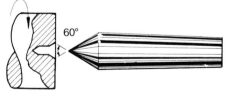
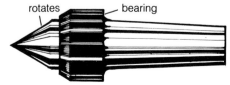

rotates   bearing

On a **half-centre**, part of the centre point has been ground away so that the tool can cut up to the centre hole of the work while it is being supported by the tailstock.

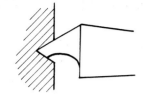

TURNING BETWEEN CENTRES
The main advantages of turning between centres are that the work can easily be removed and replaced accurately, and that the whole length of the work can be machined simply by turning it round in the lathe.

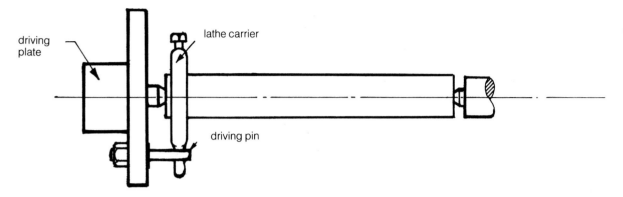

To set up work between centres:

1 Centre drill the ends of the workpiece.
2 Screw a driving plate and pin onto the headstock spindle. Put a soft centre into the end of the headstock spindle and a hard or revolving centre into the tailstock.
3 Clamp a lathe carrier onto the work.
4 Mount the work between centres, lubricating the hard centre if used with grease. Make sure that the work turns freely but without any slackness.

CHOOSING THE CORRECT LATHE SPEED
The softer the material being turned the faster the lathe speed. For a heavy roughing cut, the lathe speed is slower than for a light finishing cut.

Average cutting speeds in metres per minute for turning	
Aluminium	200 m/minute
Nylon	170 m/minute
Brass	90 m/minute
Mild steel	25 m/minute
Cast Iron	20 m/minute
Tool Steel	18 m/minute

Lathe speeds for other processes	
Knurling	1/3 cutting speed
Parting	1/3 cutting speed
Centre drilling	Full speed
Drilling	3/4 cutting speed
Using form tools	1/2 cutting speed

CALCULATING THE SPINDLE SPEED IN r.p.m.

Because cutting speeds are calculated in metres per minute and the speed of the lathe spindle is measured in revolutions per minute, it is necessary to convert the cutting speed to the correct r.p.m. for the diameter of work being turned.

$$\text{spindle speed (in r.p.m.)} = \frac{\text{cutting speed in m/minute} \times 1000}{\pi \times \text{diameter of work in millimetres}}$$

LATHE TOOL SHAPES

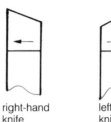 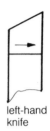   

| right-hand knife | left-hand knife | round nose | parting | form |

Round-nosed tools give a smoother finish than pointed tools, but larger cuts can be taken with a pointed tool. A knife tool is necessary to turn to a sharp shoulder, and can be used to take roughing cuts. It must have a slight radius at its tip, produced by using a slip stone, to prevent the extreme tip from burning or breaking off and to improve finish.

When roughing with a knife tool, set it to give the correct approach angle as shown, with the tool angle trailing, so that swarf is directed away from the work, and so that it will swing safely out of the way without digging into the material if the tool comes loose.

- **Right-hand knife tools** can be used to face off the right-hand end of a bar, to cut to a right-handed shoulder, or to cut along the work from right to left.
- **Left-hand knife tools** can be used to cut to a left-handed shoulder or cut along the work from left to right.
- **Round nosed tools** can be used to cut in either direction and to cut to left- or right-handed shoulders where a radiused corner is wanted.
- **Parting tool** — See parting off.
- **Form tools** can be specially ground to produce any required shape, such as the curved top of a turned screwdriver handle.

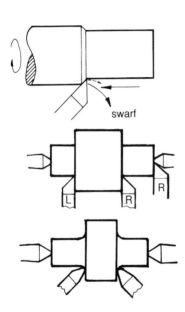

SETTING UP LATHE TOOLS

The correct height for general purposes is to set the tool at centre height, as shown.

Always support the tool in the toolpost, as near to the cutting edge as possible. A large overhang increases the risk of vibration or chatter, causing poor finish, inaccurate work and the risk of tool breakage. A tool which is set too **high** will simply rub against the work without cutting. A tool which is set too **low** will dig into the work and try to go underneath it. This may bend the work or break the tool.

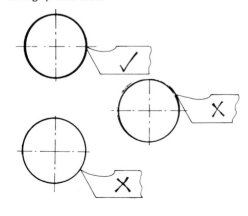

Setting up lathe tools

CUTTING FLUIDS

The main functions of a cutting fluid are:

1 To cool the work and the tool by carrying away the heat generated by friction during cutting.
2 To lubricate the point of contact between the work and the tool to reduce friction.

It also helps to prevent welding of the chip to the tool and tool breakdown, improves surface finish, gives some protection against corrosion and washes away the swarf.

The correct cutting fluids are:

Aluminium	none, soluble oil or paraffin
Brass	none
Mild steel	soluble oil
Cast iron	none
Tool steel	soluble oil

Soluble oil is a mixture of one part soluble oil to lubricate and ten parts water to cool the work. This makes a white milky suds.

GETTING A GOOD FINISH

The factors which combine to give a good finish to a piece of work when making a final finishing cut are:

1 A high cutting speed.
2 A slow tool feed, ensuring that the tool moves uniformly without any stops or starts.
3 A round-nosed tool.
4 A light cut.
5 A highly polished tool.
6 The correct lubricant.

All these factors should be checked before taking the final cut.

LATHEWORK PROCESSES

SURFACING OR FACING OFF

When the tool moves across the end of the work, at right angles to the axis of rotation of the work, a flat surface is produced on the end.

SLIDING OR PARALLEL TURNING

When the tool moves sideways, parallel to the axis of rotation of the work, a cylindrical shape is produced.

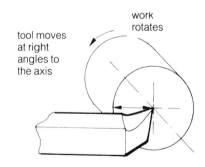

work rotates

tool moves at right angles to the axis

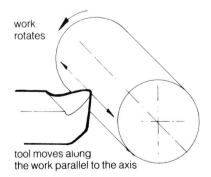

work rotates

tool moves along the work parallel to the axis

TAPER TURNING

When the tool moves along the work, at an angle to the axis of rotation, a conical shape is produced.

(a) To turn a **very short chamfer** use a form tool.

(b) To turn a **short taper** rotate the compound slide to the required angle, tighten the clamping screws, and move the tool with the compound slide handle. The maximum length of taper which can be turned is limited to the length of feed on the slide.

(c) To turn a **long gradual taper** offset the tailstock or use a taper turning attachment. The work must be mounted between centres for this.

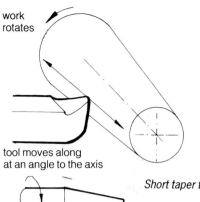

work rotates

tool moves along at an angle to the axis

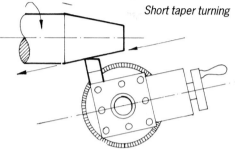

Short taper turning

DRILLING IN THE LATHE

This is more accurate than drilling on a drilling machine. Because it is not possible to centre punch work held in the lathe before drilling, we use a centre drill instead.

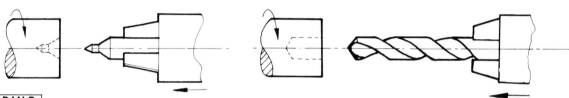

BORING

When a single-point tool is used to turn inside an existing hole, the process is called boring. Special care is needed in measuring the depth of the hole and plotting the position of the tool accurately. Light cuts only should be taken if using a long unsupported boring tool.

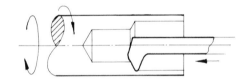

PARTING-OFF

A narrow tool is fed into the work, exactly square to the axis, to cut it to the correct length and face it off at the same time.

The tool is offset to the left so that you can part off as close to the chuck as possible. The sides of the tool taper 1° or 2° from the cutting edge to the back, to prevent the tool jamming in the groove. The sides also taper 2° from top to bottom, and the tool has a front clearance of about 5°.

The top rake is 5° for steel and aluminium, flat for cast iron and 2° negative for brass. The cutting edge slopes so that the workpiece is cut off cleanly, and the pip remains on the spare material where it is faced off.

The tool must be fed slowly and smoothly by hand. Withdraw the tool frequently and move it slightly sideways before feeding in again so that the groove cut is slightly wider than the tool.

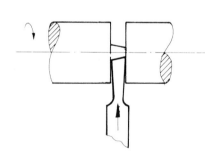

KNURLING

Knurling tools are used to **press** (not cut) a diamond or straight pattern of lines into metal, usually to provide a grip. Two very hard steel wheels mounted in a swivelling head are needed to make a diamond knurl, but only a single wheel for straight knurling. Fine, medium, and coarse knurling tools are available. Oil should be used to lubricate the wheels when knurling steel.

Feed the tool into the work and adjust it until the impression made by the wheels is equal and even from left to right. Then increase the pressure until a full knurled print is being made on the metal, and slowly move the tool along the work.

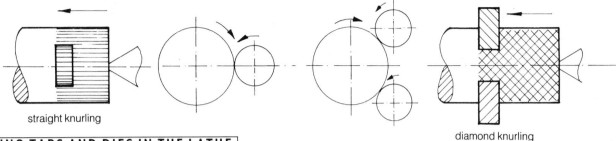

straight knurling

diamond knurling

USING TAPS AND DIES IN THE LATHE

Although hand taps and dies should not be used in the lathe under power, it is helpful to use the lathe as a means of ensuring that threads are cut square.

Taps can be held in the tailstock chuck or in the usual tap wrench with the tailstock centre located in a centre hole in the end of the shank of the tap. Use taper, second and plug taps as for hand tapping.

Dies can be held in a tailstock die holder or in the usual die holder held flat against the end of the tailstock barrel. A short taper is first turned on the end of the work to help locate and start the die, and the first cut is made with the die fully open.

The lathe must be switched off and the spindle must be out of gear, so that the chuck can be rotated by hand using the chuck key as a handle. Use the same cutting lubricants as for hand threading. Always cut the internal thread first if possible, so that the external thread can be adjusted to fit it.

CNC Machine tools

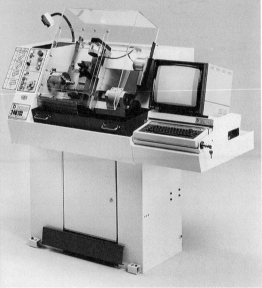

Boxford CNC milling machine programmed using BBC computer

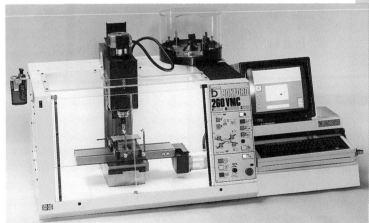

Boxford CNC lathe programmed using BBC computer

CNC stands for computer numerically controlled. A CNC machine runs under the control of a computer, and the moving parts are driven by special electric motors called stepper motors. The computer switches these on or off, and controls their direction and speed. After the computer has been programmed to make a machine tool perform a sequence of operations, the programme can be run over and over again to produce many identical components.

A CNC computer programme uses step-by-step instructions called 'G' codes, each of which is a recognised command. There are now software packages that enable the programmer simply to draw an outline of the required component on a screen, and the software then converts this image automatically into a set of 'G' codes.

The CNC lathe and CNC milling machine illustrated can be controlled using a BBC computer.

The main beam for the landing gear of a jumbo jet—finished by chemical milling

Chemical milling: cutting metals by etching

Chemical milling is a process that does not really fit into either the machine- or hand-wasting categories. In essence, it involves masking out parts of a surface and exposing it to a corrosive fluid or etchant that eats away the exposed metal.

In the Middle Ages, etching was used to decorate armour with elaborate patterns. Today, the same process — but more controlled and on a larger scale — is used to 'machine' to final shape large titanium parts for aircraft.

A maskant is applied to the metal surface and then carefully cut away to expose areas that need wasting. The part is then suspended in an etchant until all unwanted metal is removed. Sometimes, it is masked again and re-etched. Shapes impossible to machine or produce using a lathe or milling machine can be achieved by chemical milling.

In school, materials such as brass, copper and aluminium can be etched using warm ferric chloride providing that strict safety precautions are observed (see page 183). The metal surface can be stopped out with paint, nail varnish, Sellotape — even rub-down lettering. If the metal is left too long in the etchant, however, **undercutting** at the stop-out edge will occur.

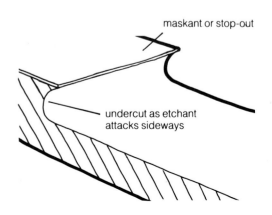

maskant or stop-out

undercut as etchant attacks sideways

If one side of very thin sheet material is completely stopped out, any shapes stopped out on the other surface can be 'cut' out by etching right through the sheet. The advantage of this method is that no distortion is produced, as might be the case using tinsnips. Because the stop-out can be produced either by printing or photographic means (see page 132), many commercial products are made cheaply by chemical milling. The very precise modelling components shown were made in this way.

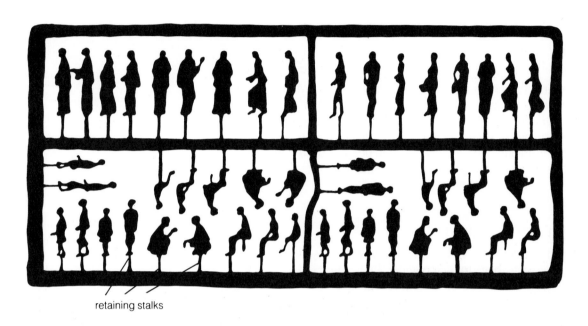

retaining stalks

Silhouettes of small figures for architectural models etched through in brass sheet

Laminating

When two or more layers of any material are bonded together to form a single thicker section, the process is called laminating. It is usually used to obtain material which is longer, thicker or wider than is available in one piece (such as in plywood and block board making), to obtain shapes which could not be cut from one piece (such as curved beams), or to obtain materials with improved properties (such as the stability of plywood or the heat and water resistance of Formica).

LAMINATING AND BENDING WOOD

Thin strips of wood can be bent to curved shapes, but unless they are fixed to a frame they will spring back to their original shape when released. This problem is overcome by laminating several layers together. While the glue between the laminates is wet they can be bent to shape, but if they are held in a curved shape and pressed together until the glue has set, the laminates will no longer be free to move and they will retain the curved shape.

TIMBERS FOR LAMINATING AND BENDING

Strips up to 3 mm thick of either natural or man-made timbers can be bent. All the laminations must be of equal thickness to obtain a smooth curve, and where they are difficult to bend, slight damping of what will be the outer curve of each lamination will help bending. Laminates must not, however, be glued wet, and if damping is used the laminates are cramped in the former overnight to dry in their new shape, before being glued in the usual way.

More expensive decorative woods can be used for the outside laminates, with cheaper materials used inside, provided that this does not leave an unsightly edge. Alternatively, layers of contrasting colours can be used to give a striped pattern to the edges.

The main laminating timbers are:

■ **Veneers:** thin decorative veneers 1.5 mm thick and constructional veneers 3.0 mm thick.

■ **Plywood:** thin plywood up to 3 mm thick, especially 1.5 mm thick mosquito ply for tight curves.

■ **Solid wood:** naturally pliable timbers up to 3 mm thick, e.g. ash, elm, beech, oak, sycamore, birch, African mahoganies.

■ **Hardboard:** oil-tempered hardboard can be bent and pinned to a shaped framework.

GLUES

Most types of wood glue, except impact and animal glues, can be used. PVA glue is cheap, easy to use and does not stain the wood, but will not withstand high stresses, heat or moisture. It is, therefore, suitable for most indoor work. Synthetic resin glues such as cascamite are more expensive and require mixing, but produce a stronger, moisture resistant and almost colourless joint.

Curing is slow because the laminations are partly enclosed by the former, but the glue will usually set overnight at room temperature.

Avoid putting on too much glue as it is difficult to remove when dry and blunts cutting tools.

WAYS OF BENDING

1 RIGID FORMERS

(a) **Solid wooden formers.** The simplest way to make mating formers is to cut the required shape from a solid block of wood. This method is suitable for small or simple shapes such as salad servers and sledge runners. Allowances must be made in the design of the former for the thickness of the laminates to be used. The surfaces which press against the laminates must be smoothed, either by careful cleaning up or by covering them with rubber or cork. These coverings also give some flexibility to allow for slight inaccuracies in the former or laminates.

(b) **Built-up wooden formers.** Larger rigid formers are built up from softwood slats screwed onto blockboard or softwood rails. There is no need to fit slats together accurately. Stiff cardboard can be used to cover the slats and bridge the gaps when laminating thin veneers which might be marked by the slat edges.

To avoid the need to make accurately matched male and female formers, we can hold single shapes, such as curved chair seats and backs, in place on built-up formers with thick strips of wood held by G-cramps. Alternatively, put the whole job into a vacuum forming envelope. (See Flexible formers.)

2 FLEXIBLE FORMERS

(a) **Flexible steel bands.** Where rigid formers are difficult to make or to use, flexible spring steel cramping bands are used. The examples here show, first, the use of a flexible female former with a solid male former to form a stool leg frame and, secondly, the use of flexible male and female formers. The male former is mounted on a sheet of block board with steel angle brackets, and the female former and the laminates are cramped onto it with G-cramps and blocks. This method enables complicated shapes to be set up quickly and all the parts are re-useable.

(b) **Vacuum forming envelope.** This allows laminates to be shaped easily using only one former, and makes possible the forming of complicated shapes which would be difficult to cramp in any other way. It is also useful for veneering both flat and curved surfaces. A built up wooden former is made, waxed and covered with paper to prevent glue sticking to it. The laminates are located on the former with staples or panel pins and covered with a further sheet of paper to keep glue off the bag. The work is placed in the envelope and the air is sucked out so that

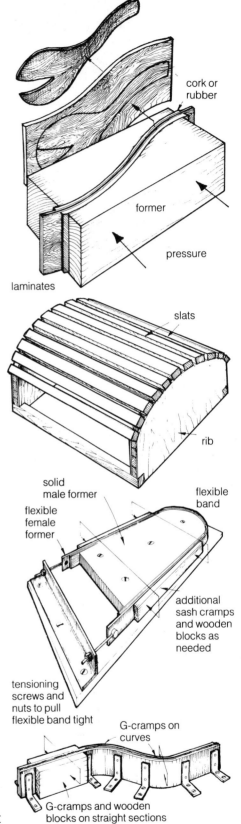

cork or rubber

former

pressure

laminates

slats

rib

solid male former

flexible female former

flexible band

additional sash cramps and wooden blocks as needed

tensioning screws and nuts to pull flexible band tight

G-cramps on curves

G-cramps and wooden blocks on straight sections

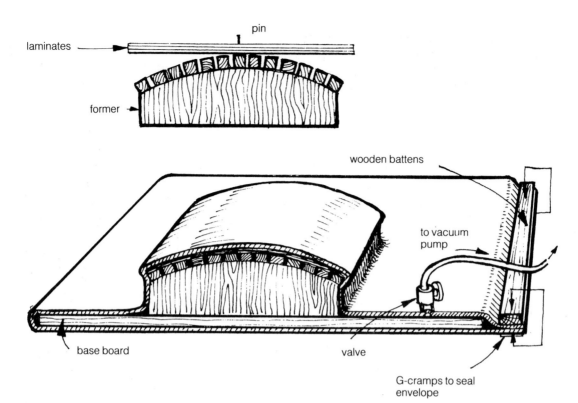

atmospheric pressure on the bag presses it onto the laminates, thus pressing them to the shape of the former. Pressure is equal over the whole shape, however complicated. Care must be taken to prevent the bag being pulled up between laminates and former as the air is sucked out. Drying time is the same as for other methods of laminating.

STAGES IN LAMINATED BENDING

1 **Make the former**, or clean and wax an existing one. Cut polythene sheet or paper to prevent surplus glue from sticking to it and tape in place.

2 **Cut the laminates to size** allowing 25–75 mm extra on the length for movement of one layer over another and for trimming. Allow about 5 mm at the sides.

3 **Assemble the job dry** to make sure that the laminates are the correct size and will bend to the shape of the former. If damping is needed leave the damp laminates cramped up overnight. Check that cramping arrangements work.

4 **Glue the laminates** evenly and without excess glue; stack them in the correct order.

5 **Position the laminates carefully in the former and gradually tighten the cramps**, starting in the middle so that excess glue and air bubbles are squeezed out.

6 **Leave to dry overnight.**

7 **Remove, mark out and cut to shape.** Wear safety glasses when cleaning up as dry glue is brittle and fragments may fly about.

LAMINATING THERMOSETTING PLASTICS

Making plastic laminates

Layers of paper or cloth are impregnated with thermosetting resins and forced together under high pressure in a heated press.

Plastic laminates such as Formica consist of sheets of paper soaked in phenol formaldehyde, with the patterned surface made by printing the design on the top sheet of paper and soaking it in a clear resin such as melamine formaldehyde. Laminates such as Tufnol used for electronic circuit boards and electrical switchgear consist of either fabric or paper soaked in phenol formaldehyde.

LAMINATING GLASS REINFORCED PLASTICS – GRP

Glass fibre mat is embedded in polyester resin to produce a strong hard-wearing material commonly known as fibreglass. This can be used to make almost any shape and size of construction from cars, caravans and boats to chair seats, trays and toys. Weight for weight, glass reinforced plastics are stronger than steel, and other important properties include high tensile and compressive strength and excellent corrosion resistance.

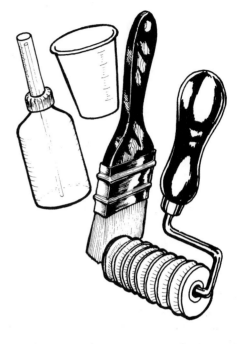

The resin provides the shape, colour and surface finish and the glass fibre mat provides the strength. The resin must be mixed with a catalyst or hardener to make it set, and an accelerator or activator to speed up the reaction time. If both catalyst and accelerator are to be added to the resin **they must never be mixed together** as they might **explode**. Many resins can be bought pre-accelerated and this is more convenient and safer than mixing accelerator yourself.

MOULD MAKING

Most GRP mouldings are made by laminating on a mould, and the quality of this is one of the most important factors in getting a good result. The side of the finished product which is in contact with the surface of the mould will come out smooth, and the other side will show the rougher texture of the mat. On a female mould the lamination is built up on the inside of the mould, and the outside of the product will be smooth (e.g. on a canoe), while on a male mould the lamination is on the outside, and the inside of the product will be smooth (e.g. on a tray or a fishpond lining).

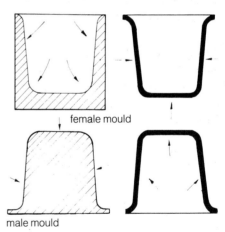

female mould

male mould

Since the surface of the completed moulding will be an exact copy of the mould surface, it is important to obtain a good finish on the mould.

The first or master mould can be made from almost any material available, and wood. plasticine, plaster and clay are commonly used. The finished moulding can be made from this or from a fibreglass mould taken from this master mould. It is often easier to make the master mould as an exact model of the finished product, and then to take a fibreglass mould from it, than to build a negative mould. Fibreglass moulds may also be better for repeated use and are easier to store.

Important points to remember when designing a mould are that you must:

1 Be able to get at all parts of the mould with brush, resin and glassfibre.
2 Be able to remove the finished job from the mould. Therefore, the mould must have tapered sides.
3 Avoid sharp corners. They are weak spots and are often difficult to laminate without trapping air bubbles.
4 Avoid large flat surfaces as they usually become curved. Make all surfaces large convex curves to increase strength and improve appearance.

STAGES IN LAMINATING

The lay-up of glass fibre can be a very messy job, and it is therefore very important to be well organised and to work carefully.

Protect your hands with barrier cream or by wearing disposable polythene gloves, and your clothes with an apron.

1 **Prepare the mould** Porous moulds such as wood and plaster must be sealed with several coats of french polish or special sealers. Non-porous moulds such as fibreglass, perspex, glass and metal, and sealed porous moulds must be polished with three coats of non-silicone wax and/or coated with a release agent.

2 **Cut-up sufficient glass-fibre mat for all the layers** This consists of strands of glass about 50 mm long stuck together into a mat with a binder. When polyester resin is added it dissolves the binder, allowing the strands to become a loose mat, which will then follow the shape of the mould.

There are three common grades or weights of mat — 300 g, 450 g and 600 g per square metre.

Two thicknesses of 450 g mat are strong enough for most purposes. Allow a 25 mm overhang round the edges and a 25 mm overlap where two pieces in the same layer join. Use the smallest possible number of pieces and avoid waste. Simple paper patterns can be made to work out the number and shapes of pieces needed.

3 **Gel-coat the mould** Gel-coat resin is the first layer of a GRP lay-up and it must provide a smooth, glossy, hard-wearing, waterproof surface. So that it does not run off the mould before it cures, it is a **thixotropic** (thick) paste.

Mix the gel-coat resin with colour pigment if required and catalyse it. Brush it evenly all over the mould to a maximum thickness of 1 mm. Leave it to cure until it will not stick to the fingers when touched although it is still tacky (usually about 30 minutes).

4 **Lay-up glass fibre** Mix pre-accelerated lay-up resin with colour pigment if required. You will need approximately $2\frac{1}{2}$ times as much resin as glass fibre mat by weight.

Brush a thick coat of resin onto the cured gel-coat using a stiff bristled brush. Lay the first layer of mat in position and stipple it into the resin. Do not brush as this will pull the mat to pieces. Stipple until the mat softens and curls up, resin rises up through all parts of the mat, and all air bubbles have been released. Do not add more resin unless you have to.

Continue stippling on layers of resin and mat, without waiting for previous layers to dry, until the required thickness is reached.

A smoother rough side to the lamination can be achieved by using a very fine glass fibre surface tissue for the final layer, and/or by pressing a sheet of polyester film onto the surface to squeeze out excess resin and air bubbles. Leave the polyester film on until the lay-up has cured and then peel it off.

5 **Leave the lamination to cure** and then remove it from the mould. The complete job can most easily be removed from the mould when it is still rubbery or 'green'. Complete curing takes at least 24 hours. Clean up equipment immediately using brush cleaner to dissolve off the resin.

6 **Trim to shape.** This can be done with a sharp knife while the job is still green or using wood and metalwork tools after it is completely cured. Trimming is often done while the job is still on the mould, using the mould edge as a guide.

USING CONTINUOUS ROVINGS
These are continuous strands of glass fibre made into a string which can be wound into cylindrical shapes such as lampshades, or used to reinforce lay-ups. Rovings are used in the proportion of seven parts glass fibre to three parts resin, by weight.

USING CLEAR RESIN
To produce laminates through which light can shine as in lampshades and skylights we use a clear lay-up resin. This can be tinted using translucent colour pastes.

Shaping thermoplastics

There are two types of bend: single curvature and double curvature.

In **single curvature bending**, thermoplastic sheet, usually acrylic, is heated until pliable and bent to shape over simple formers. The sheet is formed in one direction only and this is a simple operation.

In **double curvature bending**, the sheet is formed in two directions to make such shapes as dishes, trays, lamp shades and covers. This is more difficult and requires special equipment. The usual methods are press-forming, blow-moulding and vacuum forming.

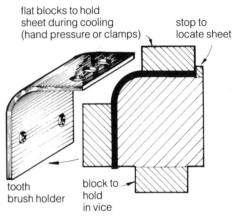

flat blocks to hold
sheet during cooling
(hand pressure or clamps)

stop to
locate sheet

tooth
brush holder

block to
hold
in vice

Simple former for single bends

SINGLE CURVATURE BENDING

DESIGN OF FORMERS
To obtain an accurate bend a simple former must be made to support the sheet during cooling. It must be smooth because the softened plastic will be marked by any blemishes. Formers are usually made from wood, but pieces of pipe will also be found useful for larger curves.

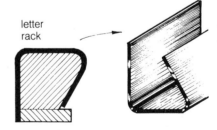

letter
rack

Simple former for double bends

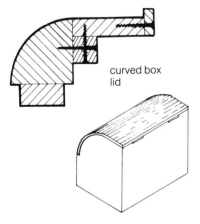

curved box
lid

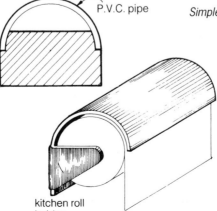

P.V.C. pipe

kitchen roll
holder

Built-up formers for larger curves

It is bad practice to try to form a sharp square bend in thermoplastics as this can overstretch and weaken the material. You should design radiused corners when using plastics.

It must be possible to put the heated plastic onto the former and shape it quickly. The jig must be designed to slightly over-bend the curve, because during cooling it will spring back a little.

HEATING FOR BENDING

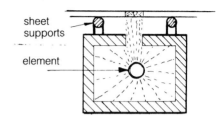

Heaters

Strip heater

This is used where only a narrow strip is to be heated across the sheet in order to form a small curvature bend. It is a single electric element enclosed in a box which has a slot above the element.

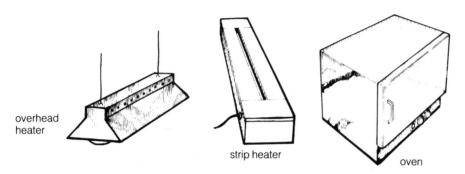

overhead heater

strip heater

oven

The sheet is placed over the slot so that a strip is heated. If the sheet supports can be adjusted for height, the width of the strip heated can be varied to suit the thickness of material and sharpness of bend. The higher the supports, the wider the strip heated. The sheet should be turned over at intervals to ensure even heating.

Oven and infra-red heaters

Where a wide strip is to be heated, it is necessary to either put the whole sheet in an oven or under infra-red heaters. Even heating of the sheet is important. Take care to protect the sheet from damage during heating.

Bending should not be attempted until the sheet is heated right through and completely flexible.

■ 3 mm thick acrylic should be heated to 160/170°C for 20 minutes.
■ 6 mm thick acrylic should be heated to 160/170°C for 30 minutes.

Heating to 180°C will damage the sheet.

DOUBLE CURVATURE BENDING

To form in two directions, it is necessary to make an accurate former of the required shape and to exert considerable pressure on the softened plastic.

Vacuum forming is used to shape thin sheets because they would not stay hot long enough to be taken from the oven and placed on the former. (See Vacuum forming.)

Thicker sheets can be shaped by press-forming or blow-moulding. For both of these the sheet is heated in an oven or under infra-red heaters and then placed on the former for shaping.

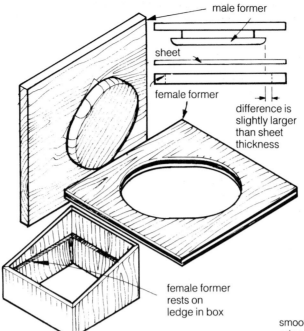

male former

sheet

female former

difference is slightly larger than sheet thickness

(a) Finished dish

female former rests on ledge in box

(b) Guide box

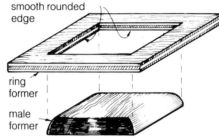

smooth rounded edge

ring former

male former

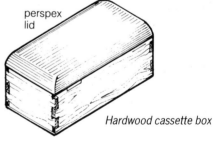

perspex lid

Hardwood cassette box

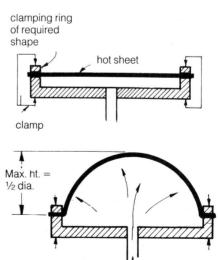

clamping ring of required shape

hot sheet

clamp

Max. ht. = ½ dia.

air blown in

PRESS FORMING

In the first example shown here, the sheet of thermoplastic is softened and then placed on top of the female former, which is in a guide box to make lining up of the parts easier. The male former is placed on top of the sheet and pressure is put on by standing on top of it until the sheet has cooled. This is a very good way to make small dishes and covers.

Once a guide box strong enough to stand on has been made, pairs of formers to fit it can be made from 12 mm ply.

The sheet and formers are always cut to fit the box so that locating the hot sheet is easy.

An alternative method is to make an accurate male former with a simple ring former to press down the sheet. This is a good method for making larger lids and covers. A small taper is needed to make sure of the easy removal of the finished shape, and the ring must be larger than the male former to allow for the thickness of the sheet.

BLOW-MOULDING

There are three main types of blow-moulding. In the simplest, **free blowing**, a sheet of softened thermoplastic is clamped into a jig and air is blown in to inflate it to a dome shape. In the second, **blowing into a mould**, the softened sheet is blown into a female mould instead of into space, so that the shape of the finished bubble can be controlled. This method produces shapes such as stereo unit lids and food containers, and is an alternative to press forming. The third method, **extrusion moulding**, is used in industry to mass produce plastic containers of all shapes and sizes from bottles to barrels. Either rigid or squeeze containers can be made simply by varying the types of granule used. This process is a mixture of two processes, extrusion and blow-moulding. Details of this process will be found under 'Extrusion' in chapter 13.

FREE BLOWING

1 Cut a piece of thermoplastic (usually acrylic) to fit the jig, and heat it in an oven until soft.
2 Quickly clamp it into the jig and inflate gently.
3 Allow the shape to cool before reducing pressure, and removing from the jig.
4 Trim to shape using bandsaw and sanding machine or hand tools. Polish the edges.

(a) Free blowing

(b) Blowing into a mould

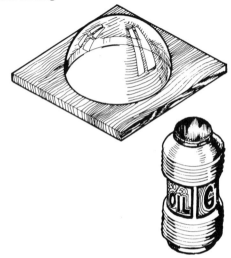

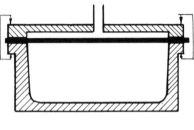

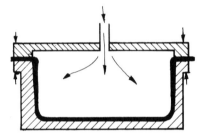

air blown in

BLOWING INTO A MOULD

The stages are similar to those of free blowing. The mould must be made to the high standards already described for other forming processes.

MATERIALS FOR BLOW MOULDING

Most thermoplastics can be blow-moulded. In school, free blowing and blowing into a mould are most often done with thin acrylic sheet. In industry polyethylene, polystyrene and PVC are widely used for extrusion blow moulding (see page 279).

VACUUM FORMING THERMOPLASTICS

In vacuum forming, a sheet of thermoplastic held in a clamp is heated until soft and flexible, and the air is sucked out from underneath it so that atmospheric pressure forces the sheet down onto a specially made mould. This process enables thermoplastics to be formed into complicated shapes such as packaging, storage trays and seed trays.

Vacuum forming machine

STAGE V1

Clamp the sheet across the top of the box and heat it until it is soft and flexible. This can be judged by watching the material, which will start to sag under its own weight when soft. If touched with a stick it will feel soft and rubbery.

STAGE V2

Suck the air out of the box so that the sheet is pressed down over the shape of the mould.

DRAPE FORMING

The disadvantage of vacuum forming is that if the sheet is drawn deep into the box it will be stretched until it is very thin in places. In drape forming, this problem is overcome by forcing the mould upwards into the hot sheet before the air is sucked out. This is done by raising the platen, and can only be done on a machine with a moveable platen.

Stage D1

As for vacuum forming (V1).

Stage D2

Raise platen.

Stage D3

Suck the air out of the box. It can be seen that there are no deep drawn sections.

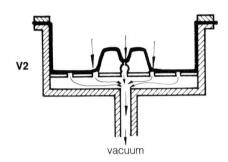

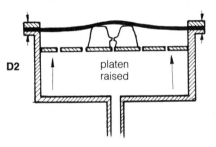

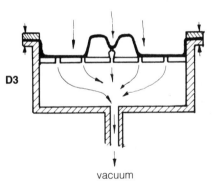

Hot forming of metals — forgework

Forging is used to produce strong, tough shapes. The hammering received during forging refines the grain of the metal and increases its toughness. By correct forging the grain can be made to follow the shape of the job without any breaks, thus making the job stronger. It is also often more economical in materials and quicker than machining shapes from solid steel.

MATERIALS

The metals most often shaped while hot are black mild steel and tool steel.

CORRECT HEAT

One of the most important things to remember when forging is that the metal must only be worked at the correct temperature: for example, mild steel at a bright red/yellow heat (1200°C) and tool steel at red heat (900°C). These heats can be reached either by heating with a gas-air torch or in a blacksmith's hearth.

TOOLS FOR FORGING

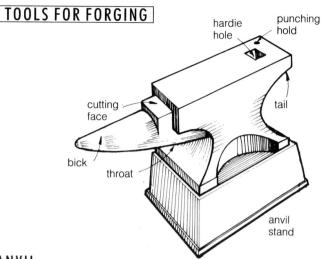

hardie hole

punching hold

cutting face

tail

bick

throat

anvil stand

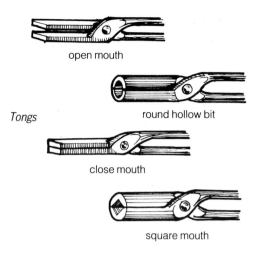

Tongs

open mouth

round hollow bit

close mouth

square mouth

ANVIL

This is made from mild steel with a hardened steel working face welded onto it. It is mounted on a cast-iron anvil stand to raise it to a good working height.

The bick is used for forming curves, the cutting face for cutting metal with a chisel or rough work which might damage the main working face, and the working face for general forming. Part of one edge is rounded for making radiused bends. The hardie hole is used to mount various forging aids (hardie, swage, fuller) and the punching hole when making holes.

TONGS

These are used to pick up and hold short lengths of hot metal. A pair must be chosen which grips the metal firmly. Some of the most used shapes are shown here.

HAMMERS

Ball-pein hammers are used for most general forging. They are usually from $\frac{1}{2}$ to 1 kg in weight. A sledge hammer is used for heavy work (see Driving tools).

SWAGES

These have semi-circular grooves which are used to finish-off metal to a circular shape. The bottom swage fits into the hardie hole while the top swage is struck with a hammer. Several pairs of different diameters are needed.

FULLERS

These have a smooth rounded shape and are used when necking down large sections of metal as the first stage of forging a shoulder, or for making rounded grooves and corners. The bottom fuller fits into the hardie hole while the top fuller is hit with a hammer. This process is a good example of how forging squeezes the fibres of the metal into a new shape without cutting them.

FLATTERS

These are used to smooth the surface of the metal after other processes. The metal is trapped between the flatter and the anvil, and the flatter is struck with a hammer.

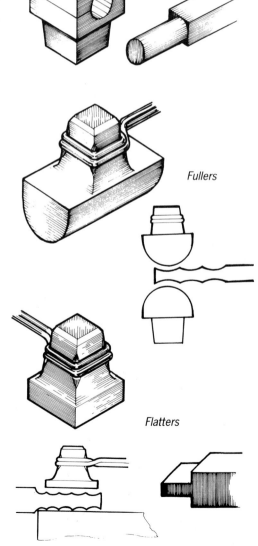

Swages

Fullers

Flatters

FORGING PROCESSES

The most important thing to remember here is that the hottest part of the metal will bend more easily. The temperature should, therefore, be controlled very carefully by a combination of heating and pouring on water to keep cool the parts which are not to be forged. Do not try to forge metal which is too cold, as this will result only in hammer marks on the metal and bad shaping.

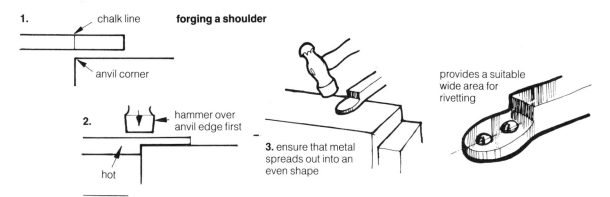

forging a shoulder

1. chalk line / anvil corner

2. hammer over anvil edge first / hot

3. ensure that metal spreads out into an even shape

provides a suitable wide area for rivetting

DRAWING DOWN

This reduces the cross-section of the metal by increasing its length. For heavy jobs, swages, fullers, or flatters may be needed, but on light sections it usually consists of forging a tapered point or a shoulder on the end of the metal.

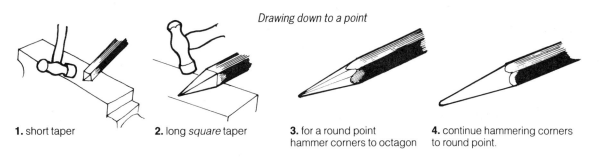

Drawing down to a point

1. short taper

2. long *square* taper

3. for a round point hammer corners to octagon

4. continue hammering corners to round point.

BENDING

The simplest bend is to form a radiused bend on the curved edge of the anvil. A square bend needs extra metal to be added to the corner to avoid over-thinning through stretching. This is done by **upsetting** the metal. Only the metal being upset or bent must be hot during shaping, the rest being kept cool by pouring on water.

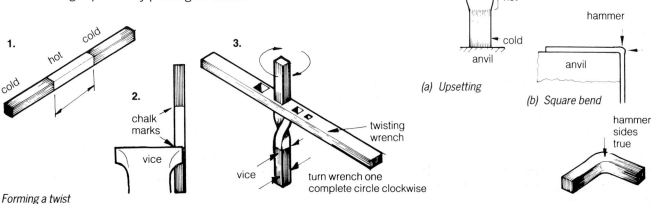

1. cold / hot / cold

2. chalk marks / vice

3. twisting wrench / vice / turn wrench one complete circle clockwise

Forming a twist

hammer / thickens / cold / hot / cold / anvil

(a) Upsetting

hammer / anvil / **curved bend** / hammer / anvil

(b) Square bend

hammer sides true

FORGING AN EYE

It is important to follow the stages shown. Unless a right angle is formed first, and the eye by bending the end outwards from this, a P-shape will result.

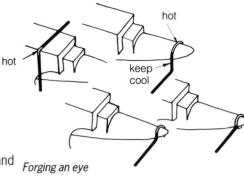
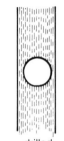

Forging an eye

PUNCHES

These are used to punch holes through the heated metal instead of drilling them and are another good example of how to shape rather than cut the grain fibres. This is done by placing the metal over the punching hole and hammering the punch into both sides of the metal in turn until it breaks through. A small pilot hole is often drilled to make the punching easier.

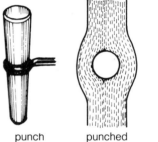

punch   punched   drilled

DRIFTS

These are used to enlarge, tidy up, or change the shape of holes; for example, from round to square. They have a large taper and no handles.

HEAVY DUTY CHISELS FOR FORGEWORK

Hardie

This is a chisel which fits into the hardie-hole on the anvil. To use, either lay the hot or cold metal on the hardie and strike the metal with a hammer, or trap the metal between the hardie and the correct set, and strike the set with a hammer. Wedge angles of 30° (hot) or 60° (cold) are used, because hot metal is softer and easier to cut.

Hot set

- ■ Used to cut hot steels and wrought iron on the anvil.
- ■ A heavy duty chisel fitted with a wooden or metal handle.
- ■ Used on the cutting face of the anvil or with a hardie.
- ■ Wedge angle of 30°.
- ■ Not hardened and tempered because hot metal would re-soften it.

Cold set

- ■ Used to cut cold metals on the anvil.
- ■ Similar to the hot set.
- ■ Wedge angle of 60°.
- ■ Hardened and tempered.

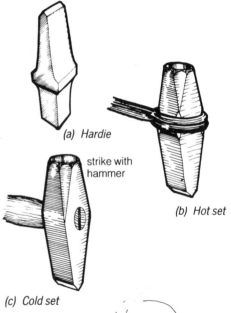

(a) Hardie

strike with hammer

(b) Hot set

(c) Cold set

Cold forming of metals

SIMPLE BENDS

Thin sections of metal can be bent cold, usually after annealing (softening). Black mild steel can be bent without annealing, but bright mild steel would probably crack in tight bends.

Simple jigs can be made where several pieces must be bent to the same shape. An adjustable jig can be made by drilling holes in a thick steel plate, and turning pegs of any required diameter to fit.

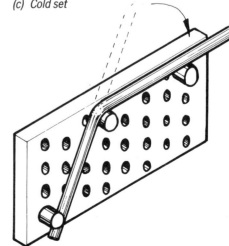

BENDING SHEETMETAL

Where a long bend is to be made, folding bars are used to give a straight line. Bend a small amount at a time all the way along the bend to avoid over-stretching. For larger jobs bolt or clamp two lengths of angle-iron together. In industry, bending of sheetmetal is done on folding machines.

Take care not to damage the surface of the sheet during bending.

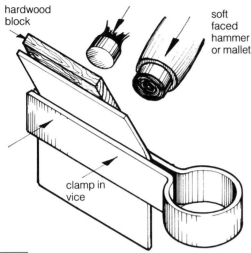

hardwood block

soft faced hammer or mallet

clamp in vice

SPINNING

This is an important mass production process in industry, used for making saucepans, and stainless steel and aluminium hollow-ware. It is not often used in school because it can be dangerous. A thin metal disc is mounted in a lathe between an accurately made former and a tailstock pad which revolve with it. A heavy steel finger-shaped bar with a polished end is pressed firmly against the revolving disc to push it over the former.

spinning tool

blank

spun shape

pad

tail stock

former

finished vessel

PRESSING

This is a mass production process used to make all types of thin metal containers, car body panels, heating radiators, etc.

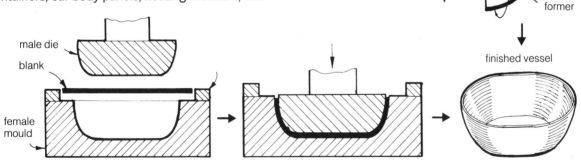

male die

blank

female mould

BEATEN METALWORK

Malleable metals such as copper, brass, gilding metal and silver can be shaped, after annealing, into container shapes such as jugs, bowls and vases. There are several ways of working these materials, the most used ones being hollowing, sinking and raising, all of which are usually followed by planishing. More advanced work usually involves a combination of these processes and fabricating, where shapes such as cylinders and cones are folded from flat sheet, silver-soldered along the seams and then soldered to each other. For example, a tankard might be made by folding and soldering a cylinder, raising it to shape and soldering on base, plinth and handle.

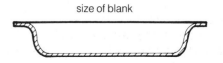

size of blank

SINKING

This is a method of thinning the centre of a piece of metal to form a shallow tray with the edge of the metal being left almost untouched.

Marking-out

On the annealed and cleaned blank, draw a pencil line to mark the width of the lip which is to be left round the tray.

Method

The simplest method is to make a wooden block as shown, cut to the cross-section required, and with two pins to limit the width of the lip.

Hold the annealed metal against the pins and hammer with a sinking hammer just inside the pencil line. A gradual depression should be made all the way round the tray. Hammering is repeated as many times as necessary gradually moving away from the line, and annealing and cleaning frequently. This is a slow and difficult process.

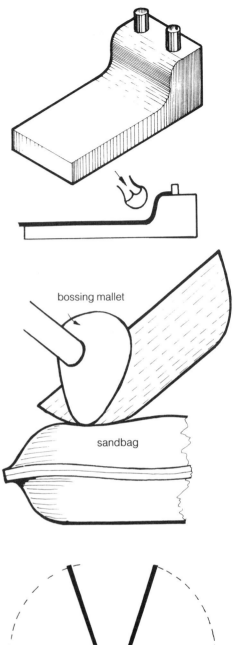

HOLLOWING

This is a simpler process used to make shallow dishes. The metal is thinned so that the diameter of the finished dish is again approximately the same as that of the blank used.

Marking-out

After annealing and cleaning, draw concentric rings in pencil round what will become the inside of the dish and a radial starting line.

Method

Using the smaller face of a bossing mallet and a leather sandbag, work round the outside line and then each line in turn, working towards the centre. Anneal and clean as necessary. After each round of hollowing, use the large face of the mallet to true up the shape and remove any wrinkles in the edge of the bowl. You must get the bowl as smooth and even as possible at each stage.

RAISING

This is a way of making taller shapes by bending up the sides of a blank. It is the opposite of hollowing and sinking where the centre of the blank is pushed down. During raising the thickness of the metal is increased as the circumference of the vessel is reduced. **The blank must first be hollowed to turn the sides inwards.**

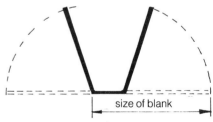

Marking-out

Draw concentric circles about 10 mm apart and a radial starting line on the outside of the hollowed shape of the job. Use a flat-faced planishing hammer unless the centre will show the diameter of the base of the finished vessel.

Method

The metal is placed on a raising stake and struck with a raising hammer or mallet (stage 1). The blow strikes the part which is just above the stake and forces it down onto the stake and into a smaller area, thus thickening it. The force of the blow must stop before the metal is trapped between the hammer and the stake, and thinned. This is repeated all the way round the circle. The job is moved to a new position on the stake and

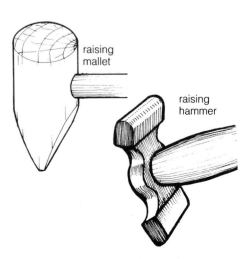

raising continues round the second line (stage 2). After the whole blank
has been raised in this way, dress out any wrinkles in the edge, and
anneal and clean ready for further raising. Raising gets more difficult as
the sides get higher and continues in smaller steps. If the shape is
uneven raise part of the way round to even up the shape.

PLANISHING

After we have shaped our job we finish it by planishing to smooth the
surface, true up the shape and work-harden the metal so that it will keep
its shape.

Marking-out

Draw concentric circles and a radial starting line on the outside of the
annealed and cleaned shape.

Method

Choose a stake which curves slightly more than the shape of the job, and
a flat-faced planishing hammer unless the shape of the job would cause
the edges of the hammer to dig in. Both stake and hammer must be
smooth and highly polished. If a flat stake is used, a curved hammer face
will be needed. To check that the stake is correct, put the job onto the
stake and tap it with the hammer. If the sound is hollow the stake is
wrong or you are striking in the wrong place. If solid it is correct.

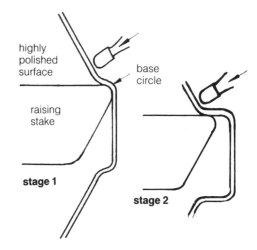

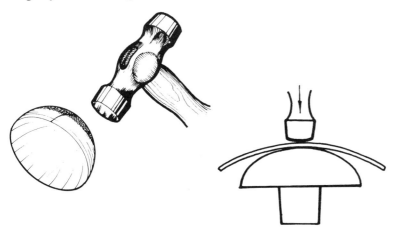

When planishing, start in the centre of the job and planish round inside
the first circular line, then the second, etc. To make sure that the finished
shape is the same all the way round always strike the same spot on the
stake with the hammer, and slowly move the job in order to planish the
whole surface. Every planishing mark must just touch the next one, so
that the whole surface is covered evenly with no gaps, like the scales of a
fish. It is important to make sure that the corner of the hammer does not
dig into the surface by keeping it square to the work. Hold the end of the
hammer shaft, and deliver the blows by moving the wrist so that they fall
lightly and evenly on the work exactly over the point of contact between
the job and the stake. Do not swing the hammer from the elbow or
shoulder as this increases the danger of digging in.

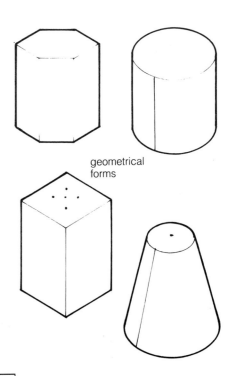

geometrical
forms

FOLDING AND SEAMING

Instead of raising deep shapes from a flat sheet we can draw the
development of the nearest simple geometrical shape, cut it out, bend it
and silver solder it. This is easier than raising such shapes as cylinders
and cones, and the best way to make such shapes as square, hexagonal

and octagonal vessels. After soldering, the basic shapes can be modified by raising and then finished by planishing if needed. The base can be a flat piece soldered on, a simple hollowed shape soldered on, or a flat piece set about 3 mm inside the seamed shape, so that the joint does not show.

To make a square corner, a V-groove is first cut with a simple scraper made from hardened and tempered silver steel, so that a neat sharp fold can be made.

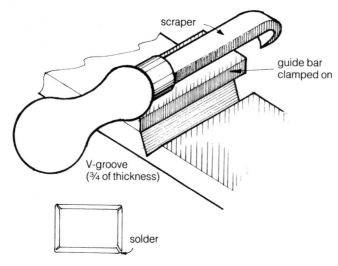

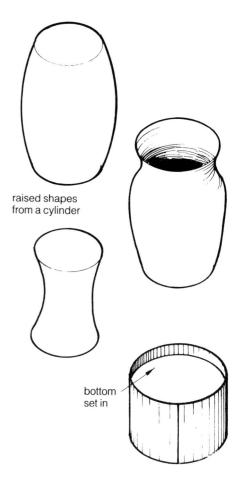

raised shapes from a cylinder

bottom set in

Press forming of sheet metal

Metal components varying in size from a cigarette lighter to a car body panel can be formed by squeezing sheet metal between two matched metal moulds or dies. One die half is a mirror image of the second, and complicated die sets can therefore be very expensive and difficult to make.

The main body of the cigarette lighter (far left) and other products seen here were made by press forming of sheet metal

In a process known as rubber block forming, only one metal die half is required. The sheet metal is squeezed between this die and a block of rubber. Under high pressure the metal sheet is pushed against the die by the rubber and takes up the exact shape of it.

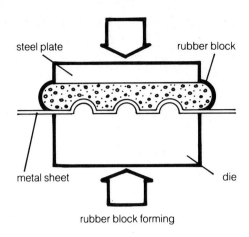

steel plate

rubber block

metal sheet

die

rubber block forming

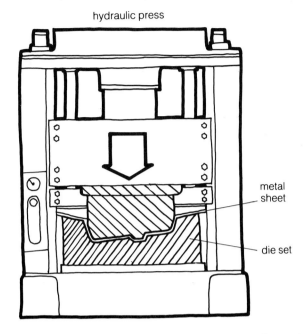

hydraulic press

metal sheet

die set

Dies used commercially in rubber block forming are normally made from steel, but for pressing aluminium, brass or copper sheet, aluminium — or even softer materials — can be used instead. Rubber sheeting, old car tyre inner tubing or even a thick wad of newspaper can also be used in place of the special commercial rubbers.

Pressure can be applied to the rubber and die with a large metalworking vice, but a preferred method uses a hydraulic car jack operating in a very strong metal frame. The example shows large and small hub caps for models pressed formed against aluminium dies made from scrap. The impression in each die was produced by turning on a lathe.

Rubber block forming is ideal where several identical components are needed, but some experimentation is required. The sheet material must always be annealed prior to forming and, in general, the thinner the sheet, the less relief it can be given when formed. Sharp edges should be avoided in the die otherwise the sheet will tend to shear through under pressure at these points.

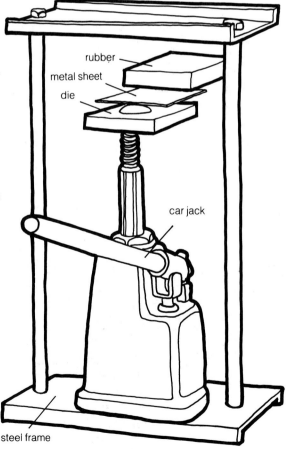

rubber

metal sheet

die

car jack

steel frame

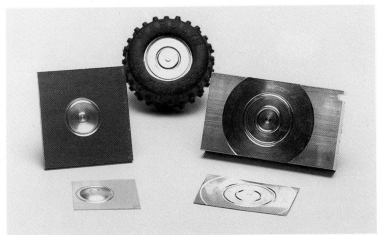

19 Ways of working materials.
PART 3—moulding and casting

Casting is where shapes are made by pouring molten metal or thermosetting plastics resins into moulds of the required shape and leaving the castings to solidify. Moulding originally described the process of making the sand moulds for casting metals, but the term is now also used to describe processes where plastics granules are heated to make a soft paste which can then be shaped in processes such as injection moulding. In these processes the material is never completely liquid.

Casting metals

GREEN SAND MOULDING

This means simply that the mould is made from damp ('green') sand. It is the most used foundry method in school, and in industry it is used for small production runs and large or intricate castings.

The simplest type of mould is a hollow of the correct shape in the sand into which molten metal can be poured. This is adequate when the top of the casting does not have to be smooth, but most sand moulds are made in two parts so that the whole casting is enclosed, giving a smooth finish to all sides.

The mould is made in a **flask** consisting of two parts which locate accurately together, but can easily be taken apart. The top part is called the **cope** and has pegs which fit into holes in the lower part or **drag**. The pegs are offset so that the cope and drag cannot be fitted together the wrong way round.

MOULDING SAND

A good moulding sand must have:

(a) **Refractoriness** so that it will withstand heat.
(b) **Permeability** to allow steam and gases to escape.
(c) **Sufficient bond** to hold the mould shape together when the pattern is removed and the metal is poured in.
(d) **Smoothness** to give a good surface finish.

Refractoriness is increased by the presence of silica which fuses at a temperature higher than the melting points of the common metals. Bond is provided by a 3% to 6% clay content which acts as a binder when water is added. The moisture content should be 8%. It is dangerous to make the sand too wet, because when hot metal touches it steam is generated. This can cause the metal to splash back, or when trapped in the mould can cause blow holes in the casting, or even a blow back where the mould breaks up under the pressure of the steam.

To check the sand for dampness:

(a) Take a handful of sand and squeeze it together. It should bond together.
(b) Break the lump of sand carefully in half. The edges should stay firm and not crumble.
(c) Drop the lumps onto the moulding bench. They should break up.

IMPROVING THE MOULD SURFACE

There are several ways of doing this. For example:

1 Oil-bound sand, such as Petrabond, can be used to cover the pattern or for the whole mould. It is finer than green sand and because it has no water to cause steam it can be rammed harder. This gives a very good finish to the casting.
2 A mould coating can be sprayed onto the surface after the pattern has been withdrawn.

PATTERN MAKING

Patterns can be made from any material which will give a smooth, water-resistant surface and which is strong enough to withstand the ramming of the sand around it.

Close grained, easily worked hardwoods (such as jelutong) or softwoods are usually used. Metal is used in industry for patterns which will be used repeatedly. When designing a pattern you must remember the following points:
(a) The metal will shrink as it cools. Therefore, make the pattern slightly oversize.
(b) Parts which must be machined or filed to shape after casting will need an extra machining allowance left on.
(c) All corners should be radiused and all sides tapered so that the pattern can easily be removed from the mould.
(d) There should be no sudden changes in metal thickness as this would weaken the casting.
(e) Work out how the finished casting will be shaped. It may be necessary to cast in a mounting lug to hold the work in the lathe or vice. This can be cut off after shaping.
(f) Time spent in finishing the pattern is time well spent because it is much easier to make a smooth, accurate casting than to clean up a bad casting.

TYPES OF PATTERN

FLAT-BACK PATTERNS
These are the simplest type having one flat and one shaped side. They are moulded in one half of the flask only. (See Making a flat-back moulding.)

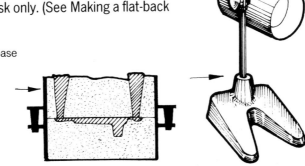

lamp base

ODD-SIDE PATTERNS

This type does not have a flat side and must be moulded in both halves of the flask. The parting line between the cope and the drag must be carefully chosen so that the pattern can be removed without damaging the mould.

Making a mould using an odd-side pattern is complicated because the pattern must first be temporarily supported by burying it up to the parting line in the sand-filled cope so that the drag can be made up. The drag and pattern are then carefully removed and turned over so that the cope can be broken up and remade properly with runner, riser, etc.

There are two ways of redesigning the pattern to overcome this difficulty.

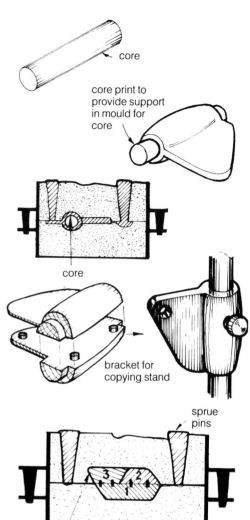

core

core print to provide support in mould for core

core

SPLIT PATTERNS

The pattern can be made in two parts located together with tapered metal dowels. This makes it possible to build up the bottom half of the mould as with a flat-back pattern and then fit the other part of the pattern to complete the mould. Split patterns are also used when moulding shapes which are too complicated to remove from the mould in one piece. In the example shown, the problem of an **undercut** shape which could not be withdrawn in one piece has been solved by using a three-piece split pattern.

bracket for copying stand

MATCH-PLATE PATTERNS

The two halves of a split pattern can be mounted on either side of a piece of 12 mm thick plywood which fits between the cope and drag. The mould can then be made simply by filling the drag, turning the flask over, placing the sprue pins and filling the cope. The pattern can include the shapes of the gates so that these do not have to be cut separately. Match plates are a simple aid to the quantity production of castings.

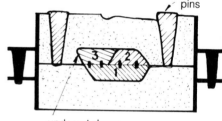

sprue pins

undercut shape

CORES

These are used where internal shaping is needed in a casting. It is easier and more economical to cast in shaping than to machine it afterwards. For example, the large hole in the bracket above would only require finishing to the correct size, while to set up and drill a solid casting would be quite a lengthy task.

Cores can be made by mixing a special silica sand with a binder and ramming this into a mould to form the shape. After removal from the mould, the core is baked in an oven ready for use and carefully placed in position, resting in core prints in the mould made by the pattern. After pouring, the core can easily be broken out of the casting.

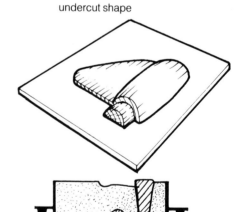

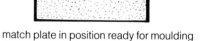

match plate in position ready for moulding

MAKING A FLAT-BACK MOULDING

1 Put the drag upside down on a flat board. Place the pattern inside the drag, making sure that there is at least 25 mm space all round, and that there is room for the sprue pins later. Shake parting powder over the pattern to prevent sand sticking to it.

1

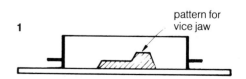

pattern for vice jaw

2 Riddle a covering of sand over the pattern, and fill up the rest of the drag by throwing in unsifted sand and ramming it down. Strickle (level) off the top with a straight edge to give a flat surface.

3 Turn the drag and the board over together so that the pattern does not drop out. Fit the cope. Sprinkle on parting powder. Put sprue pins in place to make the runner and riser. Riddle sand over the pattern, fill up with unsifted sand and strickle off.

4 Cut a pouring basin at the top of the runner with a lip to prevent sand or slag being washed down. Smooth all the edges especially round the top of the runner and riser. Tap loose and carefully lift out the sprue pins. Finish smoothing the edges.

5 Remove the cope and place it carefully aside. Cut gates or channels from the runner and riser to the pattern, and smooth the edges. Screw a woodscrew into the pattern, tap it all over to loosen it and carefully lift it out. Blow out any loose sand.

6 Refit the cope. Place the flask in a tray of sand and pile sand around it as a precaution against leaks between cope and drag during pouring.

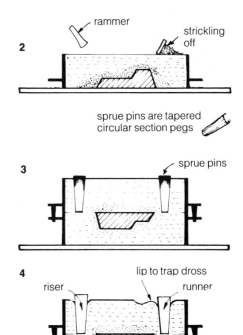

sprue pins are tapered
circular section pegs

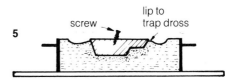

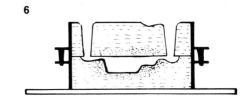

SOME OTHER METAL CASTING METHODS

GRAVITY DIE CASTING
Green sand moulding is slow and does not produce a high quality surface finish. These problems can be overcome by die casting, where the metal is poured into a cast iron or steel die. This process is only economical where large numbers of the same casting are needed.

PRESSURE DIE CASTING
Where very large numbers are needed, pressure die casting becomes economical. Here the metal is forced into alloy steel dies under hydraulic pressure. This enables intricate shapes such as cylinder heads to be cast accurately and automatically in die casting machines. The process is similar to the injection moulding of plastics.

LOST WAX CASTING
This is a very old process where an expendable pattern of a shape too complicated to be withdrawn from the mould is made from wax. This is then coated with refractory material to make the mould and buried in sand.

The mould is heated so that the wax melts and runs out, and the molten metal can then be poured in.

This process is used both for the production of intricate one-off designs, such as jewellery, and for the small-scale production of parts requiring great dimensional accuracy, such as turbine blades.

CASTING WITH EXPANDED POLYSTYRENE PATTERNS
This is a modern variation on lost wax casting. Because expanded polystyrene vaporizes away when hot metal is poured onto it, patterns of any shape or size can be made and left in the mould during pouring. Take care to ram the sand firmly into all parts of the shape. The mould must be well vented, and have large runners and risers so that the metal can flow in quickly, and the fumes can easily escape. Pouring must take place outside or in a well ventilated area, and the metal should be slightly

hotter than usual so that it will melt the pattern and flow to all parts of the mould. This method is not suitable for precision work and does not produce a good surface finish. It is ideal for producing ornamental castings such as lamp bases and sculptures.

Moulding and casting plastics

COMPRESSION MOULDING

This is a way of shaping **thermosetting** plastics into such things as electrical fittings and melamine 'unbreakable' crockery. Powdered plastic is placed in the heated lower half of the mould, and the mould is closed. A combination of heat and high pressure is then used to plasticise the powder and force it into the shape of the mould.

The main materials used are melamine formaldehyde, urea formaldehyde and phenol formaldehyde.

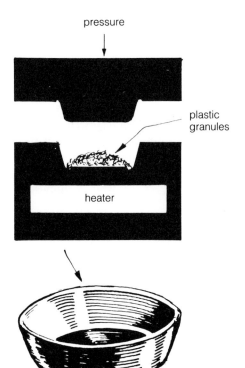

pressure

plastic granules

heater

ROTATIONAL CASTING

The correct amount of **thermoplastic** paste (usually plasticised PVC) is poured into a hollow mould. This is then rotated on a special machine in two directions at once while being heated in an oven. The paste is spread evenly over the whole of the inside of the mould. After cooling the mould is opened and the completed shape removed. Products of this process include footballs, squeezy toys and dolls heads.

SLUSH MOULDING

This is a similar but simpler process now being replaced by rotational casting.

COLD RESIN CASTING WITH THERMOSETTING RESINS

Polyester resins and epoxy resins can be cast into solid blocks which can then be used as cast, for example in making lamp bases and small statues, or they can be machined and worked with hand tools in the same way as metal castings.

Clear polyester resin can also be used for **embedding** small items, in order to preserve and display them, or to make decorative paperweights, jewellery, etc.

Instructions for the safe handling and mixing of resins have been given in the section on glass reinforced plastics, and must be followed.

MOULDS FOR CASTING

These must have a smooth polished surface to give a good finish to the casting, and if needed a slight taper so that the casting can be removed after curing.

Ready-made moulds can be polythene, PVC, glass, porcelain, waxed paper, aluminium foil and other materials. Polystyrene should not be used as it is sometimes melted by resins. To make your own mould, first make a wood, clay or plaster pattern of the required shape and finish it to the standard required on the finished casting. Seal porous patterns with french polish or a suitable sealer and then polish all patterns with non-silicone release wax or brush on release agent. This pattern is then used in one of several possible ways to make the mould.

For a complicated shape we can use flexible mould-making materials, such as remeltable PVC, rubber latex or silicone rubber. For a simple shape which can easily be withdrawn from the mould, we can vacuum form a PVC sheet over it, lay-up a GRP mould or cast a plaster mould round it.

CHOICE OF RESINS FOR CASTING

Most **polyester resins** can be cast, but special casting resins and clear embedding resins are available to give the best results.

There are three problems to beware of in using these resins.

1 **Cracking.** During curing a lot of heat is given off and this reaction can cause cracking of the casting.
2 **Shrinking.** During curing the casting will shrink by at least 5%. While this often helps removal from the mould it can also be a cause of cracking around hard objects embedded in the resin, and when a new layer of resin is poured onto a layer which has shrunk it can seep down between casting and mould causing serious cleaning-up problems later.

Both these problems can be overcome by using less activator (if the resin is not pre-activated) and less catalyst, by building up the resin in layers of not more than 10 mm thick to control the amount of heat given off, or by using special resins which do not crack when made into large castings in one go.
3 **Stickiness.** A further problem is that with some clear embedding resins the surface which is left exposed to the air during curing will remain sticky. There are several ways to overcome this. A piece of **melinex** polyester film laid on the surface during curing will reduce the problem; a thin final layer of a non-sticky opaque resin, suitably coloured, can be poured on to cover the stickiness; the stickiness can be cleaned off with acetone or brush cleaner and after further drying with wet and dry paper; or a piece of felt can be stuck on to make a base.

CASTING METHOD

Almost any type of resin can be used for opaque castings. Inert fillers such as calcium carbonate (powdered chalk) can be added to economise on expensive resin and to reduce the amount of exothermic heat produced during curing. For most castings a 50:50 mix of resin and filler is suitable. Other fillers such as sawdust, metal filings and sand can be added to vary the texture and colour of the casting. Alternatively, a gel-coat containing the required finish can be put on the mould before casting.

Opaque colour pastes can be added to give the required colour.

The amount of resin needed for a casting can be worked out by filling the mould with water and then pouring it into a graduated waxed mixing cup. The resin must be mixed and poured carefully to avoid trapping air bubbles in the casting, and to make sure that any fillers are well mixed in. Mix the resin carefully to the manufacturers instructions, and do not add more than recommended in one go.

CLEAR CASTING AND EMBEDDING

For this, clear resin must be used, but some or all of the layers can be tinted using translucent colour pastes. Special care must be taken to keep dirt out of the mould, which must always be covered during curing.

Before starting to cast, coat the mould with a release agent to prevent sticking of the completed casting and set up the mould absolutely level.

1 Pour the first layer of resin into the clean, waxed mould and leave to cure.

2 As soon as the first layer has gelled enough to support it, place the article being embedded in position and pour on the second layer of resin. If you are embedding a large object several layers may be needed to cover it. If embedding an object which will float, stick it down with a very thin layer of resin. If embedding several objects at different levels place them on different layers of resin. Take care not to trap any air bubbles under objects.

3 Pour in the final layer of resin. A translucent colour paste in this layer will appear to tint the whole casting. An opaque coloured layer will provide an attractive base to the finished job. In choosing your final layer or layers think about the problem of stickiness already discussed.

In a clear casting built up in several layers you will be able to see the joints between the layers slightly. This is unavoidable.

Decorative patterns can be made in the resin by mixing small amounts of opaque or translucent coloured resins and applying them in a variety of ways, such as dripping them into the still wet resin, trailing them in with a spatula, or painting them onto a dry surface before adding more clear resin.

1
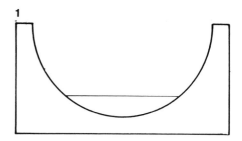

2
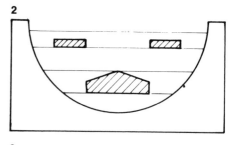

3
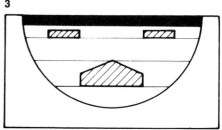

EXTRUSION

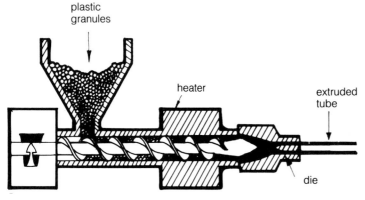

plastic granules

heater

extruded tube

die

Extruding

This process converts granules of thermoplastic into such products as pipes, rods, mouldings and films. The granules are fed into the hopper and fall into an electrically powered rotating screw which forces them towards the die at the other end of the extruder. The pressure on the plastic is increased as it moves towards the die by the increasing core diameter of the screw and the tapered aperture leading up to the die. It is also heated to the correct temperature by the heaters surrounding the barrel, so that when it reaches the die it is in a plastic state, and can be forced through it. It is then quickly cooled so that it keeps its shape.

To put plastic covering on wire, such as electrical insulation, the wire is fed through the centre of the die as the plastic is extruded.

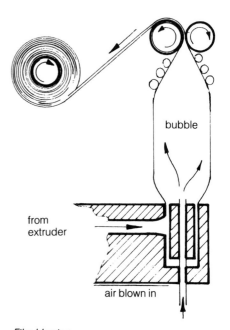

bubble

from extruder

air blown in

Film blowing

Many schools have a pug mill in their pottery room which can be used to demonstrate a similar process.

In **film blowing**, a continuous plastic tube is extruded and blown into a large bubble. This stretches the plastic into a thin film which cools and is wound onto a roller to make materials such as wide polythene sheeting for building and packaging. The bubble is blown vertically and may be 10 m or more high.

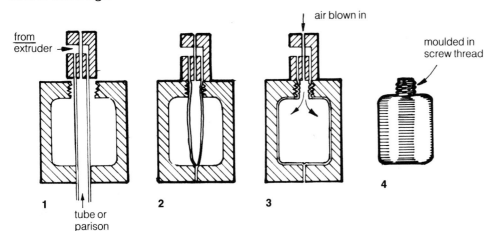

Extrusion blow moulding

In **extrusion blow moulding**, a tube of molten plastic is extruded between the two halves of a die (1) which close, sealing the ends of the tube (2). Air is blown into the tube to enlarge it to the shape of the die (3). The waste is trimmed off and the finished shape is ejected (4).

INJECTION MOULDING

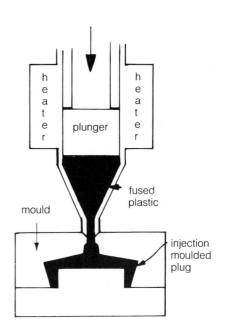

This process is similar to extruding, except that the screw is replaced by a plunger which injects a shot of thermoplastic into a mould. The mould is warmed before injecting and the plastic is injected quickly to prevent the plastic hardening before the mould is full.

Pressure is maintained for a short time (the dwell time) to prevent the material creeping back during setting. This prevents shrinkage and hollows, and therefore gives a better quality product.

When the plastic has solidified sufficiently to be removed without damage, the mould is opened and the moulding ejected.

Injection moulding is now the most important manufacturing method for small consumer products, including bottle tops, sink plugs, containers, model kits, bowls, dustbins, milk crates, etc. It has also become the most important manufacturing method for consumer-durable products such as radio cases, television cabinets, and even complete items of furniture.

During the last few years, it has become possible to produce extremely large mouldings such as dingy hulls and very small high-precision components. Precision injection moulded parts for cameras, razors and a host of other small goods have enabled the price of these things to fall dramatically. Previously, some precision parts such as small gears had to be machined individually at a much higher cost.

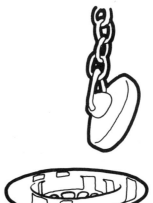

Injection moulding in industry is a favoured manufacturing method when products are to be moulded in very large numbers. The capital cost of tooling (making the mould) is usually very high, but a single mould can produce many thousands of mouldings — making the unit cost of each one very low.

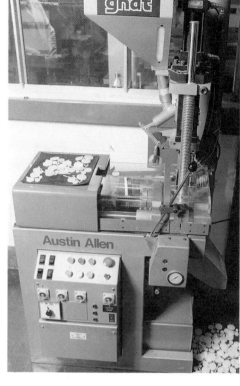

Injection moulding machines found in school are generally quite small and have to be operated manually. In industry, the machines are generally much larger and capable of fully automatic operation. The mould is closed, material injected, and the mould opened again to eject the product in a regular repeating cycle. A single operator can now look after a factory full of such machines.

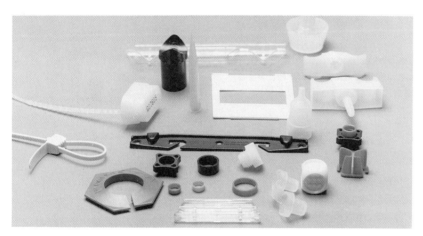

MOULD DESIGN FOR INJECTION MOULDING

Good injection mould design is essential to injection moulding, and provides great scope for projects in school. A mould consists of two or more pieces in which the shape of the moulding has been cut. Steel is normally used for long production runs, but aluminium can be used if there are to be hundreds rather than thousands of mouldings. Aluminium is widely used in industry for prototype moulds, and is an easy material to work with in school.

It must be possible to open the mould and eject the moulding easily and without misusing tools. A slot can often be made along the joint line so that a screwdriver can be inserted and turned to separate the parts. Deep shapes must be tapered to help removal and an ejector pin can be built into the mould to push out the moulding if necessary.

All surfaces must be very smooth and highly polished to ensure a good finish to the mouldings and leakproof mating surfaces on the mould, so that there is no flash to clean off the finished job.

The channels through which the molten plastic flows must be carefully designed. The nozzle of the machine fits against the **sprue**

which carries the plastic to the mould cavity. Close to the cavity is a **gate** — a narrow opening through which the plastic flows, but where the moulding can easily be broken off when set. Multiple mouldings can be injected from one sprue using a system of **runners** to link the sprue to the cavities, as for example when moulding all the parts of a plastic model kit in one operation. Each part is linked to the runner by a separate gate.

The sprue is usually placed along the parting line of the mould for ease of ejection, and to avoid any cleaning out problems between mouldings. Sprues, runners, and gates are round or half round in section so that they can be made by drilling wherever possible and to give a smooth flow. They must be large enough to allow quick filling of the mould.

Sharp corners and sudden changes in section must be avoided because they interrupt the flow of plastic and weaken the moulding. **Large flat surfaces should also be avoided** because the finished moulding will often not come out completely flat.

LAMINATED MOULDS

The simplest type of mould to construct requires just three plates of steel or aluminium. The centre plate is cut out by hand or machine so that when sandwiched between the other two a cavity is formed, into which the fused plastic is injected.

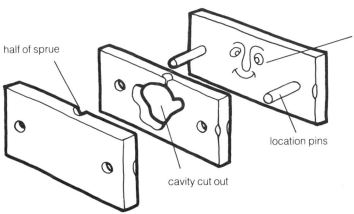

half of sprue

detail etched, punched or drilled into surface

location pins

cavity cut out

final product

The sprue hole is drilled between the centre and one of the two outer plates when these are clamped together. Holes for location pins may also be drilled when the three plates are clamped. The surfaces of the plates facing into the mould can be etched or punched to give texture or relief detail to the finished moulding.

CALENDERING

This process is used to produce plastic sheet, packaging films, sticky tape and plastic coated fabrics and papers. Examples of products made in this way include vinyl washable wallpapers, PVC leathercloth upholstery materials and plastic-coated playing cards.

The machine consists of large heated rollers which squeeze softened plastic into a continuous sheet. The surface can be smooth or a pattern can be embossed on it by feeding the warm sheet through patterned rollers. If the plastic is to be bonded to a backing material, this is fed through the rollers with the hot plastic. The sheet finally passes through cooling rollers.

The softened plastic can be supplied from an extruder fitted with a wide slot, or granules can be plasticised on the calender.

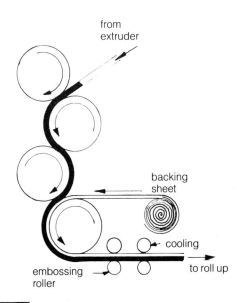

from extruder

backing sheet

cooling

embossing roller

to roll up

20 Ways of working materials.
PART 4—fabrication

In order to choose the best way of joining any combination of materials in any situation which is likely to arise, we must have a good general knowledge of methods of joining.

Joints can be classified in several ways such as temporary and permanent, flexible and rigid, and hot and cold formed. Below we have listed temporary and permanent joints, but you should also be able to list them in other ways to make sure that you know the important features of each.

	Wood	Plastics	Metal
Temporary joints	Screws ————————→	→	————————→
	Nuts and bolts ————→	→	————————→
	Knock down fittings ——→	→	————————→
	Hinges, catches and stays ——→	→	————————→
Permanent joints	Glues ————————————→	→	————————————→
	Nails	←	————Rivets
	Carcase joints	X	Sheet metal joints
	Frame joints	←	————Frame and tube joints
	X	X	Soldering
	X	X	Brazing
	X	←	————Welding

In the pages which follow we have given enough details of the common ways of joining for you to be able to choose the best method and use it correctly.

Nails

Nailing is the quickest way of making a permanent joint in wood. Nails cannot be removed easily or without damage, and therefore should not be used as temporary joints.

The nail punches the fibres of the wood away from the nail head. They grip the shank of the nail and resist attempts to withdraw it. The serrations round the shank, below the head, give extra grip. The treaded pattern on the head stops the hammer from slipping. Always nail through the thinner piece of wood into the thicker piece. The nail length should be about $2\frac{1}{2}$ to 3 times the thickness of the thinner piece.

Nails are sold by length, type, material and weight (not number).

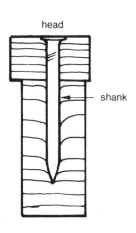
head

shank

COMMON TYPES

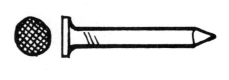

Round wire nails have a round shank and a flat head. They are made from steel wire and can be galvanised to stop rusting. The usual sizes are from 12mm to 150mm long and they are used for general joinery work.

Oval wire nails have an oval shank and a narrow head which is driven below the surface. Turn the long axis of the oval shape in line with the grain to prevent splitting. They are made from steel wire and can be galvanised. The usual sizes are from 12mm to 150mm. Because they have no heads they do not hold the wood as firmly as round wire nails, but they are neater and are therefore used for interior joinery. The nail holes can be hidden by filling.

Standard panel pins have a thin round shank and a small head which is driven below the surface with a nail punch. The usual sizes are from 12mm to 50mm and they are used for strengthening joints and fixing thin sheets.

Hardboard pins have a hard square shank to penetrate hardboard without bending and a pointed head which does not need punching below the surface.

Clout nails are short nails with extra large heads for fixing roofing felt, canvas chair webbing, etc. They are usually galvanised to prevent rusting.

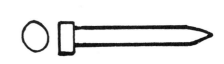

Hardened fixing pins are hard, round shanked nails designed to withstand persistent hammering and to penetrate bricks, etc. They should be long enough to go through the job being fixed, any plaster on the wall, and then 15mm to 20mm into the wall.

Staples are square for crate-making and upholstery, and round for holding wire. Square staples are usually fired in by a staple gun. Round staples are heavier and are hammered in.

DOVETAIL NAILING
To give extra strength to a joint, drive in pairs of nails towards each other dovetail fashion.

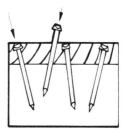

STAGGERED NAILING
When nailing a frame together stagger the nails across the width of the wood to avoid splitting the grain.

If the wood is brittle or tough, bore a small hole and blunt the nail point. These precautions help to prevent splitting, especially when nailing close to the end of a plank.

CLINCHED NAILING
This is used to prevent nails being easily pulled out when nailing into thin wood. The process is shown here. Note that the usual rule is still used to calculate the length of the nail (3 × thickness of piece A). A convenient round bar, such as one handle of a pair of pincers, is used to help in turning the nail point back into the wood to give a strong, safe joint. Simply bending the nail over leaves a dangerous point exposed.

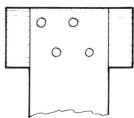

Gimp pins are small wire nails, often of brass, with a large head used in upholstery where the nail heads will show.

Cut tacks are short, sharp-pointed, flat-headed nails, usually with a blued or black mild steel finish. They are used in upholstery where the nails will be hidden.

Corrugated fasteners are short strips of corrugated steel with one sharp corrugated edge, used to make crude joints in cheap work. They are hammered in across the joint lines at each corner to hold the frame together.

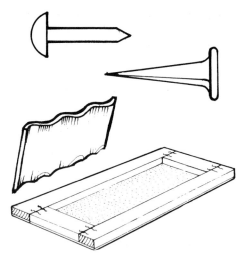

Screws for wood

Screws are an effective way of making a permanent or temporary joint in wood. The thread of the screw becomes enmeshed with the grain fibres to make a strong joint. Screws are stronger, neater and more accurate than nails, and can be taken out without causing damage.

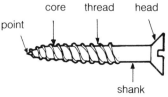

USING SCREWS

1 Select the correct length of screw. This is $2\frac{1}{2}$ to 3 times the thickness of the top piece of wood. Always screw through the thinner piece of wood into the thicker.

2 Drill the pilot hole to slightly less than the screw length. A bradawl hole may be enough in softwood, but in hardwood and for large diameter screws, use a drill equal to the core diameter. Failure to drill properly causes chewed-up screw heads and split wood.

3 Drill a clearance hole for the shank.

4 Countersink for the screw head if needed.

5 When using brass screws which easily break, screw in a stronger steel screw first to cut a thread, and in hardwood, lubricate the screw with soap or wax.

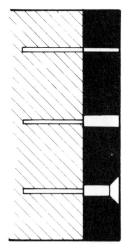

COMMON TYPES OF SCREW

Countersunk head screws are used to join wood to wood where the head has to be flush with the surface, and for fitting hinges. They are the most commonly used type.

Round head screws are used to screw thin metal fittings to wood (e.g. tee hinges and shelf brackets), and for joinery work where the head need not be flush. They are often of black japanned steel to resist rusting.

Raised countersunk head screws are less common and are used to screw fittings to wood. They are often of chrome plated brass to look attractive or plated to match fittings such as door furniture.

Twinfast screws have two threads instead of one, so that fewer turns are needed to screw them in. They have more holding power than ordinary screws, and this is especially useful for joining difficult materials such as chipboard and blockboard.

Coach screws are large heavy duty screws with a square head onto which a spanner is fitted to turn them. They are used to join large pieces of wood such as bench tops, and to screw heavy metal fittings such as vices, to wood.

Screw caps and screw cups are used where appearance is important or where the screw must be removed frequently.

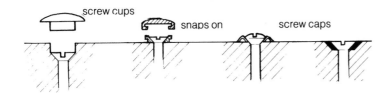

TYPES OF SCREW SLOTS

■ **Straight slot.** A screwdriver can slip out of a straight slot and damage both screw head and wood.

■ **Phillips slot.**

■ **Posidriv slot.** The main advantage of Phillips and Pozidriv slots is that the screwdriver blades do not slip out of the slots so easily.

The common **materials** are steel and brass, and screws are often plated with chrome, zinc, nickel, or black japanning. Steel screws are the strongest and cheapest. Brass screws look better and do not rust, but are not very strong.

The common **sizes** of steel countersunk screw are 6 mm to 150 mm long and 0 to 22 gauge number sizes. The gauge number indicates the diameter of the shank and the size of the head. The higher the number, the thicker the screw.

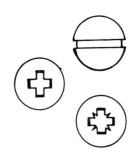

Screws are sold by:

1 Quantity (How many?)
2 Length (How long?)
3 Gauge (How thick?)
4 Material (What is it made from?)
5 Type of head (What shape? What sort of slot?)

e.g. 100, 25 mm × No. 6 steel countersunk.

SCREWING INTO END GRAIN

Screws will not hold in end grain without special methods being used, and nails are often better because the screw thread cuts through the grain fibres and they crumble away.

Two ways of solving this problem are shown here.

■ **Method 1.** Let a dowel into a hole across the width of the wood to provide a nut for the screw.

■ **Method 2.** Insert a rawlplug into a hole bored down the end grain. The rawlplug holds firmly in the wood and the screw holds firmly in the plug.

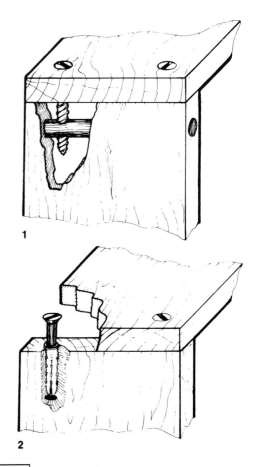

1

2

Glues

CHOOSING THE CORRECT ADHESIVE

The following list suggests suitable adhesives for most jobs, but there are many other glues and it may be necessary to experiment when faced with an unusual combination of materials.

Acrylic to acrylic	— Tensol cements.
Acrylic to others	— It is not usual to glue acrylic to other materials. Use screws, etc., if possible, or experiment with the various types of Bostik.
Polystyrene to polystyrene	— Polystyrene cement.
Polystyrene to others	— Contact adhesive.
Expanded polystyrene to expanded polystyrene Expanded polystyrene to others	PVA, natural latex (e.g. Copydex), or contact adhesives used sparingly.
PVC to PVC	— PVC cement.
PVC to others	— Contact adhesive or PVC cement.
Wood to wood	— a wide range of wood glues suitable for all purposes.
Wood to others	— Epoxy resin or contact adhesives.
Metal to metal	— Epoxy resin.
Metal to others	— Epoxy resin, or contact adhesive.
Rubber to rubber	— Rubber solution, contact adhesive, or natural latex.
Rubber to others	— Contact adhesive or natural latex.
Leather to leather	— Contact adhesives, epoxy resin or PVA.
Leather to others	— Epoxy resin or contact adhesive.
Textiles to textiles	— Natural latex.
Textiles to others	— Natural latex, contact adhesive or PVA.
China to china or glass to glass	— Epoxy resin.
China or glass to others	— Epoxy resin or contact adhesive. Do **not** stick glass to wood. If the wood shrinks or warps the glass might break.

(For further details, see Some common glues and their uses.)

HINTS ON GLUING

Surfaces to be joined must be clean, dry and grease free. Do not apply any finishes to the parts to be joined and remove any old paint, varnish, glue, etc.

Whenever possible, slightly roughen the surfaces to be joined, to help the glue to wet the surface more thoroughly.

Plastics should be washed in warm water containing a small amount of liquid detergent, rinsed in clean warm water, and left to dry. Always

dry-cramp the job before gluing to make sure that the parts fit, and to work-out the best method of cramping. (For details of cramping, see Holding tools.)

Follow the manufacturers instructions carefully. Most glues have a setting time during which pressure must be applied to hold the parts together, and a longer curing time during which the job must not be roughly handled or used.

Always check for squareness and correct assembly before the glue sets and wipe off surplus glue.

SOME COMMON GLUES AND THEIR USES

SCOTCH GLUE
This is an animal glue made from bones and hide which is used **hot** to stick wood. It is available in slab or pearl (bead) forms.

To use it, break a slab wrapped in cloth into small pieces and soak these in water overnight to form a jelly. Put the jelly and more water into the inner pot of a glue kettle, half fill the outer pot with water, and heat slowly until the glue melts into a liquid. The water in the outer pot prevents overheating. Pearl glue is ready for heating after a short soaking.

The glue is ready for use when it just runs from the brush and a thin skin forms on top. Remove the skin.

- ■ **Advantages.** It is cheap, does not stain wood, is very strong if the joints fit well, and there is no waste because it can be reheated several times.
- ■ **Disadvantages.** It must be used quickly before it cools, leaving little time to fit the job together and the job must be left in cramps overnight to set. It is not heat or water resistant.

CASEIN GLUE
This is an animal glue made from the curds of sour skimmed milk which is used **cold** to stick wood. It is sold as a white powder which must be mixed with water to make a thick cream and left for 20 minutes before use.

- ■ **Advantages.** It is heat and water resistant, but only semi-waterproof. It is very strong and can be used for several hours after mixing.
- ■ **Disadvantages.** It is liable to stain hardwoods and must be left in cramps overnight to set.

SYNTHETIC RESIN GLUES
These are made from plastics resins and make joints in woods which are stronger than the wood itself. There are two main types.

The **one-shot** type (e.g. Cascamite) consists of a resin and a hardener ready-mixed in a powder which must be mixed with water to make a thick cream.

The **two-shot** type (e.g. Aerolite 306) consists of a resin powder which is mixed with water and spread on one half of the joint, and a separate hardener which is spread on the other half. The two are then pressed together and cramped. Take care not to mix up the brushes.

- **Advantages.** They make very strong, almost colourless and waterproof joints which set in only 3 hours. They will fill small gaps in the joints and have a long shelf life.
- **Disadvantages.** They stain some woods and you must mix only as much as is needed straight away to avoid waste.

PVA (POLYVINYL ACETATE) GLUE

This is sold as a white ready-mixed liquid in a plastic container (e.g. Evostick Resin W). It is the most widely used wood glue and is also useful for some other materials.

- **Advantages.** It is easy to use, non-staining, strong if the joints fit well and water resistant. It has an unlimited shelf life and joints set in 2 hours.
- **Disadvantage.** It is not waterproof.

CONTACT (IMPACT) ADHESIVES

These are synthetic rubbers and resins in a solvent (e.g. Evostick impact, Bostik, Dunlop Thixafix). They are used to hold sheets of light and usually dissimilar materials together, such as Formica to a chipboard worktop and PVC leathercloth upholstery to a plastics chairshell. They work because two dry films of synthetic rubber will stick under light pressure. The glue is spread evenly over both surfaces with a comb and allowed to become touch-dry, usually after about 15 minutes. One part is located over the other without allowing them to touch, and then they are pressed together. Once touched together the parts cannot be separated or moved into position.

- **Advantages.** No cramps are needed, and this allows large difficult items to be joined.
- **Disadvantages.** The joints are not very strong and they are not suitable for such jobs as furniture making. Once opened, the glue has a short shelf life.

EPOXY RESIN GLUES

These (e.g. Araldite) will stick wood, metal, glass, china, stone, concrete, rubber and plastics. Equal amounts of resin and hardener are mixed together, spread on very clean surfaces, and cramped together.

- **Advantages.** They will stick almost anything.
- **Disadvantages.** They are very expensive, and should only be used when there is no cheaper alternative. The joints are not strong enough to handle for 24 hours and do not reach their full strength for 2 or 3 days.

RESORCINOL AND PHENOL GLUES

These are considered the ultimate for high stress joints in wood. They are used mainly for such purposes as making laminated beams and boat building.

- ■ **Advantages.** The joints are very strong and completely waterproof.
- ■ **Disadvantages.** They are very expensive and leave dark brown glue lines.

PLASTICS CEMENTS

Joints can be made in many thermoplastics by using suitable cements containing a powerful solvent for the material being joined. Some thermoplastics (e.g. polypropylene, polythene and PTFE) cannot be cemented together because suitable solvents are not available.

Other adhesives can also be used to join plastics and to join plastics to other materials, but the joints are usually less strong than cemented joints.

Acrylic (e.g. perspex, oroglass) can be joined to itself using Tensol cement. Tensol No. 6 is a ready-mixed acrylic solvent which is easy to use for most purposes, but does not give a clear joint. Tensol No. 7 is a two-part pack which must be mixed with care, but has the advantages of making a completely clear and waterproof joint suitable for use outdoors.

Perspex is not usually stuck to other materials. Try to use screws, etc., if possible.

PVC can be joined using Tensol No. 53 cement or a number of readily available PVC adhesives, some of which will also stick PVC to other materials (e.g. Gloy PVC repair and Vinyl weld). Acetone (nail varnish remover) can be used to clean joints and remove excess glue.

Rigid polystyrene can be joined using the polystyrene cements widely sold for use with polystyrene model kits such as Airfix. They dry quickly and give a clear joint. Glue can be removed with acetone or carbon tetrachloride.

EMA Solvent Cement will bond a wide range of dissimilar plastics and its use results in little or no squeeze-out of softened material.

Soldering, brazing and welding metals

Soldering makes a permanent joint between two pieces of metal, by using an alloy which has a lower melting point than the metals being joined as a 'glue'. This alloy makes the bond by forming an alloy with the base metals which are not melted during the process.

Soft soldering, hard soldering and brazing are all examples of this process, while welding works by melting the edges to be joined so that they fuse together. A filler rod of similar metal is added to fill the weld.

These joints all involve heating the metal, and the higher the temperature needed the stronger will be the joint made. Where several joints are to be made on the same job, the first is made at the highest temperature and the others, in turn, at progressively lower temperatures.

The following chart shows the correct temperature, flux and filler rod for each process.

Process	Filler rod	Flux	Approx. temperature
Welding	Same as parent metal	None needed for mild steel Depends on metal being welded	Melting temperature of metal.
Brazing	Brazing spelter 65% copper 35% zinc (brass)	Borax (usually in a proprietory flux)	875°C
Silver soldering or hard soldering	Enamelling (81% silver plus copper and zinc) Hard (78% silver) Medium (74% silver) Easy (67% silver) Easy-flo (50% silver)	Borax Borax Borax Borax Easy-flo flux	800°C 775°C 750°C 720°C 625°C
Tinman's soldering or soft soldering	40% lead, 60% tin	Active — zinc chloride Passive — resin	200°C
Electronics soldering	40% lead, 60% tin	Resin (contained as fine cores in the 'multi-core' solder wire)	180°C

FLUXES

The purposes of a flux are:

1 To protect the cleaned surfaces from oxidisation during heating. Solders only stick to clean metal.
2 To break down the surface tension of the filler rod so that the solder will run into the joint.
3 To chemically clean the joint. Only active fluxes, such as zinc chloride for tin soldering, do this. Active fluxes can only be used where the job can be washed to remove surplus flux after cleaning.

SOFT SOLDERING

SOLDERING IRONS
The bit is made of copper because it has a high heat storage capacity, is a good conductor of heat and is easily wetted with solder. Soldering irons are heated in a gas soldering stove or by internal gas or electric heaters. When the gas flame turns green the copper is hot enough.

TINNING THE BIT BEFORE USE
Heat the soldering iron to soldering temperature, quickly file the copper clean, flux it and roll it in a tin-lid full of solder, to coat it with fresh solder.

hatchett bit

straight bit

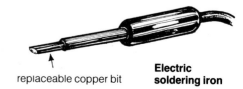

replaceable copper bit

Electric soldering iron

STAGES IN SOFT SOLDERING A JOINT

1 The joint must be clean and close fitting so that the solder will flow in by capillary action.

2 Flux the joint. Active fluxes should be used if possible as they are more effective. Passive fluxes are used for such jobs as soldering electronics components, where the job cannot be washed afterwards and an active flux would corrode the metal.

3 The surfaces to be joined are tinned with a film of solder using a soldering iron. It is necessary to allow time for the job to heat up so that the solder flows from the iron to the surfaces.

4 The tinned surfaces are refluxed and pressed together. Heat is applied with either a flame or a clean hot soldering iron, to remelt the solder and join the surfaces.

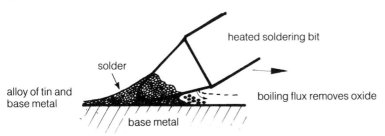

STAGES IN SOLDERING ELECTRONICS COMPONENTS

1 All surfaces to be soldered must be cleaned, i.e. component legs/pins and copper tracks on printed circuit boards.

2 The component legs/pins and their intended positions on the copper tracks are tinned using a soldering iron and 'multi-core' solder. The soldering iron tip is first applied to the work, followed immediately by the solder wire. **Do not** melt solder onto the soldering iron tip and then offer it to the work: the flux will burn off before it can have any effect.

3 Bring the component leg/pin in contact with the tinned track and simply reheat the joint with the soldering iron.

Note: Components such as transistors can be heat damaged by conduction along the legs. When soldering, these should be held with pliers which act as a heat sink.

HARD SOLDERING AND BRAZING

STAGES IN HARD SOLDERING OR BRAZING A JOINT

1 Clean the joint with file and emery cloth and make sure it fits together well.

2 Mix the correct flux to a thick creamy consistency.

3 Paint the flux onto the joint and onto the end of the filler rod.

4 Wire the joint together if necessary.

5 Heat the joint to the correct heat with a blow torch, gently at first to dry the flux.

6 Touch the solder onto the joint. If the joint is hot enough, the heat from the job will melt the solder, and it will run along the joint.

7 Remove the heat and allow the joint to cool.

WELDING METALS

Two pieces of the same metal are heated using either a very hot oxy-acetylene flame or an electric arc, until the surfaces to be joined melt. At the same time a filler rod is melted into the joint to fill in the gap between the two pieces of metal. The molten pool of metal formed during welding rapidly solidifies, fusing the surfaces together. A properly welded joint should be as strong as the surrounding metal.

When welding thick metal, the joint is prepared by bevelling the edges to form a vee. In industry there is a much wider range of welding processes, including automatic and continuous methods.

WELDING PLASTICS

The process is basically the same as when welding metals. Two pieces of the same material, and if needed a filler rod of this material, are heated until they soften, and pressure is applied to fuse them together.

There are two methods commonly used in school. These are **heated tool welding**, to fuse thin sheets up to 1 mm thick and films, and **hot air welding** for thicker sheets. In industry a wider range of methods is available.

In heated tool welding a tool similar to an electric soldering iron is drawn across two thicknesses of thin sheet to soften them, followed by a roller to press the joint together. Heated tool and roller can be combined into one heated roller which is wheeled across the joint.

To prevent the sheet melting and sticking to the hot roller, a sheet of polyester film such as Melinex is placed between the roller and the sheet being welded.

In hot air or hot gas welding, a stream of hot air or gas is used to heat the surfaces being joined and the filler rod, exactly as when oxy-acetylene welding. The simplest hot air welding tools are similar to hair dryers with interchangeable nozzles and temperature control. The joint is prepared by bevelling the edges to form a vee and by cleaning them. When the material has been heated to the correct temperature, the softened filler rod is pressed into the vee to fuse the parts together. This is often done by feeding the filler rod through a tube attached to the nozzle so that it can be heated and pressed with the same tool.

SUITABLE PLASTICS FOR WELDING

Only thermoplastics which do not burn or decompose when heated to their softening temperature can be welded. Polythene, polystyrene, polypropylene, PVC, nylon and some acrylics are examples of thermoplastics which can be welded by both the above methods.

Rivets

Rivets are used to make permanent joints in metal, to join metal to soft materials and for joining soft materials to each other.

SOLID RIVETS

Snap or round head rivets are used for general purposes where a flush finish is not important and countersinking would weaken the job.

Countersunk head rivets are used for general purposes where a flush surface is needed. They are the most commonly used type.

Flat head rivets are used for joining thin plates which cannot be countersunk.

Bifurcated rivets are used for joining soft materials such as leather, plastics and occasionally thin plywood.

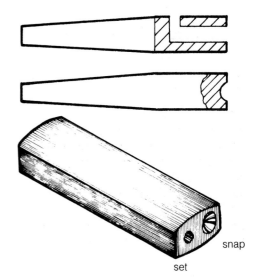

washer

allowance

To choose the correct rivet you must know:

1 The length.
2 The diameter — 3 mm is the commonest size in school.
3 The shape of the head.
4 The material from which it is made — low carbon steel, brass, aluminium, stainless steel, copper, etc.

In order to work out the correct length you must know how much of the rivet shank to leave projecting, ready to be shaped into a second head: on a countersunk rivet allow an extra $1 \times$ the diameter of the rivet; on a roundhead rivet allow an extra $1\frac{1}{2} \times$ the diameter of the rivet.

RIVETING TOOLS

The **rivet set** is used for setting or pressing together metal plates and making sure that the rivet is pulled all the way into the hole. The hole in the set is the same size as the rivet diameter.

The **rivet snap** (or dolly) is used to support the head of a round head rivet while riveting (dolly), and to finish a round head rivet to the correct shape (snap). It has a concave hole the same size and shape as the rivet head, and two are needed to complete a round head rivet.

Both set and snap can be combined into one tool and are available in several sizes to fit different rivet diameters.

snap

set

STAGES IN ROUNDHEAD RIVETING

1 Drill both plates. Clean off any burrs.
2 Support the rivet head with a dolly held in the vice.
3 Swell the rivet with the flat face of a hammer until it is tight in its hole.
4 Use the ball-pein to shape the head.
5 Finish the head with the snap to make a smooth shape.

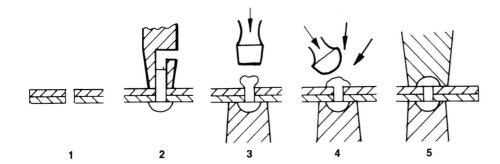

1   2   3   4   5

STAGES IN COUNTERSUNK RIVETING

1 Drill and countersink both plates. Clean off any burrs.
2 Put in the rivet and press the rivet and the plates together with a set. Support the countersunk head on a flat block.
3 Swell the rivet with the flat face of a hammer until it is tight in its hole.
4 Use the ball-pein to fill up the countersink.
5 Finish with the flat face and file the head smooth. A good countersunk rivet should be almost invisible.

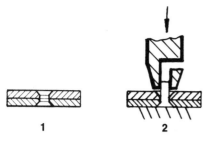

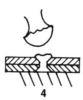
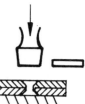

1   2   3   4   5

DRILLING

It is impossible to drill several holes in two different pieces of metal and get them to match up exactly. To avoid this problem, drill all the holes in one piece, but only one in the other. Clean off the burrs, join the pieces with one rivet, and then drill and rivet one hole at a time.

POP RIVETS

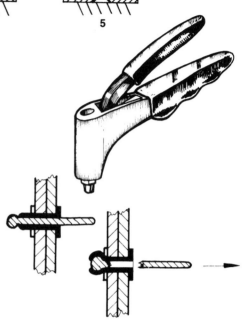

These have the advantage that they can be set quickly from one side only. They are weaker than solid rivets because they are made from soft metal and are hollow. They are used mainly for joining thin sheet metal, but they can also be used for other thin materials. Washers can be put onto the rivets to enable soft materials such as leather and rubber to be riveted.

As the mandrel is pulled through by the pop riveting pliers, it expands the rivet head. When the correct pressure is reached, the head breaks off and stays in the rivet.

Nuts, bolts and machine screws

All these fixings are usually made of steel or brass and can be coated either to rustproof the steel or to improve their appearance.

Bolts usually have either a square or a hexagonal head. They are ordered by the diameter of the thread and the length to the underside of the head. Bolts may be threaded for all or part of their length.

Coach bolts are used to join wood to wood, or wood to other materials. They have a domed head with a square collar underneath which is pressed into the wood to prevent the bolt turning. They are usually used for strong structural woodwork.

Machine screws are available in a wide range of thread diameters, lengths and head shapes.

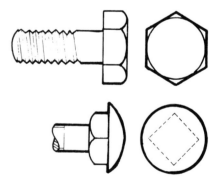

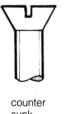

counter   round   pan   cheese
sunk   head   head   head

Nuts are either plain square, plain hexagonal, wing nuts for easy removal, or special locking nuts to prevent vibration loosening them.

wing
nut

hexagonal

square

lock
nuts

castle nut
and split pin

nylon or
fibre lock
nut

Washers are used to protect the surface when the nut is tightened, to spread the load or to prevent vibration loosening the joint.

plain
washer

lock
washer

Self-tapping screws are used to join thin sheets of metal and plastics, and as chipboard screws where ordinary woodscrews would cause the chipboard to crumble. They are made of hardened steel so that they can cut their own thread as they are screwed in.

Common sizes are 6 mm to 50 mm with Phillips, Pozidriv and straight slots.

Drill a tapping size hole equal to the core diameter of the screw.

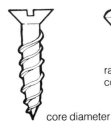

raised
countersunk

round
head

pan
head

mushroom
head

core diameter

countersunk

Furniture fittings

HINGES

The sketches show a few of the common types of hinge. There are many others.

Butt hinges are used for room and cupboard doors, small boxes and windows. They are usually made of steel, nylon or brass, and may be plated, They fit onto the edge of the wood and are usually recessed so that when the door is closed they are neat and almost hidden. The main disadvantage is that because the screws are close together and in a straight line there is a danger of splitting the wood.

Back flap hinges are used for drop-down leaves and flaps, and strong tool box lids. They are usually made of steel, nylon or brass, and may be plated. They fit onto the surface of the wood and the screw holes are spaced out for greater strength.

Piano hinges are long lengths of butt hinge. They are used on box and furniture lids. They are neat and allow the screw holes to be spread out over the whole door length. They conceal the edges of man-made slabs.

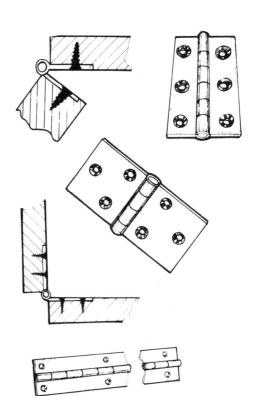

Laid-on hinges are used where doors fit onto the outside edge of a cupboard and must open within the width of the cabinet, for example, when a row of kitchen unit doors fit closely together in a row. The doors can usually be opened through 180°. The hinges are usually made of plated steel.

Flush hinges are lightweight hinges where one flap fits into the other when closed. The hinge is thin and does not need recessing. They are usually made of plated steel.

Tee hinges are used on shed doors, gates, and workshop cupboards. The long arm spreads the load across several planks of a tongue and grooved door, while the short arm fits onto a narrow frame or post.

Stays are used to control the opening of fall flaps and to keep lift-up doors open. They are usually fitted so that the fully open stay is at 45° to the cabinet when the lid or flap is opened to 90°.

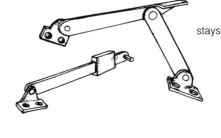

laid on hinges

flush hinges

tee hinges

stays

CATCHES

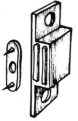

(a) Magnetic

(b) Ball

(c) Spring

LOCKS

Surface fitting cupboard and drawer locks are screwed onto the inside surface of the door or drawer.

Cut cupboard or drawer locks are recessed into the door or drawer edge. The two keyholes enable the lock to be used vertically or horizontally.

Box locks are used for lift-up lids and sliding doors where a cupboard lock would pull open. A sliding bolt in the lock engages with the hooks on the keep.

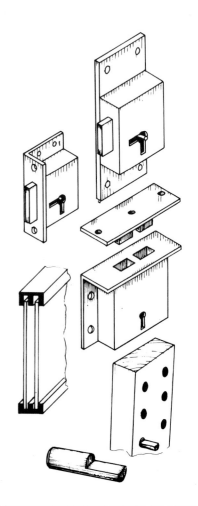

SLIDING DOORS

So that the doors can be lifted out, the top track is twice as deep as the bottom track. To remove a door, lift it and pull the bottom outwards. The tracks can be made by cutting grooves or by using ready-made channels.

ADJUSTABLE SHELVES

There are many ready-made adjustable shelving systems available, but we have shown here one simple way of fitting adjustable shelves into cabinets.

1 Drill 6.5 mm diameter holes 10 mm deep into the sides.
2 Cut lengths of 6 mm diameter nylon, aluminium or brass rod, and file or face off to 20 mm long. Chamfer the ends to ease fitting.
3 File approximately halfway through for half of the peg length.
4 The shelf resting on the dowels prevents them from falling out.

Constructions in wood

There are four types of construction in wood: carcase construction, stool frame construction, flat frame construction and slab construction. Many pieces of work contain examples of more than one type, and there are usually at least two possible constructions for any job.

1 **Carcase or box construction** is where planks of wood are joined to make box shapes such as cabinets, drawers, tool boxes and bookshelves.

2 **Stool frame construction** is where a supporting frame is made from several legs and rails, such as in tables, chairs, stools, underframes for cabinets and frames covered with lightweight panels, as an alternative to carcase construction.

3 **Flat frame construction** is where several pieces of wood are joined together to make flat shapes such as doors, window frames and picture frames.

4 **Slab construction** is where sheets, usually of man-made boards, are joined together using simple permanent or knock-down joints. The widespread use of man-made boards, modern adhesives, and ready-made joints has caused slab construction to replace the three traditional methods above for many purposes, such as built-in furniture and self-assembly furniture kits.

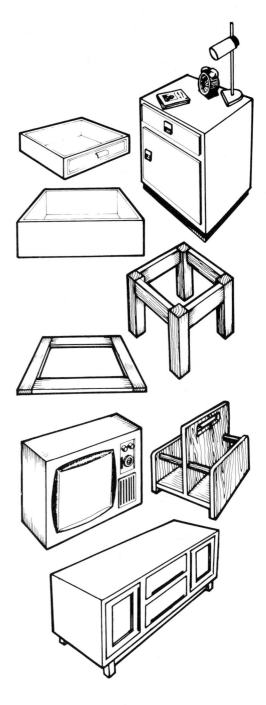

Each method of construction is governed by a set of rules designed to ensure that the final product is sound and pleasing in appearance, and although modern materials and adhesives have made woodworking easier it is still necessary to follow them. In particular there are appropriate joints for each material and purpose.

Before making each job, examine your design carefully and make sure that:

1 **The construction will be strong enough.** For example, if making a coffee table remember that people will sit and perhaps stand on it at some time.

2 **You have not misused the chosen materials.** For example, you should not join two pieces of natural timber with the grain in one piece at right angles to the grain in the other. You must allow for movement in natural timber (see Faults in timber and Fixing table tops).

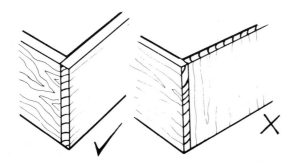

3 **You have used the correct joints in the correct way.** For example, a double tenon should be used to join a wide rail into a leg to avoid weakening it. A dovetail should only be pulled apart in one direction. Make sure that this is the direction which takes the smaller strain.

Many joints are designed to reduce the risk of warping. A shelf of natural timber which has been housed at both ends should stay flat, but the same shelf simply resting on brackets is likely to cup. Therefore, an adjustable shelf might be better made from man-made board.

4 **It will be possible to assemble the job when you have cut the joints.** It is very easy to design joints which cannot all be assembled at the same time because they go together in different directions.

JOINTS

On the pages which follow we have shown the most used joints, together with examples of how they are used for each type of construction.

FLAT FRAME CONSTRUCTION — CORNER JOINTS

The sketches on this page and opposite show in some of the simple joints which can be used to make a flat frame such as a flush door, and then some of the more advanced joints used in better quality work.

Butt joints are the quickest and simplest joints to make, but they are not very strong and must usually be strengthened by dovetail nailing, corrugated fasteners, or wood or metal reinforcing plates. On the flush door shown, the ply- or hardboard panels would provide most of the strength.

Mitre joints are neater than butt joints because the end grain is hidden, but they are harder to make because the ends must be cut at 45° and fitted accurately together. The mitre can be strengthened by nailing or by inserting veneer keys into saw cuts across the joint.

Corner halving joints are stronger than butt joints and simple to make, but still need strengthening with screws or dowels for heavier work.

Dowelled joints are neat and strong. The holes must be lined up exactly but this can be done using a dowelling jig. The dowels are coned at the ends to make them easier to drive in, and grooved to let surplus glue escape. (The making of dowel jigs is discussed in chapter 13 — Holding tools.)

Corner bridle joints are strong and fairly easy to make. They can be strengthened with dowels.

Dovetail bridle joints are stronger than corner bridle joints and can only be pulled apart in one direction. They will therefore carry more weight.

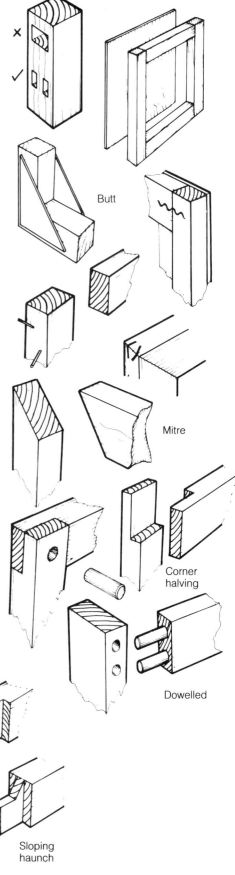

Flush door

Butt

Mitre

Corner halving

Dowelled

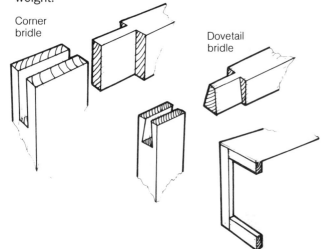

Corner bridle

Dovetail bridle

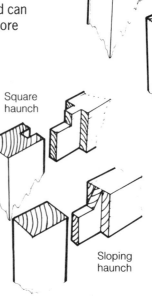

Square haunch

Sloping haunch

Mortise and tenon joints are the strongest and most important frame joints for more advanced work, such as panelled doors and frames for furniture making.

Square haunch mortise and tenon joints are used where a mortise is at the end of a piece of wood. The haunch is designed to join the rail to the leg for its complete width, while preventing the mortise breaking out of the top of the leg.

Sloping haunch mortise and tenon joints are not quite as strong as square haunch joints but the haunch does not show on the top of the leg.

Grooved and square haunch mortise and tenon joints are used where panelling is held in a frame. The square haunch fills the open end of the groove.

Long and short shoulder mortise and tenon joints are used where glass is held in a frame. The glass can be fitted into the rebate after the frame has been made, and held with loose beads so that it can be replaced if broken.

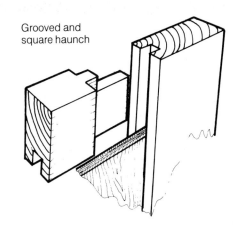
Grooved and square haunch

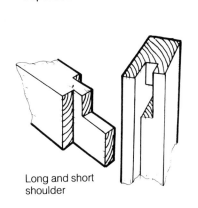
Long and short shoulder

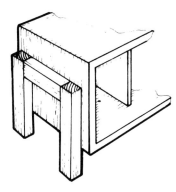

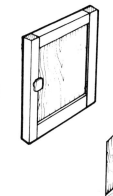

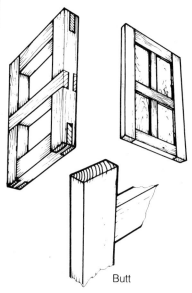

Butt

Tee halving

FLAT FRAME CONSTRUCTION — TEE AND CROSS JOINTS
When a flat frame has a horizontal centre rail or a vertical **muntin**, tee and cross joints are needed.

Butt joints are made and strengthened in the same ways as corner butt joints.

Tee halving joints can be strengthened by dowels or screws or by the use of a dovetail halving joint.

Dovetail halving joints can only be pulled apart in one direction.

Dowel tee joints are fairly simple to make using a dowel jig, as for dowelled corner joints.

Tee bridle joints can be strengthened by dowels.

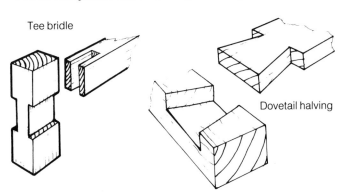
Tee bridle

Dovetail halving

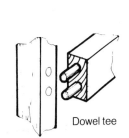
Dowel tee

Mortise and tenon joints are the strongest tee joints, and can be further strengthened by wedging or dowelling. This is a through mortise, but a stopped mortise can be used to hide the end grain on the tenon.

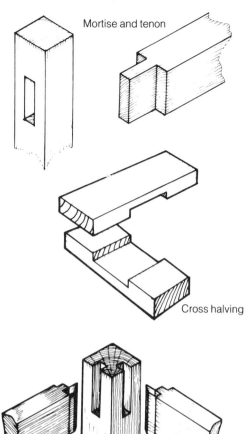

Mortise and tenon

Cross halving joints are the usual way of joining two rails which cross without cutting right through either piece. Alternatively, cut a through mortise in one piece, cut the other piece in half, and make a tenon on the end of each to go into the mortise, or use dowel joints.

Cross halving

STOOL FRAME CONSTRUCTION

All the joints shown in the preceeding section can also be used in stool frame constructions, but in addition there are special combinations of joints used where two rails join into a leg at the same level.

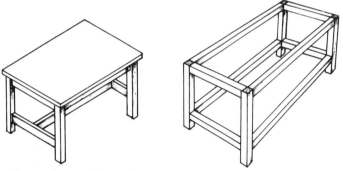

Square haunch mortise and tenon joints are used where rails join into the top of a leg. If two rails join at the same level the tenons are mitred so that they fit together inside the leg. The haunches will show on the top of the leg.

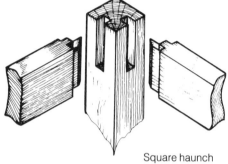

Square haunch

Secret haunch mortise and tenon joints are used where the haunches must not be seen on the top of the leg, for example where there is no stool or table top to hide them.

Single dovetail joints can be used to make frame constructions as shown below, where the rails and legs are joined in a 'box' construction. More details of dovetails will be found in the section on carcase construction.

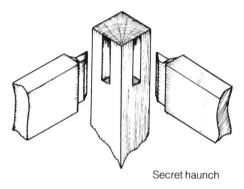

Secret haunch

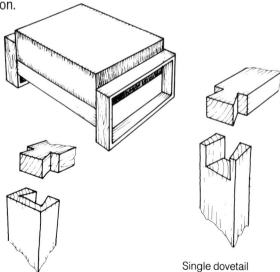

Single dovetail

CARCASE CONSTRUCTION — CORNER JOINTS

Carcase constructions range from simple butt jointed boxes to the more complicated pieces of furniture shown here. This section starts with the simplest joints and then shows more advanced joints suitable for furniture making using solid timber.

Butt joints are the quickest and simplest to make, but they are not very strong, and show a lot of end grain. They are reinforced by dovetail nailing, wooden blocks glued or screwed in, or metal angle brackets.

Corner rebate or lap joints are stronger than butt joints because they increase the area being glued, and neater because less end grain shows. They are simple to make, and as the diagram shows are convenient for use with grooves or rebates as the lap hides the end of them.

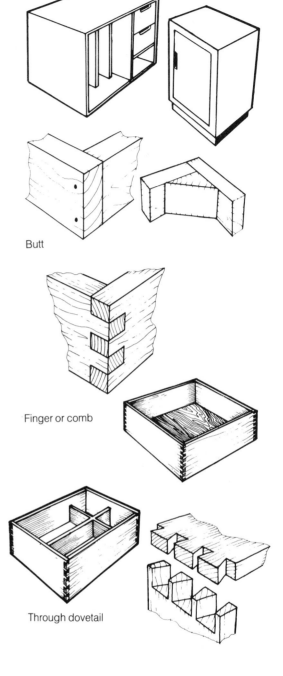

Butt

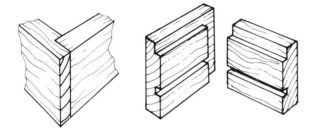

Corner rebate
or lap

Finger or comb joints are simple to make because there are no dovetail-type angles, and strong because of the large gluing area. They are often used for machine-made joints.

Through dovetail joints are the strongest carcase construction joints because they can only be pulled apart in one direction and have a large gluing area. They can also be an attractive feature if well made.

Lap dovetail joints are used where the joint must not show on one surface such as for the front corner joints of drawers, and the tops of cabinets where a smooth surface with no end grain is important. Lap dovetails allow grooves to be cut without making special dovetail joints to hide the ends.

Finger or comb

Through dovetail

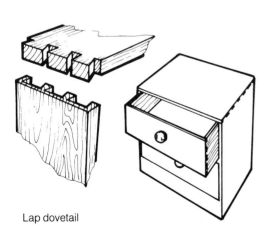

Lap dovetail

CARCASE CONSTRUCTION — TEE JOINTS

Housing joints are the most used method of fitting shelves and partitions into carcases.

Through housings are simple to make and are suitable where the two parts being joined are the same width.

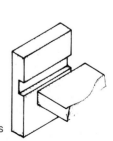

Through housings

Stopped housings are harder to make, but are neater because the joint does not show on the front edge. They are also used where the shelf is narrower than the side.

Dovetail housings are used to give strong joints where there is danger of them being pulled apart, as when books are wedged into a bookcase. They can be through or stopped, and dovetailed on one or both sides.

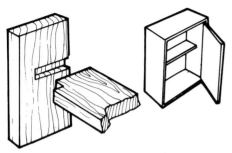
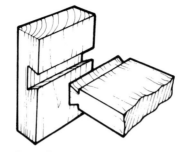

Stopped housings

Dovetail housing

Mortise and tenon joints can be used to make a stronger tee joint, especially for fitting vertical partitions which must bear heavy weights. They can be through or stopped, but are often taken through so that they can be strengthened by wedging. Strong attractive joints can be made by using housings with tenons near the edges to help prevent warping.

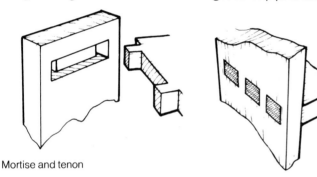

Mortise and tenon

Edge jointing of solid timber

Solid timber is often too narrow for cabinet work and it must therefore be jointed along its edges, by one of the methods shown.

The timber is prepared by planing the edges true with a try-plane, so that they are perfectly flat and square to the face-side.

Butt joints depend on the quality of the preparation and of the glue for their strength. There are several ways of strengthening them.

Tongue and groove joints can be made using matching tonguing and grooving cutters in a combination plane, or by ploughing grooves in both pieces and inserting a loose tongue of plywood.

Dowelled joints are made by using a dowel jig on both prepared boards to make sure that the holes line up.

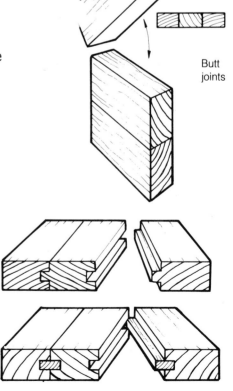

Butt joints

Tongue and groove joints

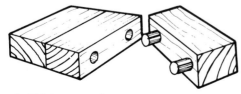

Dowelled joints

JOINT PROPORTIONS IN WOOD
Mortise and tenon.

Length of haunch (L) = thickness of tenon.

Match thickness of tenon to the nearest mortise chisel size, usually 6, 8, 10 or 12 mm.

Length of tenon (T) = width of wood containing mortise for a through joint, and two-thirds of the width for a stopped joint.

Bridle.

Dovetail. Mark out and cut the tails first and draw round the tails to mark the pins.

T = thickness of the wood.

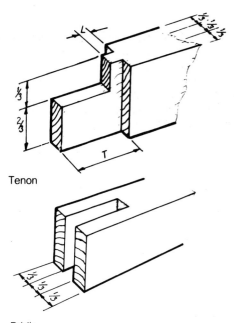

Tenon

Bridle

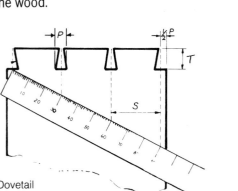

Dovetail

The dovetail slope is 1:6 for softwood and 1:8 for hardwood. Remember the average slope of 1:7.

P = approximately $\frac{1}{4}$S.

Stages in marking out tails.

1 Before dividing up the width of the wood, leave half the width of a pin ($\frac{1}{2}$P) at each side so that the outer pins will be strong enough to resist splitting when the joint is assembled (3 to 5 mm is usually a convenient amount to leave).
2 Then decide on the number of tails needed and divide up the remaining shape as shown into equal spaces (S).
3 Mark out the pin widths (P) and use a dovetail template or adjustable bevel to complete the shape.

Housing. Depth of joint (D) = $\frac{1}{3}$ to $\frac{1}{2}$ the thickness of the wood (Th).

Halving. Depth of joint (D) = $\frac{1}{2}$ the thickness of the wood (Th).

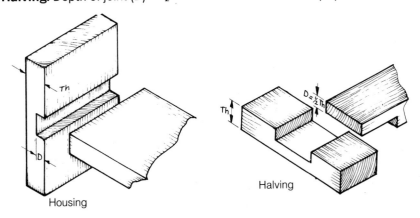

Housing

Halving

SLAB CONSTRUCTION — CORNER JOINTS

Since man-made boards are stable, no allowance has to be made for expansion, contraction or warping. This allows simple constructions to be used, especially where later veneering or painting will conceal them.

Butt joints are simple and quite strong when used with man-made boards to make box constructions. The joint can be strengthened by screwed or glued corner blocks, and exposed edges can be lipped, veneered, painted or stained as appropriate.

Corner rebate or lap joints are neater and do not need strengthening. Chipboard is not joined in this way, but plywood and blockboard can be lapped, taking care to cut along a joint in the laminations.

Mitre joints conceal the edges of the boards, and are especially useful when joining veneered material. Well cut mitres are quite strong when glued, but blocks are usually used as for butt joints.

Tongue and groove joints into a corner block or leg provide a strong construction which conceals the edges of the boards, allows shaping of the cabinet corners, and protects corners from chipping of veneers.

Dowelled joints are a strong and fairly simple method of joining these man-made boards and are especially suitable for veneered chipboard. Where a number of similar dowelled joints are to be drilled, make a metal drilling jig as shown and pin it in the correct position on each piece in turn, to guide the drill. Use a thick piece of metal to help keep the drill square. (See Dowel jigs.)

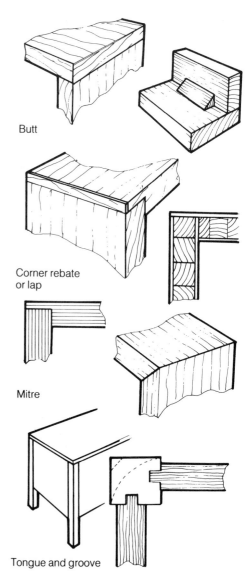

Butt

Corner rebate or lap

Mitre

Tongue and groove

SLAB CONSTRUCTION — TEE JOINTS

Butt, through housing, stopped housing and dowelled joints can all be used for tee joints in man-made boards as they are in carcase construction.

COVERING THE EDGES OF MAN-MADE BOARDS

The edges of plywood, blockwood and chipboard can be covered in several ways depending on the quality of the job and the use to which it is to be put.

1 **Paint.** Carefully finished plywood edges can be painted, usually either black or a shade of brown similar to the veneer colour.

2 **Veneer.** Wood veneer can be applied to the edges of any man-made board. The simplest methods are using either pre-glued iron-on edging strips or strips cut from a sheet and glued with contact adhesive.

3 **Solid wood.** Where the edges have to withstand knocks, strips of solid wood can be glued on. The corners are mitred. This method is the best way of edging boards which will be veneered later. The butt joint can be strengthened by using either a tongue and groove joint or a loose tongue.

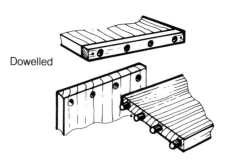

Dowelled

4 **Plastic and metal edging strips.** A wide variety of strips which either glue, screw or nail on are available. Alternatively, where a plastic laminate such as formica is used, matching strips can be cut from the same sheet.

FIXING TABLE TOPS AND UNDERFRAMES

Solid wood tops
Solid wood usually shrinks, mainly across the grain, in centrally heated buildings and expands in damp conditions. This movement is allowed for when fixing a solid wood top to an underframe.

Methods

1 **Wood buttons.** A set of buttons is made across the end of a board so that the grain is in the strongest direction.

Fit the projecting tongue into a shallow groove or mortise on the inside of the rail. Screw into the top.

The button top is sloped to make sure that the top is pulled tight down onto the rail.

Allowance for movement at the end is made in the mortise, and at the side by a space between the rail and button shoulder.

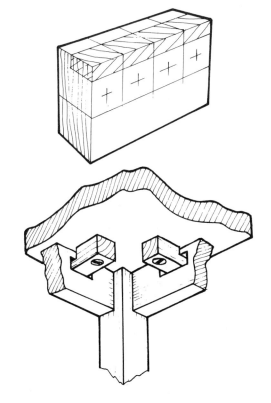

2 **Metal plates.** Straight or right-angled 3mm thick steel or brass plates are screwed to the rails with countersunk screws in round holes, and to the top with round head screws in slots (see below).

The diagrams show how the slots are arranged to allow for movement across the grain on a table corner, and a dual-purpose bracket with slots for screwing at end, or at side of top.

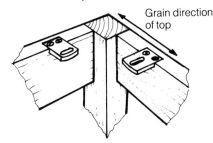
Grain direction of top

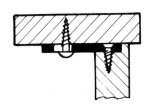

Man-made tops
Man-made boards are almost free from movement, and therefore fixing is much simpler.

Methods
It is possible to screw through a flat top rail, but with a thick rail other methods are needed to avoid very long screws.

1 **Pocket screwing.** Cut a row of pockets inside the top rails with a gouge and drill down from the top into these pockets.

Drill up through the slot into the top and put in the screw. Choose the screw length carefully.

2 **Counterboring.** Drill a clearance hole through the rail and then bore a hole equal in diameter to the screw head. It is important to check the screw length and depth of counterbore carefully.

3 **Knockdown fittings.** To make a removeable top, one half of a bloc-joint fitting is screwed to the rail, and the other half to the top. The halves are joined by a screw so that the job can be easily taken apart and reassembled. (See Knockdown joints.)

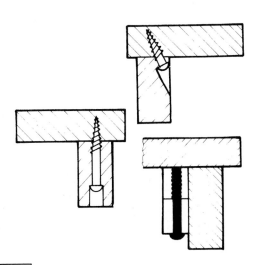

---

4 Screwed blocks and glued blocks. Either square-section wooden blocks are drilled with clearance holes at right angles to each other, and screwed to rails and top; or a number of plastic modesty blocs are used (see knockdown fittings); or square or triangular blocks are glued between rails and top.

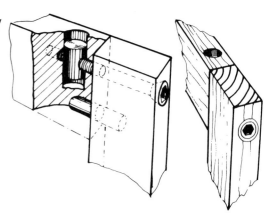

KNOCKDOWN JOINTS

'KD' fittings are used to make furniture which can be taken to pieces for moving and reassembled later. There are many different types and only a few examples are shown. They also provide a simple way of making permanent joints in carcase and slab constructions, especially in difficult materials such as veneered chipboard.

- **Bloc-joint fitting.** A two-piece plastic KD joint which screws together to make a 90° angle joint in slab construction.
- **Modesty bloc.** A small one-piece plastic block for making light slab constructions, for strengthening butt and mitred joints, and for fixing shelves, etc.

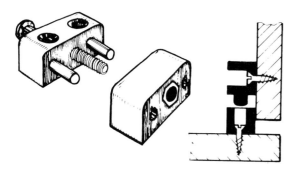
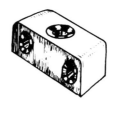
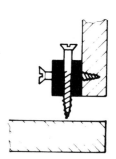

- **Scan fittings.** These fittings are the most frequently used way of making KD frame constructions. They can also be used for slab constructions. Each joint consists of a countersunk head machine screw with a socket for an Allen key, a brass collar to protect the wood where the screw head is tightened against it, and a cross-dowel into which the screw is tightened. Brass dowels can be used to prevent any rotation of the two pieces being joined.
- **Leg fastenings.** This fitting is used where the joint has to be taken apart frequently and especially for joining legs. The hanger bolt remains in the leg, and the wing nut is unscrewed to take off the leg.

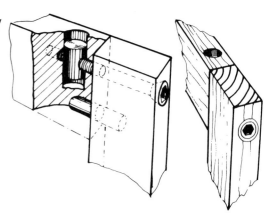

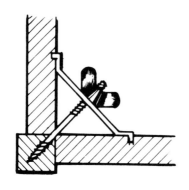

Joints in metal

FRAME JOINTS

When making metal frame constructions, such as stools or tables, it is sometimes necessary to make joints similar to woodwork joints. This is in order to increase the area of contact for brazing or hard soldering, to obtain a flush joint where two pieces cross, or to give a neat appearance, especially when joining tubes.

BUTT JOINTS

These are used when welding, but are often not strong enough for brazed joints because of the small area of contact.

MITRED JOINTS

These are neat and especially useful for concealing the ends of square and round tubes.

DOWELLED JOINTS

These are a neat, easy way to make a stronger frame joint, for example when making a wrought iron gate. Spigots can be turned by holding the metal in a four jaw chuck or filed by hand. Alternatively, loose dowels can be used.

HALVING JOINTS

These are an alternative to dowelled joints. The cross-halving is the most used, because it is the best way to make a flush cross joint. The U-shapes are hard to cut out by hand.

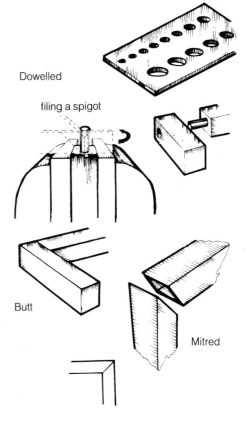

Dowelled

filing a spigot

Butt

Mitred

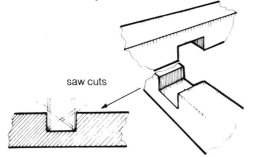

saw cuts

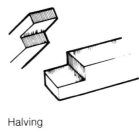

Halving

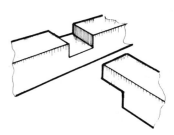

DOVETAIL JOINTS

These are used to make very strong corner joints in flat pieces of metal.

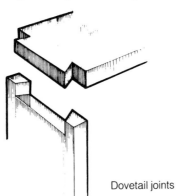

Dovetail joints

SHEET METAL JOINTS

Edge-to-edge butt joints are only suitable for joining thick sheet materials where the edges have a large contact area or where a strong method of joining is to be used. For example, they are used where mild steel is to be welded, or brass, silver and copper are to be silver soldered.

Thin sheet metal and coated sheet such as tinplate need special joints to increase the joint area for soft soldering, or to make the parts interlock.

The exposed edges of thin sheet metal are rarely strong enough to be self-supporting and may be dangerously sharp. They can be stiffened and made safe by forming a safe edge, or further reinforced by using a wired edge.

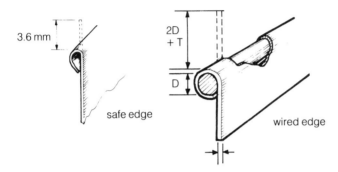

3.6 mm

safe edge

2D + T

D

wired edge

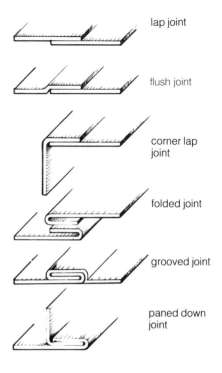

lap joint

flush joint

corner lap joint

folded joint

grooved joint

paned down joint

21 Materials for design and technology: Wood

PART 1: How a tree grows

Roots These absorb water and mineral salts, and make crude sap.

Sapwood This carries crude sap to the leaves.

Leaves Plant food is manufactured in the leaves by the process of photosynthesis. In this process sugars are formed out of water (from the sap) and carbon dioxide (from the air) using energy absorbed by chlorophyll from sunlight.

Bast This carries plant food down from the leaves to all parts of the tree.

Medullary rays carry plant food from the bast into the cambium layer, sapwood, and heartwood, and store it.

Cambium layer This contains cells capable of division to produce sapwood cells on the inside and bast cells on the outside, to make the tree grow.

Sapwood is the living part of the tree. It consists of cellulose cells which have thin walls capable of absorbing moisture from the roots, and plant food to grow.

Heartwood is the commercially most useful part of the tree. It consists of cells which have become clogged with gum and die. They are stronger, more durable, and more resistant to insect and fungal attack than sapwood, and provide the strength to support the tree. A young tree consists mainly of sapwood but as it grows it makes heartwood. Waste products are stored here.

Pith is the centre of the trunk consisting of the original sapling, from which the tree grew, and is often soft.

Bark is a protective covering to protect the tree from damage and extremes of temperature. It is made from the outer layers of bast as they die, and consists of a soft inner layer which expands as the tree grows and a hard outer layer.

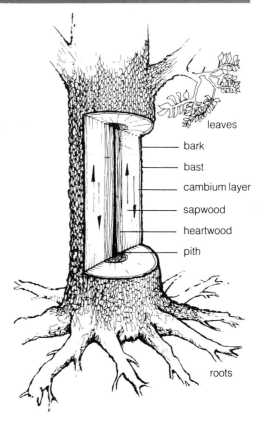

leaves
bark
bast
cambium layer
sapwood
heartwood
pith

roots

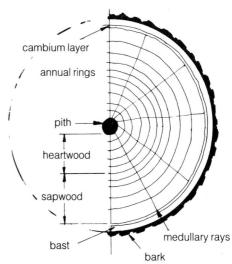

cambium layer
annual rings

pith

heartwood

sapwood

bast

medullary rays

bark

Annual rings each represents one year's growth. In spring, the cambium layer makes wide thin-walled cells so that a large amount of sap can reach the leaves quickly. These cells are pale, soft and weak. In summer, the tree needs less sap, and so it makes narrow cells with thick walls which are dark, hard and strong. In winter, the tree rests and no sap flows. This cycle gives alternate pale and dark annual rings from which we can count the age of softwood trees.

Some hardwood trees (e.g. oak and ash) produce light and dark growth rings similar to, but less distinct than, those of softwood. Others (e.g. beech and mahogany) grow at an even rate throughout the spring and summer and so we cannot tell their age.

PART 2: Hardwoods and softwoods

Hardwoods

These are produced by broad leaved trees (having leaves broad in width in proportion to their length) whose seeds are enclosed in fruit (e.g. apple, acorn). They show a wide range of colours and grain patterns and are divided into two groups.

DECIDUOUS HARDWOODS

These trees lose their leaves in winter. They grow in warmer **temperate** climates (including the British Isles, Europe, Japan, New Zealand, Chile and central USA), and are slow growing (100 years) and expensive. Common examples include: Oak, Ash, Elm, Beech, Birch, Chestnut, Lime, Sycamore, Walnut, Apple and Pear.

EVERGREEN HARDWOODS

These trees keep their leaves all the year round, and therefore grow more quickly and to a greater size. They are usually softer and easier to work than deciduous hardwoods. They grow mainly in **tropical and sub-tropical** climates (including most of South America, central America, Indo-China, Africa, Burma, India, and the East and West Indies). Common examples include: Mahogany, Teak, African Walnut, Afrormosia, Iroko, Rosewood, Ebony, Balsa and Sapele. There are two European evergreen hardwoods, the holly and the laurel.

Softwoods

These are produced by conifers (cone bearing trees). They are usually evergreen with needle-like leaves, and grow mainly in colder and cooler temperate climates (including Scandinavia, Canada, Northern Russia, and at high altitudes elsewhere. They grow quickly (30 years) and are therefore cheaper, softer and easier to work than hardwoods. The seeds are not enclosed, but are held in cones. Common examples include: the many types of Pine, Spruce, Fir, Cedar, Larch and Giant Redwood.

Yew is a coniferous tree which does not produce cones. Larch is the only deciduous coniferous tree.

Note: The names softwood and hardwood describe the leaves, seeds and structure of the trees, and not necessarily the timber produced. As a result, some hardwoods (notably Balsa) are light in weight and very soft to work, while some softwoods (e.g. Yew and Pitch Pine) are heavy and hard to work.

Commonly available forms of hardwood and softwood

Remember when ordering timber that the widths and thicknesses of all timbers are given as the rough sawn sizes. You can buy machine-planed timber either planed on both sides (PBS) or planed all round (PAR), but its size will still be described as the nominal (rough sawn) size, although it will actually be approximately 3 mm smaller in thickness and if PAR in width too.

A **board** is a piece of wood less than 40 mm thick and 75 mm, or over, wide.

■ Common thicknesses are 12, 16, 19, 22 and 25 mm.
■ Common widths for softwood are from 75 mm to 225 mm.
■ Common widths for hardwood are from 150 mm to 330 mm.
■ Lengths normally start at 1.8 metres and go up to 6.3 metres.

A **plank** is a piece of wood over 40 mm thick.

Squares are square sections.

Common sizes for squares are 25 mm × 25 mm, 38 mm × 38 mm, and 50 mm × 50 mm.

Strips are rectangular sections narrower than 75 mm wide. Common sizes for strips are 25 mm × 38 mm and 25 mm × 50 mm.

PART 3: Conversion of timber

Conversion means the sawing of logs into usuable sizes with the minimum of waste. There are many different methods to suit different timbers and purposes.

The two main ones are:

■ **Plain sawing** (also known as flat, through, and through and slash sawing). This is the simplest, cheapest and quickest method, but the boards warp and shrink badly because there are long annual rings in most boards. Only the centre board has short annual rings and will stay flat. (see Shrinkage.)

  Plain sawing is used mainly for softwoods.

■ **Quarter or radial sawing.** True quarter sawing produces boards with short annual rings which are less liable to warp and shrink, are stronger, and show the figure of the wood. This is the attractive grain exposed by sawing along the medullary rays of some hardwoods.

  True quarter sawing is more difficult, more expensive and slower than plain sawing, and wastes a lot of wood. Therefore, several near-radial methods are used to reduce wastage and simplify sawing.

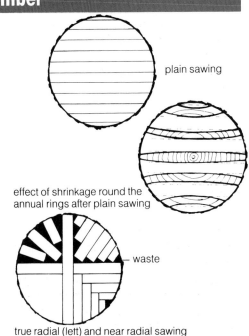

plain sawing

effect of shrinkage round the annual rings after plain sawing

— waste

true radial (left) and near radial sawing

Properties and uses of a few common hardwoods

Name	Sources	Colour	Advantages
Beech	Europe including Britain.	White or pinkish brown, with flecks in grain from rays when quarter sawn.	Hard, tough, very strong and straight. The close grain polishes well and withstands wear and shocks.
Elm	Europe, including Britain.	Light reddish brown.	Tough, elastic, durable, fairly strong, fairly easy to work, medium weight, does not split easily. Good for use under water.
Iroko	East and West Africa, e.g. Nigeria, Ghana.	Initially yellow but darkens to dark brown.	Looks like Teak and has the properties of Teak, but is only half the price. Naturally one of the most durable timbers because it is oily. Needs no preservative outside.
African Mahoganies, e.g. Sapele Utile	West Africa, e.g. Nigeria, Ghana.	Pink to reddish brown.	Plentiful supply, available in wide and long boards, fairly easy to work, fairly strong, medium weight, durable. Finishes fairly well.
Meranti	Malaysia, Indonesia, Philippines	Dark red or yellow.	Red Meranti looks like Mahogany, but is cheaper. Fairly strong, fairly durable.
European Oak	Europe, including Britain, Russia, Poland.	Light to dark brown, with silver grain or ray figure when quarter sawn.	Very strong, very durable, hard, tough. Little shrinkage. Usually works fairly well with sharp tools. Finishes well.
Japanese Oak	Japan.	Yellowish brown.	Strong, durable, slightly lighter, milder and easier to work than European oak. Knot free. Cheaper than European oak.

Disadvantages	Uses
Not suitable for outdoor work because it is not durable when exposed to changes in moisture. Heavy, difficult to work, narrow planks and warps.	Most used hardwood in Britain. For furniture (especially chairs), floors, wooden tools, veneers, plywood, toys, turnery. Good for steam bending.
Tends to warp unless well seasoned. Cross-grained.	Garden furniture when treated with preservative, construction work, turnery, furniture.
Heavy, cross-grained.	Teak substitute. Furniture, interior and exterior joinery, cladding, floors, veneers, constructional work.
Some interlocking and variable grain, warps, hardness varies.	Shop fitting, furniture, cladding, floors, veneers, joinery plywood. Because the name includes a wide range of timbers, the properties and colours inevitably vary.
Does not polish as well as Mahogany. Fairly hard to work.	Interior joinery, furniture, construction work, Mahogany substitute. Red and yellow faced plywood. Can be used outside with suitable preservatives.
Heavy, expensive, open-grain. Contains tannic acid which corrodes iron and steel fittings and causes permanent blue stain on wood. Splits. Some British Oak is harder to work. Sapwood needs preservative.	Boat building, garden furniture, gate posts, floors, construction work, veneers, high-class furniture and fittings.
Slightly weaker and less durable than European Oak.	Interior woodwork and furniture. Good for steam bending.

Properties and uses of a few common hardwoods — contd.

Name	Sources	Colour	Advantages
Teak	Burma, India, Thailand.	Rich golden brown.	Hard, strong, one of naturally most durable timbers because it is oily. Highly resistant to moisture, fire, acids and alkalis. Very attractive straight grain. Works fairly easily. Does not corrode iron and steel.
Obeche	West Africa, e.g. Cameroon, Nigeria, Ghana	Pale yellow	Straight-grained variety works well, and stains and finishes well after filling the open grain.
Afrormosia	Africa generally.	Yellow to light brown with darker streaks. Tends to darken on exposure to light.	Works fairly well. Fairly durable.
Makoré	West Africa, e.g. Ghana, Nigeria, Sierra Leone.	Light red with a striped figure.	Very durable. Stable when dry. Fairly easy to work. Stains and polishes well. Strong.
African Walnut	West Africa.	Bronze yellowish-brown with irregular dark lines.	Works fairly well. Attractive appearance. Available in larger sizes.

Properties and uses of a few common softwoods

Name	Sources	Colour	Advantages
Redwood (Scots Pine, Red Baltic Pine, Fir)	Northern Europe, Scandinavia, Russia, Scotland.	Cream to pale reddish-brown heartwood, cream sapwood.	One of cheapest and most readily available timbers. Straight grain. Fairly strong. Easy to work. Finishes well. Fairly durable.
Whitewood (Spruce)	Northern Europe, Canada, USA.	Plain creamy white.	Fairly strong. Easy to work. Very resistant to splitting.

Disadvantages	Uses
Difficult to glue because oils form a barrier that will not readily absorb adhesives. Gritty nature, blunts tools quickly. Very expensive.	High class furniture, veneers, laboratory benches, ships' decks.
Tends to be 'corky' when cutting joints. Not durable outside. Sometimes cross grained and difficult to work — avoid this type.	Hidden parts of furniture. Interior joinery, plywood core making and for veneering on. Work to be painted.
Stains in contact with iron in damp conditions. Grain is variable.	High class interior and exterior joinery. Floors, windows, sills, doors, gates, stairs, external cladding, furniture, constructional work.
Cross grain can make planing difficult.	High class interior and exterior joinery. Cladding, floors, veneers, plywood, furniture.
Cross grain can make planing and finishing difficult.	High class internal and external joinery, veneers, furniture. Sometimes used as a Teak substitute in furniture.

Disadvantages	Uses
Knotty. Sometimes has a blue stain from a harmless fungus.	Most used softwood in Britain. Suitable for all inside work and with suitable preservatives for outside work. Also for woodturning.
Small hard knots. Contains resin pockets. not durable.	General inside work. Whitewood furniture.

Properties and uses of a few common softwoods — contd.

Name	Sources	Colour	Advantages
Douglas Fir (Columbian Pine)	Canada, USA.	Attractive reddish-brown heartwood. Cream sapwood.	Available in long and wide boards. Knot free, straight grain, slightly resinous, therefore water resistant. Fairly strong, fairly durable, tough, fairly easy to work.
Western Red Cedar	Canada, USA.	Dark reddish brown.	Contains natural preservative oils, therefore resists insect attack, weather and dry rot. Knot free, light weight, soft, straight grained. Fine, silky, attractive surface. Very durable, stately. Very easy to work.
Parana Pine	South America, especially Brazil.	Pale yellow with attractive red and brown streaks in heartwood.	Available in long and wide boards. Often knot free. Hard, straight grain. Fairly strong, works easily and well. Smooth finish. Fairly durable.

PART 4: Seasoning

Seasoning is the removal of excess moisture from the wood by drying it after conversion.

Green timber is saturated with moisture (85% water). Timber with less than 20% moisture content is immune from decay, especially dry rot, and therefore seasoning aims to reduce moisture content to below 18% for general use, and 12% for use in centrally heated and air-conditioned buildings.

Correctly seasoned timber has:

1 Increased strength.
2 Increased stability.
3 Increased resistance to decay.

The two methods of seasoning are air and kiln seasoning.

1 AIR SEASONING – THE NATURAL METHOD

Boards are stacked in the open air with **sticks** (thin strips of wood) between them to allow air to circulate. The stack is raised clear of the ground on piers and has a roof to protect it from the weather.

The ends of the boards are painted, or have cleats (wood or metal strips) nailed across them to prevent the end grain drying more quickly than the rest of the board, as this causes splitting (checking).

Identifying a quarter sawn board

Look at the growth rings on the end of the board.

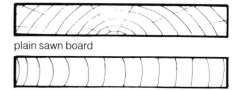

plain sawn board

quarter sawn board

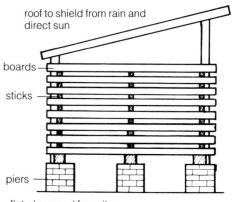

roof to shield from rain and direct sun

boards

sticks

piers

flat, dry, wood free site

Disadvantages	Uses
Splits easily. Open grain with pronounced annual rings.	General outside construction work, masts, ladders, plywood.
More expensive than red and whitewood. Not very strong.	All kinds of joinery, especially outside. Widely used for cladding the outside of buildings, for roof shingles, for kitchens and bathrooms, and for panelling walls.
Lacks toughness. As expensive as some hardwoods. Tends to warp if not carefully seasoned and used.	Best quality internal softwood joinery, especially where attractive grain colour will show, e.g. staircases, and built-in furniture.

■ **Advantages.** It is cheap and needs little skilled attention.
■ **Disadvantages.** It takes 3 to 6 years to dry. (Allow one year for every 25 mm thickness of wood.)

The moisture content can only be reduced to 15–18%.

2 KILN SEASONING – THE ARTIFICIAL METHOD

Boards are stacked on trolleys with sticks between them, and pushed into a kiln. The kiln is sealed and seasoning proceeds in three stages.

Stage 1. Steam is injected at low temperature to force free moisture out of the wood cells.

Stage 2. Steam is reduced and the temperature is increased to dry the wood.

Stage 3. Finally there is a flow of hot, almost dry, air.

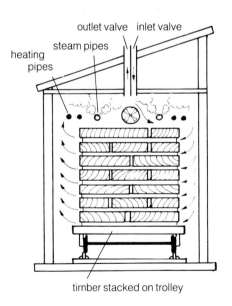

timber stacked on trolley

■ **Advantages.** It takes only a few days or weeks and kills insect eggs in the wood (e.g. woodworm). It is possible to reduce moisture content to below 12%, making the wood suitable for use in centrally heated and air-conditioned buildings.

■ **Disadvantages.** Kilns are expensive to build and to run.

It needs more attention and a lot of skill as incorrect drying will ruin the wood.

Testing moisture content

Wood is never completely dry in normal use and moisture content (m.c.) is the amount of water contained in the wood, as a percentage of its oven-dry weight. During seasoning, a sample is usually put in with the main stock and checked at intervals.

METHOD 1 WEIGHING

(a) Weigh a sample of the wood to be tested (initial weight).
(b) Dry it in an oven until there is no further weight loss.
(c) Weigh the dry sample (dry weight).
(d) $\dfrac{\text{Initial weight} - \text{dry weight}}{\text{dry weight}} \times 100 = \%\text{m.c.}$

METHOD 2 ELECTRIC MOISTURE CONTENT METER

This works on the principle that wet wood is a better conductor of electricity than dry wood. Two prongs are pressed into the wood, and the meter gives a direct reading of the moisture content by measuring the current which flows between them.

PART 5: Faults in timber

(A) Shrinkage

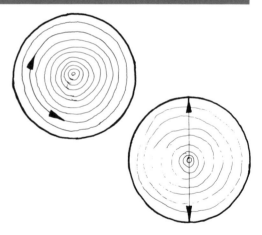

When seasoning removes water from timber, it shrinks considerably.

Most shrinkage takes place round the annual rings.

About half as much shrinkage takes place across the diameter as around the annual rings.

Very little shrinkage takes place along the length. (Can be ignored.)

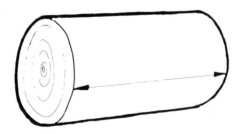

If a log is allowed to dry before conversion it will split along the medullary rays as the annual rings shrink and try to shorten themselves.

When timber is seasoned after conversion, shrinkage affects the shape of the boards. As shrinkage shortens the annual rings, the most shrinkage occurs in those boards with the longest annual rings, and the shape of each board depends on which part of the log it comes from and on how it is sawn. (See Conversion.)

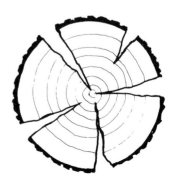

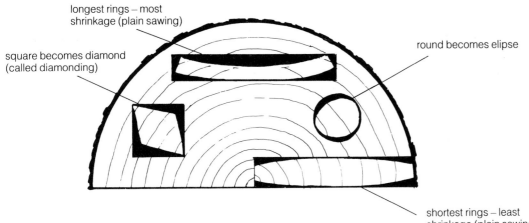

longest rings – most shrinkage (plain sawing)

square becomes diamond (called diamonding)

round becomes elipse

shortest rings – least shrinkage (plain sawing)

(B) Warping

Warping is the general name for any distortion from the true shape. There are four ways in which wood warps.

1 **Cupping** — a curve across the grain.
2 **Bowing** — a curve along the grain on the wide surface of the board.
3 **Springing** — a curve along the edge of the board.
4 **Twisting or wind** — curved like a propeller (remember use of winding strips to test face-sides for twist).

These faults are caused by poor seasoning, uneven shrinkage and poor vertical stacking.

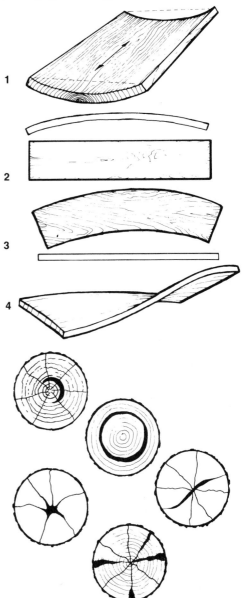

(C) Defects in timber

Defects are faults in the structure of the timber, which may reduce its strength, durability or usefulness. Natural defects are caused by strong winds, lightning, fire, insect and fungal attack. Artificial defects are caused by careless felling, conversion and seasoning.

1 **Shakes.** The separation of adjoining layers of wood usually caused by strong winds, poor felling, or shrinkage.

■ *Cup shake* — a partial separation of the annual rings.
■ *Ring shake* — a cup shake which has separated all the way round an annual ring.
■ *Heart shake* — a split along the medullary rays starting in the pith.
■ *Star shake* — several heart shakes forming an approximate star shape.
■ *Radial shakes or splits* — splits along the medullary rays starting on the outside, and caused by shrinkage around the annual rings after felling.

2 **Knots** are where branches grew from the tree. A large knot weakens the timber.

Live knots are where a living branch joined the tree. They are hard, tightly knit into the wood, light in colour and free from decay.

Dead knots are where a branch died or was cut off while the tree was growing. They are often dark in colour, soft, decayed, or loose.

3 **Pitch pockets** are saucer shaped hollows along the grain full of resin. The resin runs out when the pocket is opened. They are caused by damage to the growing tree.

4 **Checks** are splits in the length of a board caused by bad seasoning.

5 **Thunder shakes** are hair-line cracks across the grain which are often impossible to see until the timber is converted. The board will usually break along the shake. This is especially seen in mahoganies.

6 **Irregular grain** is any variation of the grain from approximately parallel to the surface, which makes planing very difficult and weakens the wood.

Cross-grain is where the grain fibres are at varying angles to the surface, usually only in small areas of a board. Caused by cutting from logs where the grain is not straight, or around a knot in the wood.

Short or diagonal grain is where the fibres are not parallel to the surface although the board is cut from straight-grained timber. Caused by careless conversion.

Interlocking grain is where adjacent strips of grain fibre are angled in opposite directions so that whichever way you plane, some strips tear.

7 **Waney edge.** A board which shows part of the natural circumference of the tree.

8 **Sapwood** is the young, soft part of the tree, and is much more vulnerable to fungal and insect attack than heartwood.

It should, therefore, be removed during conversion before the timber is used for most purposes.

9 **Case-hardening and honeycombing** is when the timber is seasoned too quickly in a kiln, leaving the outer layers very hard, and causing the cell walls in the centre to collapse, resulting in short splits along the medullary rays.

pitch pockets

checks

thunder shakes

heartwood

sapwood

bark may still be on

case-hardening

(D) Insect attack

Most insect damage to wood in Britain is caused by beetles. They all have a similar four-stage life cycle, and the three most important are furniture beetle (commonly called woodworm), death-watch beetle, and powder post beetle (lyctus).

THE LIFE CYCLE

1 Eggs are laid by beetles in cracks in timber.

2 Eggs hatch into larvae which bore into the wood, and feed on it for 1–50 years.

3 When full grown, the larvae hollow out tiny caverns just below the surface and grow into pupae.

4 Pupae hatch into beetles and bite their way out of the wood through the flight holes which we see in infested timber, mate, and restart the cycle.

The infestation is not visible until the flight holes appear, by which time it may be too late.

FURNITURE BEETLE

This attacks hardwood, softwood and some plywoods, especially sapwood and old wood, and is responsible for 75% of known damage to timber in buildings. It produces pellets of coarse, gritty powder, and honeycombs the inside of the timber with tunnels.

DEATH WATCH BEETLE

This attacks hardwoods, especially old oak structural timbers, and occasionally softwood, usually where there is also damp and fungal attack (see section E). It is not normally found in houses or furniture and produces bun-like pellets of coarse dust which are easily seen.

POWDER POST BEETLE

This attacks only the sapwood of hardwoods. It reduces the inside of the timber to a very fine powder and produces flour-like bore dust.

PREVENTION

1 Apply preservative to timber, e.g. creosote or insecticides.
2 Keep furniture clean and wax polished to seal small cracks.

TREATMENT

1 In a building, cut-out and burn infested timber wherever possible. This may not be possible when repairing furniture.
2 Apply a deep penetrating insecticide to kill larvae and give protection from renewed attack.
3 Fill old holes with stopper so that new holes can be spotted.

Treatment of serious infestation requires expert help.

(E) Fungal attack

All fungi which attack timber develop under similar conditions. They require:

1 Food. The cells of non-durable wood, especially sapwood.
2 Moisture. The moisture content of the wood must be at least 20% (see Seasoning).
3 Oxygen from the air.
4 Correct temperature. Unfortunately the temperature in Britain is never too hot or too cold for fungus.
5 Lack of air circulation.

Decay can be recognised by:

1 Softening and change of colour of the wood.
2 Loss of weight of wood.
3 A musty smell.

The main types of fungal attack are wet rot and dry rot.

WET ROT (OR WHITE ROT)

This is a general name for a group of fungi which attack timber with 30% or more moisture content. It is the commonest form of rot, especially on outside woodwork. The wood becomes dark and spongy when wet, and brittle when dry.

- **Prevention.** Treat with water-repellent preservative.
- **Treatment.** Cut out badly affected timber and dry the rest. Treat with fungicidal preservative.

DRY ROT (OR BROWN ROT)

Dry rot thrives in damp, unventilated conditions, on timber with 20% or more moisture content. It is called dry rot because it leaves the wood in a dry crumbly state. It is the most serious form of fungal attack and is very difficult to eradicate. It spreads either by sending out strands in different directions or by releasing millions of fine rust-red spores (like seeds) from the fruit bodies which grow on it. These can be carried by wind, animals or people to all parts of the building, while the strands can penetrate through walls to adjoining rooms.

- **Prevention.** Keep woodwork dry and well ventilated and treat with preservative. Use naturally durable timbers.
- **Treatment.** The cure must be prompt and thorough as even brickwork, concrete and steel girders will not prevent the spread of spores. Remove and burn all affected timber and debris up to at least 500 mm beyond the decay. Then sterilise all timber, walls, etc., in the area with a blow lamp and dry-rot fluid.

Correct causes of damp and bad ventilation, and prevent direct contact between new woodwork and brickwork.

PART 6: Veneers and man-made boards

Veneers

Veneers are thin sheets of wood. They can be made in several ways, including:

- **Rotary cutting.** After softening by steaming, the log is mounted between centres on a lathe, and slowly rotated against a knife to unroll a continuous sheet of veneer which is then chopped into sheets.

  This method usually produces a plain veneer which is used to make the plies of plywood. It is the most used and cheapest method.
- **Slice cutting.** After softening by steaming, the log is mounted on a machine bed which moves it against a knife to produce flat sheets.

  This method usually produces interesting grain patterns for face veneers.

rotary cutting

slice cutting

Man-made boards

Very wide boards of hard or softwood are rare, expensive and liable to warp. Narrow boards joined edge to edge are time consuming to prepare and liable to warp.

Man-made boards are available in large sheets and are stable. Plywood, blockboard, and laminboard have great strength in both directions because of the crossing of the grain in the layers.

PLYWOOD

This is made from layers or plies of wood glued together so that the grain of each ply is at right angles to the next. There is always an odd number of plies so that the grain runs the same way on both outside pieces and hence stresses are balanced.

Plywood can be faced with a veneer of decorative hardwood to improve its appearance, or with melamine to give a harder wearing surface.

Plywood is graded for interior or exterior use depending on the water resistance of the glue used, and this is shown by code letters on each sheet.

WBP — Weather and boil proof.
BR — Boil resistant
MR — Moisture resistant
Int. — Interior use only

Plywood is also graded by the smoothness of the surface and number of defects in it. Plywood can be nailed near the edge without splitting. Thin plywood is flexible and can be formed into curved shapes.

Usual sheet sizes are 2440 × 1220 mm and 1525 × 1525 mm.

Common thicknesses are 4, 6, 9 and 12 mm.

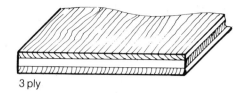
3 ply

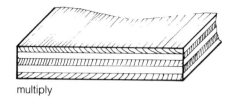
multiply

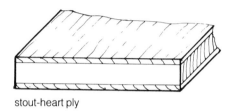
stout-heart ply

BLOCKBOARD AND LAMINBOARD

These are made by sandwiching strips of softwood between two plies. The strips are narrower in laminboard than in blockboard. They are usually made in interior grade only. The grain of the face plies runs at right angles to the core strips. The core strips are arranged with the heartside alternately on top and underneath (as when edge jointing boards) to avoid warping. Both block and laminboard can be faced with veneers of decorative hardwood.

It is usually cheaper to make blockboard than to make multiply over 12 mm thick.

Usual sheet size is 2440 × 1220 mm.
Common thickness is 18 mm.

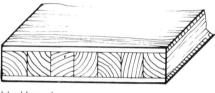
blockboard

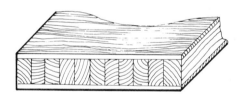
laminboard

CHIPBOARD

Chipboard is made by gluing wooden chips together under heat and pressure. Most chipboard is of **graded density**, having smaller chips packed tightly together on the outside to give a smoother and stronger face. It is suitable only for interior use. Veneered and melamine-faced chipboard is widely used for worktops, shelves and furniture making.

Usual sheet size is 2240 × 1220 mm.
Common thicknesses are 12 mm and 18 mm.

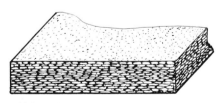
chipboard

HARDBOARD

Hardboard is made by mixing wood fibres with water and synthetic resin glue, hot-pressing it into sheets and leaving it to dry. It is not very strong and is usually fixed onto a wooden frame.

Standard grade is for interior use.
Tempered grade is impregnated with oil for exterior use and for bending to make curved shapes.
Can be melamine-faced or ready painted.

Pegboard is hardboard with holes to hold display hooks.
Usual sheet size is 2440 × 1220 mm.
Common thickness is 3.2 mm.

SOFTBOARD (FIBRE-BOARD)

This is made in the same way as hardboard, but less pressure is used. It is used for notice boards, and sound and heat insulation boards. Its low density makes it light, but weak.

Usual sheet size is 2440 × 1200 mm.
Common thicknesses are 9 mm and 12 mm.

Cleaning up and finishing wood

As much cleaning up and finishing as possible is done before assembly, but joints need to be levelled off and the outside of the job cleaned up and finished, after the cramps have been removed. The stages are:

1 **The smoothing plane** is used to remove marking-out lines and to clean the surface.

It must be sharp and set fine. For cross-grained wood move the cap-iron close to the cutting edge and move the frog to reduce the width of the mouth. Be careful not to plane off too much, especially from joints, and to keep the work square.

2 **Scrapers** are used to produce a very smooth surface on hardwoods only, especially on cross-grained timbers where a plane is not entirely effective.

They take off very fine shavings and there are two types:

(a) **Simple tool steel blade** (flat or curved) which is held between thumbs and fingers.
(b) **Cabinet scraper** (flat only) which has a blade held in a cast iron body similar to a spokeshave.

3 **Abrasive papers** are used to remove small faults from the surface. They scrape wood away by rubbing and should always be used wrapped tightly round a cork block to prevent damage to the wood. Take care not to round corners or rub hollows in flat surfaces.

There are three types:

(a) **Glasspaper** consists of pieces of ground glass, graded into sizes and glued onto backing paper. There are ten grades of cut. Sheet size 280 × 230 mm.
(b) **Garnet paper** consists of very hard stone, crushed, graded and glued onto backing paper. It is more expensive.

There are two types of garnet paper. The first is **open coated paper** with abraisive grains spaced out so that the paper does not clog when rubbing down paint or soft resinous woods, and when machine sanding.

The second is **close coated paper** with grains packed together to give a regular surface suitable for rubbing hardwoods (all glasspaper has a closed coat).

(c) There are also special, tough, hardwearing grits used mainly for sanding machine discs, sheets and belts, and metal backed hand rubbers (e.g. aluminium oxide). These are graded by grit sizes.

4 **Wire wool** (steel wool) is used as a very fine abrasive, mainly in the final stages of polishing. Take care not to leave fine pieces of black wire stuck in the grain.

Grades of abrasive

Grit size		Garnet paper	Glasspaper
220 ⎫ 180 ⎬	Extra fine	6/0 5/0	Flour 00
150 ⎫ 120 ⎬	Fine	4/0 3/0	0 1
100 ⎫ 80 ⎬ 60 ⎭	Medium	2/0 0 ½	1½ F2 M2
50 ⎫ 40 ⎬ 36 ⎭	Coarse	1 1½ 2	S2 2½ 3

5 **Finishing.** After cleaning up, but before assembling, apply the chosen finish to as many parts of the job as possible. All inside surfaces should be finished before assembly because it is difficult to get a good finish in corners after gluing. Mask areas which are to be glued with tape because glue will not stick on many finishes.

It is essential to check the surface of the wood very carefully before applying any finish because any faults will look worse afterwards. Small dents may be removed by damping the surface with water or ironing over a damp cloth and allowing to dry.

Wood finishes

These are used to protect the surface of the wood from weather, insect attack, fungal attack, heat, liquids and dirt, and to improve the appearance of the timber. The type chosen depends on the type of wood and the use to which it is to be put. The ones listed below are only a few of the many available.

French polish is made by dissolving Shellac in methylated spirit. It is available in a range of colours, mainly white (an amber shade) and browns. The wood may be stained first.

To use it, apply the first coat with a brush to seal the grain. If necessary fill the grain with filler and leave to dry. Lightly rub down and apply polish in long strokes along the grain with a cloth rubber and allow to dry. Apply more polish with a circular motion of the rubber and finish with diluted polish.

Oil produces a good natural finish. It is especially suitable for naturally oily timbers (e.g. Teak and Iroko). It is suitable for inside and outside use, but requires regular recoating. Some examples include teak oil and linseed oil. Olive oil is used for woodware which will come into contact with food.

To use oil, rub in well with a cloth and wipe off the surplus. Allow 1 week between coats.

Wax polish produces a dull gloss finish and shows the natural grain of the wood. It was originally made by shredding beeswax and dissolving it in turpentine.

To use it, seal the grain with white french polish. Then lightly rub down with fine glasspaper when dry, rub wax into the grain and allow to dry again. Finally, polish with a brush and/or soft cloth.

Plastic finishes (e.g. clear polyurethane varnish, etc.) produce a good gloss, eggshell or matt surface and show the natural colour of the wood. They are widely used for furniture because they are heat proof, immune to most liquids and very durable. Some are also suitable for outside use.

To use, apply with brush, spray or cloth and rub down lightly between coats. They can be diluted with white spirit (turps subs.) to help them soak into the grain and obtain a natural finish.

Varnish is a solution of resins in oil or spirit. It produces a hard, durable, waterproof, glossy, transparent finish, and is used on internal and external joinery, but not usually on furniture.

It is used as for plastic finishes but using a brush only.

Filler is a paste used to fill the grain to make the surface smooth. The colour must be matched to the wood and applied after staining, if needed. Then clean off the surplus by rubbing across the grain and leave to dry.

Wood is **stained** to imitate other woods or to enhance its appearance. Matching colours is difficult so always test stains on scrapwood. Do not stain after filling because filler stains darker than wood.

Paint is suitable for internal and external use. There are many types so select for the job and read the instructions.

To use it, key the surface by glasspapering at 45° with coarse glasspaper (S2). Treat knots with knotting or french polish to prevent resin staining the finish, or causing peeling. Apply one coat of primer and fill nail holes and cracks with putty or filler. Then apply one or two coats of undercoat followed by one or two coats of gloss, eggshell or matt finish. Rub down lightly between coats.

Wood preservation

Some timbers are naturally immune from decay (see Some common hardwoods and softwoods), and all wood finishes protect the wood to some extent, but exterior woodwork and structural timbers may require more thorough treatment than painting or varnishing.

Wood preservation means treating wood with solutions which make it poisonous to fungus, insects and marine borers, as well as protecting it from the weather.

COMMON TYPES OF PRESERVATIVES

1 **Tar oils**, for example **creosote** which is the best known preservative. It soaks into the grain and gives a matt brown finish. It is cheap, permanent, safe to handle and does not affect metals.

2 **Water soluble chemicals** (e.g. zinc chloride) are for use where timber will be used in dry conditions.

3 **Preservatives contained in non-water soluble solvents** penetrate deeply into the timbers and then evaporate leaving the preservatives in the wood cells. They are usually proprietary preservatives which are more expensive than creosote, but penetrate better when brushed or sprayed on.

HOW TO USE PRESERVATIVES

1 Brushing or spraying on is a simple way of treating timber already made up, but gives only surface protection because the preservative does not penetrate far into the timber.

2 Soaking the timber in tanks of hot and/or cold preservatives gives better penetration than brushing and spraying and needs only simple equipment.

3 Forcing the preservative into the timber under pressure gives the greatest penetration, but requires expensive equipment.

CLEANING BRUSHES

■ French polish — methylated spirits.
■ Cellulose paint and varnish — cellulose thinners.
■ Polyurethane varnish and paint — white spirit or cellulose thinners.
■ Oil-based paint and varnish — white spirit (turps subs.).
■ Emulsion paint and some modern oil-based paints — soap and water.
■ Creosote — paraffin.

There are a number of brush cleaners and paint removers on the market which will soften hard brushes used for all but cellulose finishes.

The production of iron

Iron ore, usually in the form of iron oxide in rocks, is mined or quarried and taken to a steelworks. There it is graded and crushed to reduce it to a maximum size of 100 mm cubes. Small particles are mixed with coke and heated to form a clinker of similar size called **sinter**.

Once lit, a blast furnace runs continuously until the heat-resistant bricks of the refractory lining start to burn away, usually after about 2 years. The raw materials, coke, limestone, iron-ore and sinter, are continuously poured in through the double bell charging system which prevents hot gases from escaping during charging.

Heated air is blasted into the bottom of the furnace from the blast or bustle pipe, through the tuyères, to make the coke burn fiercely.

The iron in the ore melts and collects in the well at the bottom of the furnace. The limestone acts as a flux to make impurities float on the surface of the molten iron in the form of a liquid slag, which can be tapped off. The iron and slag are tapped off at regular intervals.

The hot waste gases go through a gas cleaning plant before either being reused to heat the blast to 800°C, or being burnt off.

The iron produced is 90 to 95% pure, and it is used in one of three ways.

1 In a modern integrated steel works it is conveyed in its molten state straight to the steel-making furnaces.
2 It is fed into a pig casting machine which makes it into small iron bars (pig iron) for future remelting, for example, in an electric arc furnace.
3 It is refined into cast iron which is a strong but brittle metal especially suitable for making intricate castings such as engine cylinder blocks and cylinder heads simply, easily and economically.

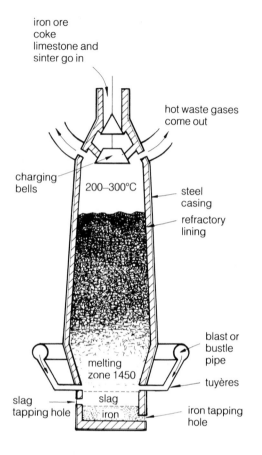

The production of steel

The raw materials for steel making are iron from the blast furnaces, scrap iron and steel. The amount of each used depends on the type of steel being made and the process used. Because there are many different types of steel, for example, mild steel, tool steels, stainless steel and steel alloys, there are many variations in the techniques used. All steelmaking however, involves removing impurities and excess carbon from the iron, and adding small amounts of other elements.

THE BASIC OXYGEN FURNACE

This is the most important method for making large tonnages of widely used steels and one furnace can make 350 tonnes or more in 40 minutes.

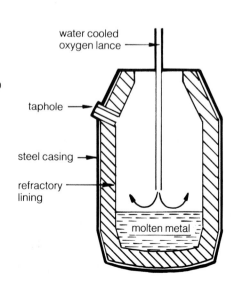

The furnace is tilted and charged first with 30% scrap and then with 70% molten iron. With the furnace upright, a water-cooled oxygen lance is lowered to just above the surface of the metal, and oxygen is blown into the melt at very high speed. It combines with carbon and other unwanted elements to remove them from the charge. During the blow, lime is added as a flux so that the oxidised impurities form a slag on the surface ready for tapping off later.

After the blow, the steel which has been made is tapped out through the taphole into a ladle. The converter is then tipped upside down to empty out the slag.

THE ELECTRIC ARC FURNACE

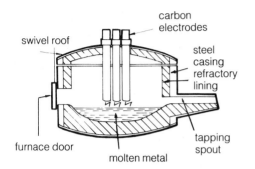

This method is used to make both large tonnages of widely used steels and, because of the precise control it gives over the composition of the steel, special high quality steels. A large furnace can make 150 tonnes of steel in 4 hours.

The furnace is charged only with cold scrap. To charge the furnace, the carbon electrodes are withdrawn and the swivel roof is swung open so that the cold metal can be dropped in. The roof is swung closed and the electrodes are lowered. When the electric circuit is completed between the electrodes and the metal, a powerful arc is struck which produces a temperature of about 3500°C to melt the metal.

Lime, fluorspar and iron oxide are added to combine with the impurities in the metal and form a slag. Additions are made to get the required type of steel. The slag is poured off through the furnace door by tilting the furnace which is then tilted the other way to tap off the steel.

CONVERTING THE MOLTEN STEEL

After tapping from the furnace, the molten steel is first cast in one of three ways.

(a) It can be cast into ingots by pouring it into moulds to solidify. The size of each ingot depends on the use to which it will be put. Red hot ingots can then be rolled between heavy rollers to make slabs, blooms, billets and heavy sections such as girders, or forged by pressing or hammering into shape.

Slabs are usually 75–254 mm thick and up to 2 m wide. They are used to make plates, sheets, strips, pipes and tinplate.

Blooms are usually 150–300 mm square, while **billets** are usually 50–125 mm square. They are used to make structural shapes, bars, rods and wire.

All these shapes are in 7 to 10 metre lengths.

(b) It can be cast into slabs and blooms by the continuous casting process where molten steel is channelled down through a water-cooled tube until it has solidified on the outside. It is then passed through water sprays and rollers until completely solidified, and it is finally cut to length.

The advantage of this method is that the steel travels straight from the furnaces, through the continuous casting plant to the rolling mill. The casting of ingots, the reheating of the ingots, and the rolling of ingots into slabs, blooms and billets ready for further processing are all eliminated, and the inevitable wastage of some steel at each extra stage avoided.

(c) It can be poured into sand moulds to make steel castings.

BLACK STEEL AND BRIGHT STEEL

Metal which has been rolled to shape while hot is known as black bar, because it has a coating of black oxide all over it. The best example of this is the black mild steel used for forgework.

To convert this to a bright finish (as, for example, on bright drawn mild steel), and to make the sizes more accurate, the black steel is first pickled in dilute sulphuric acid to remove the oxide, washed, dried and oiled, and then rerolled cold.

The bright steel is finally drawn through a series of gradually reducing dies to make accurately shaped rods, flats and wire.

The production of aluminium

Aluminium ore, known as bauxite, is mined or quarried, crushed and dried before being refined into alumina (aluminium oxide). This is done by dissolving the bauxite in a hot caustic soda solution, filtering out impurities and collecting the aluminium oxide which remains in precipitation tanks.

The filtered oxide is washed and heated to 1000°C to give alumina. This is ready for the second stage of refining where it is dissolved in a flux of molten cryolite in a steel furnace. This furnace has a refractory lining and an inner lining of carbon which forms a cathode. Blocks of carbon are suspended in the melt to form anodes, and a large current is passed between the anodes and the cathode to heat the furnace to about 1000°C. As the alumina melts, molten aluminium of 99 to 99.8% purity collects in the bottom of the furnace. The oxygen from the aluminium oxide combines with carbon from the anodes to form carbon dioxide which escapes as a gas.

The aluminium is tapped off and cast into ingots ready for further processing.

The production of copper

Copper ore, often containing a very low percentage of copper, is mined or quarried and then crushed and ground into a fine powder. Large quantities of waste can then be removed by the flotation process, where grains of copper float on the surface of the liquid while the rock particles sink.

The resulting copper concentrate is smelted in a reverberatory furnace, where lime is added as a flux to form most of the impurities into a slag, which is then tapped off.

The **matte** of copper and iron sulphides remaining after smelting is taken to a converter where compressed air is blown through it. This oxidises the iron to make a slag, and blows off the sulphur as a gas. The copper, which is now 99% pure, is cast into cakes known as **blister** copper.

To obtain pure copper blister, copper is used as the anodes in electrolytic cells where the copper is gradually dissolved and redeposited on cathodes made from pure copper sheet.

When the cathodes have grown into blocks of copper, they are melted and cast into copper ingots ready for conversion into wire, plates, sheets, strips, tubes, rods, castings and powders.

Definitions of properties of materials

Various words are used to describe the properties of materials and for this purpose they have exact meanings. In general conversation the same terms are often used inaccurately, and it is important that when we are discussing materials we should understand exactly what they mean, and use them accurately.

The most commonly used terms are defined below and are used in the following chapters.

■ **Hardness** is the resistance of the material to cutting and surface indentation.
■ **Toughness** is the amount of energy the material can absorb without breaking and measures its ability to withstand shocks. It is the opposite to brittleness.
■ **Tensile strength** is the maximum force the material can stand in tension (pulling apart), compression (crushing), torque (twisting) and shear (sideways pressure), without breaking.
■ **Malleability** is the amount of shaping which can be done by hammering, rolling or pressing without the material breaking.
■ **Ductility** is the length to which the material can be stretched without breaking.
■ **Elasticity** is the length to which the material can be stretched and still return to its original length when released. The elastic limit is the point beyond which it remains stretched.
■ **Heat and electrical conductivity** is a measure of how well the material will conduct heat or electricity.

FERROUS AND NON-FERROUS METALS
All metals belong to one of these two groups.
■ **Ferrous metals** are those which are made mainly of iron with small amounts of other metals or other elements added, to give the required properties. Almost all ferrous metals can be picked up with a magnet.
■ **Non-ferrous metals** are those which do not contain iron, for example, aluminium, copper, lead, zinc and tin.

PURE METALS AND ALLOYS
All metals are also either pure metals or alloys.

■ A **pure metal** consists of a single element, which means that it is a substance having only one type of atom in it. The common pure metals are aluminium, copper, iron, lead, zinc, tin, silver and gold.
■ An **alloy** is a mixture of two or more pure metals, or one or more pure metals mixed with other elements. Alloys are made in order to create materials which have combinations of properties not all available in the pure metals, and to fulfil needs for which no pure metal is suitable. For example, while pure aluminium is soft and ductile, the addition of small amounts of other elements can produce aluminium alloys which are stronger than mild steel, have improved hardness, and are corrosion resistant while still retaining the lightness of aluminium.

The identification of ferrous metals

Metal	Test		
	Drop on anvil	Nick and hammer in vice	Grind
Mild steel	Medium pitched ring	Bends before breaking. Shows uniform grey lustre on fracture.	A long thick stream of pale yellow sparks which explode and fork.
Carbon steel	High ringing note	Bends a little and then breaks. Silvery white, fine, crystalline structure.	Orange sparks burst from a thick stream of lines.
High speed steel	Medium metallic ring	Resists blow and then breaks cleanly. Very fine, crystalline structure.	Dull red sparks barely visible close to the wheel.
Grey cast iron	Dull note	Snaps easily. Coarse, dark fracture.	Dull orange stream of sparks close to the wheel.
White cast iron	Very dull note	Breaks cleanly. Finer, white fracture.	Dull red stream of sparks close to the wheel.

The heat treatment of metals

Heat treatment is a way of making metals more suitable for processing or for the jobs which they have to do. For example, a piece of high carbon steel being used to make a cold chisel must be annealed (softened), so that it can be shaped, and then hardened and tempered so that it can cut other metals.

There are three stages in heat treatment.

1 Heat the metal to the correct temperature.
2 Keep it at that temperature for the required length of time (soaking).
3 Cool it in the correct way to give the desired properties.

Annealing makes the metal as soft as possible to relieve internal stresses, and to make it easier to shape.

■ **Mild steel** is heated to bright red heat, soaked for a short time, and left to cool slowly.
■ **Tool steel** is heated to bright red heat, soaked for a short time, and left to cool **very slowly** in hot ashes. The more slowly the metal cools, the softer it will be.
■ **Copper** is heated to cherry red heat and quenched in water.
■ **Gilding metal** is heated to salmon pink heat and quenched in water.
■ **Brass** is heated to dull red heat and left to cool.
■ **Aluminium** is covered with soap, heated gently until the soap turns black and left to cool.

Normalising returns work hardened steel to its normal condition after forging or previous heat treatment. **Steel** is heated to red hot and left to cool.

Hardening increases the hardness and tensile strength of tool steel in order to make cutting tools, springs, hard, wear-resistant bearing surfaces, etc. Hardening can only be carried out on carbon and alloy steels. The higher the carbon content of the steel, the harder it will be.

Steel is heated to cherry red heat, soaked for a short time and quenched vertically in oil, brine or tepid water. Quenching horizontally or in cold water can cause cracking. Hardened metal is brittle and unusable.

Tempering removes the extreme hardness and brittleness from hardened steel, and makes it tougher so that it can be used. Increasing the tempering temperature reduces hardness, but increases toughness, and the final compromise between hardness and toughness depends on the purpose for which the steel is to be used. The hardened steel is cleaned so that the tempering colours can be seen, heated to the required tempering colour and immediately quenched in water.

Tempering colours — as the metal is heated it changes colour, and below are given examples of different degrees of tempering.

Colour	Approx. temperature	Uses
Light straw	230°C Hardest	Planer blades, lathe tools, scribers, scrapers, dividers, emery wheel dressers.
Dark straw	245°C	Drills, taps, dies, reamers, punches.
Orange/brown	260°C	Lathe centres, shears, hammer heads, plane irons.
Light purple	270°C	Knives, scissors, woodwork chisels.
Dark purple	280°C	Saws, cold chisels, rivet sets, axes, table knives.
Blue	300°C Toughest	Springs, screwdrivers, chuck keys, vice jaws, spanners, needles.

Case hardening is a method of putting a hard surface coating onto steels which do not contain enough carbon for hardening and tempering. Carbon is burnt into the surface of the metal so that it can be hardened to give a wear resistant shell and a tough break resistant core.

Mild steel is heated evenly to dull red heat, and dipped or rolled in carbon powder which melts and sticks to the surface. Repeated heating and dipping burns the carbon into the metal and thickens the carburized shell. When the required thickness of shell has been built up, surplus powder is cleaned off with a wire brush and the metal is heated to bright red heat and quenched in water to harden it.

Properties and uses of common non-ferrous metals

Name	Melting point	Composition	Properties	Uses
Aluminium	650°C	Pure metal.	Greyish-white, light, soft, malleable, ductile and highly conductive to heat and electricity. Corrosion resistant (a thin inert film of oxide forms and protects the metal from further attack). Can be welded and soldered by special processes.	Aircraft, boats, railway coaches, engine cylinder heads, blocks, pistons and crankcases, window frames, saucepans, aluminium foil for packaging and insulation, electrical conductors and cables, castings.
Aluminium alloys, e.g. Duralumin	650°C	Aluminium + 4% copper and 1% manganese.	Ductile, malleable, light, work-hardens, and machines well.	Aircraft and vehicle parts.
L.M.4 casting alloy		Aluminium + 3% copper + 5% silicon.	Good fluidity in pouring, good machineability, improved hardness, toughness and corrosion resistance.	General purpose casting alloy.
L.M.6 casting alloy		12% silicon.	High fluidity.	Complex castings.
Copper	1100°C	Pure metal.	Red, malleable, ductile, tough. High heat/electrical conductor. Corrosion resistant. Hot or cold working is possible. Cold working increases hardness and strength and requires frequent annealing. Easily hard and soft soldered.	Wire, especially electrical cables and conductors. Water and central heating pipes. Soldering iron bits and welding nozzles. Copper foil for car radiators, printed circuits and gaskets. Roofing, castings.
Copper alloys Brass	980°C	65% copper + 35% zinc (approximately).	Yellow, very corrosion resistant though it tarnishes easily. Harder than copper. Casts well, easily machined and easily hard and soft soldered. Good heat/electrical conductor.	Castings, forgings, ornaments, valves, propellers.

Name	Melting point	Composition	Properties	Uses
Copper alloys Bronze	980°C	90 to 95% copper + 5 to 10% tin. Sometimes other elements, e.g. phosphorous for phosphor-bronze.	Reddish-yellow, harder and tougher than brass, hard-wearing, corrosion resistant and easily machined.	Bearings, springs, instrument parts, gears. Air, water and steam valves and fittings. Pumps, castings for statues.
Gilding metal		85% copper + 15% zinc.	Golden colour, corrosion resistant and easily hard and soft soldered. Enamels well. Annealed and worked cold.	Beaten metalwork, jewellery, architectural metalwork.
Lead	330°C	Pure metal.	Bright and shiny when new, but rapidly oxidizes to a dull-grey. The heaviest common metal. Soft, malleable, corrosion resistant and immune to many chemicals. Very easy to work. Readily joined by 'burning'.	Coverings for power and telephone cables. Protection against X-rays and radiation. A main constituent in many soft solders, paints, printing type, bearing metals. Roof-coverings and flashings.
Tin	230°C	Pure metal.	White, soft, corrosion resistant in damp conditions.	Tinplate, making bronze, soft solders, printing type metal.
Tinplate		Thin sheet steel coated with pure tin.	Mild steel core is strong and ductile. Tin coating bends with the steel without separating and protects it from corrosion. Resistant to and non-toxic for use with a wide variety of foods.	Tin cans, etc. Light sheet metalwork.
Zinc	420°C	Pure metal.	Bluish-white, ductile, a layer of oxide protects it from further corrosion. Easily worked.	Making brass. Zinc chloride soft soldering flux and wood preservative. Coating for steel galvanized corrugated iron roofing, tanks, buckets, etc. Rust-proof paints, intricate die castings.

Properties and uses of common ferrous metals

Name	Melting point	Composition	Properties	Uses
Cast iron	1000 to 1200°C	Remelted pig iron with small additions depending on use, and scrap steel.	A wide range of alloys with varying properties. Hard, brittle, cheap, strong, rigid in compression and self-lubricating.	Used for heavy crushing machinery.
			White cast iron is very hard, brittle and almost unmachineable.	
			Grey cast iron is readily machineable, easily cast into intricate shapes, and corrosion resistant in damp conditions.	The most used type. Used for car cylinder blocks and heads. Vices, machine tool parts, car brake drums and discs.
			Malleable cast iron is white cast iron annealed to make it softer, more ductile, more machineable and to increase tensile strength.	Horticultural machinery and agricultural implements. Machine handles and gear wheels. Intricate shapes which must withstand rough work such as plumbing fittings.
Steels	1400°C	Alloys of iron and carbon.	Properties, working, qualities and uses vary considerably with the different types of steel.	
Low carbon steels		Less than 0.15% carbon.	Soft, ductile, tough and malleable.	Wire, rivets, thin sheets, cold pressings, drawn tubes.
Mild steels		0.15 to 0.30% carbon.	High tensile strength, ductile, tough, fairly malleable, softer than medium and high carbon steels. Because of low carbon content it cannot be hardened and tempered. Must be case-hardened.	General purpose steel, girders, angle iron, plates, sheet, tubes, drop forgings, nuts and bolts etc.
Medium carbon steels		0.30 to 0.70% carbon.	Stronger and harder than mild steel, but less ductile, tough and malleable.	Garden tools, shafts, axles, springs, wire ropes.

Name	Melting point	Composition	Properties	Uses
High carbon steels		0.70 to 1.40% carbon.	Hardest of the carbon steels, but less ductile, tough and malleable. Hardness and toughness are improved by heat treatment.	Hammers, wood, metal and plastic cutting tools, such as chisels, drills, files, lathe tools, taps and dies. **Silver steel** is a high carbon steel.
Alloy steels		Any steel to which other elements have been added.	Properties depend on elements added.	
Stainless steel		18% chromium and 8% nickel added.	Corrosion resistance.	Sink units, kitchen ware, tanks, pipes, aircraft.
High speed steel		Medium carbon steel, tungsten, chromium and vanadium.	Retains hardness at high temperatures. Brittle. Can be hardened and tempered.	Cutting tools for lathes, etc.
High tensile steel		Low carbon steel, nickel and chromium.	Exceptional strength and toughness.	Gears, shafts, engine parts.
Manganese steel		High carbon steel and manganese.	Extreme toughness.	Chains, hooks, etc.

Commonly available forms

Metals can be bought in a wide range of shapes and sizes, and you should always try to design jobs which use these standard sections. It is advisable to check what materials are in stock before starting, or to look in a stockholder's catalogue to find out what is available. The following sketches show the common shapes and some of the most used sections.

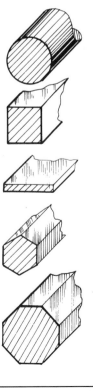

- **Round rod** 5, 6, 8, 10, 12, 16, 20, 25, 32, 40, 50 mm diameter.
- **Squares** 5, 6, 8, 10, 12, 16, 20, 25 mm square.

- **Flats** 12 × 1.5 mm   20 × 1.5 mm   25 × 1.5 mm
        12 × 3 mm   20 × 3 mm   25 × 3 mm
        32 × 3 mm   40 × 3 mm   50 × 3 mm
        12 × 6 mm   20 × 6 mm   25 × 6 mm
        32 × 6 mm   40 × 6 mm   50 × 6 mm

- **Hexagons** 6, 8, 10, 12, 16, 20, 22, 25 mm across flats.

- **Octagons** 6, 8, 10, 12, 16, 20, 22, 25 mm across flats.

- **Sheets** 0.60, 0.80, 1.00, 1.2, 1.6, 2.0, 2.5, 3 mm thick.

- **Round tubes** 5, 6, 8, 10, 12, 16, 20, 25, 32, 40 mm outside diameter.

- **Square tubes** 12, 20, 25 mm square.

- **Rectangular tubes** 50 × 30 mm.

- **Angles** 12 × 12 mm, 18 × 18 mm, 25 × 25 mm.

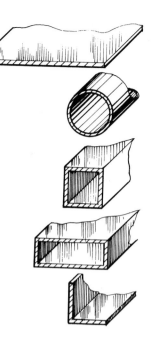

Cleaning-up and finishing metal

FINISHING BRIGHT STEEL

STAGE 1
After shaping with coarse file and smooth file, complete filing by drawfiling. Always work in the same direction along the metal and make sure that each stage removes all marks left by the previous one. Keep your files clean to avoid pinning.

STAGE 2
Finish by using different grades of emery cloth, first coarse, then fine, and finally after all marks have been removed add a little oil to the fine cloth for final finishing. Always wrap emery cloth round a flat file to avoid rounding corners and work in the same direction as the drawfiling marks.

STAGE 3
To protect the metal from rust, smear it with Vaseline or light grease.

OIL FINISHING BLACK STEEL

STAGE 1
Remove all loose scale from forging, grease, etc.

STAGE 2
Either dip the metal in machine oil and burn it into the metal, or heat the metal to dull red heat and quench it in oil. Old sump oil containing carbon can be used to give a blacker finish and reduce costs.

STAGE 3
Wipe off surplus oil and polish with black boot polish.

PAINTING METAL

STAGE 1
Thoroughly clean and degrease the metal. Paraffin or special degreasers will clean badly affected parts while hot water with soda or detergent will remove light oil and dirt.

STAGE 2
Find a dust-free place to work, and make arrangements for supporting the work while painting and drying before starting.

STAGE 3
For maximum protection apply primer, undercoat and topcoat. For inside work, one or two coats of topcoat alone are adequate. Do not allow the paint to collect in corners or run. Paint awkward parts first, and then larger, flat, more noticeable areas. Two thin coats are always better than one thick one. Keep brushes clean and paint tin lids sealed.

CLEANING COPPER AND BRASS

STAGE 1
Dip into an acid pickle consisting of one part sulphuric acid to ten parts water. Always use brass tongs as steel will contaminate the pickle.

STAGE 2
Clean the metal with pumice powder and a damp cloth, and then remove any blemishes with wetted water of Ayr stone.

STAGE 3
Finally polish on a polishing machine with a linen mop and tripoli buffing compound and/or by hand using metal polish.

LACQUERING

STAGE 1
Thoroughly clean, polish and degrease the metal.

STAGE 2
Apply the lacquer or varnish with a best quality soft paint brush to preserve the finish.

Coating with plastics

There are several widely used ways of coating metal with plastics. This is usually done to protect the metal from corrosion, to provide electrical insulation, or to improve its appearance.

Common examples include vegetable racks, refrigerator shelves and baskets, dish drainers, supermarket trolleys and baskets, metal furniture, steering wheels and tool handles.

The method most suitable for school is to dip the pre-heated metal into a tank of fluidised thermoplastic powder such as polythene, PVC, nylon or cellulose acetate butyrate. Polythene is the most used coating powder because it is reasonably cheap, pleasant to handle, tough and durable.

FLUIDISATION

Fluidisation is where air is blown through a powder to make it behave like a liquid, so that when an object is dipped into it all parts are evenly coated.

The fluidising tank has a porous base so that air can be blown at low pressure through the powder above, until the powder bubbles.

METHOD

1 Clean and thoroughly degrease the job. Arrange a suitable method of suspending it during heating and dipping.
2 Heat the job to 180°C in an oven. A thin wire construction will need to be hotter than a thick piece of metal.
3 Dip the job in the fluidised plastics powder for a few seconds.
4 Return it to the oven to fuse the coating into a smooth glassy finish. Overheating will discolour or burn the coating.
5 Hang it up to cool without touching it. Trim any rough edges with a sharp knife.

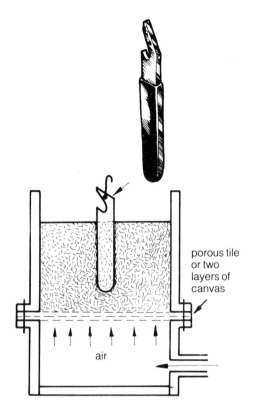

porous tile or two layers of canvas

air

Electroplating

In electroplating, a thin film of metal is deposited on the surface to be covered using an electroplating bath. It is a common means of improving the appearance of metal products, and protecting surfaces from chemical attack. Chromium plating, for example, is used widely on steel products (e.g. car parts) to prevent corrosion and provide visual interest. Silver and gold are often plated onto less expensive metals for jewellery and tableware. It is also possible to electroplate plastics by first giving their surface a special treatment.

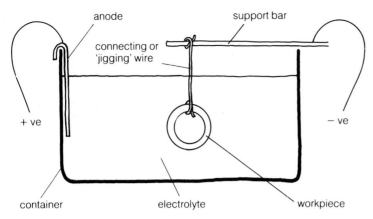

Electroplating bath

An electroplating bath consists of an electrolyte — a solution of salts of the metal to be deposited — into which is suspended an anode and cathode. The anode is a piece of the metal to be deposited and the cathode is the workpiece to be plated. When the anode is connected to the positive side of a power supply and the cathode to negative, metal goes into solution in the electrolyte at the anode and an equivalent amount deposits out on the cathode.

A simple copper-plating bath consists of an electrolyte of copper sulphate, water and a small percentage of sulphuric acid to make the solution conductive. Copper sheet or rod is hung in as the anode. Such a bath, though, is not suitable for plating onto ferrous metals.

In industry, very large electroplating baths are employed, and hundreds of products can be put in as the cathode at one time. Normally, though, the electrolytes used contain highly toxic chemicals.

The Philip Harris electroplating unit, for use in school, is shown here in operation. The anode is a piece of nickel foil and the cathode is a piece of work held in brass tongs — connected to the negative side of the power supply. The power supply itself is a battery comprising three cells to give 4.5 V. This unit is especially useful for giving a uniform bright nickel finish to small products such as jewellery fabricated from brass and copper. The nickel plates over soft- and hard-soldered joints.

The plated products shown include cylindrical boxes made from copper tubing and the hub cap for a model vehicle press formed using the rubber block technique (page 271).

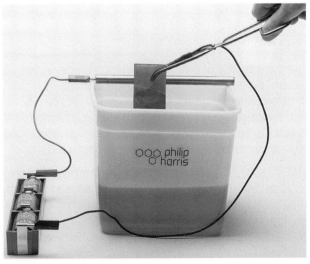

23 Materials for design and technology: Plastics

The manufacture of plastics

Unlike wood and metal, plastics are man-made materials. They are often thought of as one material called plastic but this is wrong, and they are really a group of materials with widely varying properties. Suitable plastics can be found to take the place of the traditional materials, such as wood and metal, for many purposes.

Plastics are distinguished from other chemical compounds by the large size of their molecules. While most substances have molecules made up of less than 300 atoms, plastics molecules contain thousands of atoms. They are therefore known as **macromolecules**.

SOURCES OF PLASTICS

A few plastics are made by modifying natural substances which already have large molecules (see figure 23.1) but most of those used today are man-made, and are therefore known as synthetic plastics.

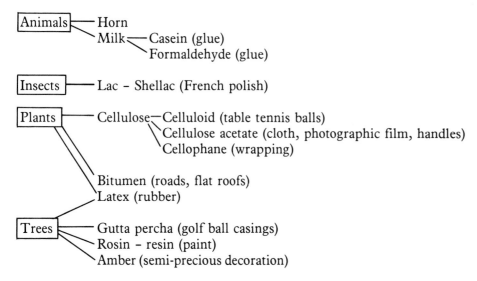

Figure 23.1 Sources of natural plastics

The main source of synthetic plastics is crude oil, but coal and natural gas are also used. During the refining of crude oil, liquids of various densities, such as petrol, paraffin and lubricating oils, and highly volatile petroleum gases, are produced. These gases form the basis of the plastics industry. Although complex and expensive equipment is needed to manufacture plastics, the basic process is simple.

The gases are broken down into **monomers**, which are chemical substances consisting of a single molecule, and thousands of these are then linked together in a process called **polymerisation** to form new compounds called **polymers**. Most polymers are made by combining the element carbon with one or more of the elements oxygen, hydrogen, chlorine, fluorine and nitrogen.

THE TWO MAIN METHODS OF POLYMERISATION

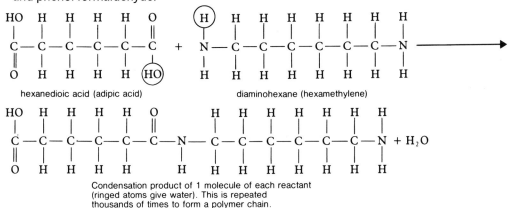

H₂C=CH₂ → polymerization →

ethene (ethylene) monomer → polyethene polymer

Figure 23.2 Polyethene (commonly called polythene)

ADDITION POLYMERISATION

Polymers produced by addition polymerisation result from the chemical linking of thousands of identical small molecules (see figure 23.2). Other common addition polymers include polypropene (polypropylene), polyethenyl ethanoate (polyvinyl acetate), polyphenylethene (polystyrene), polymethyl 2-methylpropenoate (acrylic).

CONDENSATION POLYMERISATION

This is where two different monomers which react with each other are linked together to give a larger molecule with the splitting off of a small molecule, usually water. After the reaction the resulting larger molecule still contains two reactive groups, and therefore the reaction goes on and on, making a larger and larger molecule (see figure 23.3). Common addition polymers include urea formaldehyde, melamine formaldehyde and phenol formaldehyde.

hexanedioic acid (adipic acid)   diaminohexane (hexamethylene)

Condensation product of 1 molecule of each reactant (ringed atoms give water). This is repeated thousands of times to form a polymer chain. + H_2O

Figure 23.3 Polyamide (commonly called nylon 6.6)

WAYS OF CHANGING PLASTICS

The properties of plastics materials can be changed in three ways.

1 **We can lengthen or shorten the chains making up the polymers.**
For example, fifteen ethene monomers combine to make a paraffin wax, while several thousand combine to make polyethene (see figure 23.2).

2 **We can change the basic monomer.** For example, if we replace one of the hydrogen atoms in the ethene monomer (see figure 23.2) with a chlorine atom we have a vinyl chloride monomer. These can then be linked to make a polyvinyl chloride (PVC) polymer (see figure 23.4).

polymerization →

Figure 23.4 PVC

3 **We can combine two or more monomers** to make a new material. This is called **copolymerisation** and the new material is a **copolymer**. For example, a small amount of vinyl acetate monomer mixed with vinyl chloride monomer makes PVAC (vinyl chloride/vinyl acetate copolymer), (figure 23.5) which is easier to process than PVC for such jobs as pressing gramophone records and vacuum forming, because it combines the toughness of PVC with greater heat stability during shaping.

THERMOPLASTICS AND THERMOSETTING PLASTICS

There are two basic types of polymer chain formation and each behaves differently when heated. This difference allows us to separate plastics into two main groups.

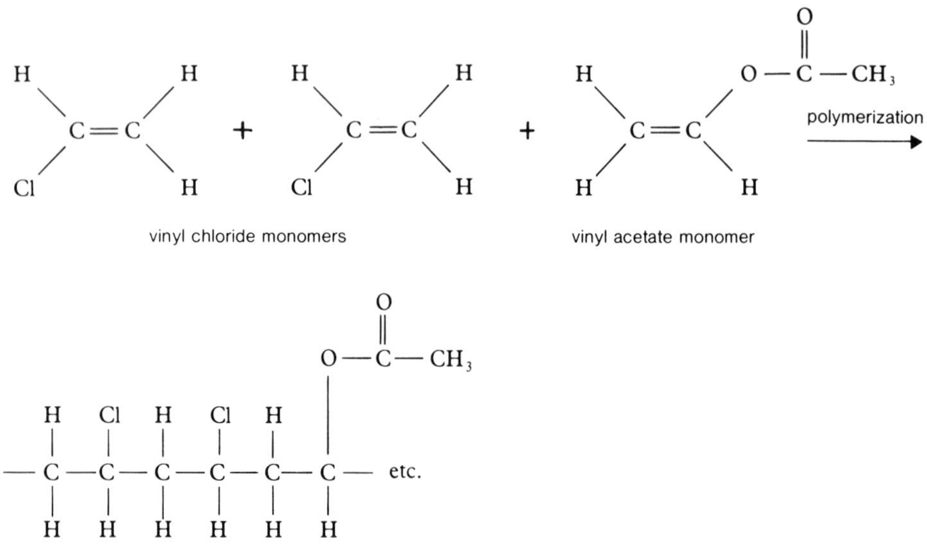

vinyl chloride monomers   vinyl acetate monomer

Figure 23.5 PVAC

THERMOPLASTICS

These plastics are made up of lines of molecules with very few cross linkages. This allows them to soften when heated so that they can be bent into different shapes, and to become stiff and solid again when cooled (see figure 23.6). This process can be repeated many times. (See also figures 23.2 to 23.5.)

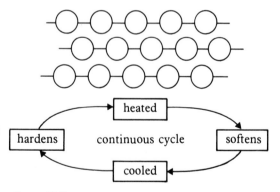

Figure 23.6

Plastic memory

Each time a thermoplastic is reheated, it will try to return to its original flat state, unless it has been damaged by over-heating or over-stretching. This property is known as plastic memory.

Three quarters of the plastics used are thermoplastics.

THERMOSETTING PLASTICS

These plastics are made up of lines of molecules which are heavily cross-linked. This results in a rigid molecular structure (see figure 23.7). Although they soften when heated the first time, and can therefore be shaped, they then become permanently stiff and solid, and cannot be reshaped (e.g. condensation product of phenol and methanal (e.g. Bakelite)).

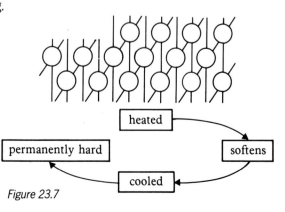

Figure 23.7

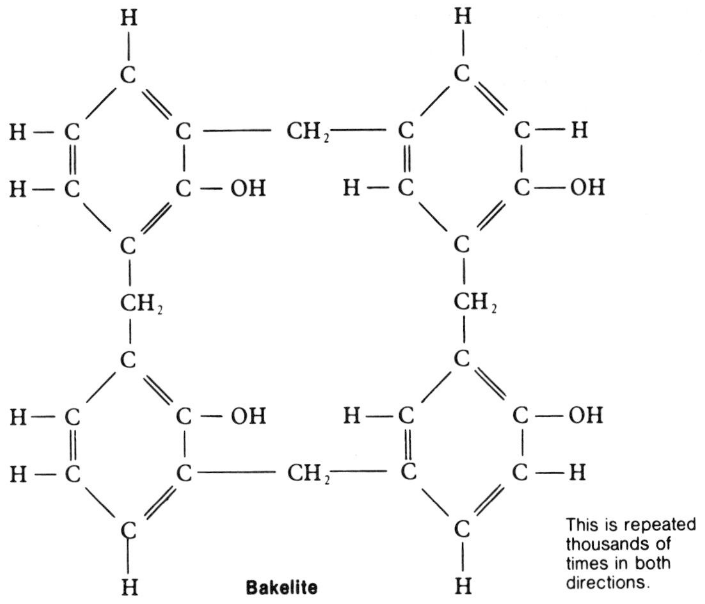

This is repeated thousands of times in both directions.

Bakelite

Figure 23.8 Bakelite

Properties, uses and commonly available forms of plastics

Before the raw materials can be converted into finished products, other substances may have to be added to give the required properties.

These may include:

- Plasticisers to soften the final product and make it less brittle.
- Dyes and pigments to give the required colour.
- Heat stabilisers to give resistance to heat during manufacture or in use.
- Inert fillers to improve the properties by increasing flexibility, hardness, or toughness for example, or to save money by increasing the bulk of the material.
- Catalysts to control the speed of a chemical reaction.
- Fire-retarding additives.
- Foaming agents to make plastic foams.

Raw materials manufacturers produce plastics in many convenient forms for use by other industries. These include powders, granules, pastes and liquids, and semi-finished products such as sheets, slabs, rods, tubes and films.

Many of these forms are either not available in small quantities, or are not suitable for working by the methods available in school or at home. We have, therefore, included in the properties and uses chart only those which are readily available for school and home use.

THE IDENTIFICATION OF PLASTICS

Although it is very difficult to identify all the many different plastics, especially where two or more have been used together, or when additives have been used to alter their properties, it is useful to be able to recognise the most used ones.

The following chart shows some simple tests which will help in this, and the results of them for some common plastics.

In general, most thermoplastics will cut cleanly, become flexible at 200°C or less, and melt to a viscous liquid if heating continues, while thermosets will produce powdery chips when cut, and bubble and decompose before softening.

The identification of common plastics

Common name	Technical name	Cut with sharp knife	Hit with hammer	Bend at room temperature	Put in water	Scratch with finger-nail
1 Polythene	Polythene	Easy and smooth	Very strong	LD — flexible HD — fairly stiff	Floats	Yes
2 Polyvinyl chloride (PVC)	Polychloroethane	Easy and smooth	Fairly strong	Plasticised — flexible Rigid — stiff	Sinks	Plasticised — yes Rigid — no
3 Polystyrene	Polyphenylethene	Fairly hard	Weak	Stiff	Sinks	No
4 Expanded polystyrene	Expanded polyphenylethene	Crumbles	Crumbles	Breaks	Very buoyant	Yes
5 Acrylic or PMMA or poly-methylmethac-rylate	Polymethyl (11)methylpropenoate	Splinters	Brittle	Breaks	Sinks	No
6 Polypropylene	Polypropene	Easy and fairly smooth	Very strong	Stiff	Floats	No
7 Nylon	Polyamide	Fairly easy and smooth	Very strong	Stiff	Sinks	Yes
8 Cellulose acetate	A modified natural material	Easy and smooth	Strong	May be flexi-ble	Sinks	No
9 Urea formaldehyde	Urea methanal	Chips	Brittle	Very stiff	Sinks	No
10 Melamine for-maldehyde	Melamine methanal					
11 Phenol formal-dehyde	Phenol methanal					
12 Polyester resin	Unsaturated polyes-ter resin	Difficult and chips	Brittle	Very stiff	Sinks	No

Effect of burning

Softens	Ignites	Colour of flame	Smoke	Nature of flame	Continues to burn on its own	Smell
1 Yes	Easily	Blue with yellow tip	Little	Burning droplets go out when hit floor	Yes	Candle wax
2 Yes	With difficulty	Yellow	White, heavy soot formation	May drip	No	Hydrochloric acid
3 Yes	Easily	Orange/yellow	Black with sooty smuts	Burning droplets	Yes	Sweet
4 No	Easily	Orange/yellow	Black with sooty smuts	Drips continue to burn	Yes	Sweet
5 Yes	Easily	Yellow with blue base and clear edges	None	Drips continue to burn. Bubbles before burning. Spitty flame (crackles)	Yes	Strong, sweet, fruity smell
6 Yes at a higher temperature than polythene	Easily	Yellow with clear blue base	Little	Burning droplets go out when hit floor	Yes	Candle wax. Different from polythene
7 No	Difficult	Blue with yellow tip	Little	Melts to a free flowing liquid which drips carrying a flame	Yes	Like burning hair.
8 Yes	Easily	Dark yellow	Little	Material crackles and shrivels.	Depends on type	Like vinegar
9–11 No	Difficult	Pale yellow with light blue green edges	Little	Plastic swells, cracks, turns white at edges. Glows red after flame is put out.	No	Pungent burning smell
12 No	Easily	Orange/yellow	Lots of black smoke with smuts	Very smoky	Depends on type	Fruity

Common name	Chemical name	Properties
Low density polythene	Low density polyethylene	Wide range of colours. Tough. Good chemical resistance. Good electrical insulator. Flexible, soft. Fades unless light stabilised. Attracts dust unless anti-static. Service temperature 60°C, provided there is no mechanical stress.
High density polythene	High density polyethylene	Wide range of colours. Fairly stiff and hard. Stiffness and softening point both increase with density. Can be sterilised. Good chemical resistance. High impact and shock resistance (special grades). Fades unless light stabilised. Service temperature 80°C, provided there is no mechanical stress.
Rigid PVC (polyvinyl chloride)	Rigid polychloroethane	Wide range of colours. Stiff, hard. Tough at room temperature. Can be used outdoors if suitably stabilised. Light weight. Very good acid and alkali resistance. Particularly good for fabricating.
Plasticised PVC (polyvinyl chloride)	Plasticized polychloroethane	Wide range of colours. Soft, flexible. Good electrical insulator.
Polystyrene	Polyphenylethene	Stiff, hard. Wide range of colours. Can be made impact resistant.
Expanded polystyrene	Expanded polyphenylethane	Very buoyant. Light weight. Absorbs shocks. Very good sound and heat insulator. Crumbles easily. Burns readily unless flame-proofed.

Uses	Common forms
Squeezee bottles and toys. Plastic sacks and sheets. Packaging film. Telecommunications cable insulation. TV aerial lead insulation.	Powders. Granules. Films. Sheets. Wide range of colours.
Milk crates. Bottles, barrels, tanks, pipes. Chemical pumps. Machine parts (e.g. gear wheels). Houseware (e.g. buckets, bowls).	Powders. Granules. Films. Sheets. Wide range of colours.
Pipes, guttering and fittings. Bottles and containers. Gramophone records. Chocolate box liners. Curtain rails. Roofing sheets. Shoe soles. Brush bristles.	Powders. Pastes. Liquids. Sheets. Wide range of colours.
Leathercloth, suitcases, tabletop coverings. Sealing compounds, Underseal. Dip coatings. Hosepipes. Electrical wiring insulation. Wall coverings (vinyl wallpaper). Floor coverings (vinyl tiles, etc.).	Powders. Pastes. Liquids. Sheets. Wide range of colours.
Food containers. Disposable cups, cutlery, plates. Model Kits. Refrigerator linings. Film. Kitchen ware. Toys, radio cabinets.	Powders. Granules. Sheets. Wide range of colours.
Sound insulation. Heat insulation. Packaging.	Sheets Slabs } Usually white. Beads

Common name	Chemical name	Properties
Acrylic or polymethyl methacrylate (PMMA)	Polymethyl(11) methylpropenoate	Stiff, hard, glass-clear. Very durable outdoors. Easily machined, cemented and polished. Good electrical insulator. Safe with food. Ten times more impact resistant than glass. Splinters easily. Scratches easily.
Polypropylene	Polypropene	Very light, floats. Very good chemical resistance. Good fatigue resistance (e.g. integral hinges). Hard. Can be sterilised. Impact resistant even at low temperatures. Service temperature of 100°C. Rigid. Good mechanical and electrical properties.
Nylon	Polyamide	Hard, tough, rigid, creep resistant. Good bearing surface. Self-lubricating. Resistant to oil, fuels, and chemicals. Good fatigue resistance. High melting point. Very resilient. Wear and friction resistant.
Cellulose acetate	(A modified natural material)	Tough. Can be made flexible. Hard, stiff. Resilient. Light weight.

PROPERTIES AND USES OF A FEW COMMON THERMOSETTING PLASTICS

Common name	Chemical name	Properties
Polyester resin	Unsaturated polyester resin	Good electrical insulator, good heat resistance. Stiff, hard, brittle alone but strong and resilient when laminated. Resistant to ultraviolet light for outside use. Strongly exothermic, this can lead to cracking. Contracts on curing.
Urea formaldehyde (UF)	Urea methanal	Stiff, hard, strong, brittle. Heat resistant. Wide range of colours.

Uses	Common forms
Light units and illuminated signs. Watch and clock glasses. Record player lids. Simple lenses. Aircraft canopies and windows. Car rear light units. Skylights. Furniture. Baths. Perspex sheet. Cladding for buildings.	Rods } Tubes } Usually clear. Sheets are clear, translucent and opaque. In a wide range of colours.
Crates. Chair shells and seats. Waste and chemical pipes and fittings. Packaging film. String, rope, sacks, cloth, carpets, strapping tape. Car and domestic appliance parts, e.g. air-cleaners, battery cases. Medical equipment (e.g. syringes). Containers with integral hinges.	Powders. Granules. Sheets. Rods. Colour naturally pale pink/white, but can be pigmented.
Gear wheels, bearings, automotive, agricultural, general communications and telecommunications equipment parts. Power tool casings. Curtain rail fittings, packaging, film, clothing, combs.	Powder. Granules. Chips. Rod. Tube. Sheet. Extruded sections. Usually white or cream. Other colours including black obtainable.
Photographic film. Tool handles. Transparent, flexible box lids. Pen cases. Toothbrush handles. Car steering wheels.	Powder. Sheet — clear and in a range of colours. Film. Rod — yellow/amber shade. Extruded sections — usually fluted.

Uses	Common forms
GRP boats, car bodies. Chair shells, ducting, garden furniture, etc. Translucent panels for building. Encapsulating and embedding castings.	Liquids. Pastes.
Light coloured electrical fittings and domestic appliance parts. Adhesives (especially for wood laminating).	Powder. Granules. Colours: white, cream.

Common name	Chemical name	Properties
Melamine formaldehyde (MF)	Melamine methanal	Stiff, hard, strong. Heat resistant. Wide range of colours. Resistant to weak chemicals. Stain resistant.
Phenol formaldehyde (PF)	Phenol methanal	Stiff, hard, strong, brittle. heat resistant. Makes high strength fabric or paper reinforced engineering laminates. Limited colours because it darkens under light.

Cleaning-up and finishing plastics

The following instructions apply particularly to acrylic, but will be found suitable for most hard plastics. Take care to avoid scratching the surface of plastics at all times. Leave the protective paper covering on, where supplied, for as long as possible. After removing the paper the last traces of adhesive can be washed off with warm, soapy water.

STAGE 1
After cutting, **plane, file or sand** the edges to remove saw marks. If using a disc or belt sander on thermoplastics, use a coarse abrasive and light pressure to avoid overheating. If filing, finish by draw filing.

STAGE 2
Use a scraper or wet and dry paper, to obtain a completely smooth edge. Scraping will leave the edges ready for machine polishing. By using progressively finer grades of wet and dry paper, the edges can be made ready for hand finishing. Use the wet and dry paper on a cork block to keep the edges square.

STAGE 3
To avoid overheating when **machine polishing** thermoplastics, keep the work moving lightly against a soft mop coated with a mild abrasive.

When **hand polishing** use progressively finer grades of abrasive polish. Rubbing down compounds, as used for rubbing down car paintwork, valve grinding pastes or special polishes, can be used. For example, on Perspex we would use Perspex No. 1 (abrasive polish), Perspex No. 2 (fine polish) and Perspex No. 3 (anti-static polish).

Domestic metal polish is a fine finishing abrasive.

Deep surface scratches can be removed from most plastics by using progressively finer grades of wet and dry paper, valve grinding paste, or rubbing down compound. Shallow scratches can be removed by using special polishes or domestic metal polish.

Uses	Common forms	
Tableware such as Melaware. Decorative laminates e.g. formica. Electrical insulation. Synthetic resin paints.	Powder. Granules. Laminate sheets. Colour- clear unless pigmented.	
Dark coloured electrical fittings and parts for domestic appliances, such as electric kettle, iron and saucepan handles. Bottle tops, door handles. Paper and fabric reinforced laminates.	Powder. Granules. Reinforced sheet and rod e.g. Tufnol. Colours include black, brown, red and green.	

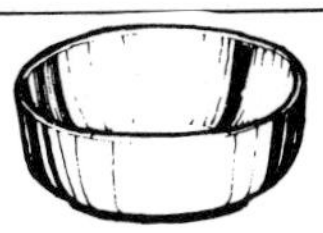

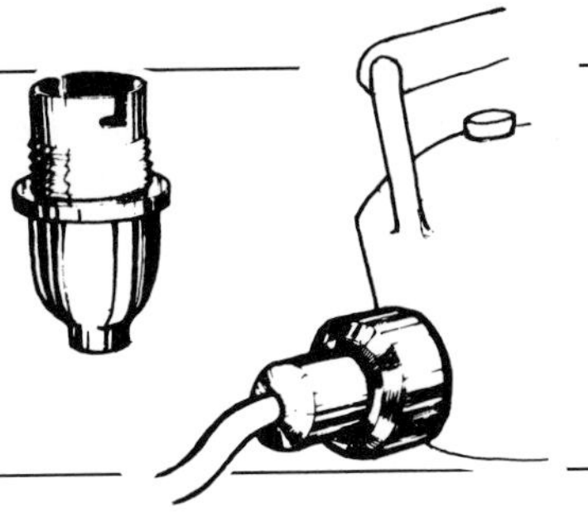

Heating thermoplastics will cause marks which have been removed to reappear (plastic memory). Therefore, final polishing should be left until all heating is finished.

Wet and dry paper (silicone carbide paper) is graded by grit sizes. Common grades are:

  60–120 grit coarse
200–320 grit medium
400–600 grit fine

The following questions are taken from specimen and actual GCSE examination papers, and reproduced by permission of the examining groups. Abbreviations are used to identify the origin of each question ('S' indicates that question was published as part of a specimen paper):

Northern Examining Association	NEA
London and East Anglian Group	LEAG
Southern Examining Group	SEG
Midland Examining Group	MEG
Welsh Joint Education Committee	WJEC

You will find the questions useful both during your course and for revision. For detailed information on the individual exams, contact the appropriate examining group.

Remember: In many cases it is now appropriate (and acceptable) to represent your final design ideas as a model (see page 37).

Design Tasks

1 Everything in its place

Storage is often a problem. Sometimes the difficulty can be overcome by following the old saying *a place for everything and everything in its place*. This applies to the storage of almost everything from large bulky objects down to things as tiny as a pin.

Think of a particular situation where you know storage is a problem, for example in your home, in the shed or garage, at school, at a club you belong to.

Investigate the problem. Identify the items that need storing.

Using any suitable combination of materials, design a container (or some other system) that can be used to store these items safely and tidily.

In your design solution there must be *a place for everything*. It must be easy to identify, remove and replace each individual item. *(WJEC)*

2 Helping Others

With the help of your teacher, contact an elderly, disabled or handicapped person. (This could be a relative or friend).

Discuss with the person the types of difficulty they have. Identify with them a particular problem that can be overcome by a simple inexpensive aid.

With advice from your teacher and other experts, design and build the aid.

Keep in touch with the person regularly so that the aid is designed to suit their particular needs.

Take as much advice as possible from other experts to ensure the aid is safe and well made. *(WJEC)*

3 Gyroscopes and Magnets

Find out as much as you can about gyroscopes and magnets, including electro-magnets and reed switches.

Use the information about the gyroscopic effect, magnetism and electro-magnetism to help you design and build a toy or some other device that will interest and amuse young children. The toy or device should also help the children understand about one or more of these phenomena.

Your design must be functional **and** visually attractive.

(WJEC)

4 Alternative Technology

Alternative Technology is not **just** to do with building hydro-electric power stations and windmills, it is something we can **all** become involved with. It is described as: 'living with the natural systems and resources on which all our lives depend'.

What do you think this means?

Look at the 'Alternative Energy Web' (figure 24.1). This shows key areas of concern. Study the diagram. You may be surprised at some of the words included.

Using the diagram as a starting point, discuss with your teachers, friends and relatives, what you understand by this term — *Alternative Technology*. Try picking out a series of words and linking them together, for example: small is beautiful; craftsmanship; appropriate materials; recycle; repair and DIY.

Identify a personal situation, or a problem in or near your home, your school or in the local area, that could be improved. Then design and build a self-help, low-tech solution.

environmental concern   renewable energy   solar power
windpower   resource conservation   bio-fuels
wavepower   hydropower   clean rivers   mixed farming
compost   small farms   festivals   diversity
allotments   fish culture   tree planting   hedges
earthworms   wildlife   stability   intermediate scale
craftsmanship   appropriate materials   recycling
repair   do-it-yourself   valuing labour   low growth
re-use   friends of the earth   balance   freedom
personal responsibility   democracy   open government
practical action   decentralisation   local industry
regional identity   community   demystification
social audit   village schools   equality of opportunity
participation   hand tools   pollution control   quality
simplicity   adaptability   durability   beauty
creativity   vision   greater self-sufficiency
local politics   vote green   villages   local shops
wholeness   world concern   ecological perspective
self-build   insulation   organic vegetable growing   love
families   preventive medicine   non-violence
self-reliance   appropriate technology   honesty
natural materials   mental well-being   nuclear mistrust
long-life products   low energy   canals   bicycles
sail ships   airships   railways   fulfilling work
cooperatives   intuition   low-meat diet   wholefood
gentleness   caring   sharing   awareness
physical activity   humour   sustainability
small is beautiful   individuality   whales
free range people and animals

Figure 24.1 Some threads of the 'Alternative Technology Web'

5 'Now you see it, now you don't.'

Optical illusions of all types have fascinated people for many, many years. Find out as much as you can about this subject.

Using the inspiration from your research, design and make a visually interesting device that includes some form of optical illusion.

The device may be mechanical or powered by batteries. It may be based on an old idea but must **not** be a direct copy.

The purpose is to attract attention. It will be sited on a table in a public place such as the school entrance hall, a shop window, the public library or the town hall. Suggest a suitable site for your device. *(WJEC)*

6 Training Aid for Handicapped Children

Figure 24.2 shows a simple training aid. Handicapped children develop their grip, hand and arm movements by threading the coloured blocks on to the rods. This also helps them develop language by the use of words like left, right, tall, short and so on.

Improve the design for the following parts of the training aid:

(a) The Coloured Blocks.
(i) Choose a suitable material for the blocks.
(ii) Change the size of the hole so that the blocks fit more easily on to the rods.
(iii) Change the shape of the blocks so that they can be picked-up and gripped more easily.

(b) The Base and Rods.

(i) Choose a suitable material for the base.
(ii) Choose a suitable material for the rods.
(iii) Choose a material for the balls.

(c) Sketch a way of joining the balls to the rods.

(d) The aid is unstable. Improve the design of the base. *(WJEC)*

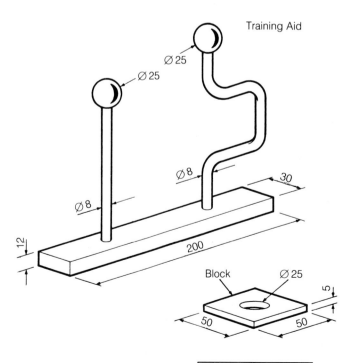

Figure 24.2

7 A Learning Aid for a Primary School

Figure 24.3 shows the outline of a light-weight *Trundle Wheel* used to help primary school children measure distances. The children push the wheel along the ground.

The wheel revolves freely on the axle. The wheel travels a distance of one metre each revolution.

Complete the design for this learning aid:

  (a) The Wheel and Handle.
    (i) Choose a suitable material for the wheel.
    (ii) Choose a suitable material for the handle.

  (b) The Axle.

    (i) Choose a suitable material for the axle.
    (ii) Sketch a way of joining the axle to the handle.
    (iii) Sketch a way of mounting the wheel on to the axle. It must be possible for the teacher to remove the wheel using simple tools.   (WJEC)

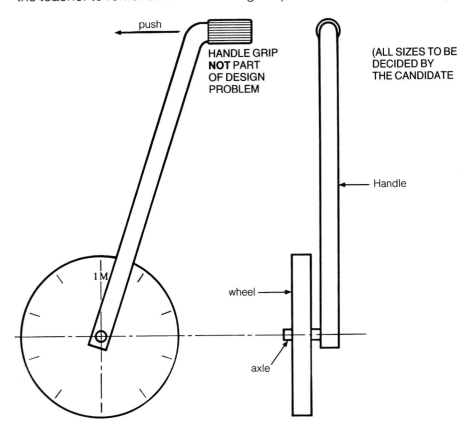

Figure 24.3

8 A Sellotape Holder

Figure 24.4(a) shows a small reel of adhesive tape, e.g. sellotape. Figure 24.4(b) shows a design for a simple sellotape holder.

The design has a number of faults, e.g. it is impossible to install the reel. Re-design the holder.

Design requirements:
  (a) When the reel is empty, it must be possible to fit a new one quickly and easily.
  (b) Your design should enable a handicapped person, with the use of only one hand, to remove a piece of tape from the reel.

Show **all** constructional details, **all** main sizes and the materials used. (You may choose any materials you think suitable.) (WJEC)

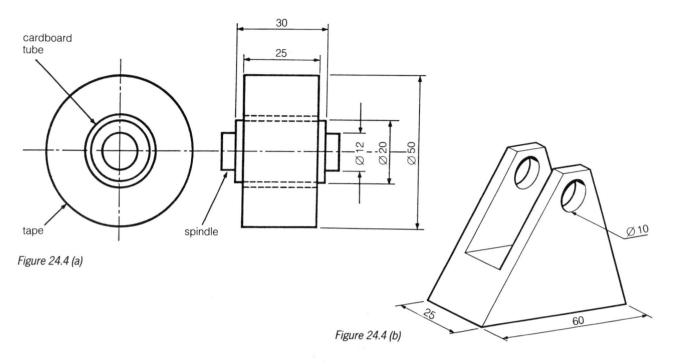

Figure 24.4 (a)

Figure 24.4 (b)

9 With a diagram show how you would arrange **six** of the 1.5 V cells shown in the photograph to produce a total voltage of 9 V. (LEAG)

10 Figure 24.5 shows the circuit diagram for the torch/lantern.

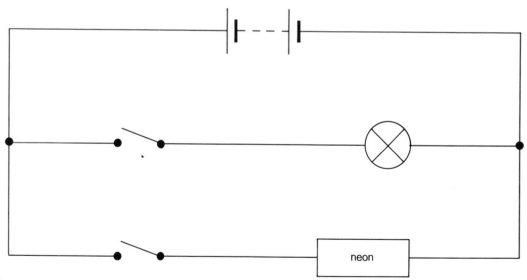

Figure 24.5

The manufacturer wishes to modify the system so that only **one** switch is used to operate both the bulb and the neon. With the new system it must still be possible to operate the bulb and neon independently of each other.

(a) Draw the circuit diagram for the new system.

(b) Name the type of switch you would use in the new system. (LEAG)

11 The catch mechanism on the base of the torch/lantern shown in the photograph and Figure 24.6 can easily become jammed.

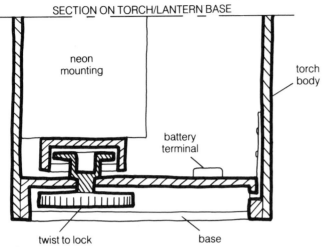

SECTION ON TORCH/LANTERN BASE

neon mounting

torch body

battery terminal

twist to lock   base

Figure 24.6

(a) Using clear sketches show how you would modify the catch (and/or the base), to stop it from jamming.

(b) Use a flow chart or pictogram to produce a simple instruction sheet for the fitting of the batteries and base of the torch/lantern.   (LEAG)

12 A pupil, as part of a research project on lighting has obtained a trade catalogue. A page from the catalogue showing electric light bulbs is illustrated below.

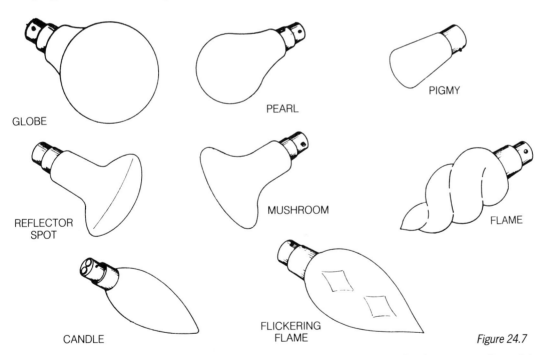

GLOBE

PEARL

PIGMY

REFLECTOR SPOT

MUSHROOM

FLAME

CANDLE

FLICKERING FLAME

Figure 24.7

(a) Select **two** bulbs which are suitable for use when designing non-adjustable wall lights. In **each** case suggest the type of room setting in which they might be found.

(b) Select **two** bulbs which are suitable for adjustable lights which are used to highlight certain areas of the room. In **each** case suggest both the room and which areas are to be highlighted.

(c) The pupil is working on solving the need for an adjustable lamp for a desk, which is to be used when studying at home. Suggest **three** bulbs which will be suitable for this project. In **each** case give reasons to support your choice.

(d) The pupil has decided to investigate the suitability of the bulbs for this adjustable lamp project. One aspect to be researched is the risk associated with the heat generated by the bulb on different materials for the shade, and the ventilation required. Suggest **two** other areas which will need to be investigated in this project.

(e) Outline a method of investigating each of the following:

   (i) heat generated by a bulb;
   (ii) suitability of shade material.

(f) Take **one** of the areas that you have suggested in (d), and outline how the problem would be investigated. *(LEAG)*

13 A group of five pupils have set up a mini-enterprise project to design, make, and sell toy yachts. The basic design has been agreed, and you have been appointed Production Manager. Your task is to organise materials, resources, equipment, and workers (the rest of the team) to produce a batch of 50 toy yachts as shown in the drawing.

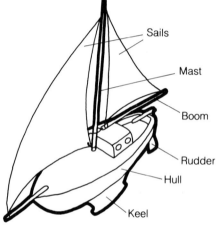

Sails
Mast
Boom
Rudder
Hull
Keel

Figure 24.8

(a) State a suitable material for **each** of the components given below.

   (i) Hull
   (ii) Keel
   (iii) Sails
   (iv) Mast and Boom
   (v) Rudder

(b) Having stated the materials to be used, the method of "making" needs to be decided. By making a list of stages and processes describe how the HULL **only** will be made.

(c) Economic use of materials will be essential. State **two** particular instances where careful planning will save material when making the components of the yacht.

(d) State briefly how the team of workers (five including yourself) will be organised to make a batch of 50 toy yachts.

(e) The yacht will need to be attractive to customers. Give details of how you will "finish" the toy yacht to make it attractive. *(LEAG)*

14 Simple toy automata (toys involving mechanisms and linked movement) are enjoying a revival. The drawing below shows a pupil's idea for such a toy.

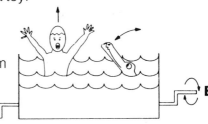

(a) The characters are to be made from sheet material. State a suitable material and its thickness.

(b) Within the base box there will be a mechanical system which makes the swimmer rise and then disappear below the water, when handle A is turned. Show how this movement can be achieved.

Figure 24.9

(c) The crocodile rises out of the water in an arc.
  (i) Show how the crocodile is fixed to "make" it move in an arc.
  (ii) Show how the crocodile can be made to rise and disappear below the water by turning handle B.

(d) The pupil then decides that two rows of waves are to alternately oscillate to give the impression of movement. Show how this could be done; if necessary a third handle may be added.

(e) Finally, the pupil realises that the toy would be greatly improved if all three systems were operated by one handle. Show how this could be achieved.

(LEAG)

15 Toys made of tin plate and lead used to be very cheap and popular presents for children. Today these materials are no longer used for the manufacturing of toys and are in fact banned.

(a) Give **two** reasons why they are banned.

(b) Tinplate and lead have been replaced by modern materials. State **two** such materials used for toy making and add an appropriate process for making toys from **each** material.

(c) On the toy veteran car shown on the left of the page, the bonnet is to be made of sheet material.
  (i) Name a suitable modern material for the bonnet.
  (ii) Give complete details of how the **bonnet** can be made in school; include any nets or developments, jigs and moulds.

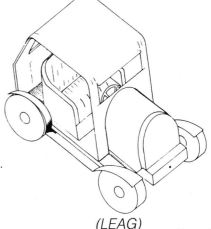

(d) The chassis, number plate, wings, roof and windscreen front are all to be made from sheet material.
  (i) Draw and detail the nets/developments required to make the above using the least number of pieces.
  (ii) Name the sheet material that would be used.
  (iii) Give details of the method used for joining the parts.

(LEAG)

Figure 24.10

16 A local builder has taken you on for work experience and you are assisting the bricklayers building the walls of some new houses.

You find it difficult to read the spirit level. You are told that spirit levels are easily damaged.

It is suggested that when you return to school you might be able to come up with a better design.

Investigate the problem with a view to designing an improved 'Builders' Level'. The bricklayers tell you that they do not mind putting in batteries or doing things to it provided that it becomes better and easier to use.

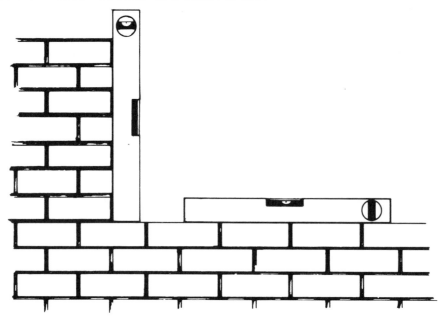

Figure 24.11

On returning to the bricklayers for further help they tell you that the minimum length of the level must be 900 mm and ideally it should check levels both horizontally and vertically.

If your design includes any moving parts, they should be locked in position before the level is put away.

Design an improved 'Builders' Level'. *(LEAG)*

17 In a modern small kitchen it is often difficult to store large packets of soap powder away from the food. Automatic washing machines need to have an exact amount of powder if they are to wash efficiently. Too little powder and the wash is not clean; too much powder and the machine overflows with suds. The machines also need to have hot and cold running water as well as a convenient power socket.

The normal size of a soap powder pack is an E10 which contains 3.1 kg of powder and has a volume of 7500 cc or ml.

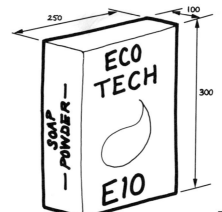

Figure 24.12

The washing machine needs

   $1\frac{1}{2}$ cup for normal loads;
   1 cup for economy loads.
   (1 cup = 300 cc or ml.)

Design a wall-mounted soap powder storage device which can be fitted close to the machine and will be able to dispense the right amount of powder. *(LEAG)*

18 When visiting a large supermarket you are taken on a guided tour around the warehouse at the back of the store. Lorries reverse into the loading bay and the goods are pushed on trolleys from inside the lorry into the warehouse. Empty trolleys are pushed back again onto the lorry.

However, there is a problem in that not all of the lorries are of the same height.

An investigation of the range of heights shows that the lowest lorry is level with the loading bay but the highest one is 150 mm above the loading bay.

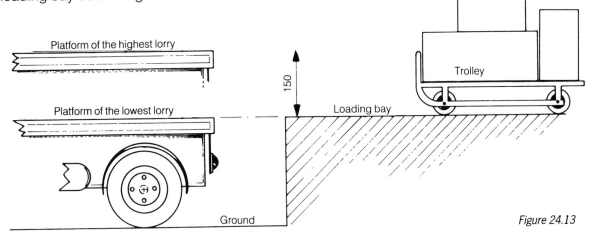

Figure 24.13

Maximum width of lorry = 2 metres
Trolley size = 1 metre square.

Design a solution which will ensure that the trolleys can be pushed on and off ALL the lorries onto the loading bay.

The maximum width of the lorry is **2 m** and the trolleys are **1 m** square with rubber wheels 150 mm in diameter.

You may make any alterations that are required to the loading bay — but NOT the lorries.   *(LEAG)*

19 Your football team has won the FA Cup which will be displayed in a room in your local town hall. The display room has two doors and two windows, as shown in figure 24.9 below, and is on the first floor of the building.

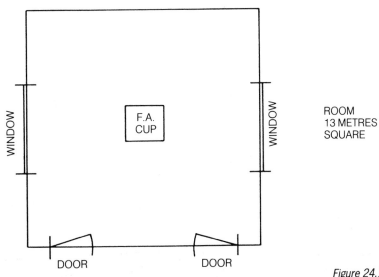

Figure 24.14

All entry and exit points in the room are to be made burglar proof.

Design a security system for the room that will alert the caretaker (who lives in a flat above the room) that someone is attempting to break in.

Your device should show the caretaker where the room has been breached and if the trophy is removed from its display stand. Due consideration must be given to "packaging" the security system.   *(MEG, S)*

20 Figure 24.15 shows a small electric drill which is to be used for drilling holes in electronic printed circuit boards (PCB).

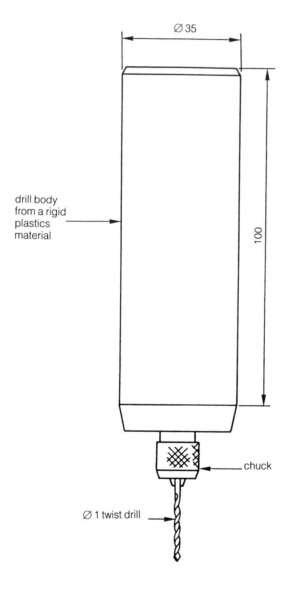

Figure 24.15

A device is required which will hold the drill in a vertical plane and also allows it to be moved through a vertical distance of 30 mm.

Accurate vertical control of the drill is essential and this may be accomplished by either manual or by automated means.

You are required to design 'a device' that will hold the drill and also allow it to move vertically as described. Your design should also have the facility for supporting the PCB on a firm base during the drilling operation.   *(MEG, S)*

21 The illustrations show three battery-powered lights. NOTE: The illustrations are not to the same scale.

a bicycle lamp

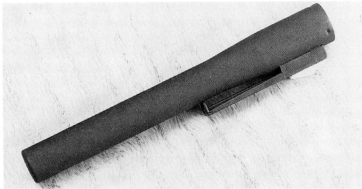

a large hand torch

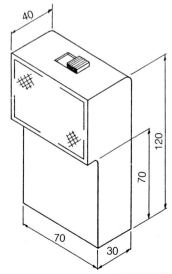

a small pen-sized torch

(a) Give a situation in which each light would be used.

(b) For each light state two factors which make it suitable for the situation you have given in (a).

(c) Describe two design features important to the working of all three lights.

(d) The drawing shows an isometric drawing of a bicycle lamp.

40

120

70

70

30

Figure 24.16

A fitting is required to attach the bicycle lamp to the handlebar in the area indicated by chain line on the drawing below.

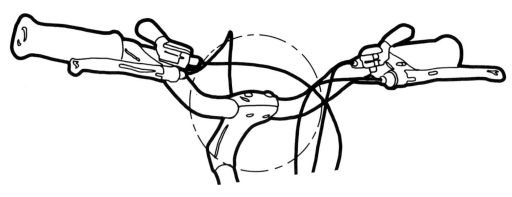

Figure 24.17

Design the bicycle lamp fitting using the space provided on the following pages, providing information and sketches in the positions indicated.

The information required is summarised as follows:

(i) a list of design requirements indicating the features you would expect the final design to possess;

(ii) your initial design ideas in the form of free-hand sketches;

(iii) your final solution;

(iv) the initial elements of the parts list completed to show an accurate list of the materials and fittings you require to make the attachment you have designed. Clearly state the name of the component, the dimensions, material, and surface finish.

(SEG, S)

22 A student has designed a mechanism (figure 24.18) which will be used to compress newspaper pulp into logs for burning. Wet pulp is placed in the mould and water squeezed through the holes during compression. A lever is used to gain mechanical advantage and the force is transmitted to the pressure plate.

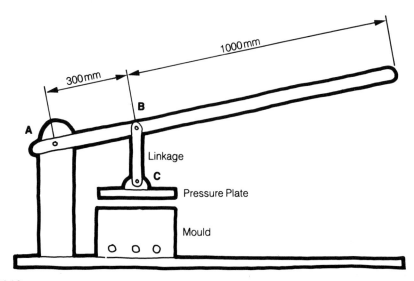

Figure 24.18

(a) Explain using the example of the pulp press, what is meant by mechanical advantage.

(b) (i) Why is a long lever necessary for this application?
(ii) If the force applied by the student at the end of the lever is 100 N what force is transmitted to the pressure plate through the linkage?

(c) (i) Which type of force is acting on the pin **A**?
(ii) Which other component is acted on by this type of force?
(iii) Sketch a common example which illustrates this type of force.

(d) Difficulties have arisen in removing the compressed block from the mould.

(i) Make a sketch of a mechanical arrangement which would make removal very easy or automatic.
(ii) Make a sketch of an improved new design which would produce more speedy operation.
(LEAG, S)

23 Many people are now actively interested in physical fitness and this in turn has given rise to an increase in the sale of home fitness equipment. Some of the equipment is very expensive and there is a need, therefore, for a fitness machine for home use which is inexpensive to make and will enable the user to perform safely a wide variety of exercises.

Design a home fitness machine which meets the above requirements. The machine which you design should also

(a) allow for a wide range of resistance in the exercises,

(b) be collapsible and portable,

(c) be easy for one person to assemble and take apart without tools or specialised equipment.
(LEAG, S)

24 The range and variety of indoor plants now available has increased during the past few years. Many of these plants are very expensive and require regular care and attention. This is a problem for people who go on holiday for several weeks.

Design a piece of equipment which will atuomatically water a pot plant when the owner is away from home. It is essential that the plant must not receive more water than it needs.

Your design should not involve connection to either mains electricity or the main water supply.
(LEAG, S)

25 **Push-Along Toy Which Makes Sounds**

Simple noise-making toys appeal to young children of about three years. Noise for such toys can be generated by striking, shaking, or squeezing.

Stage 1: Design a push-along toy which generates sound as the toy moves. A detachable handle (600 mm long by 18 mm diameter) enables a toddler to push the toy whilst walking. The toy without handle will have to fit inside a box of the dimensions shown in figure 24.19.

Stage 2: Make the toy that you have designed.

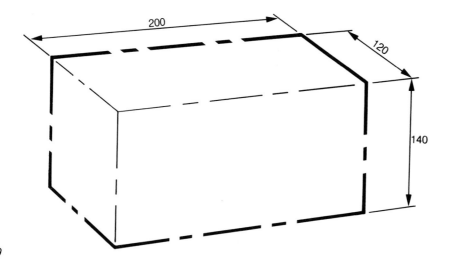

Figure 24.19

NOTE: The handle of length 600 mm and diameter 18 mm does not form part of the examination, but location and security for the handle must form part of your design.

(LEAG, S)

Design and technology theory

26 The drawing in figure 24.20 below shows a record turntable deck and arm.

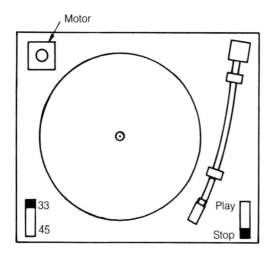

Figure 24.20

(a) (i) Complete the drawing in figure 24.20 to show how the motor is connected to the turntable.
  (ii) The speed of the turntable can be changed by making the motor go faster or slower. Explain another method that could be used to change the speed of the turntable.
  (iii) If the motor rotates at a speed of 1800 revs/min what is the velocity ratio between the motor and the turntable for the 45 revs/min playing speed?

(b) Name **two** other machines used in the home which use the same drive system as the record turntable deck.

(c) (i) Give **one advantage** and **one disadvantage** of a belt drive system over other drive systems.
  (ii) Suggest **one** way in which a belt drive system could be improved to overcome the disadvantage you have given.

(d) The diagram in figure 24.21 shows a bicycle.

Figure 24.21

(i) Explain why the bicycle has a chain drive system and not a belt drive system.

(ii) Explain why the bicycle has a large pedal sprocket and a small back axle sprocket.

(iii) Bicycles often have 3, 5 or 10 gears. Explain the advantage of having a range of gears on a bicycle   *(LEAG)*

27   (a) The diagram in figure 24.22 shows a simple gear train. The input shaft is fixed to gear **A** which has **40 teeth** and the output shaft is fixed to gear **C** which has **20 teeth**.

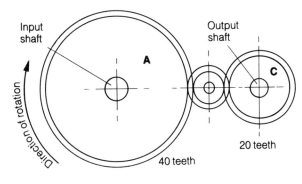

Figure 24.22

(i) What is the gear ratio of the gear train?

(ii) In which direction will gear wheel **C** rotate?

(b) The drawing in figure 24.23 shows a simplified gear box which has an input shaft **A** turning clockwise and an output shaft **B** turning anti-clockwise.

Sketch (using conventional symbols) and name a gear mechanism which will make shaft **B** turn at the same speed as shaft **A**.   *(LEAG)*

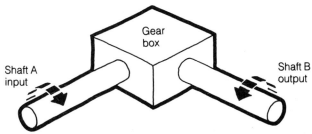

Figure 24.23

28 The diagram in figure 24.24 shows a small hand driven winch. The crank handle is fixed to spindle **A** which turns the winding drum through the two gear wheels.

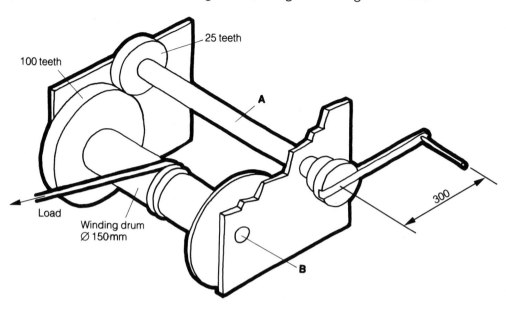

Figure 24.24

(a) (i) Give **two** examples of other machines which use a crank handle or crank wheel.
   (ii) If the operator winds the handle at 24 revolutions per minute (revs/min) what will be the speed of the winding drum?
   (iii) Calculate the velocity ratio between the spindle **A** and the winding drum.
   (iv) What is the mechanical advantage between spindle **A** and the winding drum if the winch has an efficiency of **50%**?

(b) If the crank handle is released by the operator, the winch cable will unwind and the load will fall. Sketch and name the mechanism which could prevent this from happening.

(c) The winding drum is mounted on a spindle **B** which is supported through the casing of the winch.

   Sketch and name a bearing that could be used to support the spindle **B**.

(LEAG)

29 Figure 24.25 shows a storage unit for electronic components and a range of components.

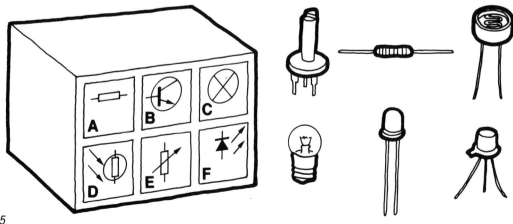

Figure 24.25

(a) The drawers of the storage unit are labelled **A–F**. In the space provided label **each** component with the letter of the drawer it should go in.

(b) Give the **full name** of **each** of the components in the following drawers: drawer **B**, drawer **D**, drawer **F**. *(LEAG)*

30 In figure 24.26 you are shown the circuit diagram and bottom view of a p.c.b. for a light sensing circuit.

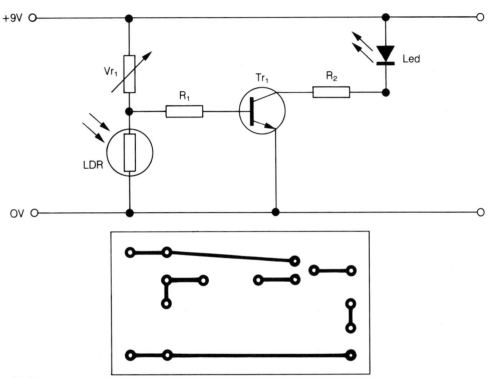

Figure 24.26

(a) What is the meaning of the term p.c.b.?

(b) (i) Using the abbreviations given for each component in the circuit diagram, clearly show where each component will be positioned on the p.c.b.
 (ii) Clearly label the +9V and 0V terminals on the p.c.b.
 (iii) Briefly describe any precautions you would take to prevent damage to component Tr_1, when soldering it on to the p.c.b. *(LEAG)*

31 When constructing the circuit shown in figure 24.26, only the following resistors are available.

$130\,\Omega$, $470\,\Omega$, $680\,\Omega$, $1.1\,k\Omega$, $1.6\,k\Omega$, $1.8\,k\Omega$.

(a) (i) Show, by using resistors in series, how you would achieve a resistance of approximately $2.2\,k\Omega$ at R_1.
 (ii) Show, by using resistors in parallel, how you would achieve a resistance of approximately $270\,\Omega$ at R_2.
 (iii) Briefly explain why the resistance obtained at R_2 would not be exactly $270\,\Omega$.

(b) Assuming that all the resistors you have used were of 10% tolerance, give the colour code for the highest value of resistor used.

Use the colour code table below to help.

1st Colour Band 1st Digit		2nd Colour Band 2nd Digit		3rd Colour Band Number of Zeros		4th Colour Band Tolerance	
Black	0	Black	0	Black	No zeros	Gold	5%
Brown	1	Brown	1	Brown	One zero	Silver	10%
Red	2	Red	2	Red	Two zeros		
Orange	3	Orange	3	Orange	Three zeros		
Yellow	4	Yellow	4	Yellow	Four zeros		
Green	5	Green	5	Green	Five zeros		
Blue	6	Blue	6	Blue	Six zeros		
Violet	7	Violet	7	Violet	Seven zeros		
Grey	8	Grey	8	Grey	Eight zeros		
White	9	White	9	White	Nine zeros		

(LEAG)

32 *(a)* Aluminium and steel are two metals which are widely used in industry.

   (i) Explain why aluminium is more expensive to produce than steel.
   (ii) Steel is more likely to corrode than aluminium and is more dense, yet is often preferred to aluminium for manufacturing car bodies. Give **two** reasons for this.

   (b) (i) Explain, with the help of a simple line drawing, the extrusion process.
   (ii) Name **one** example of a product that could be made from extruded metal.
   (iii) Name **one** product that could be made from extruded plastics.

   (c) (i) Explain what is meant by an alloy.
   (ii) Give **two** examples of alloys. For **each** example give its components.

(LEAG)

33 *(a)* Use simple sketches to show **one** method of improving the rigidity of sheet steel.

   (b) Explain, with the aid of sketches, how **two** of the following materials may be strengthened.

   (i) concrete;
   (ii) wood;
   (iii) polyester resin.

(LEAG)

34 *(a)* People are often confused by the terms *hardness* and *toughness*.

   (i) Give **one** example of a useful application for a hard material.
   (ii) Give **one** example of a useful application for a tough material.
   (iii) Describe briefly a test which could be used to compare the hardness of a range of different materials.

(b) State a method of preventing corrosion in each of the following.

    (i) Steel garden gate
    (ii) Aluminium window frame
    (iii) Steel dustbin
    (iv) Wire shelves used in a refrigerator

(c) (i) What is the main difference between thermoplastics and thermo-setting plastics?

    (ii) State the **manufacturing process** which is used to produce **each** of the objects listed below.

        Washing up liquid bottle
        Plastics light switch
        Nylon gear wheel

    (iii) You have designed a cutlery tray which is to fit in a drawer. You have decided to make the tray from plastics and figure 24.27 shows the wooden mould or 'plug' which is to be used to vacuum-form the tray.

        Describe, in detail, the process of vacuum-forming. Use sketches to help you explain the process. *(LEAG)*

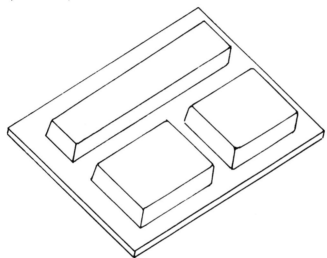

Figure 24.27

35 (a) Explain briefly why you consider the work of designers to be important.

  (b) The following are used in designing to help produce good solutions. Briefly explain each term.
    1 Mock-up
    2 Modelling
    3 Prototype

  (c) (i) Explain how the making of a mock-up often proves to be helpful during the process of designing.
    (ii) List **three** materials commonly used in modelling in order to make the process fast and effective.
    (iii) Give **two** reasons why it is essential to produce a prototype of a final design before beginning mass production.

  (d) (i) Briefly explain why testing is considered a vital part of an evaluation.
    (ii) List below **four** different ways you could evaluate a prototype of a small teddy bear. *(NEA)*

36 *(a)* (i) What do you understand by the term *man-made* boards?
   (ii) Name **one** man-made board which is used in either the construction industry or furniture making.
   (iii) List **two** constructional advantages of using a man-made board as opposed to natural timber.
   (iv) Explain briefly how the manufacture of some man-made boards helps in the better use of natural resources.

(b) Many different types of material can be used to make bathroom furniture.

Write a short specification for the materials you would use to make a small medicine cabinet to hang on the bathroom wall.

(c) Compression is one type of force that occurs in many structures and design situations. List **three** other types of forces that can be found in structures.

(d) On each diagram below show where a force would act during use and name the type of force.

(NEA)

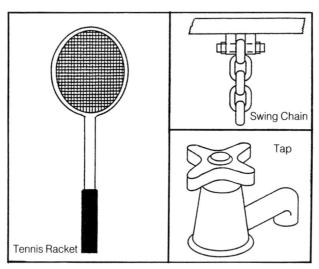

Figure 24.28

37 **Picture A** below shows a traditional manual typewriter which relies for its operation on mechanical linkages.

Dimensions — Height 240 mm, Width 610 mm, Breadth 400 mm, Weight 16 kg (35.25 lb).

Picture B below shows a modern word processor/typewriter which relies largely for its operation on an electrically controlled system.

Dimensions — Height 430 mm, Width 610 mm (860 mm with monitor)
Breadth 690 mm, Weight 16 kg (35.25 lb)

Read the information and study the pictures before answering the following questions.

(a) Select the typewriter you think has the better ergonomic qualities and explain in detail the reasons for your choice.

(b) The casing of the manual typewriter (**Picture A**) is a metal pressing, as opposed to the casing of the electric word processor/typewriter (**Picture B**) which is moulded plastics. Explain as thoroughly as you can the reasons for this change.

(c) The diagram below shows the lever mechanism used in a manual typewriter. (The levers in the diagram are shown as outlines and the linkages connecting them are drawn in heavy black lines. The pivots which connect the linkages to the levers are shown as black dots.)

When a key is pressed the type bar strikes the paper.

Show how the mechanism works from the time a key is pressed to the time that the type bar strikes the paper.

Illustrate your answer by marking the diagram clearly with:

(i)   an **arrow** to show the direction of movement of each lever;
(ii) a **cross** to mark the pivot of each lever.

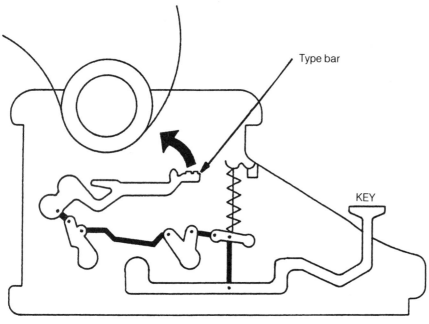

Figure 24.29

(NEA)

38 A local primary school has a brick boundary wall as shown in figure 24.30 with a pedestrian entrance which gives access to a side road. A new gate is required for this entrance and a local supplier has gates made of wood as well as metal as shown in figure 24.31. You are to assume that either gate will be hinged to the wall.

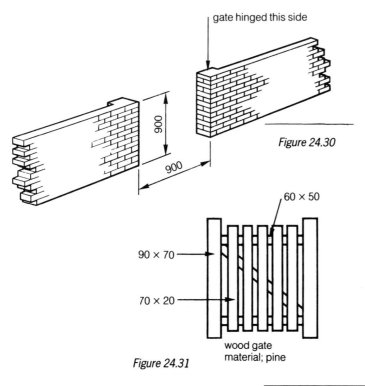

gate hinged this side

Figure 24.30

90 × 70
70 × 20
60 × 50

wood gate
material; pine

Figure 24.31

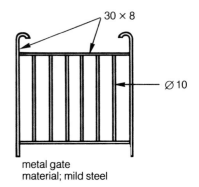

30 × 8
Ø 10

metal gate
material; mild steel

(a) State which gate you would choose and give your reason.

(b) Describe how you would finish the gate you have chosen if it were supplied without any finish applied, and give reasons for each stage in the application of the finish.

(c) Describe and evaluate the methods of construction you would expect to have been used in making the gate of your choice.

(d) Use sketches and notes to show a method of **either** keeping the gate open **or** having it self closing. *(MEG)*

39 The modern domestic kitchen incorporates features resulting from good design and recent technological innovation.

Many of the features are the result of social and economic change.

(a) The three main services found in most kitchens are water, gas and electricity.

Name **four** items of equipment found in a kitchen which use at least **one** of these services.

(b) Manufactured boards and plastics are widely used in most modern domestic kitchens and have replaced traditional materials such as solid wood and metal. Give **two** examples where this has occurred.

(c) Hygiene has always been important in kitchen design. Use **two** examples to explain how the levels of hygiene have improved.

(d) Kitchen units are increasingly being sold by DIY stores as 'knock-down' units for the consumer to construct and fit.

   (i) Give **two** reasons why units are sold in 'knock-down' form.
   (ii) Explain why this could be both an advantage and disadvantage to the consumer.

(e) The kettle in figure 24.32 is an example of technological innovation. Explain **one** aspect of the design which illustrates how the designer has taken into account functional and aesthetic considerations. *(MEG)*

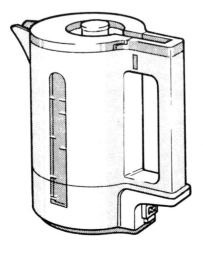

Figure 24.32

40 Figures 24.33 and 24.34 show the basic shape of a toy made mainly from wood. The front roller can be steered by turning the chimney stack left or right.

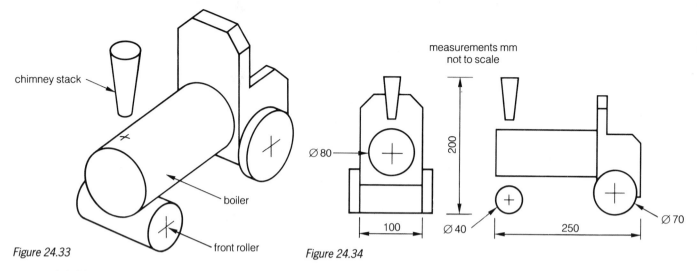

Figure 24.33

Figure 24.34

(a) Name a suitable hardwood for the toy and an appropriate finish. Give a reason for both selections.

(b) Name the machine and method of holding the material to produce the boiler to the shape shown.

(c) Show clearly how the rear wheels could be fixed to the rear part of the toy, allowing them to rotate freely.

(c) Devise a means of connecting the chimney stack to the front roller to enable it to be steered. Include clear details of materials and constructions you would use.   (MEG)

41 Figure 24.35 shows an incomplete clamping device used for securing thin sheet metal while being drilled on a bench drilling machine.

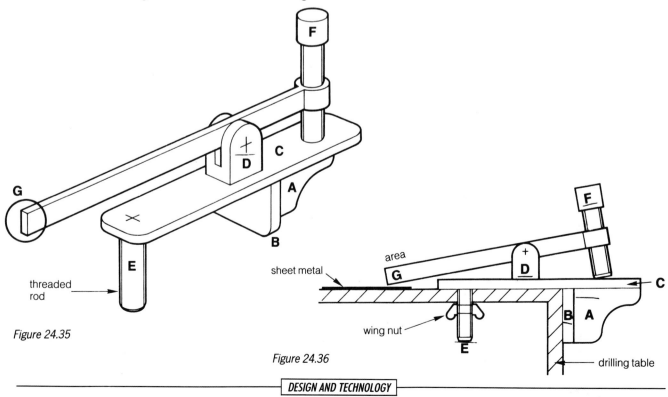

Figure 24.35

Figure 24.36

Figure 24.36 shows the clamping device in position against the drilling table.

The parts labelled **A, B, C, D** and **E** are fabricated, i.e. each piece is separately joined.

(a) Name a suitable material from which **all** the main parts could be made.

(b) Name a suitable construction for joining **A** to **B** and a different method of joining **C** and **E**.

(c) The clamp body (parts **A, B, C, D** and **E**) could be made by a process other than fabrication. Name such a process and the material from which it would be made.

(d) Describe **two** different modifications which could be made to part **F** to enable the screw to be tightened against the surface of **C**.

(e) Design a foot at **G** capable of holding thin sheet metal securely. Show clearly all constructions.

(f) Explain why part **A** is so important to the success of the device.   (MEG)

42 A plastic bottle like that shown in figure 24.37 is made to operate as a rocket. A launcher is required which will set the rocket at any angle from 30° to 60° before launch.

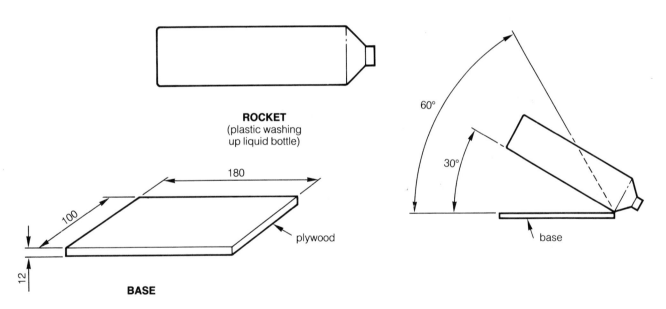

ROCKET
(plastic washing
up liquid bottle)

180

100

plywood

12

BASE

60°

30°

base

Figure 24.37

(a) Using the given plywood base, design the following:

  (i) a launch pad and a pivot mechanism which will allow the launch pad to be tilted to any angle to the base within the range shown;
  (ii) a means of locking the launch pad at any selected angle;
  (iii) a means of knowing the angle the launch pad is set to;
  (iv) a guide to keep the rocket in line as it is launched, (the rocket can be modified with simple additions if you wish).

(b) Draw a chart with headings, which can be used to record the results of trial launches of the rocket.   (MEG)

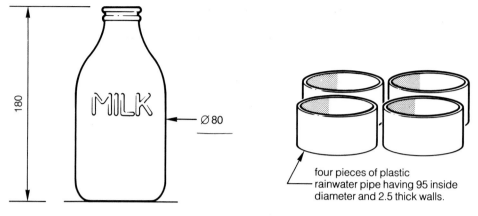

four pieces of plastic
rainwater pipe having 95 inside
diameter and 2.5 thick walls.

Figure 24.38

43 It has been decided to make a carrier for up to four milk bottles using materials of your choice but including plastic pipe arranged as shown in figure 24.38.

    (a) Show the details of your design solutions to the following problems:

        (i) a means of supporting the base of the bottles when they are placed in the carrier;

        (ii) a method of fixing together the four pieces of pipe;

        (iii) a carrying handle and its attachment to the bottle holders;

        (iv) a means of preventing birds pecking away the foil bottle caps to get at the milk.

    (b) Give **three** reasons, other than that of cost, for choosing the materials and finish you have used for your design.　　　　　　　　　*(MEG)*

44　*(a)* Identify the following British Standard graphical symbols:

    (i)　　　　　　　　　　　　　　　　(ii)

    (b) Write down the meaning of the following abbreviations: AC, DC, SPDT.

    (c) Consider the circuit in figure 24.39 and then complete the table by stating which lamp is on for **each** combination of switch positions.

    The first answer is completed for you as an example.　　　　　*(WJEC)*

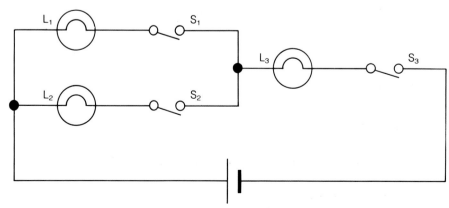

Figure 24.39

45 (a) Write down which of the following materials are metals:

aluminium; brass; carbon; copper; glass; low carbon steel; paper; p.v.c.

(b) Explain, with the aid of a sketch, the construction of **one** of the following:
blockboard; plywood; chipboard.

(c) State **one** practical application for the material chosen in part (b).   (WJEC)

46 (a) Complete the table below by choosing, from the following list, the correct property for the definitions given:

hardness; plasticity; conductivity; toughness; strength.

Property	Definition
	Deforms under load and does not return to its original shape when the load is removed.
	Resists abrasion and penetration.
	Withstands shock loads without fracture.
	Withstands loads which tend to make it increase in length.

(b) Complete the table by stating a definition for the given property.

Property	Definition
Ductility	
Malleability	
Elasticity	
Brittleness	

(c) Explain what is meant by the term *thermal conductivity*.   (WJEC)

47 (a) State **four** forms of energy.

(b) (i) Explain what is meant by the term *recycling*.
(ii) Give **two** practical examples of its use.   (WJEC)

48 The roof space in a domestic dwelling is to be covered with an insulating material.

(a) If the dimensions of a roof space are 8 metres by 10 metres, determine the area to be covered.

(b) If a roll of insulation material is 8 metres by 0.5 metre, determine how many rolls will be required.

(c) Calculate the cost of insulating the roof space if the cost of one roll is £4.00.

(d) State **four** main areas of heat loss from a domestic house, other than the roof. *(WJEC)*

49 Explain, with the aid of a sketch, **one** method by which the energy of the wind may be converted into electrical energy. *(WJEC)*

50 The diagram shown in figure 24.40 is a graph of time spent on housework for two types of families.

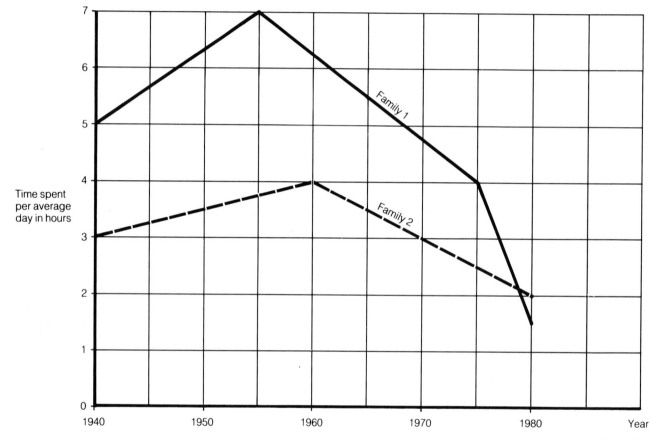

Figure 24.40

(a) State, for Family 1, the average number of hours per day spent on housework, in

    (i) 1940
    (ii) 1955
    (iii) 1975
    (iv) 1980

(b) State, for Family 2, the average number of hours per day spent on housework in

    (i) 1940
    (ii) 1960
    (iii) 1980

(c) Give **one** example of technology in the home, that may account for the decrease in time spent on housework during the last twenty years. *(WJEC)*

51 (a) Calculate the total circuit resistance caused by the two resistors as shown in figure 24.41.

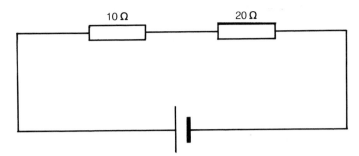

Figure 24.41

(b) State the nominal value of a resistor colour coded Brown, Black, Brown, as shown in figure 24.42, using the following resistor colour code:

Black = 0 Brown = 1 Red = 2 Orange = 3 Yellow = 4
Green = 5 Blue = 6 Violet = 7 Grey = 8 White = 9
Gold = ±5% Silver = ±10%

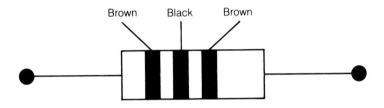

Figure 24.42

(c) Determine the colour code for a resistor of value 270 ohms.

(d) What is the maximum value of a 500 ohm resistor if its tolerance colour code is silver?   (WJEC)

52 Figure 24.43 shows a 100 ohm resistor connected in series with a cell giving a constant voltage of 2 volts.

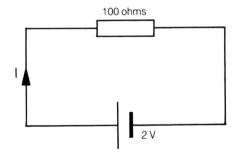

Figure 24.43

(a) Calculate the value of current I.

(b) Sketch on the circuit diagram a voltmeter to measure the cell's terminal voltage and an ammeter to measure total current flow.   (WJEC)

53 (a) Explain what is meant by the term *mechanism*.

(b) Design a mechanism that can be used by hand to produce enlarged copies of simple drawings. *(WJEC)*

54 (a) Explain, with the aid of a sketch, what is meant by the term *cam*.

(b) The direction of rotation of a cam is shown in figure 24.44. Explain what is meant by the following terms:

cycle; dwell; rise; fall; stroke.

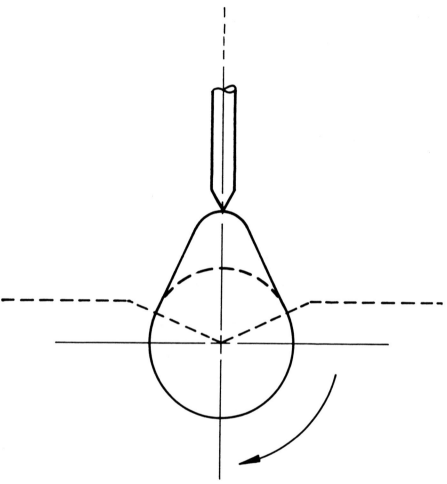

Figure 24.44

(c) Design a simple mechanism incorporating a cam, to enable a person with a weak grip to open a coffee jar with a screw top. *(WJEC)*

55 (a) Explain what is meant by the term *structure*.

(b) Draw a simple example of **each** of the following type of truss:

(i) Warren;
(ii) Bowstring. *(WJEC)*

56 Sketch a simple example of the following types of riveted joint:

(i) single riveted lap joint;
(ii) double riveted lap joint.

Give **one** example where a riveted joint could be used. *(WJEC)*

57 Name the type of plastics and the process used to make the following:

(a) Cap from a tube of toothpaste.

PROCESS	MATERIAL	DRAWING OF PRODUCT

(b) Disposable egg box from a supermarket.

PROCESS	MATERIAL	DRAWING OF PRODUCT

(c) Fizzy-drinks bottle.

PROCESS	MATERIAL	DRAWING OF PRODUCT

58 In **each** of the following, identify the errors which students have made at the designing stage and in each case state a better alternative. (The type of material should **not** be changed.)

(a) A crank handle made from wood.

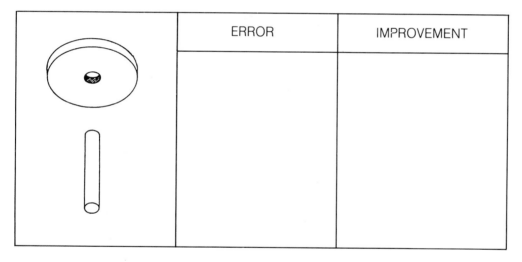

	ERROR	IMPROVEMENT

(LEAG)

(b) An aluminium wheel fixed to a mild steel axle.

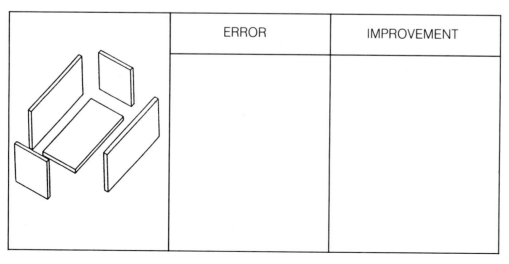

	ERROR	IMPROVEMENT

(c) A dish made from acrylic.

	ERROR	IMPROVEMENT

(LEAG)

59 Two identical components need matching paired holes. Make a
simple planning sheet to show how exact matching is achieved.

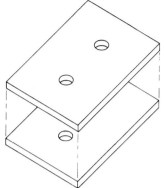

Figure 24.45

60 Safe working of MATERIALS to prevent damage is essential. Identify the problem
shown and state the correct approaches in **each** of the following.

(a) (i) Hazard .... (ii) Correct approach	*Nailing wood*
(b) (i) Hazard .... (ii) Correct approach	Rivet *Riveting Mild Steel*
(c) (i) Hazard .... (ii) Correct approach	*Centre Punching Acrylic*

(LEAG)

61 Name **four** sources of energy that can be converted to electricity.   *(MEG, S)*

62 The sketch below shows the principle of a water powered system for producing energy.

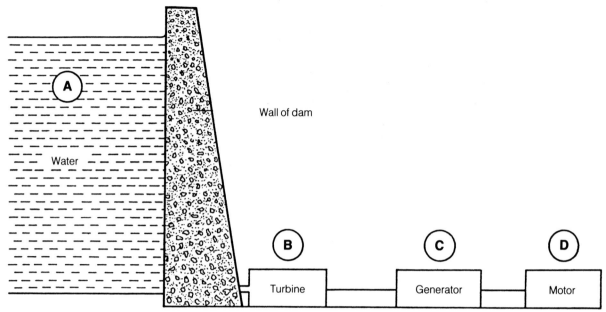

Figure 24.46

Name the **four** types of energy contained in each stage of the system.   *(MEG, S)*

63 Name the following and explain their function.

Pictorial Symbol	Name	Function

64 The sketch below shows three plugs in an adaptor which in turn is in a 13 amp wall socket.

Figure 24.47

Identify **two** safety hazards shown in the above sketch. *(MEG, S)*

65 Small size computers/micro-computers were made possible with the introduction of the 'silicon chip'.

What do you understand by the term 'silicon chip'? *(MEG, S)*

66 Figures 24.48 and 24.49 below show the 'Opella' 500 Series plastic tap for use on a wash-hand basin, and a section through this tap. It was designed many years ago as an alternative to a metal tap, is still produced and is currently available in several different models.

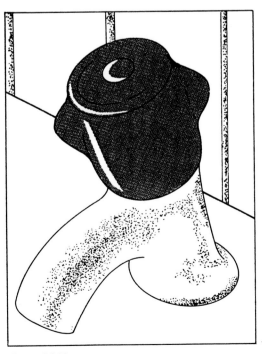

Section through tap showing lift mechanism

Coloured disc

Crosstop

'O' ring seal

'O' ring seal

Lower hexagonal head nut

Fixed washer stem

Standard washer

Integral flow straightener

Figure 24.48

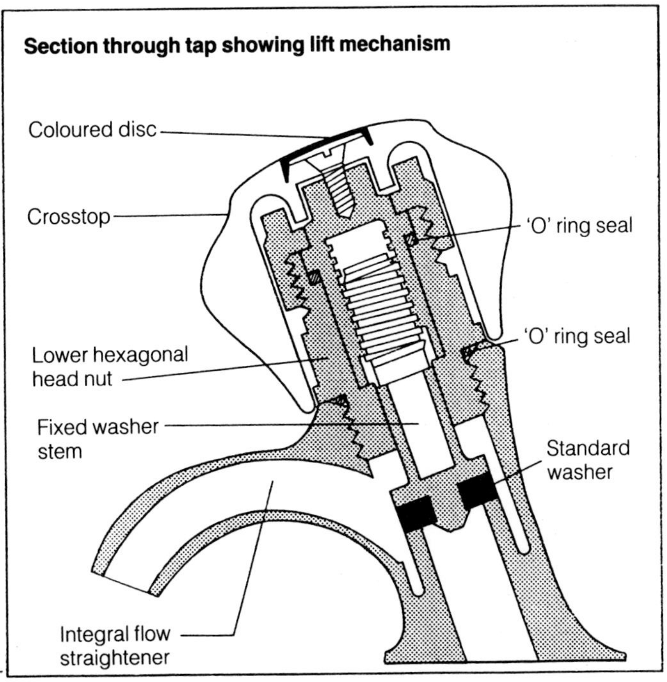

Figure 24.49

Consider a **metal tap.**

(a) (i) List the range of materials used in the conventional metal tap.
(ii) Name the process by which the body of such a tap would be made.
(iii) Name the finish usually given to metal taps and describe clearly and with a diagrammatic layout how it would be carried out.

(b) Make a concise list of the advantages that a plastic tap might have over the conventional metal model.

(c) On the sectional view, figure 24.49 (see page 389), 'O' Ring Seals are shown in two locations.

(i) What function do they perform?
(ii) From what material are 'O' ring seals usually made?

(d) Also on the sectional view, figure 24.49 (see page 389), a coloured plastic disc is shown.

(i) Name the process by which it would be made.
(ii) Draw clearly and carefully a sectional view of the tool used to produce the coloured disc.

(MEG, S)

67 (a) Draw labelled diagrams of mechanisms which could be used to produce the action shown in each of the following boxes in figure 24.50 below and give an example of the use of each.

(i)

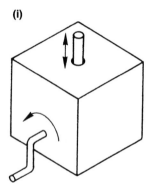

(ii)

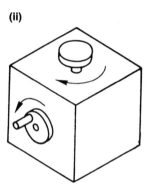

(b) Figure 24.50 below illustrates a winch used for pulling boats up a slipway.

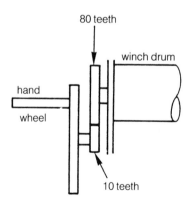

80 teeth

winch drum

hand wheel

10 teeth

Figure 24.50

Sketch and label the parts of a mechanism which, if added to the winch, would allow the operator to stop the winch without the boat sliding back down the slipway.

(c) If the operator winds the handle at 24 rpm, how many revolutions per minute will the winch drum make?

(d) Explain, in detail, why the hand wheel is not connected directly to the winch drum.

(e) Sketch and name a mechanism which, if added to the winch, will allow the operator to pull the winch cable down the slipway without the hand wheel turning.   (MEG, S)

Figure 24.51

68   (a) Name **two** working parts of the bicycle shown in figure 24.51 above which are levers.

(b) State **three** advantages that a chain drive will have over a belt drive in this application.

(c) Identify **four** areas where friction is encountered in a bicycle, **two** of which are of benefit to the cyclist and **two** of which are a disadvantage. Suggest how the undesirable friction can be reduced.

(d) On the bicycle shown above, the chain wheel has 48 teeth and the rear axle sprocket has 16 teeth.

   Calculate:
   (i) the velocity ratio;
   (ii) the mechanical advantage if the efficiency is 80%.

(e) If the diameter of the rear wheel is 500 mm, determine the velocity of the bicycle in metres/ minute if the crank revolves at 15 revolutions/minute.

(MEG, S)

69   (a) Identify the tool used to remove the shaded part of the piece of wood shown in the drawing.

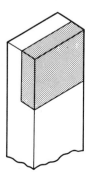

Figure 24.52

(b) Name the softwood most commonly used for general joinery purposes.

(c) What is a suitable surface material for a kitchen worktop?

(d) Give an example in which the use of plywood is better than natural timber.

(e) Draw the head of the type of woodscrew that would be used to secure a black japanned tee-hinge to a cupboard door.

(f) Sketch the section of a file that would be suitable for finishing the edges of the cut out in the piece of jewellery shown.

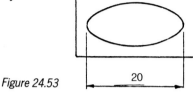

Figure 24.53

(g) Identify a suitable material for the manufacture of car-body panels.

(h) The joining of car-body panels is done on a large scale by robot. Identify the technique used.

(i) What is the lathe tool shown in the drawing used for?

Figure 24.54

(j) State one safety precaution necessary when pouring molten aluminium.

(k) Which of the lathe gearwheels A, B, or C, will rotate the fastest?

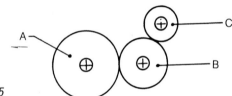

Figure 24.55

(l) The diagram shows an open three-pin plug.

Label the terminals:
L — Live; N — Neutral; E — Earth.

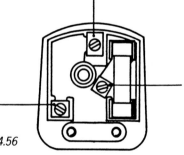

(m) Using the formula

power = voltage × current   Figure 24.56

calculate the current for a 480 watt motor, run from 240 volt mains supply.

(n) Name the type of force acting on the chair leg at A.

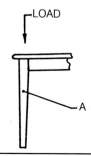

Figure 24.57

(o) What does the symbol represent?

(p) Name one thermosetting plastics material.

(q) In what way do thermoplastics differ from thermosetting plastics?

(r) Name a method of joining acrylic sheet that does not involve an adhesive.

(s) Describe a situation in which a designer could exploit the visual qualities of acrylic sheet.

(t) Make a pictorial sketch of the block shown.   *(SEG, S)*

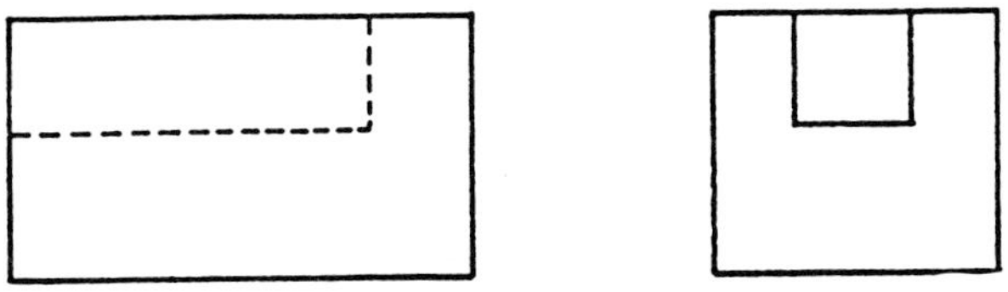

Figure 24.58

70   *(a)* For each material in the table, tick the tool most suitable for cutting it.

Materials	Tools				
	Coping Saw	Hot Wire	Piercing Saw	Hacksaw	Tenon Saw
150 mm thick expanded polystyrene					
25 mm thick beech					
6 mm thick acrylic sheet					
1 mm thick copper					
3 mm thick mild steel					

(b) Describe the cutting action of:

  (i) a hot wire;
  (ii) a coping saw.

(c) Name a tool that cuts using a shearing action.

(d) State three safety precautions which must be observed when using a drilling machine.

(e) A 70 mm diameter hole is required in a 3 mm thick sheet of mild-steel. Give a step-by-step account of how this would be cut.   *(SEG, S)*

71 The drawing shows a section through a bearing bush and part of the axle of a model car.

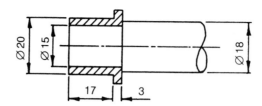

Figure 24.59

(a) Name a material that would be suitable for the axle.

(b) Name two materials that would be suitable for the bush.

(c) (i) State a possible cause of wear in the assembly.
(ii) How can this wear be reduced?

(d) Name an engineering component that could be used as an alternative to the bush.

(e) The diagram shows the shaft of an electric motor (A) which runs at 1000 rev/min driving another shaft (B).

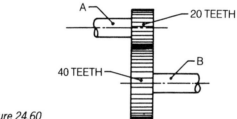

Figure 24.60

(i) What is the speed of shaft B?
(ii) State the number of teeth required on the shaft B gearwheel if the shaft is to rotate at 125 rev/min.

(f) Illustrate two methods of securing a driving gearwheel on a shaft.

(g) Explain the advantages and disadvantages of each method.   (SEG, S)

72 (a) For each material listed state whether they are metals or non-metals: concrete, copper, silicon, PVC.

(b) Explain briefly how **each** of the following materials can be protected against corrosion or decay: wood, steel, aluminium.   (LEAG, S)

73 (a) Give an example of a device which will change:

(i) mechanical energy into electrical energy.
(ii) sound energy into electrical energy
(iii) chemical energy into mechanical energy.

(b) Explain why a petrol engine is **not** 100 per cent efficient.   (LEAG, S)

74 (a) List **two** ways in which heat is lost from a house and in **each** case explain **one** way of reducing this loss.

(b) Give **three** examples of alternative energy sources.   (LEAG, S)

75 The diagrams below show **five** mechanisms in common use. **Name** the mechanisms illustrated and give **one** practical application for each.

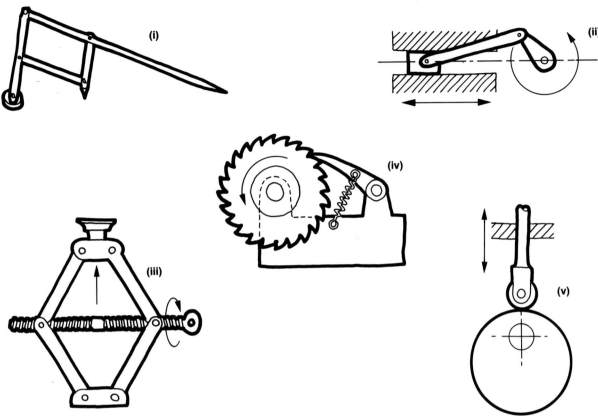

Figure 24.61

76 The diagram below shows a pillar drilling machine with guards removed.

Draw the belt in position on the pulleys for drilling a 2 mm diameter hole.

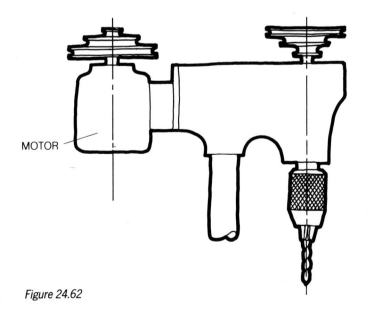

MOTOR

Figure 24.62

77 Complete the table below by naming the correct cutting tool for **each** process.

| | TOOL TO BE USED ON | | |
PROCESS	HARDWOOD	MILD STEEL	ACRYLIC SHEET
(a) Cutting 3mm thick sheet material			
(b) Making a 10mm diameter hole through 12mm thick material			
(c) Preparing an edge from which to work			

(LEAG, S)

78 (a) Gears in toys, models and kits are often made from ....

by the following process ....

(b) What is the purpose of the types of gears shown in the drawing below?

(c) Draw the tooth shapes for two gear-wheels in mesh.

(d)

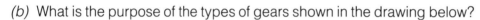

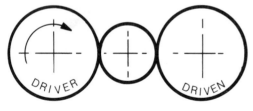

Gear train 1

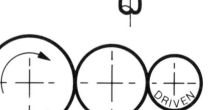

Gear train 2

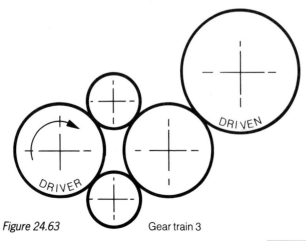

Figure 24.63　　　　Gear train 3

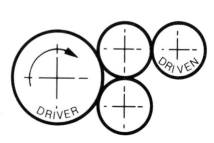

Gear train 4

Using the illustrations opposite state:

 (i) a train that will not rotate,
 (ii) a train that gives no change in rotation direction.
 (iii) a train that increases speed.
 (iv) a train that decreases speed.
 (v) a train that does not alter speed.

Figure 24.64

(e) The drawing above shows a winder for a simple rubber-band motor used for model aircraft. The winder also has a device which prevents the winder unwinding if the handle is released.

Draw the internal mechanism necessary to give **six** clockwise rotations of the winder to match **one** clockwise rotation of the handle.

(f) Draw a suitable device which prevents the winder unwinding when released.

(LEAG, S)

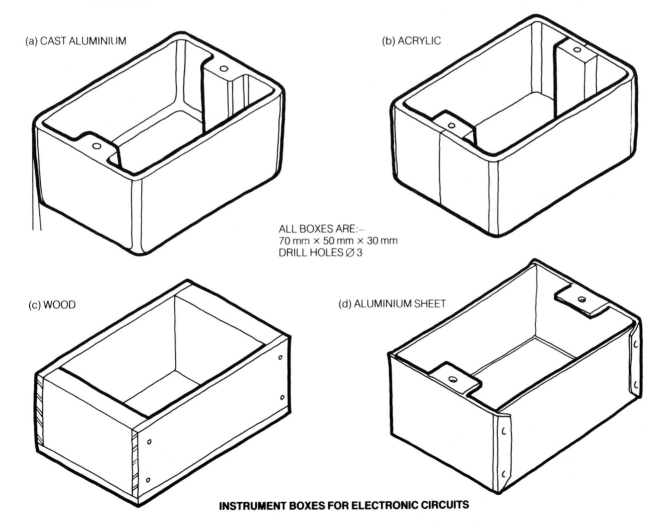

(a) CAST ALUMINIUM

(b) ACRYLIC

ALL BOXES ARE:–
70 mm × 50 mm × 30 mm
DRILL HOLES Ø 3

(c) WOOD

(d) ALUMINIUM SHEET

INSTRUMENT BOXES FOR ELECTRONIC CIRCUITS

Figure 24.65

79 (a) Four designs for small instrument boxes are shown.

   Show why each of the following help manufacture.

   BOX (a) A PATTERN   BOX (b) A FORMER

   BOX (c) A JIG   BOX (d) A TEMPLATE

   (b) Which BOX do you consider expensive in terms of time and energy. Show why.

   Under what conditions would it be worthwhile using the box you have outlined.

   (c) Selecting which to make will vary according to the number needed and production facilities available.

   Select the box you consider most appropriate for each of the following. Outline the method, and give reasons for your choice.

   MAKING ONE BOX
   Box chosen   Method of making   Reasons for selection and method.

   MAKING TEN BOXES
   Box chosen   Method of making   Reasons for selection and method.

   MAKING FIFTY OR MORE BOXES
   Box chosen   Method of making   Reasons for selection and
   method.   (LEAG, S)

80 From the following list, select the most appropriate material finish for the articles listed in the table below:

painted; varnished; polished; lacquered; knurled; glazed; textured, plastic coated; blued; natural.

Article	Finish
Brass letterbox	
Garden gate	
Tea cup	
Finger screw	

(WJEC)

81 (a) What do you understand by the term ergonomics?

   (b) State four ergonomic details (not measurements), you think a designer would require before designing a computer work station.   (WJEC)

82 Figure 24.41 shows several different materials of similar cross-section.

   (a) Name a suitable method, other than gluing, of joining them as shown in the diagram.

(b) On the diagram sketch the method chosen.   *(WJEC)*

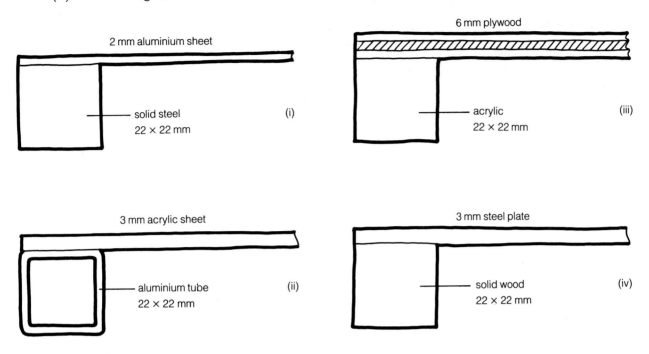

2 mm aluminium sheet

solid steel
22 × 22 mm

(i)

6 mm plywood

acrylic
22 × 22 mm

(iii)

3 mm acrylic sheet

aluminium tube
22 × 22 mm

(ii)

3 mm steel plate

solid wood
22 × 22 mm

(iv)

Figure 24.66

83 Figure 24.67(a) shows a simple lever. The load, effort and fulcrum are also shown. Practical examples of levers are shown in figure 24.42(b). On **each** of the diagrams (i)–(iv), indicate the **load**, **effort** and **fulcrum**.   *(WJEC)*

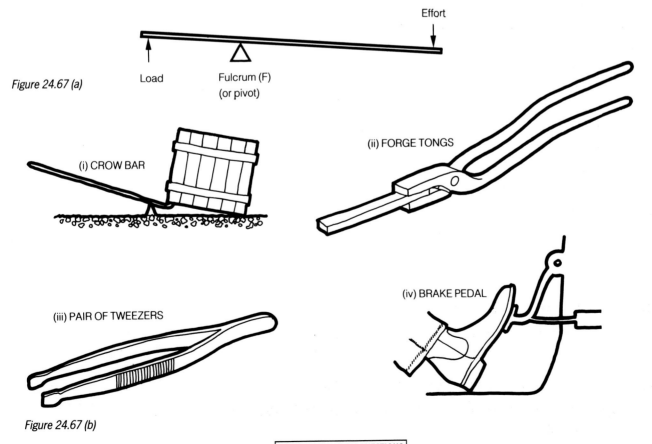

Figure 24.67 (a)

Effort

Load   Fulcrum (F)
              (or pivot)

(i) CROW BAR

(ii) FORGE TONGS

(iii) PAIR OF TWEEZERS

(iv) BRAKE PEDAL

Figure 24.67 (b)

84 Cams are used in machinery. They can be used to change rotary motion (in a circle) to reciprocating motion (backwards and forwards).

An example is shown in figure 24.68.

(a) Sketch a cam so that in one revolution the follower rises and falls twice.

(b) Sketch a cam so that in one revolution the follower rises gradually and falls suddenly.

(WJEC)

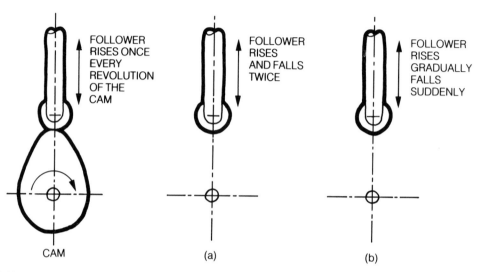

Figure 24.68

85 Outdoor Play Equipment

Figure 24.69 shows the details of a large polypropylene tray used by children in a primary school. It is to be filled with water.

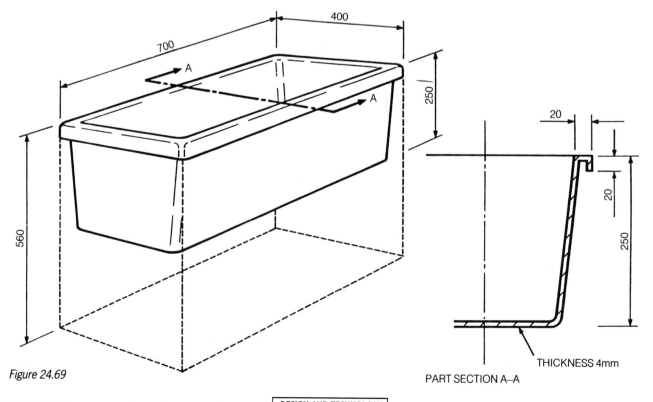

Figure 24.69

PART SECTION A–A

The tray is supported on a 'knock-down' frame. It is taken apart and stored away in the winter.

Materials

(a) Name **two** different materials that could be used to make the frame, (e.g. a specific metal, wood, plastic or some other suitable material).

(b) Choose **one** of these materials. Sketch and label a suitable cross-section for the legs and for the rails.

Processes

(c) Using clear simple sketches and notes, show how you would join the rails to the legs. Remember, the frame must be 'knock-down'.

(d) Show how the frame could be modified so that two teachers could move it a short distance while the tray is still full of water. *(WJEC)*

86 Batch Produced Spatulas

Figure 24.70 shows the outline of a spatula, 30 of which are to be made in the CDT Department and sold at the school fête to raise money for charity.

Two versions are to be made:

(i) To be used in the kitchen.
(ii) To be used for cleaning garden tools.

Materials

(a) Name **two** different materials that could be used to make the kitchen spatula.

(b) Name **two** different materials that could be used to make the garden spatula.

(For (a) and (b) name a specific wood, metal, plastic or some other material.)

Processes

(c) Choose **one** of the materials you have named. Use sketches and notes to show, step by step, how you would make **either** 30 kitchen spatulas **or** 30 garden spatulas.

You may modify the design if you wish. *(WJEC)*

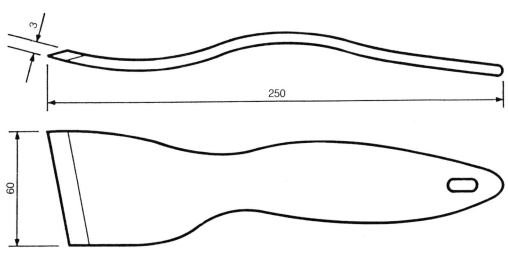

Figure 24.70

87 Preparation for Designing for the Disabled

You are asked to help a group of fourth year pupils who are beginning their CDT Design Project. It is concerned with 'designing for the disabled'.

Simulation exercises will help the pupils understand some of the problems faced by disabled people. For example, wearing a blindfold to experience what sorts of tasks are difficult for blind people.

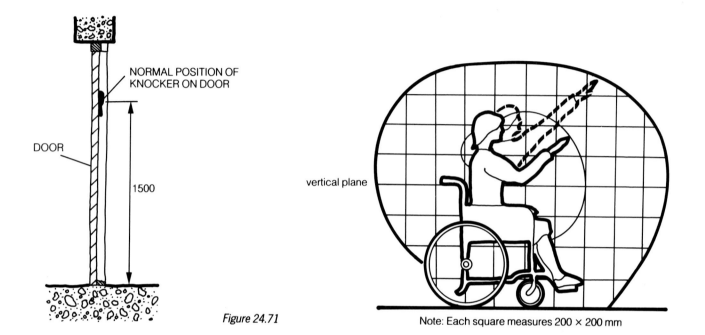

Figure 24.71

Note: Each square measures 200 × 200 mm

(a) Choose **one** of the following disabilities:

(i) one-handedness (e.g. a stroke patient);
(ii) arthritis;
(iii) no use of the legs.

Describe **four** every day activities that would be difficult for people with this disability.

(b) Produce a worksheet to be used by the pupils, which will include:

(i) instructions on how to simulate the disability;
(ii) activities the pupils must try;
(iii) questions the pupils must answer. (WJEC)

88 Designing for Younger Children

You are asked to design and make a large mobile toy for a nursery school.

(a) A meeting is set up between you, your own teacher and the nursery school teacher before you begin the project. List **four** questions you would ask at the meeting. Give **one** reason for **each** question.

(b) List **four** questions you would ask the children before you begin the project. Give **one** reason for **each** question.

(c) List **four** things you would check when the toy had been in use for a few weeks. (WJEC)

89 Technology in Society

"In society we rely more and more on technology."

    (a) Explain in **one paragraph** what you understand by this statement.

    (b) Describe briefly **one** situation in our day to day lives where you feel the effects of technology are extremely good.

    (c) Describe briefly **one** other situation in our day to day lives where you feel the effects of technology are bad.

    (d) Explain why you think 'western technology' is not always suitable in third world countries.
(WJEC)

Addresses

Specialist suppliers of modelling equipment, consumables and educational kits:

EMA Model Supplies Ltd, 58/60, The Centre, Feltham, Middlesex TW13 4BH

Suppliers of design and technology equipment, educational kits — including electroplating kits and mechanisms construction kits:

Philip Harris Ltd, Lynn Lane, Shenstone, Lichfield, Staffordshire WS14 OEE

Electronic component suppliers and distributors and suppliers of electronics equipment (minimum order quantity on application):

JPR Electronics, Unit M, Kingsway Industrial Estate, Kingsway, Luton, Bedfordshire LU1 1LP

Index

abrafile saw 208, 209
abrasives
    cutting 242–245
    papers 304, 352, 353
acrylic weaknesses 167
air brushing 30
aluminium production 330
ampere hours 108
angle plate 191
anvil 264
assembly drawings 32

back saws 205, 209
ball-pein hammers 198
band saws 242
batteries, electrical 107
beam compasses 188
beams — designing 159
bearings, types
    ball bearing races 151
    (and) mechanical modelling 154
    plain 150
    sintered 151
beaten metalwork 266
belt sanding machine 243
bending: wood, plastics
    techniques 254
    flexible formers 255
    laminated — stages 256
    rigid formers 255
bevel edge firmer chisel 216, 217
bits, wood boring 220, 221
bleed-proof paper 27
block plane 215
bolts 294, 295
bossing mallet 199
bow saw 206
bradawl 221
brass tongs 193, see also Tools
breast drill 201
brush cleaning 327
bullnose plane 216
butyrate tubing 42

cabinet screwdriver 199
    scraper 213, 324
calendering 281
calipers 187, 188
cam 145, 146

capacitance, unit 118
capacitor, electrolytic 118, 121
cap iron, plane 227
cardboard engineering 152
carpenter's — mallet 198
    ratchet brace drill 201
casting see also 'moulding'
    gravity die 275
    lost wax 275
    polystyrene patterns 275
    pressure die 275
catches 296
central bit, new pattern, 220, 236
centre lathes 245
    construction features 245
    mounting work in 246
        centres 245
        faceplate 246
        4 – jaw chuck 246
        half-centre 247
        3 – jaw centring chuck 246
    technique 247–250
        cutting fluids 249
        finishing off 249
        setting up 248
        spindle speeds 248
        tool shapes
centre lines 13
centre punch 107
centre square 188
chain pliers 201
chemical energy 171
chemical milling 252
chip 106, 124
chisels 204, 216–218, 237–239,
    266
    metal 239
        safety 239
        technique 239
    principles of morticing 237
        technique 237
    principles of paring 237
        technique 237
    sharpening/grinding 238
chucks 200, 201, 246
circuit boards 128, 129
    printed 128–132
circuit diagram 106
circuits, electronic 106

capacitor delay 128
    experiments with 128
    prototyping board 128
circular split dies 223
claw hammer 198
clear casting, embedding 277
clinched nailing 283
coach bolts 294
cold forming of metals 266–269
cold resin casting 276
cold set chisel 266
colour 67
combination: centre drills 219
    plane 215
    pliers 201
compasses 13
compression moulding 276
computer graphics 31
computer numerically controlled
    machines (CNC) 251, 252
conservation, law 172, 173
    creation/indestructibility of
        energy 173
construction in wood 297
    carcase corner joints 301, 302
        tee joints 301
    dowelled joints 302
    edge jointing 302
    flat frame corner joints 298
        construction joints 299
    tongue and groove joints 302
    slab corner joints 304
        tee joints 304
    stool frame joints 300
continuity test circuits 116
control 148
    cable 148
    hydraulic 149
    pneumatic 148
conventional current flow 107
coping saw 206, 209
copper production 330
    blister 330, 331
    matte 330
cores, pattern making 274
cramp, 'G' weaknesses 167
cramping, methods 196
crank 138
crating 4, 7, 9, 10

cross cut (cape) metal chisel 217, 218
cross-cut saw 205
cross-pein hammer 198
curved snips 209
curved tooth files 231
cutting fluids 249
cutting planes 13, 18
cutting tools 203

deformation 254–271
design and technology
    changes 2
    communication of ideas 3
    effect on living 2
    evaluation 3
    problem identification 83–105
    purpose 1
    understanding of 3
    vocabulary 59–71
designer's gouache 25
design method, stages: advanced
    brief, context 75
    investigation: factor analysis 76
        research 76, 77
    solution, synthesis:
        check final design/brief 80
        development sketches 79, 80
        preliminary ideas 79, 80
        presentation drawings 80
        realisation 80
        testing 81
        working drawings 80
    simple problem: stages —
        brief 73
        investigation 74
        realisation 74
        solution:
        final/partial solution 73
        idea sketches 73
    stock (cutting/parts) list 81, 82
design vocabulary 59–71
development sketches see
    sketching
diagrams in circuitry 106
diamond point chisel 217, 218
dies 204, 222, 223, 233, 271
die holder (stock) 223
dimensioning rules 17
dimension lines 13, 17
diodes 116
direct current miniature
    motors 124
disc sanders 242, 243
double cut files 230
dovetail nailing 283
dovetail saw 206, 209
dowell sharpeners (bits) 221

drape forming (thermoplastics) 263
drawing boards/instruments 12, 14, 15
drill gauges 189
drilling — principles/
    technique 235, 236
    machines 200, 242
drills 204, 218–221
    cutting lips 235
    land, flutes 235
driving tools 197–202
dry cells 107
dry cramp (gluing) 187

elastic limit of materials 169
electric batteries 107
electric current, flow 106, 107, 108
electric drills 201
electricity: costing/
    measurement 180
electric motors: D.C./miniature 123
electric portable saws 204
electronic components
    discrete 106
    individual 106
    soldering 291
electronic switches 109–111, 122, 126–7
energy 170
    chemical 171
    definition 170
    electrical 171
    heat/light/sound 171, 172
    mechanical 170
energy conservation 179
energy conversion 173
    efficiency/friction/wastage 173–4
energy sources 174
    geothermal 178
    heat pumps 178
    nuclear 178
    sun 174–5
    tides 174
engineer's screwdriver/vice 192, 199
etching metals (chemical
    milling) 252–3
exact product models 45–6
    advantages/disadvantages
        materials 46
expansive bits 221
exploded view 20, 33
extrusion moulding 261, 278
eye level (perspective drawing) 6, 20

fabrication 282–307

fabrication models: definition 47
    technique of construction 47–50
facing off 249k
factor analysis 77–9
    anthropometric/ergonomic
        data 79
    factors involved 77–9
    objectives 77–9
farad/microfarads 118
ferrous metals: identification
    lists 332
filament bulbs 109
files 203, 211–3, 230–2
filing principles/technique 230–2
fillister plane 215
finishes (wood) materials 325–6
fire/explosion risks with
    plastics 184
firmer chisel 216–7
first angle projection (British) 14
flat back patterns 273–4
flat bits 221
flat chisel (metal) 217–8
flatters 264
flat views see orthographic
    projection 11
flying leads (EL) 117
foam see also models
    polystyrene block 44–5
folding and seaming (metal
    work) 269
folding bars 193
fore plane 214
forgework (metals) 263–271
    correct heat/tools 263–4
forging processes/technique 265–6
form: definition 65
    natural/shape/size 65–6
formal drawings 16, 33
    rules of layout/presentation 16, 17
formers (in bending) 255, 259, 260
Forstner pattern bit 220
four-jaw independent chuck 246
four-square drill 211
free blowing moulding 261
freehand sketching, rules/
    technique 4, 12
friction – energy losses 174
fullers 264
furniture/interior models 41
furniture joints/hinges 295

garnet paper 324
    close/open 324–5
gas pliers 201
gate (injection mould) 281

gears 142–4, 153
general purpose: file 212
    saw 207, 209
    geometrical locking 137
    girders 161–2
    glass fibre rovings (strands) 259
    glasspaper 324
    glass reinforced plastics (GRP)
        laminating/mould making 257
glues (adhesives) 255, 286–9
    compatibility 286
    plastic cements 289
gouges 217
    in- out channel 217
gravity die casting 275
grids and units
    examples 68–70
    stencil/template/tracing 63
    sub- super-units 63
    tessellating geometric shapes 63
green sand moulding 272

hacksaw 207, 209
half-round file 211
hammers 198, 264
hand drill 200
hand file 211–2
hand lever bench shearing
    machine 210
hand scrapers 213
hand tools classifications
    common holding 192
    driving 197
hand vice 193
hardie chisel 266
hardwoods classifications/
    uses 254, 310–4
hatching lines 13
heat energy transfer methods 171
heat treatment (metals) 332
    annealing/case hardening/
        hardening/normalising/
        tempering 332–3
hidden detail lines 13, 17–9
hinges types 295–6
holding tools 192–3
hold saw (electric drive) 219
home – structures in –
    examples 164–5
Hooke's law 169
horizontally rotating: cutters 241
    abrasive wheels 243
hot metal glue guns 155
hot set chisel 266
hot wire cutters 210
hydraulic control 149
    advantages 149

(and) mechanical modelling 154
    systems 149

icon mouse – computer
    graphics 31
ideas, presentation 32–3
injection moulding, mould
    design 279–81
ink 25
ink-jet colour printer 31
instrument drawing, equipment/
    method 12, 14
integrated circuit (IC) 106, 124
    555 tuner 126
    LED flasher (LM3909) 125
iron production 328
isometric projection 10, 18–20

jack plane 214, 227
jelutong pattern making 273
Jenning's pattern auger bit 220,
    236
jeweller's snips 209
jointer plane 214, 227
joint proportions in wood
    structures 303
joints in metal 307
Joules 170, 179
junior hacksaw 207, 209

knives types 203, 210–211
knock-down joints (KD) 306
knurling 250

laminate cutting tool 210
laminated bending 256
laminated moulds 281
laminating stages 254, 256–9
lathes 245
lathework processes
    boring 250
    drilling in 250
    knurling 250
    parting-off 250
    sliding (parallel turning) 249
    surfacing (facing off) 249
    taper turning 250
layout, formal drawings 16
lettering 13, 16, 26
levers 134–6
light-emitting diode (LED) 116,
    118–19, 125
    continuity test circuits 116
    555 timer 126
    LED flasher (LM3909) 125
    uses 125
light energy 172
lines, standardisation of (BS308) 13

line, as indicator of:
    circuitry 106
    direction 59
    free-form design 60–1
    movement 59
    rhythm 60
    shape 60
    texture 60
line rendering 25
lining-in 4
linkage 136
lintels 160
London-pattern screwdriver 199
low voltage power supply units
    (PSU) 109

machine screws 294
machine tool cutters 243–4
machining principles 240–253
macromolecules see also
    plastics 342–3
mallets 199
man-made boards 304, 323–4
man-made tops, fixing
    materials 305–6
marker rendering 27, 30
marker streaking 29
marking gauge/knife 186
marking out 188–190
masking 22, 30
match-plate patterns 274
materials
    deformation 182
    fabrication 182
    moulding/casting 182
    wasting 182
materials principles of working 181
    (change) appearance 181
        function 181
        properties 181
materials, properties
    behaviour 169, 331
    ductibility 168, 331
    elasticity 169, 331
    hardness 168, 331
    heat/electricity conductivity 168,
        331
    Hooke's law 169
    malleability 168, 331
    plastic deformation 169, 331
    tensile strength 168, 331
    toughness 168, 331
materials, visual properties 67
mechanical advantage 135
mechanical energy types 170
mechanical modelling, techniques/
    use 152–4
mechanisms 134

membrane panel switches 55
metal finishing 338–341
metal joint in 307
metals categories
  alloys 331
  ferrous 331–2
  non-ferrous 331, 334–7
  purity 331
metals standard trade
  dimensions 337–8
microelectronics 124
microfarads(F) 118
micrometers 190
midget screwdriver 199
milled tooth file 212
millenicut file 212
models 11
  computer-generated screen
    images 37
  exact product models 45
  example, working model 57
  fabrication 47–50
  false details 53
  finishing 54
  foam, technique of 44–5
  paper and card 38–40
  relief lettering 52
  scale model, categories/uses 41
  surface detailing 51
  switches for working 54–5
  techniques 38–43
  three dimensional 37
  vacuum forming 50
moisture indicators 117, 119
mole wrench 193
monomers 342
morse-taper shank drill 218
mortise gauge 187
mould – blowing into 262
moulding/casting metals 272
  green sand 272
  mould surface 273
  pattern making 273
moulding/casting plastics 276
  clear casting (embedding) 278
  cold resin 276
  compression 276
  extrusion 278
  injection 279
    mould design for 280–1
  laminated 280
  moulds – criteria 276–7
  resins 277
  rotational casting 276
  slush moulding 276
  technique 277
mouse in computer graphics 31
multi-point cutting 241, 244–5

band saws 242
  horizontally rotating cutters 241
  reciprocating saws 242
  vertically rotating cutters 242

nails 283–4
nail setters 200
NPN transistors (BC108) 119
natural forms, use in design 66
needle file 212
new pattern centre bit 236
nibblers 210
non-ferrous metals 334–7
  list 334–7
  properties 334–7
  uses 334–7
nuts 294–5

oblique views 9, 20
odd-leg calipers 187
odd-side patterns 274
off-hand grinders 242
Ohm's law 113, 123
one-point perspective 6, 9, 20
orbital finishing sanders 243
orthographic projection 11, 14, 18–
  21, 32
  drawings 16
  first-angle (English) 14
  lettering 26
  rules for presentation 16–17
  third-angle (American) 14–15
outlines 13
outside calipers 187

pad saw 206, 208–9
panel saw 205
paper and card models 38–40
parallel turning 249
paring (chiselling) 237
parting-off 250
parts drawings 32
pattern making 273
  cores 274
  materials 273
  types:
    flat back 273–5
    match plate 274
    odd-side 274
    split 274
pencil gauge 187
pencils 13
perspective drawing 5–9
Phillips' slot screws 285
photoelastic stress analysis 167
photo etching
photovoltaic cells 108

pictorial view 11, 21, 33
piercing saw 208–9
pincers 200
pin hammer 198
pinning (in filing) 232
pin punch 200
plane geometric shapes 61
planes 203, 214–6, 227–8
planing, techniques 227–30, 324
planishing 269
plastics
  available common forms 345
  cleaning up/finishing 352–3
  identification chart 345–6
  methods of changing 343
    change basic monomers 343
    combine monomers 344
    vary length of polymers 343
  natural 342
  safety precautions 183
  synthetics 342
    making 342–3
    monomers 342–4
    polymerisation 343
  thermoplastics 344
  thermosetting plastics 344
plastics cutting tool 210
plastics (and) mechanical
  models 152–4
plastics mode of deformation 169
plastics scraper 213
pliers 201
plough plane 215
plug taps 222
plywood 254
pneumatic control in
  modelling 148–9, 154
polishing machine 242–3
polymerisation 342–4
polystyrene block 44–6
polystyrene patterns in casting 275
polyurethane foam 162
posidrive slot screws 285
potential dividers (resistors) 113
presentation drawings 34
preservatives (wood) 327
press forming (sheet metal) 270–1
pressing 266
pressure die casting 275
printed circuit boards (PCB) 129–
  132
product design, factors 59
product modelling 37
proportion 67
prototyping board 128
protractors 12
pulley: belts 141
  mechanical modelling 153

radius gauges 189
raising (metal work) 268–9
rasps 231
ratchet screwdriver 199
rawhide mallet 199
rebate plane 215
reciprocating saw 242
relays 122
resins 277
resistors 112, 116
    capacitors 121
    dividers (as) 113–5
    light-dependent (LDR) 116
    (in) parallel 112
    (in) series 112
    thermistor 116, 120
    variable: preset 115
        rotary 115
respiratory hazards of plastics 183
rip saw 205
rivets 292–4
riveting tools 293
rose countersinks 219–220
rotational casting 276
round nose chisel (metal) 217–8
round (rat tail) file 211
router plane 215
routing machine 242
rovings 259
rubber-block forming
    technique 271
runners (injection moulds) 281

safety at work, rules 182–3
sash-mortice chisel 216–7
sawing, technique 224–6
saws 203–9
scale drawing 15
scrapers 203, 213, 324, 352
screwdriver blades 199, 200
screwdrivers 199
screwing into end grain 285
screws 146, 284–5
screws: application of 146–7
scriber 186
second tap dies 222
sectional lines/views 13, 18–9
shading in drawings 21, 23
shapes, symmetrical/
    tessellating 63–4
sharpening planes 227–8
sheet gauges 189
sheet saws 207, 209
shelves, adjustable 296
silicone carbide paper 353
single cut files 230
single point cutting 240–244
sintered bearings 151, 328

sketching 4, 12, 32
sliding (parallel turning) 249
sliding bevel 189
sliding doors 296
slush moulding 276
smith's tongs 193
smoothing plane 214, 227
snipe pliers 201
snips/shears 203, 209, 231–2
    technique of use 233
soft-faced mallet 199
soft woods 310–316
solar cells 108
soldering 290–2
    flux 290
    hard (silver) 291
    soft 291
    soldering irons 290
    tinman's soldering 290
solenoids 122
sound energy 172
sources – electric current 106
spinning metalwork 266
spiral ratchet screwdriver 199
split patterns 274
spokeshave plane 216
Spraymount 51
spring dividers 188
sprue 280–1
staggered nailing 283
steel
    creep 169
    elastic limit 169
    Hooke's law of tension 169
    plastic deformation 169
steel production 328–330
    basic oxygen furnace 329
    electric arc furnace 329
stepper motors 124
stiffness-to-weight ratio 162
straight shank drills 218
straight snips 209
straight tooth file 212
stress concentrations 166
structures 157
    beams/girders/trusses 157–9,
        161–3
    examples 160–2
    failure causes 165–7
    modelling, uses of 167
    testing 167
stubby screwdriver 199
sub-units, hints on designing 63–4
surface: gauge 191
    plate 191
surface grinding machine 242–3
surfacing 249
surform tools 213

switches for working models
    membrane panel 54
    simple 54
systems models 41

tank (cutting) drills 219
taper taps 222
taper turning 250
taps (dies) 204, 222–3
tap wrench 222
technical pen 25
tee square 12
tenon saw 206, 209
tessellating (interlocking) geometric
    shapes 63
thermistor (LDR) 116, 120, 122
thermoplastics 259
    blow moulding 261
        blowing into mould 261
        extrusion moulding 261
        free blowing 262
    heating for bending 260
    press forming 261
    single curvature bending 259
    tabulation of properties/
        uses 348–51
    vacuum forming 262
    welding 292
thermosetting plastics 256
    making laminates 256
    tabulation properties/uses 350–3
third angle projection
    (American) 14–5
three dimensional solids 65
three-jaw self centring chuck 246
three-square file 211
threads, cutting principles 233–5
thumb (pencil) gauge 187
thyristor 121–2
timber 318
    defects 319–320
    faults 318–319
    finishing 324–5
    fungal attack 321–2
    insect attack 321
    preservation 326
timer 555 126–7
tinman's mallet 199
toggle clamp 137
tongs 264
tool maker's clamp 193
tools 181
    cutting 181, 203–245
    driving 181, 198–9
    holding 181, 192–3
    marking-out/measuring 181, 183
torsion box 162, 168

trammel heads 188
transistor 119–121
  bipolar 119
    BFY51, 120
    NPN (BC108) 119, 120
    PNP 119
trees
  sawing, 311
    plain 311
    quarter/radial 311
  seasoning 316–8
  structure/growth 309
tribology, science of 174
trimming knife 211
trusses 163
  Howe 163
  Warren 163
try square 186
twist drill 218
two-point perspective 8, 20

units and grids 63
universal snips 209
upsetting (metal) 265

vacuum formed models

surface detailing 51
technique of construction 50–1
vacuum forming envelope 255
vacuum forming thermplastics 262
vee blocks 191
velocity ratio (VR) 135, 139, 143,
  146–7
veneers 252, 322
vices
  engineers' 192
  woodworkers' bench 193
vertically rotating: abrasive
  wheels 242
  cutters 242
vertical milling machine 242
vocabulary of design 59–71
voltage 106

warding file 211
Warrington pattern hammers 198
washer cutter drills 219
washers 295
wasting of materials 181
water colouring 24
watts 179
welding 291

metals 291–2
plastics
  heated tool 292
  hot air 292
wheel brace 200
winding strips 188
wing compasses 188
wire:
  cutters 210
  gauges 189
  wool 325
witness marking 187
working drawings 32
wood constructions see
  Constructions
wood: standard sizes sawn 311
  timber 311
  machine planed on both sides
    (PBS) 311
  planed all round (PAR) 311
  rough sawn 311
  seasoning 316–8
wood tops (solid) fixing 305

yankee screwdriver 199